Very Much a Lady
SHANA ALEXANDER

"ENTHRALLING. . . . Read this book as a cautionary tale."

—*Cosmopolitan*

"FRESH, BALANCED, AND EXCEEDINGLY WELL RESEARCHED. . . . A human illumination of the contradictions which have shaped the lives of many American women."

—*San Francisco Chronicle*

"BEAUTIFULLY WRITTEN, UNFORGETTABLE. . . . Shana Alexander compels us to know Jean Harris for the first time, bound and gagged by social convention, rushing to self-destruction."

—*Gail Sheehy*

"A PERSUASIVE CASE. . . . Quite a lot more than a competent unraveling of a complicated case. It is also a sensitive portrait of Jean Harris . . . balanced, skeptical, worldly, compassionate."

—*The Washington Post*

OTHER BOOKS BY SHANA ALEXANDER

Very Much a Lady

SHANA ALEXANDER

A DELL BOOK

Published by
Dell Publishing Co., Inc.
1 Dag Hammarskjold Plaza
New York, New York 10017

for Harry

Lines from "Put the Blame on Mame" by Doris Fisher and Allan Roberts, appearing on pages 23–24, are used by permission of Doris Fisher Music Corp.

For information address: Little, Brown and Company, Boston, Massachusetts.

Dell ® TM 681510, Dell Publishing Co., Inc.

ISBN: 0-440-19270-6

Reprinted by arrangement with Little, Brown and Company.

Printed in the United States of America

June 1986

10 9 8 7 6 5 4 3 2 1

WFH

"Society must go on, I suppose, and society can only exist if the normal, if the virtuous, and slightly deceitful flourish, and if the passionate, the headstrong, and the too-truthful are condemned to suicide and madness."

—FORD MADOX FORD, *The Good Soldier*

Contents

Author's Note

I SAW HER FIRST on TV, stepping out of a police car, and thought—she reminds me of me. Same hairdo, same shoes, even the same college class. Headmistress of a select girls' school, she had just been arrested for murder. The dead man, Dr. Herman Tarnower, was someone I used to know. Later, when I began to dig back into her life story, and his, striking similarities turned up between her life and my own. Her flourishing professional career has been devoted almost entirely to private-school education, and mine to journalism, but our chronologies are roughly parallel as to dates of birth, marriage, motherhood, divorce, and the experience of becoming what the Bureau of Internal Revenue calls a "female head of household." Most important, we are women of the same era: the last generation of Americans brought up to believe that nice girls get married. The love affair between Jean Harris and Herman Tarnower had gone on for fourteen years.

After Mrs. Harris had been sent to prison, and while I was still doing research on the case, something else happened which set that tragic event into harsh perspective. A lifetime convict named Jack Henry Abbott was released from prison on parole and, within days, he had stabbed a young stranger in the heart. When Abbott was recaptured and brought to trial, in the same state which had convicted Jean Harris, he said his lifetime behind bars had rendered him "extremely emotionally disturbed," and he threw himself on the mercy of the jury. They responded with sufficient compassion to convict him of manslaughter, not murder. Harris, on the other hand, had been too principled to say she was "extremely emotionally disturbed"—or perhaps too "disturbed"—and too prideful to beg for mercy. Harris had insisted on telling the "truth," pinning all her faith on her civics class conception of the American system of justice. She had, after all, devoted her professional lifetime to instructing children in the workings of this very system, and its superiority to all others.

Seen side by side, the two cases reveal our criminal justice system to be so imperfect a machine, so terrifyingly random as it wheezes and clatters along, that it metes out to Jack Abbott the same punishment it awards Jean Harris. The hardened criminal–multiple killer and the distraught boarding-school headmistress occupy different institutions, but they are serving identical prison terms: fifteen years-to-life, without possibility of parole for fifteen years.

But I had not set out to investigate the injustice of the "justice" machine, nor the pliability of the system in the hands of the artful criminal. I was interested in a single individual, Jean Harris, someone who had always seemed to embody the highest ideals of society, not the lowest. Three times, at three schools, the headmistress had been handpicked over other candidates as figurehead and exemplar to the next generation, three times set up as a model of womanhood to some of the fairest, most privileged daughters in the land. What qualities had raised her up? What held her together? What brought her down? And afterward: why was this passionate, headstrong, and too-truthful woman apparently so incapable of utilizing the criminal justice system as it was designed to be used—to assure an accused person the benefit of the doubt?

That I would attempt to write her story was inevitable from the first moment I saw her on TV. The following day I drove to her lawyer's office to announce my intentions, and when I got home I commenced a gentle postal bombardment of his client with letters and writings I had published over the years. Less than two months after Dr. Tarnower's death, my phone rang. "You remind me of me," she said.

This was the first of scores of conversations Jean Harris and I have held in the many months before, during, and after her murder trial. In this time we have come to realize that we are not nearly so alike as either of us at first had thought, and we have become friends. Nonetheless, what follows is in no sense of the term an "authorized biography" of Jean Harris. It is my view of the story only. I hope that someday she will be permitted to publish her own. In the period during which our friendship has developed, we have never made "agreements" of any nature. I have of course told her of my intention to write about her, but I have neither formally nor informally sought her permission to do so. She has never asked my permission to read any part of my work-in-progress, nor of the final manuscript, and she has not done so. One day when we were talking in the prison visiting room another of her visitors, a woman more worldly than the former headmistress, said, "Jean, aren't you going to *read* this book before it's published?"

"No. And I may not read it afterwards either," she replied. "But it's all right. I trust her." No writer could receive a more precious gift, and I can only pray that her trust will sustain under the unforeseeable impact of the present volume.

This book is not offered as an *apologia pro* Jean Harris, but as an independent view of the case, the fruit of interviews, observations, and researches engaged in continually over the past two and a half years. In that time, I have attended every day of all the public legal proceedings involving Jean Harris, and have talked to hundreds of people who knew her and Herman Tarnower— old friends, new friends, professional colleagues, relatives, neighbors, servants, students, teachers, parents, doctors, lawyers, judges, police officers, and members of the District Attorney's office. Some of these people spoke to me entirely on the record, some entirely off, some insisted on the right to approve their quotes, some authorized the use of their quotes but not their names. When, as frequently happened, I was offered widely divergent versions of the same events, my solution was to seek out third-party witnesses where possible; sometimes to use both versions of the story, sometimes to use neither; and in general to rely on nearly forty years' professional experience in the familiar journalistic drudgery and occasional thrill of sorting wheat from chaff.

This is the occasion to thank all my sources once more for their generous gift of time, and their valiant efforts to serve truth. In addition, I should like to express particular gratitude to some special friends of this project: the Honorable Betty Friedlander, Jessica Mitford, and Robert Treuhaft, Michael and Eleanore Kennedy, Ethel Person, M.D., Ralph Wharton, M.D., A. Bernard Ackerman, M.D., Dr. Erika Freeman, and Herald Price Fahringer, all of whom spent precious hours and days instructing me in the vagaries of the law, the mind, the body, the human heart, and who aided and encouraged me in the struggle to adapt what I had learned to the gridlock demands of the manuscript page. There simply would *be* no manuscript without the rigorous attentions of my brilliant, clear-minded editor, Genevieve Young. I am grateful too to the many, many others who cannot be named, but who helped me immeasurably to see, to understand, and to prevail. Foremost among all these people, of course, is Jean Harris herself.

On November 16, 1982, Jean Harris's conviction was affirmed by the New York State Court of Appeals, the state's highest court. As in her earlier appeal to the Appellate Division, the opinion of the judges was unanimous. In consequence, the law requires Mrs. Harris to remain in prison until 1996.

New York, N.Y.
December 1982

I

Before

1

Spring Break

YOU COULD HEAR THE horses snuffling down in the barns, and far away a groundskeeper clattered his mowing machine over billows of bluegrass lawn. Otherwise on this early Monday morning in March 1980, the campus of the Madeira School lay unnaturally hushed and empty, a vast sylvan dell surrounded by several hundred acres of prime Virginia woodlands just across the Potomac and not twenty-five minutes from Washington, D.C. Spring Break had somehow, finally, arrived. The girls had gone home, and for the next three weeks the faculty was free to sort and bundle the academic debris of the last term, and brace for the next. Without the bright shoals of schoolgirls eddying everywhere about, the members of the faculty looked stranded, bleached out. Serious schoolteaching is exhausting work. At a boarding school one must also summon up the savoir faire, the resilience, the brute emotional strength to take on the management *in loco parentis* of a hive of adolescent girls. But somehow the teachers endured it, and often enjoyed it. As mentors and guardians of some of the most privileged young women in America, Madeira's little band of dedicated educators took their work with great seriousness, no one of them more so than their fragile and high-minded headmistress, Jean Harris. On this Monday morning, just as she did when school was in session, she had scheduled a ten-hour day of appointments, beginning at eight-thirty when her secretary dropped by her home to pick up the stack of correspondence she had worked on over the weekend.

But this morning no work was ready for the secretary, and the headmistress's normally immaculate living room looked as if a small tornado had passed through. In the several agitations of the weekend, bits of her clothing and scraps of her papers had got strewn over the furniture and floor, and now she could not figure out how to tidy up, what to do first. Neither woman mentioned the dishevelment. It had been a harrowing few days. Drugs and alcohol were a chronic problem at Madeira, as they are at most boarding schools, and on the previous Thursday afternoon an impressive cache of marijuana paraphernalia, along with traces of leaves and seeds, had been discovered in the suite of rooms in South Dorm where dwelled four of the school's most popular student leaders. All were seniors, less than three months away from graduation, and all held positions of special trust: two were members of the Student Council, one was head of the Student Judiciary, one was Madeira's best rider, and one was also House Mother. That evening in the headmistress's parlor, a long and highly emotional meeting had taken place. The evidence of wrongdoing was spread out on the bright gold carpet for all to see, and the fifteen Student Council members and every adult who lived on campus were in obligatory attendance. Impassioned speeches had been made espousing every conceivable opinion—hang them, enshrine them, ignore them. Near midnight came the vote, and it had been unanimous: the offenders were expelled on the spot and sent off to telephone their parents. In this manner, at this hour, four startled families—unusual families in that they had both the means and the priorities to sink over thirty thousand dollars into the precollege education of a female child—had learned of the abrupt wreckage of that daughter's educational future. Midnight phones began jangling; Board members and powerful alumnae across the United States were roused; Madeira's Old-

Girl Network twitched and heaved. On Friday the parents of the miscreants had begun arriving on campus, and by Saturday evening Jean Harris had dealt personally with the variously aggrieved and infuriated mothers and fathers. She had also had to crack her whip at the leaders of the bitter, widespread student backlash that had set in Friday morning; and on Friday night, in an unrelated incident, another girl had been found dead drunk, and swift discipline was once more required.

All in all, a nightmarish weekend, but by nine o'clock sharp on the first Monday of Spring Break Jean Harris was at her desk in her spacious, book-lined office overlooking the Potomac. Moments earlier, she had stopped at the campus post office and sent a bulky letter by registered mail to an address in Scarsdale, New York. The two senior faculty members who met with the headmistress at nine o'clock found their normally energetic leader weary, discouraged, and glazed-looking. They felt much the same.

At 9:59 Jean Harris made a six-minute telephone call to a Scarsdale number. Her next office visitor, a serious, bearded young man who had just joined the staff, thought that the headmistress handled their meeting with a level of professionalism he had rarely encountered in fourteen years in private-school education, and he headed for lunch reassured that leaving Yale University for a fund-raising job in a fancy girls' prep school might not have been such a quixotic decision after all.

At eleven o'clock the secretary brought in the morning mail. Jean Harris looked it over and buzzed for her secretary to ask the two old-time teachers to return. Through the closed door of the headmistress's office, raised voices could be heard.

When the bearded young man returned for a three o'clock meeting, the secretary told him it had just been canceled. He glanced in through the now open door and was shocked by the change in the appearance of the woman behind the desk. He scarcely recognized her as Jean Harris. He telephoned his wife in New Haven and told her that the headmistress suddenly seemed to have aged ten years. "She looks like someone who's just been told she has cancer."

At about three-thirty the headmistress stood up and buzzed again. "Cancel *all* appointments, Carol, please. I've had enough."

Carol Potts felt relieved. Later she told her husband, "By then Jean was like a person with one foot in the grave and the other on a banana peel."

The headmistress walked back to her disordered house, speaking to no one, and began to look for the will she had started to write over the weekend. When she could not find the first will, she hastily wrote out another one and ran back across campus to have it notarized before the business office closed at four-thirty. A new will was necessary, she told the notary, because three weeks ago her elder son had got married.

Back at her house, she placed a second telephone call to the man to whom she had sent the bulky letter a few hours before. He was a cardiologist who lived several hundred miles away in Purchase, New York, an exclusive estate area north of New York City, and who practiced medicine in the adjoining village of Scarsdale.

The butler answered the telephone and said that Dr. Herman Tarnower had not yet returned from his office. Jean Harris sat down at her little writing desk, took up her red-ink pen, and began composing a series of exit lines.

To the Chairman of the Madeira Board, a letter resigning her post ended with, "I was a person, and no one ever knew."

To her sister in Cleveland, after some instructions on how she wished her possessions divided between her two sons, she signed off with, "I am so desolately lonely, Mary."

She wrote two *To Whom It May Concern* letters containing instructions in the event of her death, and tucked one of these into her handbag: "I wish to be cremated as cheaply as possible and IMMEDIATELY THROWN AWAY." She stacked the other letter on top of her will, some insurance papers, and her teacher's retirement policy, and she placed them all on a small chair just inside her front door.

It was sixteen minutes past five when she dialed the Purchase number again. This time Herman Tarnower himself answered the phone. She had to see him, she said, and it had to be tonight. Tomorrow would be too late.

From the top shelf of the closet in her clothes-strewn bedroom the headmistress took down a small, heavy plastic box that contained a new .32 caliber revolver and a box of fifty bullets. The weapon had been stashed in her closet for sixteen months. To find out what it was going to sound like, she opened the cylinder as the gun salesman had shown her, dropped in a shell, and stepped out onto her rear terrace. She aimed toward the tall trees, pulled the trigger, and heard a click. She heard three or four more clicks before the hammer finally fell on the chamber that contained the bullet. The explosion was much louder than she had expected. Birds flew out of the treetops. She tried to remove the spent cartridge. The salesman had shown her how to load but not how to unload; she couldn't get it out. In her kitchen she found an ice pick and poked out the spent shell.

She filled up the gun with bullets, zippered it in her pocketbook, and put a few more bullets in the pocket of her old mink jacket. Neatly she enclosed the nearly full bullet box inside the now empty gun box. She knelt to hug goodbye to her two dogs, Cider, the big golden retriever the girls had given her, and Liza, the springer spaniel that was a gift from her sons, and hurried out to her car. The car too was a gift. Like the official headmistress's residence, The Hill, the pretty house she was now leaving forever, the 1972 blue and white Chrysler was the property of the school and was provided for the use of the school as well as for the convenience of the headmistress. That was why the car's trunk was now crammed with nine school-owned English riding saddles sorely in need of repair. On the front seat she saw a bunch of white daisies, a quiet gift left there by one of the teachers who had noted her distress that morning. She placed her pocketbook next to the flowers and stuck the gun box and bullets into the glove compartment.

It was five-thirty when she drove to the home of the school groundskeeper and asked if he would gas up her car at the school pump. She wanted to be certain of a full tank so she would not have to search for an open gas station en route.

"Hurry, please, Junior. I'm late for a dinner party," she said.

The weather was turning bad. An hour out of Madeira the rain began. She really was expected at a dinner party, in Washington, and it bothered her that she had not telephoned the hostess and made some excuse. But she was afraid if she talked to anyone she might burst into tears. It was the shame of her life. Almost anything could make her cry—a cute puppy, a crying baby, a wedding, an old song, a surprise encounter, a

sudden argument, a trivial slight. Unexpected compliments
were the most treacherous surprises; they practically guaranteed a crying jag.

But now she didn't feel the least bit sad. As soon as she knew
it was too late to call the hostess, her mind seemed to slip into a
new gear, a sort of emotional overdrive, electraglide, pantrans-
override. Everything grew strangely blank and peaceful. She
listened to the slap-slap of the windshield wipers and thought
about nothing whatever except how entirely serene she felt now
that all her problems had been solved. No more fights with the
girls, or their parents, over archaic drug laws. No more fights
with the all-powerful Board members about money, discipline,
policy. No more fights with her ill-tempered old father about
practically everything, and in particular about his shabby treatment of her two fine sons. No more struggles with Herman
Tarnower over his relationship with a much younger woman,
Lynne Tryforos, his office assistant, a rival the headmistress had
become increasingly aware of in the past four or five years. She
considered the younger woman treacherous, ignorant, and common—someone to sleep with, if that was what it took to make
Tarnower happy, but not a worthy companion to the eminent
cardiologist. *No more fights with herself.* That was the best part;
no more agonizing over her own compromised integrity in this
sordid triangle. She could not bear having him this way. She
could not bear the long, sleepless nights with no one even to
telephone. But the alternative—not ever seeing him again,
growing old by herself, facing the world entirely alone—that
was even worse. To avoid it, she would play by any rules, agree
to any terms. Even though he had changed in these last years,
had grown increasingly distant, selfish, cruel, she could never
walk away from him. Because even if the leave-taking were her
doing, not his, it was she who would be the abandoned one.

But now as she drove steadily north into swiftly worsening
weather, all her problems had been solved. How entirely peaceful she felt now that she had finally made up her mind what she
was going to do. She was going to bid a tender farewell to the
only man she had ever truly loved, to the man she believed had
literally kept her alive these past fourteen years. She knew his
many faults better than anyone; she loved him in spite of them
and in a way because of them. That she could embrace his flaws

was in the fabric of her passion. She loved him because for fourteen years he had made her feel vivid, safe, and happy in ways she had never known before. So now she was driving to his house to feel it one more time, and to say a quiet goodbye. Then, without letting him know of her intention, she was going to walk quietly away, out of the house, down to the lily pond where the daffodils grew in the spring, and she was going to put a bullet through her brain.

Jean Harris knew the route well. She had made this same drive scores of times. Normally she stopped at the Exxon station on the Jersey side of the George Washington Bridge to gas up for the return trip, but this time there was no need to stop. The car continued steady as it approached the rainswept bridge. Flashes of lightning illuminated the ragged clot of traffic at the tollbooth plaza, and thunder rumbled after. In all the higgledy-piggledy of backed-up cars and trucks and tractor-trailers, surely there was no more curious vehicle than the old blue and white Chrysler containing a distraught boarding-school head-mistress, nine broken saddles, twelve daisies, forty-odd bullets, and a new .32 caliber revolver. The car seemed to pilot itself through the heavy commercial traffic while the driver's mind hovered somewhere far above. She had a sense of vast relief. Her mind floated high and free and blank as the quarter-moon invisible now behind the black sheets of rain.

As she turned off the parkway at Anderson Hill Road and turned again onto Purchase Street, the storm banged directly overhead. Tarnower's long, winding driveway blazed white in the lightning glare; thunder split the sky. But the headmistress was more at peace now than ever. In the entire five-hour trip she had felt but one slight twinge of anxiety, and that was very brief. Just as she swung off the George Washington Bridge and arrowed northward to Westchester County, a tiny, stray thought flashed across her empty mind.

"What if he's nice to me . . . and I can't go through with it?"

2

Good Girl

WHEN JEAN STRUVEN HARRIS thinks about her early childhood in the old and affluent Cleveland suburb of Cleveland Heights, she often sees it as pages from a "Dick and Jane" reader. She remembers huge, noisy Father, tiny, loving Mother, the four children, the two dogs, her dollhouse, the little red wagon, the big white house. In fact the Struvens were decidedly better off than the parents of Dick and Jane. They usually had a maid or a cook, a weekly laundress, private schools for the children, and a big Canadian summer home to which the whole family drove every Memorial Day weekend, each parent piloting one of the family's two Packards.

Jean Struven was born in 1923, the second of the three daughters of Albert and Mildred. Mary Margaret, six years older, was considered the family good girl. Jean, always struggling but never quite managing to be as good as her big sister, was thought of as the bright girl, and her younger sister, Virginia, born in 1928, was believed to be the prettiest, and the family hell-raiser. Bobby, their baby brother, came along nearly two years later.

Albert Struven was a blustering, tremendous man. Heavy and big-boned, not fat, standing six feet two inches tall, he could hold out his arm and his gentle, four-foot-eleven wife, whom he sometimes called "Mil," for Mildred, but more often "Bill," could walk right underneath. "Struvie," as he was known, was an Annapolis graduate who could trace back his lineage as a seagoing man at least four generations. Originally his family had come from Prussia. As a young man, he helped set up the Ford River Rouge plant, and his heroes were men like Henry Ford, Thomas Edison, Harvey Firestone. He became a crackerjack civil engineer and vice-president of the worldwide construction company, Arthur G. McKee, Inc., for which he supervised the building of oil refineries and steel plants all over the world. In the late 1920s, he was sent for by the Russians to advise them on building the first cement dam in the Soviet Union. When the big dam in the Ural Mountains was at last completed, Struven supervised the building of the USSR's first modern steel plant, at Magnitogorsk, powered by electricity from the dam.

"I was raised by my mother," Jean says firmly today. "My father was almost never home." Most people were just as glad. The man had a terrible temper, and the most trivial thing could make him explode into fury—a broken light bulb, a stalled car, a lost newspaper. Whenever he was around, all the children in the neighborhood scattered, not just his own four. All who knew him seem to agree that Albert Struven was a brilliant man, and a champion tyrant, bigot, and snob.

Even though her father died in late July of 1980, at age eighty-four, Jean Harris still rarely speaks of him without tears. "My father should not have had *any* children," she said a few months before his death. "I think he was a very sick man, a manic-depressive,* an unbelievably unhappy man to be around, remembering only the ugly things. . . . There was no way not to make him mad. He never said anything good about anyone."

"I think Jean admired her father very much—and she also

---

* Albert Struven was hospitalized for this disorder on at least one occasion, and treated with electric-shock therapy.

hated his guts," says Jean's oldest friend. "He was cold, ever-complaining, impossible to please, autocratic, and nasty. Jean is like Struvie in some ways—very stubborn, it's hard for her to bend, and she's got a bad temper."

"The saving difference between us," Jean herself says now, "was that, thank God, I have a sense of humor. Dad never laughed. Nothing gave him pleasure. He always expected the worst."

There were of course many differences between Jean and her father, as well as numerous similarities. She does not enjoy contemplating the latter and she has tried all her life to put them out of her mind. For example, to this day Jean jokingly complains that, unlike other children, she never had a nickname. "I was always just plain Jean," she says. Yet the description beneath her twelfth-grade graduation picture concludes, ". . . 'Struvie' as she is . . . often called, is going to Smith next fall."

Mary Margaret seemed to be the one member of the family of whom her father approved. Jean was forever running along behind her older sister, always trying to catch up and never quite succeeding, never able to win her father's approval, only her mother's. In her zeal, Jean could become exceedingly dogmatic. Whenever she started sounding too self-righteously certain, her mother gently rebuked her by calling her "Miss Infallible." When even that didn't work, Mildred once or twice washed her daughter's mouth out with Lifebuoy soap as a punishment for "impudence."

Mildred Struven is a staunch Christian Scientist, a faith that helped her survive her husband's tirades. Calm, gentle-natured, serene, and level-headed, she has never had any use for snobbery or pretense. One of Jean's clearest recollections from her earliest childhood is noticing that other little girls curtsied to their elders when shaking hands, and telling her mother that she, too, wished to learn to curtsy.

"A curtsy doesn't mean one doggone thing," her mother told her sternly. "I want you always to look people in the eye. And tell them the truth. You measure people from the neck up, Jean."

Mildred's religious beliefs meant that her children endured the usual childhood diseases without benefit of pediatrician. Her standard treatment was to put the ailing youngster to bed for a few days, dose the invalid alternately with homemade barley soup and long stories read aloud at bedside, and never fail to mention that despite the spots and aches things really did look fine, and surely would be even better tomorrow. It always worked. The one time it didn't, and baby Bobby came down with a near-fatal case of chicken pox, his mother rushed him to Cleveland's best hospital. The woman was a believer but not a fanatic.

After eight years of public schooling, the three Struven sisters were sent to Laurel, Cleveland's "best" private girls' school, where they wore white middy blouses with green ties and skirts, and generally got excellent marks. Jean's Laurel classmates, now matrons approaching sixty, remember her vividly. *"The* most attractive and smartest girl in the class, very good-natured, and always sensible, never flirty."

"Looks, brains, talent, personality—she had them all."

"She loved hayrides, ice-skating, dancing at the country club, good music, and rolling bandages at the settlement house."

"I never could be fond of Jean, because she just wasn't interested in clothes, styles, all the giggly, dumb things we used to do—and boys, she hardly seemed to care about them at all."

"A powerful, outspoken girl. The only time I ever saw her in trouble was when she'd talk back to teachers. That wasn't done in those days. But Jean was very independent-minded, fairly nonconformist, liberal, and quick to criticize."

Jean Struven always got elected to something, from freshman class secretary to senior class president. She was the best actress in every play she was in, and she won the all-school Current Events Contest sponsored by *Time* magazine three years in a row. She also proved to be the most durable. "At our thirtieth reunion, in 1971, Jean had changed physically less than any of us."

Jean herself says simply, "I loved school. I loved having a star on my forehead when I was little, I loved sitting in the sun room of our big house on Demington Drive and doing my homework. I loved my teachers." But when her father was home, Jean hid. "I was always running away from him, always trying to hide from him, always trying not to hear him screaming." He frightened her so, even in her teens, that "if Dad said be home by eleven, I was always home by five minutes before eleven. My younger sister, Virginia, came home at ten past one. She just didn't care. She was full of hell, and she had the most fun of any of us. But then my father would start to yell at Virginia, and I'd sit in my room quaking at the sound of his voice. His anger terrified me."

This comment, if they heard it, would certainly astonish Jean's Laurel classmates. They never even glimpsed the side of her that dreaded her father. Indeed, the single thing every one of them remembers best about Jean Struven is her famous, all-Cleveland prizewinning essay, written when she was in the eleventh grade. They even remember its title: "The Man I Took For Granted." The "man" was Jean's father, and he is described in a complex, haunting tone of voice—suffused with a love that is not expressed but veiled, something like the bantering, exasperated voice that Clarence Day used in his best-seller of the period, *Life With Father*.

In retrospect, today's readers find the final paragraph of Jean's essay truly eerie. "Oh, Mr. Day," she exclaims, "had I your talent with which to tell the story of an equally deserving father!" But "I have not the eloquence to bring it forth. Or perhaps this realization is not entirely an appreciation of father, but a step toward appreciating men in general. It is possible some day my subject will be, not 'The Man I Took For Granted,' but 'The Man Who Took Me For Granted.' "

Although she did indeed love school, the joyous center of Jean's universe for the first twenty years of her life was her family's isolated Canadian summer retreat on Lake Erie some sixty miles east of Detroit. "Little Eden" and "Millionaires' Row" is what Toronto newspapers called the place. But the Struvens and the five other Midwestern families and their nineteen children who summered there together were not millionaires. The fathers were solid, ambitious businessmen, young heads of growing families, who in the booming 1920s bought a vast tract of unspoiled Canadian woodlands and named it, rather grandly, Rondeau Shores Estates. By 1926 they had built a mile-long gravel road into the bush. At the end they erected a row of six "cottages," in reality elaborate, many-bedroomed rustic lodges with verandas and huge stone fireplaces. The Struven family owned the first "cottage" at the end of the gravel road, and the house next door belonged to Naomi and Henderson Richey, then the Midwest distributor for Metro-Goldwyn-Mayer. Their tall, blonde daughter, Marge Richey, four years older than Jean, became the leader of the Rondeau kids' gang, and Jean's lifelong friend. Marge's younger brother, David Richey, was just Jean's age, and throughout their childhoods they were inseparable.

All Rondeau recollections seem extraordinarily sharp, the telescope of memory in perfect focus. Jean remembers the very day she and Marge were lying on their bellies in the warm sand, ages six and ten, and Marge introduced her to the mysteries of four-letter words. Marge remembers the day the following summer when she raced up onto the Struvens' veranda, her blonde hair flying, shouting, "You should *see* the people who just bought the old Keener house! They have a *son!*" This was the third house in the row, just beyond the Richeys' place. The new people were the Harris family, from Grosse Pointe, and their tall, shy son, Jimmie, was almost eleven. One by one, as the years passed, all the Rondeau girls developed a crush on the good-looking youth whose family seemed so much more sophisticated than the others on the lake. Mr. Harris quoted Trollope and Conrad. Mrs. Harris read the Social Register. The other girls swiftly got over their crushes. It would take Jean somewhat longer.

Many more Rondeau "estates" were envisioned as word spread of the "by invitation only" retreat. A golf course was planned, a boat basin, a yacht anchorage, even a private airstrip. But then came the crash of 1929, and the original six houses, standing splendid in their isolation just back of the high cliffs over the lake, were the only structures ever built. For the children, Rondeau Shores Estates became a literal Eden, an uninhabited wilderness untouched by the pain and grit of Depression America. Here they could roam unsupervised and free from Decoration Day weekend until long past Labor Day when, after the dangers of polio had passed, the cottages were boarded up for the winter and everybody piled children, servants, dogs, fishing poles, tents, cots, hampers, and three months' worth of laundry back into the cars for the long drive home to Cleveland or Detroit. The nineteen children grew up as permanent, unchallenged kings and queens of the castle, living in a Norman Rockwell never-never land of taffy pulls, lost kittens, swimming holes, ghost stories, costume parties, and pink lemonade. To hear them talk about the place today—and they all do talk about it, constantly, whenever they meet—is to recognize that those long-ago beach picnics and marshmallow roasts are still the most vivid, valued moments of their sixty-year-old lives. In their collective memory, the years at Rondeau have merged into one seamless, endless summer in which special events twinkle like the bits of bright colored glass they picked up on the sand: the day on the beach that all nineteen kids triumphantly constructed themselves into one shuddering, giggling human pyramid; Sunday nights when Vernon, the Harrises' Negro cook, dressed all in white and wearing his chef's hat, crooned "A Beautiful Lady in Blue" through a paper megaphone while gentle, tiny Mildred Struven, all the children's favorite mother, played the piano and sang along in her beautiful contralto. Mildred was also the only mother willing to stand on the cliffs and referee while the children competed to determine who could swim farthest out into Lake Erie and make it back alive. Afterward, she even judged their blue lips contests. Everybody remembers the day Jean's father brought home the first wonderful aluminum canoe; they recall the miraculous rafts that Jim Harris could construct from steel drums, planks, and chains; the fathers' famous fireworks nights; the summer the knitting madness overcame the girls; the Friday the road washed out in a bad storm, and the kids raised a thicket of flags, shutters, shovels, and signs to warn the daddies returning for the weekend; the nights they sneaked down to the old barn to jump off the rafters in the dark; the amateur theatricals; the magic tricks; the day they tried to dig a hole to China; the time they decorated themselves with Mercurochrome and feathers and turned into a tribe of Indians. All the performances, copies from the movies: Jean and Wilma's tap-dance routine to "Sing You Sinners"; David's gibbering impression of King Kong; the night they translated "We're in the Money" into pig-Latin; Jean's torchy, sweet soprano rendition of "Fish gotta swim, birds gotta fly . . . Can't help lovin' that man of mine."

As the Rondeau children became teenagers, the fun and games changed, but the fundamental innocence of their lives did not. They got to know the local Canadian kids and organized enormously complicated treasure hunts. They played charades, at which Jean excelled, and on Sunday nights fifty teenagers might be gathered in one big living room. These evenings ended with a special treat introduced by Mildred Struven. Other American teenagers might be experimenting with beer, or cuba libres, but this bunch was gorging itself on cinnamon toast. On Saturday nights there were dances at a nearby amusement area, Rondeau Park. Then Jean and Mary Margaret and Marge and the other girls spent all day washing their hair, ironing dresses, polishing shoes, and whole families attended the dance together, the men and boys buying strips of five-cent tickets, the girls filling in their dance programs, parents dancing with their children, with each other, with the local hardware man or fisherman, everyone dancing his fool head off. Occasionally Benny Goodman or Glen Miller came to the casino for one night, and then a carload of Canadian boys might arrive to pick up a bunch of Rondeau girls. But even on these special nights there was no two-by-two dating, and the girls knew they were to be home by eleven o'clock, midnight on Saturdays. "The music stopped at eleven anyway," Marge remembers. "They played 'God Save the King,' and after that there was no place to go but home for cinnamon toast and milk."

Jean was very much the kid sister on these dance nights; shy, not adventurous, never a flirt. She was the same back at home in Shaker Heights (the family had moved from Cleveland Heights to a big stucco house on South Woodland). Many boys pursued her, a Laurel classmate recalls. "But she was already going with Jim, at least some of the time. It was one of those on-and-off things. I remember at a pajama party, we must have been in the tenth or eleventh grade, Jean said, 'I'll probably go ahead and marry Jim—but I know it's going to be boring as hell! He's so *predictable!*' We thought she'd never do it."

Looking back on her girlhood, Jean says now, "I suppose I *was* a good girl. But I don't remember trying to be good. I was just never tempted to do anything bad." She recalls no impulses to rebel or disobey her parents, either as a small child or as a teenager. Like most young women of the time, she was a virgin when she married, and one reason, she thinks now, is that she was never tempted to break any sexual rules either. It amuses her to recall that she arrived at Smith College in 1941 not merely ignorant of the meaning of the word *virgin*, but never having been curious enough to look it up.

Nearly forty years later, in the summer of 1979, Jean S. Harris, by now headmistress of the Madeira School, was invited back to Laurel to give the keynote address at a faculty-staff retreat. "When I was here at Laurel, growing up," she said in part, "my values were easy to list. . . . I respected honesty and knew it was important, and had I been asked I would have said social equality was a nice thing, too. However, I also lived comfortably with the notion that social equality meant taking a couple of cans of peaches and a box of clean, used clothes to school or church on Thanksgiving. Somehow, I managed to spend about the first fifteen years of my life with my biggest decision being whether I wanted chocolate or vanilla."

The tone of self-mockery had become habitual. In truth, the big decision of Jean's life, made very early and only half-consciously, had been her decision to be a good girl, as good as the perfect Mary Margaret. Surely no one ever tried harder to be a good girl than Jean Struven Harris. She wanted above all to be a good girl for Daddy, and there was nothing very unusual in her passion, except perhaps its intensity. But then Albert Struven was a man impossible to please.

3

Another Grosse Pointe

ALTHOUGH SHE WAS A little younger than both, and never met either, Jean Harris was at Smith College in Massachusetts in the same years as Nancy Reagan and Betty Friedan, and the person she became in later life can be considered an unlikely amalgam of the two: extremely stiff and proper on the one hand, and uncommonly original and open on the other. Today Jean seldom speaks about her Smith years; her lasting friendships were all made in earlier or later times. In 1942, by which time David Richey had enlisted in the Naval Air Corps, she invited him to the freshman spring dance. The following year he was killed in a plane crash off the tip of Long Island. Both Jean's and Marge's firstborn sons are named for him.

At college Jean majored in economics, minored in Spanish, swam on the water ballet team, and sang in the glee club. To help the war effort, she also worked as a nurse's aide. But for three glorious months every summer she returned to Rondeau. Time and the war had scattered many of the old gang. But Jean was content with only beach, books, and wild woods for company.

Jim Harris too had joined the Naval Air Corps, and was a navigator on a PBY, picking up survivors out of the Pacific Ocean. Jean and Jim exchanged a goodly amount of V-mail and, toward the end of her junior year, Jim got leave and arrived on the Smith campus carrying an engagement ring. He asked Jean to marry him after the war, and she agreed. Meanwhile, she studied hard enough to be elected to Phi Beta Kappa and be graduated *magna cum laude* in 1945.

During Christmas vacation of her senior year, she went skiing with a bunch of Jim's friends in northern Michigan, and visited the Harris family in Grosse Pointe. Jean adored Albert Douglas "Butts" Harris, Jim's father, a short, merry, charming, warm-hearted man who was vice-president in charge of purchasing for Wyandotte Chemical. Like Jean, he was a passionate Democrat. "Butts" not only collected books, he read them, and liked to quote at length from his favorites, especially Mencken. When he died he left his vast library to his daughter-in-law. The son was taller, more handsome, and less intellectual than the father, but equally easygoing and well liked. After serving with valor in the navy, Jim spent a lackadaisical, beer-drinking time finishing his education at the University of Michigan, and then came home to a job as a sales engineer with the Holley Carburetor Company in Detroit.

Jean was twenty-three and Jim was twenty-seven when they announced they were ready to get married and set up housekeeping in Grosse Pointe. Struvie was furious. He warned Jean she was throwing her life away; he was certain Jim Harris was not good enough for her, and he made sure Jim too knew how he felt. Once, seeing his future son-in-law take a bottle of beer out of the Struvens' refrigerator uninvited, he pitched him bodily out the house. Al Struven had little use for the entire Harris family, but his chief scorn was reserved for "Butts," who had been stupid enough to vote for FDR four times running. Mildred said little and busied herself planning the wedding and choosing her daughter's trousseau for her new life in Grosse Pointe, making certain there was a matching hat for every dress.

Marrying James Harris was the first time Jean had ever disobeyed her father, and he wept openly all through his daughter's traditional Episcopalian wedding ceremony in the backyard of the family's big house on South Woodland.

"When I got married, I had no conception of love," Jean says now. "Defying Dad was the main reason I married Jim. Also, unlike Dad, he was very quiet."

Nineteen years later, during the storms of her divorce, she said she had known it was a mistake even before the wedding, but things had gone too far to stop. Marge Richey says, "I've never known why Jean married him except—well, what other way was there to get away from home in those days? But Jim was very kind and loving. He reminded me of a nice, big, sweet, dumb TV daddy."

Dick and Betty Kimbrough were Jim Harris's closest friends, and later godparents to his son Jimmie. Betty remembers, "Jim was the kind of guy who loved to wash the car on weekends, and put on the storm windows. He liked to go up to Canada and chop wood. He was happy. You know, there are different ways to be happy. Money isn't everything. Jean was so great at entertaining, it was heaven to be with her. When we would all go up to Canada with our kids and eat fresh perch and tomatoes and corn—those are just some of the most wonderful memories I have of my entire lifetime."

"When Jean was young, she had no insight into herself," recalls Leslie "Mac" MacDougal, a sharp-witted automotive parts salesman who became Jean's special friend and dinner-party debating partner in Grosse Pointe. "She was desperate to marry this Jim Harris. I never understood it. He was a little man in every way. Jim had all his hair in those days, though, and I guess he looked good to her. But Jean had the intellect. She was brainy. Everything she got into, she did well. I liked to get her riled up, because that's when she was at her best, running on all eight cylinders. But *she* liked music, and art. *He* loved to putter, to trim the hedge. As she got more interesting, he got duller. My, how he loved to mow that lawn! He used to do it up and down, and then do it diagonally. Oh, they were an ill-matched pair—like seeing a plow horse and a Derby winner in harness together."

Despite her misgivings about the marriage, Jean determined to become the perfect wife. Her first garage apartment, and later the house on Hillcrest Road, were always spotless, and Jean was perfectly groomed even if she was painting the walls, as frequently she was. Jean was not only a demon house-painter; she scrubbed floors on her hands and knees, she baked and sewed, waxed and polished. There were always fresh flow-ers in the house, even when she could only afford to tuck a few daisies or carnations into a potted plant. When her friends com-mented on Jean's immaculate appearance, her standard reply was, "Well, I'm not a housewife. I have to look good. I work."

Jean had begun teaching at Grosse Pointe Country Day School (now Grosse Pointe University School) even before her marriage. First she taught seniors, and later first and second graders, her favorites. She was an extraordinarily popular teacher who often said that to watch a child's mind expanding to embrace a new idea was one of the two or three things she enjoyed most in life. Albert Struven said he thought teaching school was "the lowliest job on earth."

Since Jim's job at Holley Carburetor paid only a modest sal-ary, Jean's small schoolteacher's stipend was necessary to the family income. Yet money in itself never meant much to her. Getting and spending, like that other American obsession, spec-tator sports, simply never attracted her, and she was always slightly uncomfortable among what she calls "the country club set." She was not much good at any sport except swimming, at which she excelled, and not much of a game player; as for "those long-legged women with the needlepoint tennis racquet covers," she still finds them "slightly terrifying."

In Grosse Pointe, Jean's ways became a constant source of comment. "She was reading, reading constantly. . . . Remem-ber her famous Sunday night suppers with lentil soup and spa-ghetti! . . . She made such an *enormous* effort, but she was extremely volatile. We had a cup of tea together every single day, and I never knew whether I'd find a happy woman, a sad woman, an angry woman. . . ."

Jean had remarkable powers of concentration. She could be-come so preoccupied with what she was doing that on one fa-mous occasion when the telephone rang while Jean was holding a glass of milk and talking a blue streak, she picked up the phone and poured the milk in her ear.

Not long after her marriage, "Butts" Harris died, and his

widow moved in with Jean and Jim. Although Jean herself never complained, her Grosse Pointe friends recall that the senior Mrs. Harris seemed to expect to be treated as a guest in the house. When Jean came home from school, her mother-in-law would ask her what time dinner would be served.

Jim and Jean Harris very much wanted children. Jean decided to take things easier and give up teaching for a few years. Two years later, in 1950, David Harris was born, and Jimmie arrived in 1952. The day she brought David home from the hospital, she flipped on the TV news and saw a naked, crying Korean baby abandoned by the roadside. Jean herself began to cry and could not stop. The next day she drove off alone in her car and cried until nightfall. Her postpartum depression lasted two days. Sometimes even today, when she recalls the picture of the abandoned infant, tears come to her eyes. One other image that produced tears was a Norman Rockwell calendar picture that used to hang in the Struvens' kitchen. A little boy's eyes brim with tears as he stares at a puppy in a pet-shop window. He has pulled his pants pockets inside out to show that he has no money, and the puppy gazes back sorrowfully at the child with eyes that are equally wet.

But Jean does not cry just at calendar art. Seemingly anything can open the floodgates. Once, over lemonade in the backyard on a hot day, her friend Dodie Blain exclaimed, "Oh, Jean, you're so naive!" and Jean found herself rushing from the scene in floods of tears. "I had no idea she was that tender!" Dodie said later. It was not tenderness, Jean thought, so much as a humiliating, involuntary habit, rather like a tic or a stammer. Jean has struggled since childhood to find ways to control her tears. Clenching her nails in her palms does not help enough, nor even chewing the inside of her cheek. The only reliable defense is to sing a rollicking song to herself, very loudly, in her head, loud enough to blot out whatever tear-provoking event is going on. She used to experiment with folk songs, show tunes, even hymns, until the great day when Jean and her Smith College roommate went to the movies and saw Rita Hayworth in *Gilda,* slinking across the stage sheathed in black, tossing her long hair, grinding her hips, twirling her long, black gloves, and smiling provocatively as she sang, *Put the blame on Mame, boys, put the blame on Mame. Mame kissed a buyer from out of*

*town, that kiss burned Chicago down, so you can put the blame
on Mame, boys* . . . The song became Jean's secret weapon.
She sang it silently all through her own wedding. She has since
sung it on countless difficult occasions at home or in school; in
board meetings, in talks with parents, whenever she must struggle hard to maintain control. She got so good at it that, by her
last year at Madeira, she was able to sing the song in her head
and carry on a conversation at the same time. Her control as an
adult became so perfect that, until Herman Tarnower's death,
even her best friend, Marge, cannot remember seeing her cry.

Jean loves to be around small children, and shortly after Jimmie was born she started a kindergarten in her basement; the
school she founded still operates in Grosse Pointe today. Jim
Harris, too, adored the kids, and was a devoted and uncom-
plaining father to his own small sons, careful to supervise their
schoolwork and tooth-brushing at home, and in summer patiently teaching woodsmanship to a boys' group called Indian
Guides. As for the Little League, nobody can recall Jim once
missing a game.

Because Grosse Pointe Farms is home to the Ford family and
other automotive moguls, the place is thought of as an enclave
of the super-rich. But there is another Grosse Pointe, a world
where the wives busy themselves with the PTA and Junior
League while their husbands make comfortable livings selling
the specialized products and services that the big auto companies require. It is a world of Saturday morning lawn mowing
and Saturday night bridge games and country club dances, and
this was the world to which the Harrises and their friends belonged. Well-off but nowhere near rich, these people lived in a
small, closed group. Neither their golf nor their yacht club admitted Jews. Indeed, Grosse Pointe itself was one of the last
restricted communities in the United States, and much as they
now wince to admit it, the Midwesterners who were the Harrises' friends thought of themselves as a rather special "society." Jean herself—the outsider from Shaker Heights—always
had doubts about her own social standing among them. As one
of them says, "Jean had certain problems with Grosse Pointe.
She believed people here thought of her as a schoolteacher, not
really one of the crowd."

Says another, "Jean is a woman who has never known her

own worth, who never felt quite accepted socially. She talked a lot about what a disadvantage it was to her sons that 'their mother is just a schoolteacher.' "

Whenever she felt inferior, she would pretend not to care, make fun of herself, and cover up her sense of humiliation with wisecracks. At a large, stand-up cocktail party, Jean once pulled a small chair out into the middle of the room and sat down on it.

"Jean, what in the world are you doing?" Dodie asked.

"Just seeing if anyone will come and talk to me."

In a sense, Jean seemed to be forever challenging her friends to snub her, and mildly surprised when they failed to do so. "Big parties have always been a nightmare to me," Jean says. "I have always felt that I am the last person anyone would want to beat a path to talk to." These feelings contrast dramatically with the impression Jean Harris makes on others. Most people describe her as "sharp," "bright," "with it," "challenging," "controversial," "opinionated," "bossy." A surprising number, especially powerful older men—bankers, lawyers, industrialists, and the like—choose precisely the same phrase: "Jean Harris? Oh yes, met her once or twice. Pretty. Didn't really know her well, but"—pause, slow smile—"she struck *me* as a pretty tough cookie."

The men may intend this as a grudging compliment; Jean takes it as an unveiled insult. *"Tough cookie!* I think that's the nastiest thing anyone could say about me," she said recently. "I've had a lump in my throat almost every day for fifty-eight years! What do they want of me?"

In the spring of 1961, Jean heard that the Choate School was sending a summer study group to Russia and needed an extra chaperone. She wangled the assignment and, to meet expenses, obtained a fellowship from Wayne State University, where she was working on her master's degree. She used the money to enroll her sons in summer camp, and took off. Passing through New York, she stayed with her old Rondeau friend Marge Richey, now a successful interior decorator and the wife of a prominent lawyer, Leslie Jacobson. The Jacobsons had two children, a Park Avenue apartment, and a country home in Scarsdale. Marge remembers that her husband and her oldest friend "fell in love on sight. Jeannie is a special person, you know, and as innocent as she is, she only appeals to certain types of men. With that mind of hers, some men don't think she's feminine. Leslie, on the other hand, was crazy about her. He loved the mental exercise."

Marge and Jean had not seen each other since before the war. Marge had become a college beauty queen, and by the time she got to New York City to attend a fashion-design school and join the Macy's Training Squad, she was a rangy, knockout blonde. She took an apartment in Greenwich Village and had soon attracted the attention of a young attorney who was associated with perhaps the most important Jewish law firm in New York, Riegelman, Strasser, Schwartz and Spiegelberg. Metro-Goldwyn-Mayer had transferred the Richey family to New York by then, and when Marge announced her intention to marry Leslie Jacobson her father took her out to dinner and said he would not permit his daughter to marry a Jew.

"Good night, Dad," she said when dinner was over.

"No, Marge, this is not good night. This is goodbye!" It sounded like a line from an MGM movie, but Henderson Richey meant what he said. Marge was flabbergasted. Her father was in the movie business. Many of his associates and his two best friends were Jews, and Marge had never heard a word of anti-Semitism at home. But when she married Leslie in 1943, her father disowned her. When Marge became pregnant, Henderson Richey declared that he was not going to be grandfather to a Jewish child. By that time Leslie had been made a senior partner in his law firm, which is known today as Fried, Frank, Harris, Shriver and Jacobson.* For some years it has been acknowledged as the biggest Jewish law firm in the nation, specializing in corporate and business law, mergers, and acquisitions. It employs about 250 lawyers, and maintains flourishing branch offices in Washington and London.

Leslie's brilliant career notwithstanding, it was not until some months after the birth of his second Jewish grandchild that Henderson Richey at last bowed to the inevitable. "If it has to be a Jew, Leslie," he said, "I'm glad it's you."

---

* The firm's name was changed in the sixties, at a time when most of the original partners had died, and Sargent Shriver, brother-in-law of the late President Kennedy, had just signed on.

"My father was an unreasonable man," Marge Jacobson says today, "but nowhere nearly so unreasonable as Jean's father. Struvie was in a class by himself. He was anti-Jew, anti-black, anti-Catholic—a man full of hate. An ignorant man, a cruel man. Brilliant in his field, yes, but he had no compassion for anyone, and no human feeling. Bobby went to Annapolis and became a captain in the navy to try to please his father, though I'm not sure he ever did.

"They retired Struvie early from the Arthur G. McKee Company, I think because he had a nervous breakdown. Then they moved to Florida where he started his own metals business and made another small fortune. But he was a tight son of a gun, and he lacked the imagination to send his kids away, to let them travel, to enlarge and expand and cultivate their lives. He liked to complain about the world going to pot, and then he'd bellow, 'And I'm running out of banks to put my money in!' You know, Struvie was really screwy. Mildred protected him, in a way."

Two years after her trip to Russia Jean took a summer course at Yale, in "Christian Ethics in Modern Literature," and briefly saw her Scarsdale friends again. Then, for five years, they lost touch. When Jean was not in summer school accumulating credits for her master's degree, she and Jim took their sons camping or fishing, and in winter they all went skiing. Among their close friends in Grosse Pointe were Mr. and Mrs. Bob Scripps, of the newspaper family, and the two couples often went boating on the Scrippses' yacht. In the early sixties Scripps had a new boat built in Maine and the four friends sailed it back through New York to Lake Erie. Jean was so appreciative that she made up an elaborate ship's log-cum-scrapbook, wrote and bound it herself, and illustrated it with her own photographs. She told the Scrippses the trip had been the Harrises' first real vacation since their marriage.

"Jean did not lead a very exciting life here," Scripps recently remarked. "Her marriage to Jim was a real drag. He was a genuine tightwad and very conservative, really a man of no imagination, whereas Jean had so much! He never had better than a mediocre job, and he was always scared to death of doing anything that might give them an excuse to fire him. When Holley Carburetor was bought by the Colt Firearms Company, Jim was willing to hang onto the old job and take a lesser salary because the alternative would be to have to find *another* job, and he wasn't sure he could. Once he tried to learn Spanish, to get transferred to their foreign department—he thought that might be a way up. But he had to give that up because he had absolutely no aptitude, and he ended up as a kind of company lackey."

Later that summer the two couples made another boating expedition on Lake Erie. One evening after supper, Scripps saw Jean and Jim walking down the beach together holding hands. "It was the first and last time I ever saw anything affectionate happen between them. And it kind of made me feel better. That must have been about 1963."

By 1964, Jean was feeling like the Maurice Sendak character who goes around saying, "There must be more to life." She knew that Jim was a good husband and a fine father, that he did not drink too much or chase other women. But she had reached the moment when she was not sure she could settle for spending the rest of her life in Grosse Pointe Farms raising children, teaching school, playing bridge, paying off the mortgage, and answering the question: "Where do you want to go for dinner?" She did not want to be asked. She wanted to be told, and that, she knew, was never going to happen.

Like a great many girls of her age, she had really married to get away from home, and because it was the thing to do. The end of World War II had left them besotted on V-mail and sexually parched. Nineteen years later, having accumulated hardly any additional self-knowledge, she was going to get un-married because she simply could do it no longer. The critical turning points of Jean's life all seem to have happened in the same detached way. It was as if she herself did not make the really big decisions; as if they somehow made themselves, and she then carried out whatever actions the fateful decision required.

Jean Harris is a passionate woman, yet a somnambulist of the emotions. This is largely the training of her generation and class. Well-bred little girls of Jean's era are conditioned from childhood to ignore or deny feelings that might ruffle the serene surface of life. They are taught to become "ladies" of a particular northeastern upper-class WASP variety. Parents are "strict." "Personal responsibility" is stressed above most other values. If something goes wrong, if someone at school is rude or hurtful to the little girl, she is taught that first she must look to herself and ask, "What did *I* do wrong? Where did *I* fail?" She must never blame others, only herself. She is schooled to believe in the perfectibility of man, or at least of woman. The shadowy image of the "perfect lady" is always before her—modestly understated, infinitely considerate of others, always superbly controlled. She does not flirt. Unlike the Southern girl, she does not automatically bat her eyelashes, sigh and faint, and turn all pink and cuddly at the mere approach of a man.

In Jean Harris's own case, her achievements as an "intellectual," and her Phi Beta Kappa key from Smith, put still further distance between herself and her "animal instincts." She is not entirely aware that she even has such emotions. It is as if an iron door shuts off all communication between her deep, true feelings and the surface of her life. In particular, Jean seems to have conditioned herself from early childhood not to feel hurt, and if one never permits oneself to feel hurt, soon one grows less and less certain what one is feeling; and the greater the injury, the more nonchalantly one seems to experience it. *Put the blame on Mame.*

By August of 1964, Jean Harris had determined to file for divorce. One hot day, accompanied by her good friends Ann Kinzie and Dodie Blain, all three of them sporting white gloves and summer tans, Jean went down to the Wayne County Courthouse, and when the judge asked Ann and Dodie whether they saw any hope for this marriage, they each found it very easy to say no.

Jean's attorney and friend Jeptha Schureman (a bachelor who considers himself something of an expert on matrimony, having handled over 2,700 divorces) maintains, "Some people should never marry, and Jean is one of them. She is a superior person, and there are not too many suitable matches available for a person like that. Jean can be abrasive," Schureman recently told a visitor. "She does not suffer fools gladly, and she never did. But, oh, I'm sorry you didn't meet Jean years ago. What a superb woman she was!

"One other thing struck me about her," the lawyer continued. "She was never accusative about Jim Harris. Everyone

knew what he was—he was never guilty of false advertising
about himself. But Jean would never say a word against him.
She was an admirable client in a real rotten divorce."

"I hated to see her leave here," Jean's old dinner-table debating partner, Leslie MacDougal, said recently, "but that divorce
just had to happen. The rest of the Grosse Pointers were not
smart enough to have Jean's kind of fun with. I knew she'd be
better off in an atmosphere that was not so small-townish.
Grosse Pointe people are all a classic example of people who
have small minds. You see, there was nothing superficial about
Jean Harris, and there was everything superficial about Grosse
Pointe."

Jean's divorce was granted in February 1965, and by the end
of that year her dear friend Dodie found herself going through
the same ordeal. Twenty years after V-J Day, the men and
women all over the country who had created the postwar baby
boom were now discovering they could no longer live with one
another. Notwithstanding, there could scarcely have been two
more self-surprised, bewildered divorcées in the land than
Dodie Blain and Jean Harris. They had always envisaged themselves and their families as lifetime practitioners of "together-
ness." When they and their husbands were growing up in Michigan and Ohio, the very word *divorce* was spoken in whispers
and conjured up an image of a "fast" woman with scarlet fin-
gernails and a long cigarette holder. Even now, the only
divorcées Jean and Dodie actually *knew* were each other.

Dodie dreaded her first Christmas with her four children but
without their father. Jean felt wretched about what her divorce
had done to her boys. Gallant in disaster as a pair of Scarlett
O'Haras, the two women determined to join forces and manufacture for their six children the most perfect traditional Christmas ever. For days they decorated Dodie's house inside and out
and strung the colored lights. They tried to ignore the steady,
gray rain that began on the morning of Christmas Eve and
continued to fall all day as mothers and children finished trim-
ming the tree, wrapping their presents, baking cookies, and setting up the crèche. They prepared a traditional turkey dinner
with all the fixings, laid the table with the "good" china and
linen, hung up the stockings in front of the fireplace, sang the

old carols, and prepared for the reading aloud of "A Visit from Saint Nicholas," always the high point of the evening. It was important for "morale," the mothers decided, that they all dress for the feast in their finest; even the littlest boys wore jackets and ties, and Jean came to the table in a black chiffon gown with spaghetti straps and high-heeled black sandals. The evening, strangely, was very happy. Jean's wit sparkled. Having taught school at every level from kindergarten to the senior class, she was much at ease with children and kept the entire company in a state of sustained, genteel merriment. The women had decided to serve champagne, even though Jean rarely drank. Early in her marriage she had had two old-fashioned cocktails before going out to a dinner party, then gone upstairs, fallen asleep, and never got there. "That was the beginning and end of my drinking period," she told Dodie.

After the children had hung up their stockings, said their prayers, and gone to bed, Jean and Dodie lingered by the fire, finished the champagne, and wondered how their once-perfect lives had gone so wrong. It seemed obvious in retrospect that each had picked the wrong man, though at the time of course they had thought him ideal. Who, then, *was* the ideal husband? Jean said she thought very probably he was a Jewish doctor. Dodie was astounded. There were no Jews in Grosse Pointe and Dodie, of course, had never met Marge's paragon, Leslie Jacobson.

"Being Jewish, he'd be a man of superior intelligence *and* education," Jean explained. "I mean, a real intellectual." His Semitic background would also make him "warm-hearted and passionate, yet protective. Jewish husbands really take care of their women," she told Dodie. "They put them on a pedestal." She felt great compassion for what she knew of the Jews' history of suffering and persecution, and a deep, unformulated yearning to "make it up to them." Then there was the doctor factor: professional, protective, all-knowing, the doctor is the one who saves you from hurt, stops the pain, keeps you safe.

"Isn't every woman at some time in life convinced that the doctor is just one jump away from God?" Dodie asks now, with a wry smile. "This beautifully educated, magnificently trained specimen who loves humanity and is so kind and gentle and loving and understanding and patient and wise—well, I mean he just *must be* the superman husband!"

4

A Fine Romance

IN 1966, JEAN HARRIS was a bright, very pretty, provincial schoolteacher and divorcée, forty-three years old, highly educated, high-minded, and about as worldly as Winnie the Pooh. Except for her years at Smith and her trip to Russia, she had scarcely ever been out of the Middle West. Her chief concern in life—she probably would have said it was her only one—was the future well-being of her two sons, then sixteen and fourteen. She felt great guilt toward her children for disrupting their lives by divorcing their father. The one thing that might make it up to them, she believed, was an absolutely first-class start in life, which to her meant a topnotch college education, and this she had vowed to provide. She would have to do it entirely alone. "Struvie" had not only hated his son-in-law; he seemed to hate his grandsons because Jim was their father, and he flatly refused to contribute to the cost of their education. (Finally, at Marge Jacobson's urging, he did begin giving each grandson the tax-free maximum of $3,000 a year, but he tied the money up in a trust fund until each boy reached the age of twenty-one.) Jean's own resources amounted to $8,500 a year as a first-grade teacher, plus $200 a month in child support; she had refused to ask for alimony. That her educational aspirations for her sons might thus be extremely difficult to achieve, if they were not entirely unrealistic goals for a single mother in midlife, was a subject Jean simply refused to discuss. She *would do it.*

Her first step was to move immediately from school-teaching to school administration, because the pay is somewhat better. Accordingly, she advised the Smith College Vocational Office of her new goal, and gave notice to the school where she had taught for nineteen years. She shelved her own plans to complete work for her Ph.D. in philosophy and, when she was offered $12,000 a year to become the new Director of the Middle School at Springside, a strict and starchy girls' academy in the affluent Philadelphia suburb of Chestnut Hill, she accepted at once, and made preparations to move East.

In a teasing salute to her heroic new efforts, her strapping, football-playing sons had taken to calling their mother "Big Woman," or just "Big." Big was barely five feet four and weighed one hundred and ten pounds. Trim, fair, and fine-boned, she could look as sleek as the hood ornament on an old Packard, and in a few years she would. For now, her classic Nordic beauty remained blurred behind her out-of-date college-girl get-up—the sweaters and skirts, pearls, white gloves. In the twenty-one years since 1945, when she was graduated with honors and had gone home to marry the boy next door, Jean's style, like her appearance and values, had changed scarcely at all.

She tackled her new job at Springside with a level of determination that would have brought joy to the heart of Vince Lombardi. She saw to it that both of her sons got ample scholarships to good private schools, and she made their new home attractive and immaculate. She was capable of great spurts of concentration and energy, and the day before the moving van from Detroit arrived with their furniture, she stayed up the entire night roller-painting all the walls of their modest little rented house.

Two months later, in December 1966, she impulsively called Marge Jacobson in New York City. "Come up this weekend!" Marge exclaimed. "I'm having a dinner party." Jean demurred but Marge insisted. "Hang the expense! Get a sitter. I got a guy for you."

That evening at the Jacobsons' Park Avenue apartment Jean Harris met a man who looked to her like an Egyptian Pharaoh. He was tall and dark, with olive skin, white teeth, prominent nose and ears, and hypnotic brown eyes flecked with amber lights. His manner was cool, correct, intelligent, and soft-spoken. Jean knew nothing about him except that he was an old friend of the Jacobsons and an unmarried doctor.

Around the Century Country Club in Westchester, which had long been the hub of Dr. Herman Tarnower's vigorous social and sporting life, he was gossiped about as a "ladies' man," a reputation he did nothing to discourage. Paradoxically, they also spoke of him there as "a man's man," because of his dedication to game and fly fishing—Florida and Bahamian tarpon, Icelandic salmon, New Zealand or Adirondack trout—and his great pleasure in stalking game and shooting birds and wild animals of every variety. That he was neither, nobody's man but his own, self-assured to the point of arrogance, was part of his attraction. His many devoted friends and patients valued him for his intellect and stability, and prized him most of all because they considered him to be a brilliant, dedicated, and—favorite adjective—*caring* doctor.

When Herman Tarnower sat down next to Jean Harris at the dinner table, she immediately was captivated by his air of authority, the hawklike face, the strong-looking hands. After dinner they sat together on a small sofa and sought to impress each other with their knowledge of Russia. Tarnower had been a dedicated world traveler for many years. The evening sped by, and when Henri, the doctor's haughty Belgian chauffeur, arrived promptly at eleven o'clock to drive his employer back home to Westchester, Jean watched him disappear into the elevator and thought of Cinderella. She was certain that she would never see him again. Marge Jacobson knew better. Ever after, she used the same phrase to describe that first meeting, under her aegis, of the fair little schoolmistress and the powerful doctor. "Instant take!" she would exult, tossing back her handsome white-blonde head and whinnying like the very expensive palomino pony she much resembles.

A few days after the Jacobsons' dinner party, while Jean was bedded with chronic back trouble, a get-well present arrived from the doctor. It was the handsome picture book *Masada,* detailing the new finds at the ancient Israelite fortress where, in A.D. 73, nearly a thousand Jewish men, women, and children slaughtered themselves rather than accept inevitable defeat at Roman hands. "It's time you knew more about the Jews," the card said.

The next week Jean received a Christmas card. "You were a delight to be with," he wrote. "—kept wondering if you could keep up the 'pace.' Also whether or not you were a good dancer . . ." The front of the card carried a photograph of a serene woodland pond with an island on which a large Buddha appeared to float. The printed caption read simply, "Purchase Street, Purchase, New York."*

A few weeks after Christmas, a letter arrived from a safari camp near Nairobi, Kenya. "Is there any day you might be in New York in March?" In fact, Jean was planning to attend a three-day March meeting of the NAIS—the National Association of Independent Schools, a group that is to her profession what the American Medical Association is to Tarnower's. They arranged dinner for Friday, and that afternoon Jean slipped away from the school administrators to hurry to I. Miller's shoe salon on Fifth Avenue and blow forty dollars on a pair of patent leather pumps with ribbon bows to go with her good black and white silk dress. Promptly at seven Tarnower and his chauffeur picked her up at the Barbizon-Plaza Hotel and they drove to a little-known, expensive restaurant which serves fancy food that must be ordered in advance. Jean was enchanted to be *told,* not asked, where they would dine. All day long in her work she was expected to know the right answers, make all the decisions, and although she was willing, firm, and some thought even precipitate in her decision-making, it was never a role she found comfortable. Decisions did not come easily to Jean Harris, which is not to say that she lacked a mind of her own. The nickname "Miss Infallible" had been well chosen, but when Jean was try-

---

* Purchase is the northeast section of the town of Harrison, and is zoned for estates only. When John Harrison purchased the land for the town in the 1600s, someone wrote across the top of the map "Harrison's Purchase," and the designation stuck.

ing to make up her mind about something, she tended to hang onto it, chew it over, and near-worry the idea to death, like a dog with a bone.

After dinner Herman Tarnower, or "Hi" as he was universally known, suggested they go dancing at the Pierre Hotel. The doctor proved to be a marvelous partner, smooth, sure, and perfectly oiled. Jean held herself ramrod-stiff, as if she had left her portable ironing board inside the black and white silk dress, but she hoped that in his arms, with time, she too might become at ease and Arthur Murray–impeccable.

"Oh, Hi, you're *such* a good dancer!" she exclaimed as they swirled on the polished parquet.

He smiled. "A bachelor has to know that sort of thing." They were having such a good time that Hi drank two Manhattans and Jean drank two whiskey sours. The cocktails made her feel sprightly, this time, not sleepy, and it was with considerable reluctance that, shortly before eleven o'clock, she slipped on her plain black cloth coat and stepped out to the blue Cadillac where Henri was waiting to drive them back to her hotel.

Seeking to find their way into the lobby through a rear door, Hi and Jean found themselves caught in a cul-de-sac. "I guess we've gone about as far as we can go," she said.

"Oh, no, we haven't."

Now Jean smiled. It was the beginning of a delicious flirtation. The roses and phone calls began the next day.

Before we begin to trace the tortuous course of the fourteen-year romance that ensued, it may be worthwhile to reflect for a moment on the general state of romance today. Liberation may indeed be almost at hand in the ninth decade of the twentieth century, but in the secret hearts of American women, all is far from serene. Women's appetite for romance, and the farrago of fiction that nourishes it, appears to have become unappeasable. Suppliers cannot keep up with demand. Romance sells and sells and sells. More than half of all softcover books bought in this country are romances, known in the trade as "contemporaries," an apt term. American women today not only believe more strongly than ever in romantic love. They now seem rather desperately to crave it.

Women control the paperback romance market at both ends.

Men do not read these books. The successful "contemporary" author is almost always female, always over thirty. Publishers have discovered that younger women cannot write romance, because romance is not in their experience. Women under thirty know only the act itself, skin on skin, whereas what makes a romance *romantic,* indeed, what makes it erotic to fanciers of the genre, is all the fuzz, the veils, the pink light, the richly described foreplay, the silhouettes, the lavender afterglow.

Levels of sexual explicitness in the books differ, and there are other variables, but the underlying plot structure never changes: a plucky heroine encounters heart-rending obstacles, always including job problems and Other Women, usually in multiples, as she struggles to capture in fact the man who already fills her dreams. The three other essential plot elements, the publishers agree, are foreign travel, rich people, and a glamorous-sounding occupation.

In the real-life romance of Jean Harris and Herman Tarnower, all five essential plot elements are authentic and strong—plucky heroine, Other Women, travel, wealth, and *two* glamorous-sounding jobs. But there is a significant departure from the formula. These lovers are middle-aged. Their values were formed in another era and, by the time they meet, they have lived by those values more than half a lifetime.

Two weeks after their dance at the Pierre was Herman Tarnower's fifty-seventh birthday, and the date coincided with the start of Spring Break at school. The doctor suggested to Jean that she bring her sons to New York for a festive weekend. They could stay with the Jacobsons. On Friday night he would take everybody to see Angela Lansbury in *Mame,* and on Sunday they could all come up to Purchase for lunch. It was Jean's first glimpse of his mannered way of living—the curious glass-and-brick house in *faux* Frank Lloyd Wright style, surrounded by handsomely landscaped gardens and woods; the graceful pond, fringed now with daffodils; the huge, nineteen-twenties-style swimming pool and tennis court out in back; the handsome, prideful Belgian servants, Henri and Suzanne Van der Vreken, in constant, discreet attendance.

The house presented itself to the world in the grand manner, but once inside, the proportions were oddly foreshortened, like a stage set. Dr. Tarnower's home was really a much-expanded, made-over pool house. It had a dumbbell-shaped floor plan, the shaft of the dumbbell being the long, narrow, glass-fronted corridor that connected the vast living room and the dining room at either end. A steep flight of brick steps rose from the spacious circular driveway to a front door that was really one sliding glass panel in the glass-fronted wall. Directly ahead, facing the front door, was a cramped, windowless kitchen suggestive of a railroad dining car. The interiors of the grand rooms at either end of the hallway had gradually become shrines to the doctor's passions and his friends' tastes. Over the basic, by now slightly worn furnishings, done in hotel-suite neutrals, lay a mulch of giftwares. For many years the doctor's numerous girl friends and grateful patients had pelted him with expensive birthday presents, Christmas presents, thank-you presents, and carefully chosen love gifts. A great many of these items were monogrammed, embroidered, stitched, and woven by the loving hands of women whose fingers the doctor had nonetheless managed to slip through. The total effect was part Abercrombie & Fitch, part Museum of Natural History, part Alice Maynard. The living-room cushions, the cocktail glasses, the napkins, and even the card table were decorated with the rich plumage, in replica, of pheasant, partridge, and quail, the birds Tarnower loved most to shoot. Some chairs were upholstered in patterns of snakeskin and leopard. In the dining room, usually referred to as the "trophy room," a pair of eight-foot elephant tusks traced a massive ivory parenthesis around the fireplace. From three walls, dozens of stuffed fish and the mounted horns and heads of African ungulates—gazelle, wildebeest, antelope, and the great, shaggy Cape buffalo—gazed glassily down upon the diners. The fourth wall, facing the doctor's place at the head of the dining table, was occupied by a massive gun cabinet displaying Tarnower's valuable collection of hunting rifles, bird guns of every variety, and antique firearms. (The collection was stolen a decade or so ago, and never recovered.)

Upstairs, reachable only by a narrow spiral staircase leading up from the subterranean garage and passing through the living room, were the doctor's rather Spartan private quarters. A simple, twin-bedded room with a deck of slatted wood overlooked the driveway and the pond beyond with its floating Buddha. An elaborately fretted and ugly work of massive cabinetry, a free-standing room divider perhaps eight feet high, ran nearly the length of the room. It was directly under the ridgepole of the so-called cathedral ceiling, which topped it by an uncathedral-like four feet. On its front side were bookshelves, and built-in headboards for two narrow, single beds, each fitted with little swing-down armrests for sitting up and watching television. On the cabinet's back side, facing a long, narrow dressing area, an array of drawers and cupboards swung open to disclose well-lit, full-length wardrobe mirrors. This dressing area with a bath-room at each end, one for the doctor, another for a guest, had a long window overlooking the big old pool, tennis court, and the flower and vegetable gardens at the rear of the house.

Originally, all this had been part of the Herbert Lehman family's vast Westchester estate. In 1929 the banker Carl H. Pforzheimer acquired the property, and later it was divided to reduce taxes and, incidentally, to create the SUNY campus and the Westchester County Airport. In 1958 Tarnower persuaded Pforzheimer's son, his friend and patient, to offer the twenty-nine-room Lehman mansion on a ninety-nine-year lease to the Westchester County Medical Society as a medically related, nonprofit organization. The Medical Society in turn provided office space for the Westchester Heart Association, of which Herman Tarnower was founder and president. At the same time almost six acres of the estate, including its hundred-foot swimming pool, pool house, and tennis court, were sheared off and, at the very attractive price of $40,000, sold to Tarnower as a kind of mini-estate. The doctor's current remodeling project was adding a new ground-floor wing, alongside the trophy room, that would consist of two more bedrooms and bath-rooms. Sometime in the short, passionate spring of 1967, the doctor confided to Marge Jacobson that one day soon the new wing would become the new home of Jean Harris's sons.

It was no secret in Westchester that the austere doctor and the bright, sassy schoolmistress had fallen swiftly, deeply in love. Gala weekend visits, lunch parties, dinner parties, cock-tails at the Century Club were planned and replanned; love letters, long-stemmed roses, and nightly phone calls flew back and forth between Purchase and Philadelphia. The love affair was stately in its patterns, if not its pace. Decorum was observed. When Jean came up for the weekend, she slept at the home of a friend. But it was apparent to all the friends as well as to the Van der Vrekens, the prized, ever-present servants who, next to Jean herself, were the most important trophies in the doctor's collection, that a middle-aged flirtation had ripened swiftly into strong, mutual love.

> Tuesday, 6:30 a.m.
>
> Darling,
>   I love you very, very much. How can I tell?—I miss you and want to share so many things with you—sharing that must be love!! Are most people who marry in love? What happens? So few are really happy. You will give me all the answers this weekend—drive carefully, you will be transporting valuable cargo.
>   Am enclosing a map which may be of some help.
>
> More love,
> Hi

Spring became summer, the social roundabout quickened, the party carousel whirled without stop as Tarnower's devoted, fun-loving, affluent, and energetic circle of friends, patients, and accomplished, fervent hostesses vied to celebrate the coming of true autumnal love to the crowd's favorite bachelor. As Memorial Day weekend drew near, Herman Tarnower seemed happier than he had ever been in his life.

> Tuesday
>
> Darling,
>   There are so many things going on that I want to share with you—very frustrating. The highlight of this week will be Sunday—cocktails with the Smiths and then dinner at the Seymour Toppings (Foreign Editor of *The New York Times*), with Knopf, Harrison Salisbury and Mr. Ronning (Canadian Ambassador-at-large, involved with various North Vietnam peace feelers). He is Mrs. Topping's father. . . .
>   Darling, my love for you grows deeper all the time— that's good? I feel that we could be very, very happy together. May I suggest that we try to spend a very, very

long weekend together around Memorial Day to see if you can really put up with me for more than a few hours without getting terribly irritated or bored.

You can stay with me, my sister, the Schultes, the Club, other friends or a nearby hotel!! I, of course, will be on my best behavior but your penetrating eye should be able to discern the real from the apparent, the true from the false. At any rate, it will be fun trying to fool you. . . .

That weekend Herman Tarnower gave Jean Harris a blazing, emerald-cut diamond ring and asked her to marry him. In the evening they dined in Scarsdale with the doctor's sister, Pearl "Billie" Schwartz and her family, and celebrated the engagement with champagne from Tarnower's fabled cellars. (The Schwartzes did not ordinarily drink wine, save for a little Manischewitz on the High Holy Days.) A few weeks later Jean and her sons drove back to Grosse Pointe so the boys could visit their father. Approaching Detroit, they watched thick smoke from the 1967 ghetto riots blackening the summer sky. Jean stayed with her friend Dodie, who by this time had completed her divorce and become engaged to James B. Lewis, a real estate executive whom she was planning to marry in the fall. As soon as Dodie saw Jean's impressive diamond ring, she brought up the matter of insurance. The fires of Detroit were far away, but one could not be too careful. Jean had no idea whether her ring was insured. At Dodie's urging, she went to an appraiser the next day. "It would never have occurred to Jean," Dodie said later. "Except for her pearls, Jean didn't pay much attention to jewelry." That evening Jean said her ring was worth $10,000, nearly equal to her annual salary at Springside, and she appeared quite overwhelmed.

Back in Westchester on the Fourth of July there had been a formal dinner dance at the Century Club, and the dreamy-eyed little blonde wearing the big diamond ring that sparkled against the doctor's shoulder as the couple twirled around under the Japanese lanterns had been the talk of the evening. Herman Tarnower had been a member of Century for nearly twenty years, and the place was steeped in the tears of women who had tried and failed to snare him. Nearly all the dancers were pleased to see that at last the club's prize bachelor had been roped and tied. But in the ladies' room, Jean had grabbed hold of her friend Marge and whispered, "Marge, I *cannot* marry Hi for a year. I *cannot* take those children out of school again! I just can't do it to the kids. I took them away from their father already." Ever after, Marge would say that this had been Jean's fatal error. "Had she done it fast, they would have been married. But she waited too long. Two years later—well, then he didn't *have to,* I guess."

Over the summer Tarnower's old friend, patient, and closest neighbor, the publisher Alfred Knopf, had told several of his guests he was certain that, despite Jean's charms, the canny old bachelor would never go through with it. Nor were the Purchase people the only ones with forebodings. Thinking back now, every one of the Grosse Pointe friends—Dodie, the Kinzies, the Kimbroughs, "Mac" MacDougal, Bob Scripps—remembers Jean herself saying she was not at all sure that marriage to Hi would work; that he had been a bachelor too long; that he might not be a suitable stepfather for Jimmie and David; that she was not entirely certain she wanted to surrender her own independence.

In late August, shortly after Jean returned to Philadelphia, the doctor telephoned his fiancée, and Jean broached a difficult subject. "Hi, the moment is approaching when we have to set a date for this. School is going to start, and I have to know where I am going to be living, and where the children are going to be in school."

There was a long silence. Then Tarnower said, "Jean, I can't go through with it."

She waited for him to say more.

"I'm afraid of it. I can't go through with it, and I'm sorry."

If Jean was devastated by Tarnower's announcement, she did not let on, not even to her closest friends. When they expressed shock, even indignation, Jean said rather dreamily, "It hurt for a while, I suppose. But I'm not really very surprised. Maybe I should be, but somehow I'm not. If he hasn't married by this time, I suppose he can't. . . . He just isn't a marrying man. I don't really know what all the reasons are." Once more the all-saving iron door had clanged shut.

Jean hid her hurt from Tarnower with characteristic flippancy. She simply wrapped up her enormous ring and sent it back with a note. "You really ought to give this to Suzanne. She's the only woman you'll ever need in your life."

The doctor telephoned at once. "I insist you keep it," he said. "If you don't want it, I'll give it to David." He drove to Philadelphia that very weekend and brought the diamond back with him. He seemed more disturbed about her rejection of the ring than she was about his change of heart. When he arrived, the boys recall, Jean and Hi locked themselves in the bedroom and their argument lasted many hours.

The ring was, of course, only the nominal subject of their dispute. There can be no question that in his way Herman Tarnower genuinely loved Jean Harris, and that just now he was trying very hard to "do the right thing" by her, despite his own shameful failure of heart or nerve. That had happened to him before; he considered it "his" problem. Jean's "problem," he said, was that she deserved a clean break and a fresh start. "You're a wonderful woman, Jean, and you *should be* married," he kept repeating. Therefore he would take himself out of the way, give her up entirely, so as not to spoil her chances of marrying someone else. As he saw it, a woman of Jean's background could never be fully respectable, never achieve the kind of social acceptance he thought she should have, unless she were married. He saw the all-important ring as both symbol and perpetual reminder of the genuineness of his love, despite the falsity of his promise. Doubtless the big gem also helped him to expiate his guilt for his incapacity to make a lasting commitment.

But Jean was not interested in a $10,000 placebo. The doctor might be doing and saying all the "right things," but his words had nothing whatsoever to do with her feelings. She had not planned to fall in love with him. It had just happened. Nevertheless, she was by now deeply, passionately in love, and even as they were agreeing not to see each other again, she feared that in her own case she might be making a promise she would be unable to keep.

Three weeks after the ring episode, Jean and her younger son drove up to Newport, Rhode Island, for a weekend of sailing. Coming home late Sunday afternoon on the Merritt Parkway, Jean suddenly noticed a sign, Purchase Street. To be this close to Hi and not even telephone him seemed suddenly preposterous.

"We were just passing by," she said cheerily.

"Come to dinner!" he said at once. His sister Billie and her family would be there too.

So Jean and Jimmie drove back to the house on Purchase Street, and that night Jean slept on a Hide-a-Bed in the trophy room, and her lover came to visit her couch under the watchful glass eyes of the horned beasts, and by morning Jean could not deny that her resolve had been seriously compromised.

Late in September, Jean began her second year at Springside. It was a full schedule. As Director of the Middle School, she supervised the education of 165 uniformed little girls in grades five through eight. Her responsibilities included handling admissions, preparing budgets, hiring and firing teachers, and planning the curriculum, which she was extremely anxious to expand in order to demonstrate her conviction that "any child at any age can be taught almost any subject in some intellectually honest form."

Jean tried with all her considerable willpower to submerge herself entirely in work. Her chronic back trouble had come back worse than ever. When Hi heard about it, he telephoned at once, filled with concern, and recommended some new pain-killing pills; he telephoned a few days later to see if they had made her feel better. It would have been unkind to tell her then that the workers finally had finished the new wing on his house, and that he had invited Suzanne and Henri to move in. Convenient both to the tiny kitchen whence issued Suzanne's increasingly fancy gourmet meals, and to the doctor's lavish grounds, which Henri tended, the new wing well suited the Van der Vrekens' pivotal position in the austere, bachelor household.

One quiet evening, late in November, Jean Harris reached for a few sheets of three-holed school notepaper and, in a firm, bold, upright hand, she wrote out the three-page letter that would change the course of the rest of her life.

Dear Hi,

What a strange and wonderful and awful three months these have been, and what a lot of soul-searing thoughts they have evoked. I know a letter from me is not what you want most in the world, but there are so many important things still to say. Everything about us is important to me Hi, because I've never experienced love before until you, and love, I've discovered, means wanting to share every thought and sensation, in fact *needing* to share. You wanted to share too a few weeks ago? What happened? Where did it go?

One of the most upsetting things about the past weeks, darling, is where does it leave you?, what do you feel about yourself? I suppose it's rather foolish to tell someone who knows more about most things than I do,—that marriage isn't a natural state of being, not a matter of genes and chromosomes that is—so not wanting to marry isn't a sign of being unnatural or cowardly, or inferior, or odd. Now that you've said "I can't marry you" you seem to want to hide me and pretend I'm not there—as though I were a reminder of something unclean or ugly. I want to be something you are proud of, Hi, because you made me happy and whole and alive. Don't be ashamed of me, or disgusted with you because we didn't end up in a vine-covered cottage. The only advantage to marriage, darling, was the opportunity to be together—to kiss you every morning and hold you every night. The responsibility of raising children and doing the mending and marketing and laundry would still have been there for me. The only thing that made it good was knowing you'd be there too.

You looked so concerned when I said I'd explain the whole truth if people wondered why we hadn't married. I realize now it wasn't just saving my little old maidenly face that troubled you. I think somehow you're ashamed of not being married because being married is part of the proper pattern of things, and the proper pattern of things matters terribly to you. . . .

Maybe I can never really know that you loved me, Hi, but I do know that for a little while you were a wonderfully strong, loving, desiring and desirable male animal, and as a rather odd but honest loving female I found every moment with you warm and satisfying and good. Maybe having too much money was the trouble. If the

bottom ever falls out of the market, darling, I'm really a
very capable housekeeper.

As far as never seeing you again is concerned I won't
let it happen however much you protest. If your social
engagements continue to be as pressing as they are this
weekend perhaps you could work me in during office
hours. . . . And anyway it doesn't make sense. I have to
know how you are.

I'm having the ring made smaller and then I will wear
it. It's beautiful—and so was having you love me—even
for such a short time—

JEAN

To Jean, the letter was a proclamation that she was a modern
woman. To Herman, it may have seemed a license to resume his
lifetime bachelor habits. In any event, it produced the desired
results and, shortly before Christmas, Tarnower called Jean and
said, "It would be wonderful to go some place without your
children." One of his friends had a villa in Jamaica. Any bachelor guest could bring a woman companion if he chose. Her
particular identity was of no consequence to the host. So when
Christmas vacation began, Jean sent the boys home to their
father, and together she and Tarnower boarded a plane for Jamaica. It was the first of dozens of trips they would make together, including three full round-the-world tours, each describing a new orbit, as well as uncounted shorter vacations to swim
and sun and relax on the yachts and estates and private islands
of Tarnower's wealthy patients and friends.

On the second or third day of their holiday, Jean wrote a
Christmas letter to her parents and asked Tarnower to give it to
the servants to mail.

"You told your mother and father you were going away with
me?"

"Why wouldn't I tell them, Herman? I'm not ashamed of
what I'm doing. If I were, I wouldn't have come."

Tarnower did not reply. But the news clearly made him uneasy. One cannot know how much of his unease was for Jean,
how much for himself. Did he yet know, for example, that
Jean's father had taken to calling his daughter a "whore" because of her relationship with "that Jew"? How troubled was he

himself about this new and free relationship with the woman he had once planned to make his wife? Certainly it can have been no simple matter for either one of these conservative, once formally engaged people, ages forty-four and fifty-seven, to transform themselves almost overnight—on no basis but an impulsive, three-page love letter—into a pair of modern lovers, bound by no formal ties, and no commitments save those of the heart.

When they think back to 1967, David and Jimmie Harris remember one other thing about that year. Their mother never liked to use the automatic dishwasher, preferring to soap each item individually, turning it in her hands under the running water until her fingers told her it was absolutely clean. Because Jean had never felt comfortable wearing her ring to school, or around Philadelphia, until she was "officially engaged," that is, until a wedding date had been announced, she wore it at home while she washed the dishes, and by the end of the year, every single glass in the Harris pantry was etched with the circles of Jean's happiness, her unhappiness, her energy, her despair.

5

The Greening of Dr. Lunch Hour

AT THE TIME JEAN HARRIS met Herman Tarnower, he liked to refer to himself modestly as "just a country doctor," and his patients appreciated the little joke. The doctor had devoted almost thirty years to building up his practice at the Scarsdale Medical Group, of which he was founder, owner, and chief physician. It was unusually wealthy for a suburban practice, and glittered with star names in Wall Street, business, banking, and publishing circles. Tarnower was their "country doctor" only because these Loebs, Lehmans, Warburgs, Sulzbergers, Rothschilds, Knopfs, Bronfmans, Cullmans, and Schultes all had city doctors too, because they had city as well as country homes, and often an Adirondack summer camp and a winter palace in Florida or the Caribbean. To be *only* their country doctor had been a shrewd decision, made years before. Yes, they all had other doctors, but Tarnower was the one who looked after them when they were at play, relaxing with their families, having fun; he was the doctor who golfed and fished and hunted with them. And, as a master social mountaineer, he was the doctor who had time to nosh with them, schmooze with them, counsel their adored children, the pampered sons and daughters and grandchildren who worried them so; who had the time to sit up all night with them if the situation required. Herman Tarnower the physician was supremely available. You could see him in his office any morning at 7:00 A.M. before catching the 7:30 to Wall Street. You could see him Saturdays or Sundays, if necessary. After the initial visit, he always made a follow-up call to ask how you were feeling *now*. Long before Herman Tarnower had money, he had something better than money; he had the capability and the will to dispense personalized medical care at any hour of the day or night. He traded on his accessibility as much as his medical expertise. "A real *doctor* doctor," his grateful patients said. He not only made house calls. He himself would pick up your blood or urine sample, if your blood was blue enough. More than one wealthy, worried matron with an ailing husband has stood at dawn at the front of her mansion, specimen bottle in hand, peering down the misty driveway for the sight of the doctor's blue Chevrolet. (The Cadillac was for social occasions. He used a Chevrolet for house calls, and it was a part of his near-obsession with firearms that he always carried a revolver in the glove compartment.) Tarnower would take the specimen to his lab, have it analyzed, and telephone to adjust the husband's daily dosage of medication while the servants of the great house were still abed.

Not all the patients of the Scarsdale Medical Group were very rich, of course. Some were merely upper middle class, and some were the cooks, maids, butlers, and gardeners of the Great Ones, and others were simple townspeople—the garage mechanic, the locker-room attendant, the people at the hardware store. The grateful patient is one of the sweetest perquisites in the practice of medicine, and Herman Tarnower had grateful patients spotted all over town. As a result, his car was always gassed up, his vegetables were always fresh, his shirts were always ready. Grateful patients of taste had decorated his house; grateful patients, female, filled the pages of his little black book and had contributed to his extensive cuff-link collection. But grateful patients, tycoon class, were the central concern of his life. Gradually, over many years of careful cultivation, their care and well-being had become his hobby, his work, his fun, his passion.

It had all begun with Frieda Fanny Schiff Warburg, daughter of the financier and philanthropist Jacob Schiff, widow of the international banker Felix Warburg, matriarch of the Warburg clan, and chatelaine of the baronial Fifth Avenue mansion that is now the Jewish Museum. She was the benign dowager empress of "Our Crowd," and by 1948 she had a bad heart. In spring that year, while in residence at her Westchester summer palace, Meadow Farm, Mrs. Warburg felt a new flutter under her ribs. A new cardiogram was in order, said her city doctor, and it might be more convenient, and just as efficient, to have it done at the nearby hospital in White Plains. Enter staff cardiologist Herman Tarnower, thirty-eight years old, EKG charts in hand. He was a most wonderfully concerned young doctor, Mrs. Warburg decided. Soon he had taken to dropping by Meadow Farm every few days just to see how the old lady was doing. She liked his attentiveness, intelligence, and industry, and his melancholy brown eyes. It was truly an unexpected pleasure to discover a Jewish doctor so far from "Our Crowd's" own Mount Sinai Hospital in New York City. When she learned he was unmarried, she tried to fix him up with some girls. This did not work out, but he turned out to be quite a *Feinschmecker,* and when she invited him to lunch, he always stayed.

Dr. Tarnower ventured the opinion that the digitalis might be more effective if administered by injection than by mouth, and he said it would be no trouble at all for him to stop by every day and give her the shot. Soon he was a part of the household. He almost always came by shortly before noon. Mrs. Warburg took her own lunch on a tray in bed, but if no one else in the family was home for lunch that day, the staff served the doctor a tray in the sitting room. The senior Warburgs were German-born, and the entire family was addicted to puns. Mrs. Warburg took to referring fondly to her visitor behind his back as Dr. Lunch Hour.

He was a very fine doctor, they all agreed, and it was not long before Dr. Lunch Hour was looking after the various illnesses of Mrs. Warburg's four children, and *their* children. He even delivered a couple of her grandnephews and nieces. The young doctor soon acquired several other elderly and wealthy patients who had summer estates nearby. One of the most important of these to Tarnower's future career was the investment banker and industrialist Carl M. Loeb, or "CM," as his son, John L. Loeb, and his daughter-in-law, Frances Lehman Loeb, as well as the rest of that large family always referred to the old man.

Although Herman Tarnower was perfectly suited to the medical needs of these families, the young doctor lacked a certain social fine-tuning that the Warburgs undertook to correct. "I like him so much," Mrs. Warburg gently told her children. "Only one thing bothers me. I don't think he should call me Frieda."

The next day one of her sons waylaid Dr. Lunch Hour on the stairs. "You don't have to 'Mrs. Warburg' her all the time," he said, "but 'Frieda' she ain't, to you."

From then on Tarnower referred to his prize patient rather sepulchrally as "Mother."

"Who the hell's mother is she anyway?" her children would complain behind his back. But they were happy to overlook his social gaucherie because Mother was so fond of him, and because they considered him medically impeccable.

The gratitude of Tarnower's wealthy patients knew no bounds. Here a contemporary dowager empress attempts to describe her feelings toward her "country doctor": "When I think *doctor,* I don't think good—bad. I don't think young—old. I don't think rich—poor. I think—I like him! Or I don't. And Hi was *terribly* nice—a sympathetic, caring, ambitious man who was intensely interested in the world around him, and absolutely tops in his profession. If you sent your butler or your maid to him, even though they were perfectly fine, he'd know who they were. And he gave them all kinds of tests, blood and urine and so on, even though there was nothing the matter with them . . . which of course *I* knew, even though I'm not a doctor. He was great in emergencies, too. When my granddaughter had her bee sting, he was here in ten minutes."

No one appreciated Dr. Tarnower more than George "Dan" Comfort, a quiet man who directs a powerful real estate empire. The bond between Comfort and Tarnower had begun at a fishing camp in the Canadian wilderness owned by Joseph Cullman III, then president of Philip Morris. Cullman's guests had been standing armpit-deep in a rushing trout stream when suddenly Comfort was stricken with chest pains. Tarnower not only got the terrified man to safety, he reeled in his prize fish. Comfort said he had suffered from a hiatal hernia for years. "Why don't you come in one day and let me look you over," Tarnower suggested, and in due course he informed Comfort that his real trouble was in his heart, not his esophagus.

What happened next is a nice example of the Tarnower style. After doing an angiogram, he told Comfort he probably needed bypass surgery. They telephoned Dr. Frank Spencer in New York City, "who is probably the greatest open heart surgeon in the world," and learned that he was booked solid for the next three months. "Well, Dr. Hi got on one extension, and I got on the other, and we started mentioning some names. Henry Helmsley is a man I work with very closely. We also mentioned John Loeb. We mentioned Dr. Howard Rusk, and one or two others, and finally the secretary said, 'You're mentioning some very heavy names there. How about next week?' "

Tarnower's tycoon patients had still another reason to be grateful to their country doctor. They are the sort of men who keep fleets of yachts and private jets on standby to transport them to work or play around the globe, and a physician who is also good company, and a good sportsman, is ever a welcome passenger. Herman never complained about the food or fussed about accommodations. He was a man of austere personal habits. He was punctual and intelligent. Away from the office, he was easygoing, well-informed, an excellent listener, a good talker and gambler, and something of a bon vivant. Being a bachelor, he was nearly always available on short notice to jet off for a few days' fishing in Iceland, or golf at Lyford Cay. On the mogul level, abroad and at home, Tarnower filled the ancient role of *Leibarzt,* a body doctor, responsive to the imperial tradition that an important personage has someone at hand qualified to attend him at all times.

Not all powerful persons were equally smitten with Tarnower's style. Says one, "Hi had an inordinate drive for recognition. His reputation was as a devoted physician, but if you were rich, he was even more devoted. He counted the remunerectomies he performed." Another wealthy and not-so-grateful patient says, "I found him a cold, desiccated man and a mediocre doctor."

But every doctor has disgruntled patients, and for each of these, there are a dozen who will assure you that Herman Tarnower was the most "caring" physician they have ever met. No episode was too trivial, or too taxing, to merit his medical attention. In the service of his topmost bigshots he would hike many miles to attend an injured native guide in a remote hunting camp, or rush over to treat a grandchild who had fallen off his tricycle. He even came when the dog was sick. Among these families, teenagers who got into drugs or sexual difficulties or had weight problems (in this set, overweight is considered a "disease") routinely were sent to "have a good talk with Hi," and invariably Tarnower was patient, understanding, and profligate with his attention. The son or daughter would be invited out to lunch, or might spend an hour in his office discussing prep-school sports or debutante dilemmas.

People's recollections of Tarnower are filled with contradictions not only because he behaved differently with different people, and not only because he always held his cards close to his vest. His essential nature was misunderstood by nearly everybody because he had a paradoxical personality—secretive and reserved in his private life, attentive, tender, and generous with his time as a physician. Some people mistook his practiced, professional, and genuinely concerned bedside manner for real warmth. Tarnower the man went out of his way for nobody. All his personal relationships were on a "take it or leave it" basis. Especially with women, Jean Harris included, his lifelong posture had been: "Suit yourself." Tarnower the doctor could not do enough to make a patient feel happy, comfortable, and secure. On the evening of the night he died, he checked on several important patients personally by telephone, as he usually did, and he made four separate telephone calls in connection with a wealthy man who had just returned from Nassau with a slight cough.

Tarnower's close friends were reconciled to his divided nature. Marge Jacobson, for example, says, "I knew all Hi's faults, but I always liked him, and Les was as fond of him as I was. When he took up with Jean, well, knowing Hi's history, I got hold of him and said, 'Listen, Hi, between her father and her husband, she's had enough hurt already. And she's a good kid, so don't hurt her any more.' After I found out they *weren't* going to get married, I got hold of him again. He told me, 'Jean understands that we won't marry. But I have promised her that I would take care of her, and I meant it. She's remembered in my will.' But money isn't everything. And the truth is, I think Hi was *incapable* of loving. He had tremendous family feeling, but without love. Hi only loved himself, and was quite insensitive to everybody else."

Another person who well knew Herman's flaws and liked him in spite of them was his boyhood chum, Dr. Allen Tanney, a genial, unpretentious man who is now an attending physician at Manhattan's Lenox Hill Hospital, Medical Director of Philip Morris, consulting physician to both the American and National baseball leagues, and who maintains an office in the Waldorf-Astoria Hotel. "We are both men who have struggled very hard to get where we have, but Hi always loved the fancy life a lot more than I did. If you didn't understand him, Hi was an easy man to dislike . . . a bit standoffish, a bit selfish, and oh, how he loved to take care of important people!"

Not so surprisingly, Jean Harris may have said it best when she told a friend, some time after Tarnower's death, "Herman Tarnower craved social acceptance more than anything else on this earth."

The company in which he sought that acceptance, schemed and fought for it, demanded it and finally triumphantly achieved it, is one of the most powerful, closed, hard-nosed, and haughty social groups in the land. Many of its members are not only enormously rich; they have the not incorrect inbuilt assurance that they can do anything they feel like. Unabashed materialists, armored in arrogance, they give an impression of invulnerability. Search in vain for the soft underbelly; all is hard and flat. They are interested fundamentally only in themselves and their children. They navigate through life plotting their course by three immutable stars: Everyone is after your money. Nobody can be too thin. I am an interesting person, and everything I do, feel, say, or shed is also of interest. Living their entire lives in a closed and padded universe, they all know every scrap of gossip there is to know about one another. To celebrate their thirtieth wedding anniversary, one grand couple threw a huge party with three tents, two orchestras, and elaborate epithalamial odes composed by the principals. The wife's toast to her husband was a witty and lengthy catalogue of every one of his major infidelities—and the guests laughed in all the right places.

The stamping ground of these people is Westchester's old-money world of vast, manicured, stone-walled estates, and their social center is not a village but a golf club. "Century," as its members invariably refer to it, is a place of emerald fairways, deeply tanned men and women, well-behaved children, and deliberately nonflashy *luxe.* Founded in 1898, Century Country Club now costs $9,000 to $12,000 to join (depending on age) and dues are $2,400 a year, but these are only starting costs. Nonetheless, there is a lengthy waiting list. Century's kitchen has been called "Westchester's only three star restaurant," and it once had Ben Hogan as its golf pro and Don Budge's brother, Lloyd, teaching tennis. Its rambling, hilltop, ivy-covered club-house is immaculate but deliberately slightly dowdy; the year seems eternally 1938; the color scheme runs to pink, white, and green; the atmosphere is wondrously genial, and all the employees have the tact and knowledge of old family retainers. The place looks like the set of an early Bing Crosby movie, and the people a lot like Edward Arnold, Priscilla Lane, Don DeFore.

Century thinks of itself as not just the best Jewish club in New York, but best in the world. If "best" means most exclusive, they are probably right, even though getting into Century today is not quite so difficult as it once was. The club is still Wall Street–based, and a goodly number of Lehmans, Loebs, Guggenheims, Schiffs, Seligmans, and Warburgs, and the other German Jewish banking families who make up "Our Crowd," still play golf and tennis there today. But so do plenty of business and professional men and what one member calls "fake German Jews"—men of sufficient power, or wealth, to overcome the severe social handicap of being a Jew from Russia or Eastern Europe. One of the very first Century members to cross that barrier had been Herman Tarnower. Back in 1948, Walter Rothschild, the son-in-law of Frieda Warburg, had put the family doctor up for membership in the family club. Despite his powerful patronage, Tarnower still probably would not have been admitted to Century had he not been a physician. Jews have a particular respect for learning; a doctor automatically is accorded special status. Besides, at that time Century had no other doctor members who practiced medicine in Westchester. Soon the bachelor physician had become a kind of permanent fixture around the place. Whenever he was not at his office or the hospital, or asleep, he could almost always be found on the fairways or the practice tee, or lounging around the locker room or dining room.

An anthropologist seeking to unravel the hierarchies of Century society today would have to begin with a backward glance at another era when New York's old German Jewish banking families still reigned supreme. These people were not only rich; they were wellborn. They felt themselves special, and entirely apart from the gentile world of wealth. Over the years, they exerted enormous power not only in the financial but also in the cultural and humanitarian institutions of the land, chiefly through huge philanthropies. By and large their descendants tend to be educated, enlightened, cultivated persons, far brighter and better company than the merely rich of Palm Beach or Grosse Pointe.

Stephen Birmingham defined "Our Crowd" as "a citadel of privilege, power, philanthropy and family pride." Its members looked down on the poor immigrant Jews who poured in later from Russia and Poland and the Baltic states. They spoke of these eastern Jews as "Orientals," which is not to say that the wealthy German Jews were uncharitable to the new arrivals. The great German-born banking families—Warburgs, Lehmans, Seligmans, Loebs, Guggenheims, Lewisohns, and so on—financed housing, care, and even employment for these hordes of newer Jewish immigrants, but they saw no reason to socialize with them. "Our Crowd" even looked down their noses at other German Jews, such as the Gimbels, who were "in trade": storekeepers, not bankers.

No anthropologist can get far in the study of Century without asking the age-old question: what does it mean to these people to be a Jew? Obviously it is more than just a race, and more than just a religion. Yet save for special occasions, few members of Century go to temple. One member who is on the Board of Temple Emanu-El on Fifth Avenue, the richest synagogue in the largest Jewish community on earth, has never attended an ordinary Sabbath service there.

The best answer seems to be that being a Jew means belonging by choice to a certain social culture—one that varies greatly with geography and class and ethnic background. At Century, the one common trait seems to be that its members do not deny their own Jewishness. (Some Century barons consider themselves so assimilated they also belong to non-Jewish clubs.) Many do not seem particularly enthusiastic about being Jewish, yet at the same time they cling to their Jewishness with tenacity, and proclaim it insistently; the phenomenon is a kind of denial of denial. Although they call themselves "German Jews," when the anthropologist asks himself what is Jewish about them, the only common answer is that they hope to be buried from Temple Emanu-El, itself a strange place where nearly every member says, *I myself* don't need this, but it is good for my [mother] [children] [grandparents] [husband's family] [business] that we belong to this temple. "Such feelings aside," one old-timer acknowledges, "no one would go there. Not until death threatens, that is, and they get a little scared. Then they start coming in."

Century members are Reform Jews. What does that mean? According to one of the elders of the club, "It really means you're not ashamed to say you're Jewish. Because it also means that you don't have to behave differently, you don't have to live differently, you don't even have to eat differently. No beards, no fasting, no kosher food. Reform Judaism reminds me of some kind of half-assed Unitarianism, where prayers are addressed not to a Diety, but 'To whom it may concern.' But what the hell, it's all part of the process of assimilation. And a sort of underground railway station along the way to the attainment of this assimilation so desired has been the Century Club. I call the place 'the assimilated ghetto.' And court physician to the assimilated ghetto was Herman Tarnower."

"Please do not be shocked," says another member, overhearing the first. "You must understand that Century is the most anti-Semitic club in the world, and that the true function of an 'Admissions Committee' is to keep people out. You make yourself better when you turn someone else down. This club even turned down Walter Annenberg, who could have bought and sold the entire place. He was good enough to be America's Ambassador to the Court of St. James's, but not good enough for Century. His money came from the wrong kind of money-lending: racetracks, not banks."

Hearing this kind of talk, yet another club member, older and wiser, says, "What you are dealing with here are the permutations of Jewish self-hatred. All minorities have it. Blacks and women talk about themselves in the same way."

Enough stories of self-loathing. Let us talk now to someone with a better perspective, a man now in his seventies and a genuine aristocrat of the old "Our Crowd": "People belong to Century because they want a place where they can take the family, play golf, and socialize. It has nothing to do with religion. The affiliation among these Jews is essentially a social one. It results from their wish to become certified members of the *in*-group. They want to be known as amongst those who have 'made it.' Herman Tarnower's greatest ambition was to be a member of the in-group. To associate with the top German Jewish families was not enough. He wanted to be part of the *kultur,* to associate with Alfred Knopf, Seymour Topping, people like that. And he did."

In considering how Century has functioned as an underground railway station to assimilation and acceptance, it is important to remember that the people who belong to it have not only done well; they have also done a great deal of good. The Century barons have set a very fast track in philanthropic undertakings. The basis of the fine social distinctions among the club's members is the size of the various charitable contributions each family has made over many years. Each man knows that once a year he will be called into a room alongside his neighbors and friends and reminded, "Last year you gave five thousand. We need a ten percent increase this year. How much can we expect this time from you?" The goad for private giving is public pressure. It is a very tiny but potentially savage public; his brother, his lawyer, his accountant, his business partners, his club-mates are all in the room with him. The system works well at even the loftiest financial levels. Recently twenty men were called into a room and told, "This year's goal for Israel is twenty million dollars." Each man thereupon wrote out his personal check for $1,000,000.

* * *

This was the world in which Dr. Herman Tarnower circled like a fish in an aquarium, ever present, ever available and agreeable for a game, a glass, a shoot, an interesting chat, a spot of medical opinion, a bit of personal wisdom. When Jean Harris came East and took up with Herman Tarnower, she found herself in an exotic, unfamiliar society that she could not read at all. The girl from Rondeau Shores Estates could scarcely be expected to understand the special attraction that a WASP princess like herself held for Herman Tarnower. "Little Russian Jews don't get to meet that kind of *shiksa* goddess. Only Lehmans and Cullmans do," as one club-mate observed. The doctor introduced her to his friends as Jean Harris *of Grosse Pointe* (italics Tarnower's). *From* Grosse Pointe would have been more accurate, but he misread the little schoolmistress just as she misread her loving *Leibarzt.* So, cocooned in romantic gauze and pink clouds of mutual misunderstanding, the happy couple whirled round and round. Some, watching them, made the mistake of attributing Jean's high spirits to her own taste for social climbing. But she was not climbing, she was infatuated, giddy as a debutante atwirl with her first stirrings of social and sexual power.

All innocence, this middle-aged Sleeping Beauty had awakened in the exotic land of Century and now fluttered wonderingly onward, unaware, seeing herself as adventurous and bold. When she looked at her prince she saw only her own myth of the warm-blooded Jewish doctor. She did not see in him the hidden anti-Semitism of the Jew. She could not, for example, appreciate the feelings that drove Tarnower calculatingly to become the physician of four consecutive presidents of a certain non-Jewish Westchester golf club, simply in hopes of himself being invited to join.* To Jean Harris, Herman's world was always to a degree incomprehensible; she never fully understood its social intricacies and costs, nor the special geography and difficulty of his climb.

When one is madly in love, it is no trick to see black as white, to turn moles into beauty spots, to see a bald pate as a noble

---

* After he became famous as the author of the Scarsdale Diet, Tarnower *was* asked to join. To his credit, he turned them down.

brow, and a long nose as a proud beak. When friends described
the doctor as "looking like a Gauleiter," and "having a Ph.D. in
ugly," Jean merely shrugged. She adored the man's lean, hard,
smooth, hungry look. To make a virtue of every flaw is the
nature of love. When they first met, Jean told several friends
rhapsodically that she saw Tarnower as "a good Sammy
Glick." She admired in him the very qualities that others despised. Tarnower's selfishness and egocentrism, for example,
caused Jean to explain that "Hi is great to be with *because* he's
so selfish. He does what *he* wants, and that makes him damned
good company! Is there anyone worse to be around than some
self-made martyr forever telling you, 'I did it for the children's
sake'?"

Of his social climbing, she said, "Hi *not* on the make was
divine. But usually he *was* on the make, and I *liked* watching
him on the make, because it made him even more alive, and
that made me feel more alive, too."

Of his snobbery, she mused, "Even at his snobbiest, Hi wasn't
putting other people down. He was just striving for a certain set
of values that to him seemed important, and to a lot of people
seem important when they're trying to make it. He was really a
wonderful snob!"

Jean admired Tarnower for being a self-made man. She was
proud of his fierce, lifelong struggle to escape the obscurity and
poverty of his background. His arrogance delighted her. He
once told her, "Listen, if I hadn't been born Jewish, it would
have been too easy." Jean loved him for that.

Sammy Glick's creator, Budd Schulberg, has tried to define
his hero's attraction. "I realized that I had singled him out not
because he had been born into the world any more selfish, ruthless and cruel than anybody else . . . but because in the midst
of a war (of life itself) that was selfish, ruthless and cruel,
Sammy was proving himself the fittest, the fiercest, and the
fastest."

This was exactly why Jean Harris loved Herman Tarnower.
But Jean Harris's wealthy, sophisticated, and powerful new
lover was more than "a good Sammy Glick." He was also a
"good" Albert Struven. "Everything made Dad mad. Nothing
made Hi mad," she noted with wonder. "Not when he left fifteen hundred dollars in traveler's checks in Bahrein. Not when

the tickets were wrong. Not when there were no hotel reservations in Afghanistan. Nothing could ruffle him, and he never yelled."

In 1969 Jean and Hi spent a couple of autumn weeks touring the Canadian Northwest, Jackson Hole, the Grand Tetons, and they made another trip out West in January. Elaborate vacations were an old habit with Tarnower, and invariably he provided himself with an attractive companion. "I don't travel alone, Jean," he always reminded her.

For Jean, these adventures were unforgettable experiences to be relived over and over in memory. But to Herman, over was over. Nostalgia had no place in his meager array of emotions. When they parted at an airport, he never looked back and waved. He was always eager to get on to the next experience. Jean Harris, by contrast, was an emotional gooney bird, always flying forward while facing backward, always less interested in where she was going than in savoring where she had been.

Dear Hi [she wrote to him in January 1970]

The shadows over the Grand Canyon were in all the right places as we flew back on Sunday afternoon, and I enjoyed the beautiful view all over again. Do you realize how much of the United States you have shared with me, my friend, and how much I have loved every mile of it? The only bad moments are when I suddenly realize that the trip is almost over and I haven't any idea when I will see you again. . . . You aren't a man one takes for granted, doctor, so I never assume a next time, I only know how important it is to me that there be one. I'm afraid where you are concerned I belong to the if-some-is-good-more-is-better-school, and so far being with you has never given me cause to change schools. I do agree though, completely, that each of us has to write his own script and I know you find mine tedious at times—but then there are times when I am not absolutely crazy about yours either. At any rate I hope you aren't suffering too badly from over-exposure to a rather serious case of love. We've pretty well established that it isn't catching anyway—so I won't worry too much. . . .

Not only did Tarnower seem to Jean to be the precise and happy opposite of her father; in certain ways he reminded her of her mother. Faced with disaster, Hi and Jean's mother had the same reaction: look on the bright side, never sweat little things, and don't talk about the bad things. Jean saw the man she loved and her mother as alike in being consummate survivors. That one survived through enormous ego, the other through towering religious faith, scarcely mattered. The point was that both were strong, and both made her feel strong. "I feel so safe with you!" she told Herman many times.

"No one is safe with anyone," was his unvarying reply.

6

Big Fish

By 1966, THE YEAR Jean Harris met him, Herman Tarnower had built up the flossiest practice of any cardiologist north of New York City. He was on the staff of Westchester's three most prestigious hospitals. Both professionally and privately, he was a man fully engagé. His professional time was divided between his flourishing private practice and his work as president of the Westchester Heart Association, which he had organized in 1950. All his life Herman Tarnower wanted to be the biggest fish in the pond. He relished power even more than he did money. His passion was authority, dominion, control; indeed, his abundance of these qualities is what made him so attractive to so many. In his pursuit of his objectives, the founding of the Westchester Heart Association had been a brilliant move. It automatically established him as the area's premier cardiologist. His invitation to the leading citizens of Westchester to serve as directors or members of the Association's Advisory Council was an honor hard to refuse. The organization had provided Tarnower with an instant power base from which to operate, and he proved himself a superb administrator and tireless worker. His flair for fund-raising soon welded this particular group of doctors and civic leaders into one of the healthiest and wealthiest Heart Associations in the nation. In 1955, under Tarnower's direction, they had established a cardiopulmonary laboratory at Grasslands, now the Westchester County Medical Center. Over the next decade, they raised more than one million dollars to set up a cardiac surgical program and a kidney dialysis center there as well.

Socially, the doctor now mingled readily with the "best" people of his community, and belonged to its most exclusive golf and shooting clubs. If success is defined as achieving one's ambitions, Herman Tarnower was a stunning success. If failure is defined as not fulfilling one's potential, then perhaps his life was a failure, although he certainly never perceived it as such. He saw himself at fifty-seven as a healthy, hardworking, and much respected physician and pillar of his community, an entirely self-made man who by midlife had been able to realize and was still able to relish every one of his boyhood dreams.

These dreams first began to take form in Flatbush, Brooklyn, where Herman Tarnower was born in 1910, only a few years after his humble parents had cleared the customs and immigration formalities of Ellis Island. Young Herman had three sisters, Pearl, known as Billie, Edith, and Jean, but he was the family's Jewish prince. He received excellent marks at James Madison High School, and still found plenty of time to perfect his skills and pick up extra money at the neighborhood pool halls. Dora Tarnower, his energetic mother, liked to talk, play cards, and cook, in that order. She was a tall, strong, handsome woman who had been born in Bessarabia and spoke English with a heavy accent. Her gentle, quiet husband, Harry, born somewhere in Eastern Europe—probably Russia now, Estonia or Lithuania then—earned a modest living in New York manufacturing caps until he went broke during the Depression and was forced to borrow money from his son. He died of a heart attack at age fifty-four while Herman was away in Europe on a yearlong postgraduate medical fellowship. Mama Tarnower kept the sad news from her son until he returned to the United States. Then she gave him the $5,000 from her husband's life insurance policy to launch his medical practice. In turn, Tarnower became the sole support of his mother for the next forty-two years. He was uncomplaining of the burden, yet he seemed to resent Dora's utter financial dependency and vicariously lived life, and he determined never to yoke himself to another person.

The Tarnowers were not a demonstrative family. They did not celebrate birthdays, and the parents did not attend any of Herman's graduation ceremonies. When their son was ready for college, he gathered together his boyhood winnings at pool and cards and hitchhiked up to Syracuse to enroll in the university. His father had augmented the kitty as best he could, and in his quiet way Herman was grateful. "Hi was a very brilliant student," recalls the man who has known him longest, Dr. Tanney. Tarnower and Tanney went through medical school together, at Syracuse University, and later they both interned at Bellevue Hospital in New York City. Tanney says Tarnower was able to get high marks without ever appearing to study, or even to take notes. Furthermore, he completed his premedical training in two years instead of the customary four, and still found time to play varsity basketball. "He practically paid his tuition with his winnings from gin games and backgammon," says another old friend.

As a college freshman, Tarnower found his Brooklyn accent a source of ridicule, and immediately enrolled in a speech course, bought a mirror, and spent two years drilling in front of it, painstakingly plucking out the tones of Flatbush and Borough Park as if they were audible crabgrass. All his social graces and refinements—the skill at golf and fishing and shooting, the flair for conversation, the encyclopedic knowledge of wines—were patiently achieved in the same way. Practice, practice, practice; emulate, emulate, emulate. He found his models in books and magazines. He became a country gentleman out of *Country Gentleman,* a connoisseur out of *Connoisseur,* a gourmet out of *Gourmet.* He read great books by the hundredweight, and he was the only man in Westchester known to have taken Mortimer Adler's famed Great Books course twice. Being good at whatever he did was supremely important to Herman Tarnower, and he was willing to work punishingly hard to achieve his goals.

For several summers young Herman was employed as a counselor at Camp Pontusic, in Massachusetts, which advertised that its boys were cared for by genuine medical students. One camper now over sixty still remembers the summer when he was eleven and had a terrible toothache. What should he do for it? he asked his counselor.

Tarnower looked up from the book he was reading and said, "Take an ax and apply it firmly to the back of your neck."

After doctors Tarnower and Tanney completed their residencies at Bellevue, in 1936, Herman surprised his friend by saying he intended to open up a practice in Scarsdale.

"Where's that?" Tanney asked. Most young men at the time wanted the big city, the big action, but Tarnower had no interest in doctoring the city riffraff brought in by the Bellevue ambulances. He dreamed of a society practice. "He was always very definite about his ideas, though he didn't say much. Hi was an intensely private man," says Tanney. "At the time he went up there he had no money. Flat broke. He slept on a cot in the back of his first little office-apartment on Garth Road, and he used his bathroom to set up his laboratory in. In the 1930s Scarsdale and White Plains were still small-townish, and the doctors up there were nothing special. But White Plains *was* the county seat. Hi saw the potential for somebody of quality moving into the area."

Tarnower became the first very good internist in White Plains, and word got around. He joined the courtesy staff of White Plains Hospital in 1939. Sedulously avoiding domesticity, he ate every meal out for twelve years. He even disconnected the gas stove lest any overnight girl friend feel matutinally inspired to cook him breakfast. He gave occasional cocktail parties—that was only smart business—but on rented restaurant premises. Personally, he led a plain, even Spartan existence.

As a Jew at Bellevue, Tarnower had not been asked to join the interns' club. In Westchester he believed himself to be the first Jewish physician. He had specialized in cardiology as well as internal medicine, he confided, because in those days the former was a minor specialty, "so they let the Jews have it." He became board-certified in both specialties in 1941, just in time for World War II.

By mid–1942 Tarnower was on active duty with the U.S. Army Medical Corps, assigned to the base hospital at Bowman Field in Louisville, Kentucky. So that he could keep his office open, he had paid Dr. John Cannon, who had a wife, a baby, and consequently a high draft number, a monthly fee to take over his practice, pay Tarnower's rent, and pay the installments on his medical equipment.

His fellow doctors at Bowman Field remember Captain, later Major, and finally Lieutenant Colonel Tarnower as sure of himself, closemouthed, and "a very good cardiologist."

"He was extremely well-trained, a very knowledgeable physician," says one of them, "and he made everyone aware that he was above the ordinary run. Socially he was an odd person, an opportunist, very smooth and polished, knowing how to climb over the backs of others, and how to ingratiate himself with the right people, particularly the colonel."

Bowman Field was a training center to teach civilian doctors army ways, and what the trainee-doctors dreaded most was being shipped out to an unpleasant, dangerous tour of duty in some place like Borneo or New Guinea. Gradually they became aware that all the bitching about the colonel at their weekly poker game was getting right back to the colonel. Tarnower, they finally agreed, was the man. No one can say that their suspicions were correct, but most of them were sent to the South Pacific, and Dr. Tarnower was assigned to duty at the general hospital at Fort Knox, where he became chief of the medical service. Later he was chief of service at two other stateside U.S. military hospitals.

It was in the army that Herman Tarnower had originally discovered country clubs. As a bachelor officer at military hospitals in Louisville and Fort Knox, and later in Texas, he was routinely entertained by the town's better families. Almost automatically, they invited the nice doctor to come out to the country club whenever he was off duty. Although "exclusive" in these parts usually meant "exclusively gentile," inviting Captain Tarnower seemed a patriotic thing to do. At the country clubs Tarnower first encountered the kind of tennis-playing, Junior League-ish, long-legged blondes he ever after preferred. Moreover, the special country club ambience, the breezy formality that overlays the deep, unspoken sense of belonging, of

"inside-ness," the very *clubbiness* of these places, strongly attracted the young loner from Flatbush.

When the war abruptly ended with the nuclear fireballs at
Hiroshima and Nagasaki, the medical effects of massive nuclear
radiation of a civilian population were entirely unknown.
American military doctors were rushed to the scene as soon as
General MacArthur could guarantee their safety. The two physicians assigned to lead the Nagasaki study were young Major
Tarnower and Major Samuel Berg. Dr. Berg is the brother of
the late, great ballplayer-scientist-spy Moe Berg and, at the time
of Tarnower's death, he was eighty-four years old and still practicing medicine in Newark, New Jersey. After the war,
Tarnower often told others he would like to have remained in
military medicine, and he spoke with particular enthusiasm of
his tour of duty in Japan. Some army colleagues thought that
Tarnower's brilliance and his ambition would surely have made
him Surgeon General one day, but Dr. Berg has always disagreed, pointing out that he lacked the right personality. "Yes,
he was very shrewd. A *Yiddishe kupf,* a nice talker, a cultured
man. But he was lousy at army politics. He could never have
made it in the army, because he was such a snob—a snob on top
of a snob. He would never have stayed in. If he could be a six-
star general, well, maybe. But I doubt he could have taken the
pressure and regimentation of military life. He's a man who
walks away. From women, or problems. When he's had it, he's
had it. Besides, the pay was not what he had in mind."

After the war, Herman Tarnower returned to Scarsdale and
formed a small group practice with Dr. Cannon and several
other young doctors. But his arrogant ways were too much for
his colleagues; one by one, except for Dr. Cannon, they dropped
away. As for Tarnower, he remained so single-minded in his
ambition that he avoided going to the movies for fear of missing
a potential patient, and he regularly put in twelve- and four-
teen-hour work days.

By 1959, Tarnower had made enough money to build his
small, modern Scarsdale Medical Center on Heathcote Road,
utilizing some low-lying property he had acquired cheaply some
years before. He signed up several other doctors with varying
specialties—a gastroenterologist, an allergist, an endocrinolo-

gist, and so on—to join him and Cannon in a group practice which he envisaged rather grandly as a mini–Mayo Clinic, qualified to deal with many varieties of illness. His very rich patients loved the idea. A group medical practice, ever available and nearby to their country homes, was the equivalent in convenience of an all-night delicatessen, or twenty-four-hour banking. The Scarsdale city fathers, the Zoning Board, and the City Council were less enthusiastic. They objected strenuously to the erection of a professional building, complete with spacious parking lots, right in the middle of a quiet, residential district. The battles went on for years. Throughout, Tarnower remained magnificently pigheaded. He claimed the entire uproar was due to anti-Semitism and simply refused to yield. He stalled, he blustered, and finally, with the guidance of grateful patient Dan Comfort, he triumphed.

In the army, Tarnower had been quick to recognize that a golf or tennis club is not just a great place to improve one's social life and golf game; it can be a fertile hunting ground for new patients, far more productive professionally than sitting in an office waiting for the sick and lame to walk in. After the war, Tarnower had put his mind to it and only three years after V-J Day, he had become Century's only doctor member who practiced in Westchester.

"There seem to be forty-four dentists here, and about nine thousand lawyers, so how come only one doctor?" Marge Jacobson once exclaimed. "At a Jewish club, it just doesn't stand to reason!" (Marge by that time had become such a model Jewish wife and mother that very few Century members guessed her true background.) Nonetheless, at the time Tarnower met Jean Harris, nineteen years after he joined the club, he still was the sole Westchester doctor on the membership rolls. Some insight into this anomaly may be gleaned from an event that occurred the following year. In 1968, another Westchester doctor, indeed, another cardiologist, about fifteen years younger than Tarnower, applied to Century for admission. While his application was under active consideration, the Admissions Committee received a startling letter from Herman Tarnower. The younger doctor was an unethical person, he wrote, and had been fired from the staff of the county hospital, Grasslands. The facts were easy enough to check, and Tarnower's charges proved to be a total fabrication. What could he have been up to? Did he really believe himself powerful enough to embarrass the younger man into withdrawing his application and simply disappearing? If so, Tarnower had misjudged his rival. The younger doctor temporarily withdrew his application for membership—not wishing to confuse the issue—but he brought Tarnower's letter to the attention of the Ethics Committee of the Westchester County Medical Society. After a full hearing on the matter, Tarnower was officially censured. Some time later, the younger doctor reapplied to Century and was admitted. (The formal minutes of the censure proceedings are locked up in a desk at the Medical Society's headquarters.)

By the time his real estate wars with the Zoning Board got under way, Tarnower already had set up his Cardiac Care Clinic and the other special heart and kidney services at Grasslands. He had also established the only cardiopulmonary laboratory between New York City and Albany, and also a cardiac care unit at White Plains Hospital. Additionally, Tarnower served as medical director of several prestigious companies, including Loeb Rhoades (now Shearson/American Express) and the Nestlé Corporation, which has its worldwide headquarters in Westchester County.

At Grasslands, Tarnower was Chief of Cardiology for many years, and after his mandatory retirement in 1975 he remained a consulting cardiologist until his death. He was a consulting cardiologist at St. Agnes Hospital in White Plains from 1973 until the night he was pronounced dead in that hospital's emergency room.

The hospital affiliation that had always meant most to him was at White Plains Hospital,* where he sent his private patients, and he managed to give them the impression that he was Chief of Cardiology there. In fact, that hospital did not have a separate Cardiology Section until 1970, and when one was set up Tarnower, although the senior man, was not chosen to head it. Nor was he chosen eight years later, when the post became vacant again, nor for the term after that. He was never chosen.

The unanimous respect and devotion that Herman Tarnower

---

* White Plains Hospital officially designated itself White Plains Hospital Medical Center in 1979.

enjoyed from his grateful patients was not shared by his medical colleagues, at least not many of them. A few had good words. "Kindliness was Herman Tarnower's most salient characteristic. Whether his patients could pay or not, it didn't matter," says his original partner, gentle Dr. John Cannon, a general practitioner now semiretired.

Walter Herbert, M.D., the cardiologist who came to Westchester from New York to take charge of the new cardiopulmonary unit, the diagnostic lab, and other specialized cardiac units at Grasslands, and who was also, with Tarnower's blessings, recently elected president of the Heart Association, says, "Dr. Tarnower was particularly famous at the hospital for the Friday cardiac conference. Even though it was late Friday afternoon, fifty or sixty people always showed up. There was good discussion, but never any question who was boss. Hi would see the patients first in their rooms, and then, in the old school manner, interview them in front of the audience. He would say to the other doctors, 'Don't you tell me. Let me get the story from the patient.' He was exceptional at interviewing. He would ask, 'What was the character of the pain? Where did it go?' Every Friday we got a lesson in eliciting succinct and pertinent information. He both liked to teach and was very good at it."

Dr. Cannon and Dr. Herbert are unusual. Many of his peers, unlike his patients, found Tarnower's personality so abrasive that by the time of his death three, and perhaps four, of his own partners at the Scarsdale Medical Group were barely on speaking terms with him. One had not spoken to him for almost three years. Most of his colleagues saw Herman Tarnower as an enormously bright man who certainly had the intellect and organizational capacity, if not the temperament, to have succeeded in academic medicine. But he had consciously chosen medicine's other career track, the big, swanky practice, and many objected to the way he went about it.

The Warburgs and their friends would have been astounded to learn how few of Tarnower's fellow doctors shared the family's high opinion of Dr. Lunch Hour, and how absurd they found it that an old woman be given daily digitalis by injection because her doctor said "it works a lot better that way." Not only does it not work better; it necessitates sticking her with a needle. Tarnower's colleagues were also amused to hear that

Tarnower was treating important, aging male patients with testosterone injections to improve their potency. They knew that such regimens are more useful to the doctor than to his patient; that they are among the infinite number of ways in which a physician can needlessly complicate a patient's medical care so as to make himself indispensable. As one of them says, "Hi had the most carefully cultivated practice I've ever seen."

Tarnower's old friend Dr. Tanney explains: "One reason other White Plains doctors didn't like him was that for surgery, even an appendectomy, he sent his patients down to New York, where he felt they would get better care. His attitude always was, 'I want my patients to have the best,' and he did't care whose toes he stepped on."

Perhaps this resentment is the reason Tarnower was never chosen Chief of Cardiology at White Plains Hospital. More likely, it was his enduring arrogance. "Even after his mandatory retirement here," one colleague marvels, "Hi had the incredible chutzpah to ask to be named Emeritus Chief of Cardiology, even though he'd never been Chief!"

The first law of medicine, older perhaps than the Hippocratic Oath itself, is "Do not speak ill of thy fellow physician." Yet such was Tarnower's personality that a reporter can find any number of sources, once anonymity is assured. Many medical Deep Throats have contributed to this portion of our narrative, all of them doctors who worked closely with Herman Tarnower at one time or another, in all of his hospitals. All are quoted verbatim. None are his erstwhile partners at the Scarsdale Medical Group; for reasons that will become apparent, those men agreed on an ironclad no-interview policy at the time of Tarnower's death.

"His famous Friday cardiac conference was a complete waste of time."

"It wasn't a conference. It was a forum for a monologue by His Highness."

"To go to it made you feel you were committing intellectual suicide."

"He was very autocratic and intimidated the other physicians. He was skillful at getting patients to talk about their symptoms, but he had a way of looking over the tops of his glasses and saying, 'You will be operated upon.' He thought he was being warm and doing it with humor, but it didn't come out that way."

"He ruled by fear. He'd make a pronouncement, and that was it. You didn't ask questions—which meant that nobody could learn much. You have to be able to ask stupid questions in order to learn."

"Hi had an image of himself which he deliberately projected: I'm arrogant. I'm a bastard. I'm cold—but I'm right."

"Some doctors are lucky, and they never get found out. Some doctors avoid situations where they could be found out. Hi did both. He was a doctor who never lost . . . or I would rather say . . . who could always recover his arrogance."

"He could not bear to be wrong, and could not bear to be corrected. He was almost unbelievably dogmatic. One day he stated, 'There is no such thing as mitral insufficiency [a disease of one of the heart valves that usually results from rheumatic fever].' 'What about Harken in Boston?' somebody asked. 'He operated on it.' 'There is *no* such thing,' he said, and his teeth got tight the way they always did when he was asserting himself. Then he just said it again. He simply could not, would not, be challenged, in the way that Stalin could not be challenged. For years Grasslands was a fourth-rate place, because no one could work with the guy."

On occasion, Tarnower could be strikingly bad-tempered. "When he felt trapped, he would put you down publicly. He could get so nasty in meetings that sometimes you'd feel like asking him to step outside," says one dignified-looking physician. On one famous occasion, Tarnower's petty, vindictive backbiting in front of a group of other doctors, nurses, and lab technicians drove a distinguished cardiologist to resign on the spot.

Herman Tarnower not only insisted on putting his own name on any papers written by doctors working under him, standard academic practice in many institutions; he also attempted to prevent other men from getting choice invitations to lecture, or academic or hospital appointments. His envy was at times ludicrous. The most respected and beloved Jewish doctor in White Plains was the late James Flexner, M.D. Once as Dr. Flexner came out of a restaurant phone booth, a drunk approached and knocked him down. When a newspaper published a picture of the fallen physician, Tarnower complained to the County Medical Society that Dr. Flexner had unduly sought personal publicity.

After Dr. Flexner's death, his fellow doctors set about raising a memorial fund to establish a James Flexner Coronary Care Unit at White Plains Hospital. Tarnower immediately wrote the hospital's Chief of Medicine, saying such a unit was unnecessary, that it was in fact just the sort of expensive, fancy new equipment a community hospital should avoid.

Whenever Herman Tarnower got off the elevator at White Plains Hospital, one of the girls on his service always stood ready to help him into his long white coat. He was the only doctor on the staff who wore such a garment. Sometimes he made rounds not only wearing his coat but carrying his little black bag. The other men on the Cardiac Service made rounds in suit jackets, carrying stethoscopes. But Tarnower saw himself here, as he did in the famed Grasslands Friday cardiac conferences, as a man of another order, a great diagnostician in the mold of Paul Dudley White perhaps, or even Sir William Osler. In truth, he was far too authoritarian and rigid to be a great teacher. Nor was he the technocrat that all cardiologists today must be. His training had gradually become so out-of-date that he simply could no longer be considered sophisticated medically.

In part, Tarnower's famous heart-to-heart talks with the children and grandchildren of his pet tycoons served to compensate for his medical obsolescence. In part, they reflected Tarnower's notion of the correct practice of internal medicine. Men of his generation were trained to give all sorts of not strictly medical advice. Coming from an era before psychiatry was well established as a medical specialty, contemptuous of it as an upstart development, and ignorant of its uses, they nonetheless act as pseudo-psychiatrists themselves.

Obsolescence was probably also a factor in Tarnower's fanatic, longtime insistence that he, and only he, be allowed to read cardiograms. Reading EKGs is something of a chore, but it is a chore with several very positive payoffs. The reader's name appears on every cardiogram, which not only confers a certain stature and ego-satisfaction; it also is likely to produce a great many consultations. Mrs. Warburg is a case in point. If all the revenue from reading cardiograms at White Plains Medical Center today were to go to one man, he would net $40,000 to $50,000 a year. But when White Plains Hospital set up its Cardiology Section, in 1970, the new chief insisted that the EKG chores be distributed equally among the half-dozen members of the department. Tarnower kicked like a steer, but eventually backed down under pressure.

Despite his mandatory retirement at sixty-five, Tarnower insisted on coming in to read cardiograms, and had read his last ones the very week of his death. Unless he were permitted to continue reading them, he had threatened, he would see to it that his rich friends did not continue making contributions to the hospital; in short, cardiological blackmail.

After his death, Herman Tarnower was memorialized and his memory richly honored by his friends and grateful patients. At White Plains Medical Center today, beside the new-minted bronze plaque, hums the just-built $100,000 Herman Tarnower Diagnostic Laboratory, busily doing all the special diagnostic studies, stress tests, Holter monitoring, echo-cardiograms, and other advanced procedures that its namesake had once written the Chief of Medicine to oppose. The money to build the lab came in the form of two $50,000 checks from Tarnower's old fishing companions, Cullman and Comfort. In addition, a small group of patients and friends, including the Loebs, Cullmans, Schultes, Comforts, and Schwartzes, came up with more than $200,000 for the Westchester Heart Association in order to establish a $30,000 annual cardiovascular research award at the county hospital in Tarnower's name.

Alongside such magnificent tributes from his grateful patients, the silence of Herman Tarnower's fellow physicians rings particularly loud. Indeed, when the staff doctors at White Plains Medical Center heard that a new cardiac unit was to be named for Dr. Tarnower, voices were raised in protest, but it was too late; the plaque was already ordered. As for the traditional memorial service that is usually organized by his fellow physicians when a respected colleague dies after long years of service to a community, this time it simply never happened.

The sometime horrors of the Tarnower temperament aside, most of the Scarsdale men and women with whom he worked for over forty years would characterize him as a more than competent physician. One man who does not agree is a doctor who worked with him for nearly thirty years, many of those years as his administrative superior. "Tarnower was a bad guy, not a nice man, and a poor doctor," he says flatly. "He was opinionated to the point where he had a complete block about learning anything. He could even be obviously mistreating a patient, and you still couldn't get him to learn anything. A patient once almost died because of his obstinacy. The man had a brain abscess, and Tarnower was treating him with the wrong antibiotics in the wrong doses. We all told him what we thought, but he absolutely refused to listen. Fortunately he went off fishing or hunting, and the man who was covering for him rechecked his medication with the experts on the hospital staff.

"Another time I saw him tell a kidney specialist, 'Jones, I'd like you to dialyze this patient.' The kidney man said he preferred to see the patient himself and decide whether dialysis was appropriate. It wasn't even Hi's own patient, just a consult, but Hi said, 'Well, Jones, if you're not gonna do the dialysis, we don't need you.' Translation: 'Do it my way or get lost!' Later Jones and I found that Tarnower had already checked with three or four other kidney centers, and they had all refused to dialyze the man without first examining him.

"To sum it all up, I would say that Hi Tarnower was a poor doctor because he had a closed mind, because he didn't know the medicine he should have known, and because he was not willing to learn. What he was was a very talented Fascist who was absolutely brilliant at attracting money for his hospitals."

7

Herman's World

BY THE TIME JEAN HARRIS met him, Herman Tarnower's reputation as sportsman, ladies' man, and gourmet was firmly established. At his famous little dinner parties, usually for six guests, never more than eight, it was hard to tell if he took the greatest pride in his guest list, his food and wine, or the lofty conversation. His interest in wine had first been stimulated by a grand tour of French vineyards with Alfred Knopf and his wife, made some years earlier in celebration of the publisher's recovery from a severe heart attack under Tarnower's care. Soon the doctor had become nearly as knowledgeable and as much a wine snob as his patient.

Tarnower had not of course been born a gourmet, and it was Chinese food, not French, that had first caught his fancy. The bachelor doctor's original servant was a black man called Washington, and as soon as Herman discovered the delights of Chinese food, he enrolled Washington in Madame Chu's cooking school in New York City. The result was a Chinese soul-food cuisine that, until the advent of the Van der Vrekens, was the household's unvarying fare. But Tarnower was always eager to try new things, and as he traveled, he learned. After eating reindeer in Finland, he asked Suzanne to cook reindeer in Purchase.

Suzanne Van der Vreken, who is five years older than her husband, did not cook at all when Tarnower first hired the couple in 1964. In France, she had been a secretary, and Henri a clerk and gardener. But shortly after Suzanne came to work, a girl friend of Tarnower's ordered a subscription to *Gourmet,* and soon the new cook was turning out just the sort of rich, fancy meals for which the magazine is known. Suzanne's culinary creations, smothered in mysterious sauces, caused the dinner guests to exclaim and at times burst into applause, although one famous food authority has confided, "You never knew what you were eating. It was a mush always, and swimming in gravy." As for Henri, he enrolled in landscaping and nursery-management classes in his spare time, and in his dress, bearing, and manner began to ape his master. Soon guests came to consider him an even greater snob than Herman Tarnower.

From the beginning, Suzanne kept elaborate records of all menus and guests, noting every detail in large black ledgers the existence of which did not come to light until after Tarnower's death. By that time she had sixteen fat volumes, one for each year of the Van der Vrekens' employment. Suzanne's sole intention, she averred, was to make sure no important guest was ever served the same dish twice. But the ledgers also turned out to contain the name of every woman guest who remained at Tarnower's house overnight, and the date of her visit. (Whether the doctor was aware of his cook's unusually meticulous record-keeping is not known.)

As each dinner party progressed at its measured, stately pace, buttled by Henri and assisted by Suzanne, thoughtful conversation rose above the clink of goblets, always guided and if necessary censored by the host. It was Tarnower's custom each evening to bone up beforehand on a suitably important topic, then toss it out for conversational scrimmage. His own considerable talent was more as a listener than as a talker. He disliked small talk and despised tête-à-têtes; if two guests began a private conversation, he did not hesitate to break it up. He once brusquely hushed the chattering lady on his right only to realize that on this particular evening he was dining out, and the startled woman beside him was his hostess.

Most of Tarnower's friends thought his little dinners were the best action around. "So thoughtful! Such interesting friends!" says a famous hostess in her own right. "The president of Pepsi-Cola, the chairman of the board of United Foods, the chief executive of Nestlé."

Other guests found the doctor's dinner parties merely pretentious. Yet his invitations were seldom refused. People were so awed by his powerful personality that they took his invitations as commands. A couple who for over a decade dined with Tarnower six or eight times a year speak in counterpoint. "I'm a pretty comfortable woman, and I was never once comfortable in Hi's house. It was hot in summer and cold in winter, and if you were even a few minutes late, Hi made you feel guilty."

Her husband interrupts. "Evenings at Hi's house were very heavy and strained. When you got to the table, each dish had to be met with oohs and aahs. After that, either he was making a speech or picking somebody's brains."

Wife: "Hi believed that a continental person doesn't eat hors d'oeuvres, and he posed as a continental person, so the hors d'oeuvres were *fablongit*. It was a little better when Jean was there. But that Henri—if he gave you vodka on the rocks, he acted like he was doing you a favor. He was the poor man's Hi."

Husband: "By nine or nine-fifteen you were out—which was the best part. The one thing you never had at his house was fun."

Most guests were more charitable. Tarnower's old friend Dr. Tanney found the dinners too formal for his taste, but if Herman loved to preside like a baron over his table, if he chose to expatiate over the wine—served from decanters, never the original bottle—and to pontificate on the issues of the day, Tanney would not judge his friend harshly. He understood. Indeed Tanney knew, as most others did not, that Tarnower had two sets of friends, call them the A's and the B's. The A's were the top-level Century crowd. The B's were everyone else. Tarnower enjoyed them equally and was kind and friendly to both. But with one or two exceptions, such as Tanney, the groups were mutually exclusive. Tarnower's family—his adored mother, his sisters, their husbands and children—were all in the B group. "I wouldn't say he was ashamed of them," says Dr. Tanney. "They just didn't fit in."

Tarnower's most intimate friend among the Century grandees, a woman who with her husband entertained Tarnower royally and saw him weekly for twenty years, confirms Tanney's view. "No, I never saw the mother," she said recently. "I met a sister once. A very dear, middle-America lady. Whereas Hi had become very much to the manner born."

These remarks are spoken in a weird, broad-A accent heard nowhere else but at the highest altitudes in Century. It sounds snooty and affected without resembling the speech of any known region. Several Century First Families speak it, and in the later years of his life, so did Herman Tarnower. All his baths became *bahths,* his halfs *hahfs,* and he liked to quote the woman who said that you *cahn't* ever be too rich or too thin.

Tarnower enjoyed certain expensive things. He used only the highest-priced fishing and hunting gear, for example, and every two years he bought himself a new blue Cadillac. But he did not enjoy spending money. Certainly he paid his share of restaurant checks; he was a good host, and very correct in most areas of social deportment. But he was cautious with money, almost penurious. When he traveled with wealthy women, as he often did, he did not hesitate to let them pay their full share, and he readily accepted cash to cover their joint out-of-pocket expenses. When he went on fishing trips or safaris with his millionaire male friends, they were more than happy to take care of all expenses. They would no more have let him pay his own way than he would let them pay him for emergency medical treatment if the need arose. "If you want to own a rich man," Tarnower used to tell Jean, "save his life and don't send him a bill." Which is not to say that Tarnower always doctored his wealthy friends for nothing. But he billed them in ways that reflected the special and often complex nature of their relationship. Men like financier John L. Loeb, for example, were accustomed to receiving a single annual bill from the Scarsdale Medical Group that covered all services to themselves, their servants, and all members of their large families. At the same time, Tarnower served as medical director of the banking house of Loeb Rhoades and, for an undisclosed fee, looked after its top executives. "You must remember," says one partner in the firm, "that when it comes to health, the Loebs get very sentimental." The banker's bitterness may stem from his conviction, shared by many, that for many years it was the practice at Loeb Rhoades for the company medical director to talk over the intimate details of each partner's health with the head of the firm. In turn, John Loeb advised Dr. Tarnower on his investments, and handled his portfolio without fee. At the time of Tarnower's death, his account at Loeb Rhoades was said to be worth over a million dollars.

Herman Tarnower's parsimony probably reflected the poverty of his youth. He wore the same suits for twenty years. He avoided expensive restaurants. When he bought his house in 1958, he asked a friend who was a professional decorator to help him buy expensive chairs wholesale. But when she took him to the showroom, he was so overwhelmed by the prices that he bought nothing, nor did he ever ask her help again. Tarnower kept his servants on a tight household budget and modest salaries. At the time of his death, Suzanne's salary was still only $90 a week, while Henri earned $200 as butler-gardener-chauffeur. Both the Van der Vrekens complained continually about the stinginess of their employer. There was never enough money for food, garden supplies, or household repairs, they said. Suzanne's cramped and outmoded "gourmet" kitchen lacked a window, a good fan, a decent-sized refrigerator, a second sink, but the doctor always told her he had no money to spend except on necessities. Her weekly budget was a strict $175, and in the last year or two of his life the wealthy doctor and his guests subsisted largely on chicken. The Van der Vrekens grumbled about having to use their own car for shopping because the doctor would not furnish one for household chores. Despite repeated pleas from Henri, Tarnower refused to spend money to repair the leaky wine cellar, to prop up the rotting porch, or even to reseed the balding lawn.

With Jean Harris, he was different. At least at the start of their relationship, Herman Tarnower was magnanimous. He showered her with roses, gave her a $10,000 diamond, took her three times around the world, and remodeled his house to make room for her sons. That Tarnower did not spend much more money on her in the early days was her doing, not his. When he tried to be extra generous, Jean often would not permit it. Acutely prideful, she warded off every openhanded gesture as if a gift could somehow injure her. She imagined a rock in every snowball. If she could not be his wife, and freely chose to be his woman nonetheless, it became crucial to her self-esteem that she never be—or appear to be—his kept or bought woman. Thus when a magazine, rehashing the case long after Jean Harris had been sent to prison, said that "he bought her expensive clothing," Jean immediately wrote to a friend, "In fourteen years he bought me two pieces of 'wearing apparel,' a Liberty scarf when we were at Jasper Park—and a pair of black and white patent leather shoes, in Palm Springs. He happened to be with me when I bought them and when I went to pay for them he said, 'Forget it. They're paid for.' I felt a little 'kept' every time I wore them. My 'expensive wardrobe' comes from being able to wear anything from one sister's size 14s to another sister's size 8s, from buying nothing until it's ½ off, and there was a third reason but I can't remember it." Her stinging pride, even at this remove, seemed to burn the page. During her trial, she was criticized for wearing fashionable, expensive clothing, and for seeming to dress up to the jury, rather than down in the traditional penitent female mode. But old friends who saw her on TV, walking in and out of the courthouse, recognized almost the entire wardrobe, which included the same mink hat and detachable mink collar on the same khaki raincoat that she had worn at Springside ten years before.

Hunting, fishing, gambling, and golfing were Herman Tarnower's favorite pastimes. He played golf and gin almost daily at Century, and loved to spend a week in Las Vegas. Prominently framed in his trophy room was the royal flush in clubs that, he liked to tell guests, had helped pay for his house. The doctor's skill at cards was a prime social asset that outweighed all other considerations. His dear friend Arthur Schulte, a retired investment banker and heir to the Schulte tobacco fortune, used to say, "When all I want is a gin game, I don't give a damn whether the woman looking over his shoulder is the headmistress of an exclusive girls' school or the madam of a whorehouse." To which Mrs. Schulte was heard to reply, "Frankly, I

don't care what he sleeps with at night, so long as I don't have
to be stuck with her all day."

On the golf course, Tarnower scorned handicaps and insisted
on playing "flat." A male golf partner says, "Hi was never
much fun to play with because he was too competitive."

A woman golfer says, "He was no fun, period! His pecker
and his golf game were very much intertwined. He always
wanted to beat you even money and for high stakes. He wanted
to slam you. But the money was not really it. The real thing was
power, power, power!"

Many others relished Tarnower's metallic self-assurance.
Smiling fondly, a regular golf companion says, "You know, I
played golf with that son of a bitch for twenty years and never
once heard him say, 'Good shot!' "

Tarnower was tough on everybody, even his animals. His
hunting dogs were English setters, and he trained them himself
on the vast Pforzheimer estate, sometimes working them with
an electric collar, and twisting the puppies' ears when they
failed to "come" on command. Once Tarnower stopped by
early in the morning to see his patient Howard Cullman,* and
his dogs were with him. "Let the dogs run," Peg Cullman said.
After the doctor's visit, she escorted him back to his Cadillac
and was astonished to see him open the trunk, shout, "Let's
go!" and kick one dog hard in the rear before they leaped into
the trunk and he slammed the lid. "Got to keep a hunting dog
in order, you know," he said before driving off.

Herman Tarnower was a regular visitor to a private hunting
club in Dutchess Valley where quail and chukar partridge are
raised for sport shooting. Among his favorite shooting companions were Arthur Schulte and Bob Jacobs, a retired architect.
Over the years, numerous minor shooting accidents occurred.
Once Tarnower winged Schulte in the chest, and on an earlier
occasion, Tarnower accidentally shot and killed Schulte's prize
Weimaraner. Once the doctor also shot himself in the leg after
failing to unload his gun before climbing a fence. But such are

---

* The late Howard Cullman, a distinguished patron of the arts, was chairman of
Philip Morris. Joseph Cullman III, a subsequent chairman, is Howard Cullman's
nephew.

the occasional mishaps of the sporting life, and nobody, including Tarnower, took them very seriously.

Hunting trips abroad became occasions when Tarnower could expound on his racial theories, and twice—on safari in Africa and again among the Maoris in New Zealand—he acutely embarrassed his companions by discoursing on the genetic inferiority of the brown and black races even as he was being attended by native servants. But back in Westchester he masked his contempt, and went out of his way to ingratiate himself with the servants of his wealthy friends. Many of these domestic workers are black, although the top Century families are partial to white butlers, chefs, and social secretaries, and Belgians rank especially high.

Tarnower knew the names of all his friends' servants, and he was professionally available to them all, black or white, forever urging them to come see him anytime with the slightest complaint. He gave them excellent care free of charge (which is to say, the employers paid the bills), but he was not averse to disclosing and discussing their infirmities with the families for whom they worked, and he appeared to view them as a kind of chattel. Deciding to perform an angiogram on the beloved family cook, he would invite the college-age daughter of the family to come down to the hospital and watch him work.

Of Herman Tarnower and women there was no end of talk. He was Century's own Don Giovanni, and in the locker rooms, over the coffee cups, in the hairdresser's, on the golf course, in boudoirs while dressing for dinner, on private planes and yachts and islands, they speculated about Hi's sex life. Some thought him a powerful stud, some a phony, some the most fortunate of men. Tarnower shrewdly said nothing and let them draw their own conclusions. Since he had the mystique of a womanizer, he took the attitude, "Let them think I'm a swordsman—I don't care. I'm flattered." And so most people sooner or later convinced themselves that the doctor was a great Lothario. The others suspected that the real reason Tarnower never married was because he was a closet homosexual. Many confirmed bachelors inspire the same speculation, and there appears to have been no truth to the rumors. Nonetheless, Tarnower confided to several women friends that the persistent gossip about the nature of his masculinity troubled him deeply.

The wife of one of his closest friends has said, "The truth about Hi Tarnower is that he was playing slap-and-tickle. But he got himself the reputation that he was laying half the broads in the U.S. He was truly a user of women and always wanted the prettiest girl in the room on his arm."

A woman who dated the doctor a few times said, "He was a Jewish bachelor-prince, accustomed to being pursued. 'You'll have to go after him,' the woman who introduced us said, and frankly I didn't think he was worth it."

But if she did not, hundreds of others did. Tarnower had been pursued by women all his life. He almost never made the first step. It was not necessary. Despite his cold nature, many women felt themselves powerfully drawn to the saturnine doctor with tawny brown eyes. In part, his very aloofness did it. He seemed a kind of *homme fatal,* with a hypnotic, rather old-fashioned sensuality, like the exaggerated magnetism of a silent movie star.

"You know, women were never a problem for me," he told one girl friend, "because there were always nurses available." The remark reveals perhaps more than he intended about the quality of his casual relationships. Tarnower showed little refinement with women, and he had no interest in courtship. Flowers, phone calls, and other small attentions were not a usual part of his repertoire. Intimacy seemed to embarrass him. Many people found him a primly formal man. He did not ever tell off-color stories or use four-letter words. Public hand-holding or nuzzling made him uneasy. He did not like to see it in a public park, a living room, even in the movies. A too-steamy love scene made him walk out of the theater. Possibly he thought of love as a kind of weakness, and weakness and vulnerability were qualities he despised. True, when Jean and Hi first met, he spoke to her of love in his own costive way. But as he grew older he seemed to enjoy mocking any expressions of human frailty or need. "I don't love anybody and I don't need anybody" became his proud and oft-repeated credo.

Nor was Tarnower a sophisticated lover. "Sexually, Hi was an elephant," one ex-mistress says bluntly. Says another, "You know, Hi didn't really like women. He had to be stimulated. He was not very potent even when I knew him, years ago, and finally I said to myself: at my age, I don't have to work this hard." Says a third ex-mistress, "I don't think Hi was capable of loving. He was not even capable of giving. He couldn't let go sexually. When you are making love you are melting, you are fluid. He tried, but he couldn't. There was always something he was fighting in a woman. He gave me the feeling, it's man *against* woman."

"You could get violently attracted to this man," another long-ago girl friend recalls. "His eyes were very good, and he was a great dancer. You felt totally *enfolded*. His mother must have been very domineering, because if you said anything about her, a veil came over his face. In bed, he was completely unemotional, uninvolved. It ended because I got too possessive and Hi dropped me flat. But I remember him very well. He's the kind of guy that starts fast and finishes fast. Then he gets into the other bed and goes to sleep while you just lie there and feel bad."

Perhaps Tarnower was a great Casanova, and these are merely the bitter voices of women who lost out. Certainly Tarnower's men friends believe that he led the most vigorous of bachelor lives. "What did women see in him?" they are sometimes asked.

"You never got into the locker room at Century, or you would know what they see," the Century men reply.

Tarnower's golfing buddies agree that his physical condition was enviable for a man his age. He was well-built and as he strode around the locker room, disdaining a towel, he gave other men the impression that he was very proud of his body.

Without question, Tarnower's primary interest was in being a doctor. Yes, he liked women, and yes, he didn't like to be alone at night, but medicine is what he really cared about. As he often said, he was married to his work. To Herman Tarnower, his professional life was his real life, and women were there for diversion. Nor did he pretend otherwise. Tarnower may not have been kind to women, but he was direct and straightforward. It was not in his nature to try to shield them from the harsh truth.

"Hi's women always knew the score," one ex-mistress has said. Tarnower never pretended to any woman that he needed her. In fact, he took no responsibility for the relationship. That it was *her* doing, the way *she* wanted it, was always his posture.

Says the Century husband who perhaps knew him best, "Like the fellows he hung out with, Hi had great insensitivity to women, and what he did to them. All those men have a 'take it or leave it' attitude. They are so self-centered they're really unaware of the effect they have on other people. At the office, everybody's in awe of them. They don't have equal partners. The associates they do have are all people who feel held down, and constantly put down, by the ruthless man at the top. These are men who take whatever they want. Their women accept this, and they always have."

In their private lives, a number of these men have managed to have two or even three wives and ex-wives, and to continue to see them all, and to see other women as well. They constitute a kind of easygoing Old Goat Society, a club within a club of men who are rich enough, and adroit and powerful enough, to do anything they feel like, all the while preserving a flawless facade of middle-class morality with their wives and children. Birthdays, major holidays, civic banquets, and such are family-only affairs; hunting and fishing and yachting vacations may be occasions for girl friends. Herman Tarnower had no wife, hence no need to maintain the facade, but he found it natural to join his friends in their two-tiered life. Whether the Old Goats were the model for the club bachelor, or vice versa, has been a topic of much debate.

Tarnower's first visit to the Arab world offers a clue to his sexual attitudes. The doctor was making a sight-seeing tour across Morocco by hired limousine, and his Muslim driver happened to mention that he had two wives. Tarnower asked him why.

"Because I can't afford four," the man replied, four being the limit even Allah allows. "But even two is much better than one. With two, *both* try a little harder." Tarnower repeated the story many, many times.

Aging, arrogant, and balding though he was, Tarnower nonetheless had the aphrodisiac qualities of power and authority, and the godliness of being a great heart doctor. Even without his white coat, he seemed to his admirers to be wrapped in the mantle of Hippocrates. Thus sanctified, Tarnower never needed to marry anybody. Once perhaps he would have. But the temper of the times had changed in his favor, and these days a great heart doctor and a school headmistress could readily maintain a discreet but open unmarried liaison. Rules and customs changed very fast in America during the fourteen years of Jean and Herman's love affair, and whereas Herman was served by the great threshing machine of time, Jean like many women of her age and class got chewed up by it. Like many of his friends' wives, Jean Harris accepted the men's attitudes toward sex and power; that acceptance was implicit in her 1967 letter to Hi proclaiming that she was a "modern woman." Jean tolerated other women in Herman's life because that is what the other wives did. The critical difference—although Jean could never quite bring herself to acknowledge it—was that Jean was not a wife, and hence had none of the protections of matrimony. Nor, later, would she have any of the protections of divorce. Nor did she ever seem to recognize that, to Hi, her fateful letter of November 1967 bore a double message: if she did not mind, indeed if she *insisted upon* being a lover, not a wife, that meant he was free to see her on the same terms as he saw any other woman. And, of course, vice versa. But freedom to do that which one has utterly no interest in doing often feels more like a kind of bondage.

As for Tarnower, he interpreted Jean's brave and liberated declaration of a love that asked no promises, a love without strings, as her permission to go on living the life he had always lived. He lost no time getting back on his old tracks. As he often said, "Women are like streetcars."

It cannot have been easy for Jean Harris to play the part of Herman Tarnower's modern liberated woman, let alone to be a mistress. A mistress is first a pragmatist. A mistress would have kept the diamond, or sold it and invested the money. Instead of investing in her own life, Jean invested her all in her dream of romantic love. As she says, "I invested *me.*" She bet her entire emotional capital on one spin of the wheel. She put it all on red, and when it came up black, she refused to accept the evidence of her eyes. In some hidden part of herself, a place so dark and secret that even she was not fully aware of it, the hope must still have lingered that someday, when they were old and gray perhaps and all fires banked, someday they *would* marry. That was the up side. On the down side, she at least had the certitude, and the consolation, that he would never marry anyone else.

Jean Harris never thought like a mistress, she always thought like a wife. A French peasant girl wandering into the court of the Sun King was far better prepared for her new role than Jean Harris in Herman's world. But she had plunged in bravely and for a time, thanks to her native wit and intelligence, she managed to do rather well. Emblematic of her efforts to fit in were her Christmas presents. In 1970, for example, the lovers spent the holidays in West Palm Beach with Vivian and Arthur Schulte, and the household was ankle-deep in brightly wrapped offerings of Steuben glass, Gucci leather, and other well-labeled status goods. Jean's gift was a homemade red felt Christmas stocking, with cutout letters spelling H-E-R-M-A-N stitched across the top, and Herman's favorite things—an elephant and an antlered deer, a duck and a school of fish, golf clubs, dice, cards, a globe, a stethoscope, a pair of horn-rim glasses—all cut from bright bits of cloth and carefully stitched in place. Cost of materials: ten dollars. Superiority of gift: unquestionable.

Some adjustments were harder on Jean than others. Occasionally Suzanne slipped up in her housekeeping, and Mrs. Harris arrived at Tarnower's house for the weekend only to find another woman's things in the bathroom. She was angry and hurt, of course, but she told herself that she had no right to complain. The heart doctor was one of the world's most attractive bachelors, and moments like this were part of the price of having him. She was madly in love; to have Hi entirely during the times when she could be with him was all she had a right to ask.

She was always to some degree aware of the doctor's relationships with numerous other women, and she dealt with them either by pretending they did not exist, or with her characteristic mockery. "You know, Hi, if I'm ever very rich," she had told him the first year they met, "I'm going to buy a great big Steuben glass hunting bowl, and I'm going to have engraved on it all the ladies' names, and all the dates the lucky lady was laid." She also convinced herself that an insatiable appetite for women is an inevitable characteristic of any interesting man. "Hi from the standpoint of women has been the same from the day I met him," she recently told a friend. "Everything he had in that house, every piece of needlepoint, or glass, or silver, or whatever was engraved, enshrined, or embroidered with some woman's name on it, and some date. When he asked me to marry him, I didn't think he had such a *large* collection, but over the years it became obvious that he did . . . but that doesn't make people hate John Kennedy, or Thomas Jefferson, or Benjamin Franklin, for God's sake! A lot of interesting men had a lot of women; in fact, most of them."

Jean's mother had nicknamed her well. Not for the first time, Miss Infallible did not know what the hell she was talking about. For one thing, it is certain now that she had no idea whatever that, by 1970, while she was still juggling her many responsibilities and meager funds so as to arrange an occasional weekend's trip from Philadelphia up to Purchase, Herman had, among other things, hotly resumed his romance with the woman who had once been the great love of his life.

Elegant, slender, German-born, and somewhat shy, Gerda Stedman for three years was Herman Tarnower's constant companion. Meeting her today, one experiences a sharp shock of *déjà vu.* Gerda Stedman, Jean Harris, and Lynne Tryforos—the doctor's longtime office assistant and the woman who eventually would more or less replace Jean Harris in Tarnower's bed —are three lovely blue-eyed blondes, each a classic Nordic type; three variations on the same theme, three models of the same expensive car. At the time of Tarnower's death, one was thirty-seven, one was fifty-six, and one, although probably in her early sixties, was still perhaps most beautiful of the three.

Gerda Stedman is tall, with good bones, fine skin—a less earthy Dietrich, dressed in expensive shades of deep blue and mink brown. She grew up among the *haute bourgeoisie* of pre-Hitler Berlin; one of her parents was Catholic, one Jewish. She is a cosmopolite but not an intellectual, a gracious and cultivated woman, a good mother but not a clinging one to two grown daughters. She communicates a sense of a woman who has lived fully, who understands love and human nature as well as she does power and money, and who is kind. One senses in this self-sufficient and normally reclusive woman a certain need to talk.

During World War II, Gerda Stedman worked in the Hungarian underground. Then, after a year or two in Paris and London, she came to the United States and met and married a brilliant young banker from Sedalia, Missouri. Sam Stedman soon became a partner in Loeb Rhoades, and became known and profiled in *Fortune* magazine as "the Wizard of Wall Street." At the age of forty-three, Stedman died quite suddenly of cancer, leaving two small daughters, ages one and six, and a very wealthy widow. A year later, in 1962, John Loeb introduced the beautiful widow of his young partner to his doctor, Herman Tarnower.

Although Gerda and Hi always lived separately, they began to travel together frequently, hunting big game in Africa, shooting birds in Spain, fishing in New Zealand, stag-hunting in Germany, grouse-shooting in Scotland, boar-hunting in Transylvania. They visited with Hi's Century friends in Westchester and the Caribbean, and gambled in Las Vegas with his sister Billie and her husband.

When Herman Tarnower met Gerda Stedman, he was a busy and prospering doctor but in no sense a sophisticated man. She probably introduced him to whatever he knew of taste and culture. She helped him to decorate his house and office. She taught him more about vintage wines. She took him to her late husband's tailor to order his first custom-made clothes. She dragged him to a few museums and concerts, but his appreciation of the arts remained primitive. His favorite contemporary music, he once remarked, was the score for the movie *Cleopatra*. He was uncommonly well read, however, and such dinner-table remarks as "I was rereading Herodotus the other day," or "I am reading *War and Peace* for the twelfth time," may have been boastful but they were not untrue. He also was extremely well informed on current events, and used to say that one day he would like to go into politics.

Tarnower in those days was not only reluctant to spend money; he was innocent of many of its pleasant minor uses. Gerda gave him the first gold watch he had ever owned, the first gold buttons for his first blazer, the first real silver and china for his dinner table. Because he seemed almost incapable of spending money on himself, Gerda quietly paid for the necessary fabric and labor to redecorate his bedroom. When they went to the theater, she often paid for the tickets. On their world travels, she always paid her own way. When Tarnower got around to hiring the Van der Vrekens, it was Gerda who ordered the subscription to *Gourmet*. She and Suzanne grew fond of each other, and they remain so. Suzanne comes to visit on occasion, and Mrs. Stedman has always encouraged her work as an artist, chiefly as a painter of wild flowers; she bakes a stollen for Suzanne at Christmastime, and sometimes gives her old clothes.

Mrs. Stedman recalls that Tarnower would never tolerate even the mildest sort of criticism. Once, at the tables in Las Vegas, she had ventured, "Hi, if we don't leave now, we'll be late for cocktails."

"If you don't like it, let's call it quits," was his immediate, icy reply.

But it was Gerda who called it quits when, late in 1965, three years after their affair had begun, she suddenly informed Herman that she intended to marry someone else, a prosperous real estate man named Jerome Greene. Most people assumed that she was seeking a stepfather for her children and that, not for the first time, or the last, the bachelor doctor was balking at matrimony. A year or so later, on the golf course at Palm Beach, Tarnower confided to Marge Jacobson that "not marrying Gerda was the greatest mistake I ever made in my life." Then he added, "Do you know a nice girl for me?" A few months later, she introduced him to Jean Harris.

In 1970, five years after her sudden marriage to Jerome Greene, came Gerda's equally sudden divorce. She resumed her previous name and, for six months or so, she resumed her association with Herman Tarnower. The Van der Vrekens were particularly happy to see her again. They did not like the doctor's latest woman friend, the teacher from Philadelphia. Like most of the servants of the doctor's rich friends, they found Mrs. Harris variously uppity, imperious, and condescending. They took Pecksniffian offense at her free usage of four-letter words, a new habit she had picked up from a number of Century dowagers who swear like sailors. Although Mrs. Harris tried hard to befriend the Van der Vrekens, and always rewarded their favors with presents, tips, thank-you notes, she simply had no knack for dealing with underlings of any variety.

"Madame, she ees cray-zee!" Suzanne would whisper to Mrs. Stedman in her near-impenetrable Belgian accent.

"Ach, Suzanne, *you* are cray-zee!" Mrs. Stedman would tease in her own pronounced Berlin accent.

At the time of her divorce, Mrs. Stedman bought a lonely but lovely tropical villa in the British Virgin Islands, and after Christmas she invited Dr. Tarnower down for a week's visit. He was keenly appreciative of Gerda's excellent cooking, and the quiet comfort of her household. He was planning a round-the-world tour in the spring, he said, and he urged her to come along. It would be like old times. They would float on the waters of Kashmir, and visit a rajah's private tiger-hunting camp in Nepal. But Gerda was busy refurbishing her new villa, and had no time for a long vacation. When Mrs. Stedman turned him down, he invited Mrs. Harris. That became Hi and Jean's first round-the-world trip.

Jean knew that Hi and Gerda had once been lovers, but she was not in the least jealous, she assured both him and herself. Of course she had no idea that the relationship had resumed. Occasionally when she was visiting Hi, the servants would announce that Mrs. Stedman was on the telephone. After Hi took the call, in another room, Jean would remark, "You know, Hi, you really should see Gerda occasionally. Take her to lunch perhaps. She was _so_ fond of you! And so disappointed."

"She bores me," Tarnower would reply.

It was some months after the doctor's death before Jean Harris was told that Gerda and Hi had for a time resumed their love affair. She refused to believe it. It was easier to believe that Gerda was making it all up, seeking to assuage her jealousy and perhaps hatred of the woman who replaced her in Tarnower's affections. That is still what Jean prefers to believe today.

Late in 1970 and early in 1971, a number of curious events occurred that at the time made little sense to either woman. During this period, Mrs. Harris picked up her kitchen phone in Philadelphia and heard Herman announce that he had just proposed marriage to a woman with four children. Since he had twice been unable to bring himself to marry a woman with two children, this bulletin from Purchase seemed needlessly cruel. Some friends saw it as evidence of Hi's sadistic streak. Jean disagreed, and handled the situation with her usual mocking banter. "When he told me she had four, I knew he would never marry her, and I said, 'Why don't you stop messing up so many women's lives, Hi, and just mess up mine?' This seemed to relax him. I think he felt very comfortable with me after that."

In fact, the doctor proposed marriage in that year to at least two women with four children. One of them, another wealthy and beautiful widow, had had fewer than ten dates with the doctor, all stiffly proper occasions in the company of other couples at dinner or the theater, when she happened to mention one evening that she had decided not to go to Africa on safari the following month.

"Wonderful!" Tarnower exclaimed. "Then you can come to Nairobi later, with me."

When Henri drove them back to the woman's apartment, Tarnower did not bid her goodbye in the lobby, as had been his custom, but came up in the elevator. "How would you like to spend the next fifteen years of your life with me?" he said.

She was stunned. "Is this a marriage proposal?" Tarnower said he guessed it was. She pointed out that they scarcely knew one another, and the relationship swiftly shriveled and died. She decided later that the doctor really had wanted to suggest a love affair, and had not quite known how to go about it.

Gerda Stedman is not only half-Jewish; she spent some time in a concentration camp. When she resumed her association with Tarnower after not seeing him for five years, she was struck anew by the intolerance of the man. "Hi had a very small Eastern European background and outlook," she has since said. "He was *really* anti-Semitic." The very wealthy Jews whom Tarnower admired reminded Gerda of the Jews of prewar Berlin. "They had the same sense of superiority. They were Jews who were really trying to get away from their own religion and background. Hi had the most terrific resentment against such people—and he was absolutely determined to become one of them!"

Nonetheless, Mrs. Stedman continued on occasion to accept Tarnower's invitations. She particularly remembers a dinner party, shortly after the doctor's return from his round-the-world tour with Jean, when his other guests were the Knopfs and one other couple. Gerda deliberately went home before any of the others, lest they conclude that she intended to remain there overnight. Tarnower telephoned her the next morning. "Can you imagine! Just after you left, that crazy woman walked in. She drove up here all the way from Philadelphia!"

Jean Harris says today that she never came up to Purchase

unless Tarnower invited her. If this is so, then it would seem either that, for some reason, Mrs. Stedman made the story up or, more likely, that Tarnower was merely up to his old trick of disparaging one woman to another.

Not long after this episode, other curious events occurred. One day Suzanne gave Mrs. Stedman a package containing an Elizabeth Arden makeup kit and some knitting that she had left in Tarnower's dressing room. When she opened it, she found to her astonishment that the kit had been ripped and slashed, and all its tubes squeezed out. She unrolled the knitting and saw it had been smeared with nail polish. Later Suzanne told Mrs. Stedman she believed Jean Harris had done it. Jean says today that she does not know what either woman is talking about.

When Gerda broke up the New York townhouse she had shared with Jerome Greene, she got back an unusual Oriental rug that fit no place in her Westchester home; it might be just the thing, she thought, to go under the dining table in Tarnower's odd-shaped trophy room. She asked her houseman to take it over, and Tarnower telephoned at once to say that it looked wonderful and fit perfectly. At his very next dinner party, Mrs. Stedman learned, possibly through the Van der Vrekens, the guests included Gerda Stedman's closest friends, whom she had introduced to Tarnower, and the hostess was Jean Harris. Mrs. Stedman telephoned the doctor in some annoyance. "I find it very funny, Hi, that you entertain my best friends with your new girl friend on my old rug."

Henri Van der Vreken rang her doorbell a day or two later. On the doctor's orders, he had brought back the rug, stoutly wrapped in brown paper, and Mrs. Stedman ordered it put away in a storeroom.

Sometimes the old love seems the best love; perhaps longtime lovers become imprinted upon one another. In any case, Mrs. Stedman saw the doctor a time or two more. The end finally came on the weekend she was visiting him in Purchase and found a filmy nightgown in a dressing-room drawer. Had Suzanne slipped up on her housekeeping again? When Tarnower got home from the golf course and went upstairs to change, Gerda Stedman was standing there holding the lacy thing in her hand. She looked reproachfully from it to the doctor, and said, "Hi, I sink ziss iss not very hi-gienic of you."

Then she dropped the nightgown on the floor and walked out of his bedroom and out of his life. Although they continued formally to exchange Christmas cards, Gerda Stedman and Herman Tarnower did not speak or set eyes on one another for the next nine years.

It was a couple of years later, cleaning out an old storeroom, that Gerda noticed the big package wrapped in brown paper. When she removed the wrappings and tried to unroll the rug, she saw that it had been methodically and entirely razor-slashed into narrow strips.

II

Midway

8

Headmistress

JEAN HARRIS AND HERMAN TARNOWER took their first trip around the world during her spring vacation in 1971. It was a romantic, honeymoonlike excursion, the sort of deluxe tour Jean had only read about in travel brochures. She never knew it was the same expedition Gerda Stedman had turned down. That year the schoolmistress watched the arrival of spring in Senegal, Morocco, Kenya, Sudan, Bahrein, Sri Lanka, Malaysia, Saigon, and Hawaii. Travel was always the best of Jean and Hi's time together. They could be alone more, and Tarnower was a truly superb traveling companion. Nothing upset him, every new experience delighted. He was organized, aware, keenly curious, and he made Jean feel more vital than ever before in her life. "I loved watching Hi *enjoy* life the way he did," she said later, "because I could enjoy it through him, vicariously. That was an entirely new experience to me. My father was incapable of enjoying life, and Jim was always afraid he might get a bill for it."

Jean is an excellent mimic, and she was so alert to the sights

of their journey that back in school she could act out entire
panoramas for her students—a crowded bazaar at Dar es Sa-
laam, or a night in a treehouse in Africa watching the baboons
on her windowsill, the mother and baby rhino in the moonlight,
and the warthogs ("the only animal that can run on its
elbows"), all coming to drink at a waterhole. Jean kept careful
travel diaries to use at school; Hi wrote lengthy "Dear All"
letters describing his adventures. Copies were made back at his
office and distributed to all his friends. Jean was never mentioned. Sitting beside Tarnower on the plane and looking over
his shoulder as he wrote, she marveled at his ability to edit her
completely out of the story.

In 1971 Jean Harris was completing her fifth year at Springside. In addition to her administrative duties, she had for several years been teaching two courses. "Developmental Reading," in the eighth grade, reflected Jean's fanatic determination
that every one of her girls *was* reading before she moved on to
the Upper School. Her favorite course was a Harvard-designed,
prefab social studies course that pondered such basic questions
as *What is human about a human being?*

But out of the classroom and away from Herman Tarnower,
Jean Harris led the lonely life of a single woman working to
earn money to raise children by herself. Her sons' companionship was not enough to dispel the dull sense of being alone,
adrift, apart from the mainstream of life. This dread of alone-
ness was nothing new. She would have divorced Jim Harris
sooner had she not been so dismayed by the thought of life on
her own. Although she, not Jim, had sought the divorce, the
reality of it left her feeling abandoned. Fighting against that
sense of abandonment was the source of her growing exhaustion, she believed. The only times she did not feel alone were the
times with Hi. Whether they were roaming the world together,
or weekending quietly in Purchase, these moments were little
oases of companionship and closeness in the vast desert wastes
of her solitude.

Philadelphia's Chestnut Hill is a citadel of the Old WASP
establishment and, socially speaking, Jean Harris was not doing
very well there. She looked the part of headmistress, but she did
not play the part. She did not know *how* to play it; she was to
some degree ignorant and innocent of that world's deeply felt,

never-mentioned rules, and to some degree contemptuous of them. As a result, she evoked uneasy feelings among certain people there, and she would do so again in Connecticut, and even more at Madeira.

"Chestnut Hill has a lot of nets," says one sharp-eyed and impeccable inhabitant, "and Jean Harris fell through them all. The net of form, social convention, and stiff upper lip—Jean complained too much. To put it another way, she was too honest. The net of friendship—she wasn't good at it. The net of money—she didn't have any but, what was worse, *she admitted it.* In Philadelphia, she was an outsider. People inside were willing to take her in and make her manager of the thing they cared about most, the next generation, so long as she played by the rules. The rules say you don't fuck around, you don't become a public alcoholic, and you're not overtly poor, because that makes them aware of the unpleasant realities of life. The prohibition against being 'overtly poor' means you don't do your own work. You don't vacuum your own house, unless the cleaning lady is sick, or paint the walls, except in an 'amusing' way. Everything she was doing was wrong, or as we prefer to say, 'terribly unattractive.' Not only are Jews terribly unattractive. Passion is terribly unattractive. Overt poverty is terribly unattractive, and so is overt wealth. The very things everybody else in the world is dealing with—sex, passion, money, poverty, discrimination—rich old WASP families are very careful not to. Their *business* is not to think, and not to feel. They live by the morality of fox-hunting.

"It's an *inside* system, you see," the dowager continues. "So long as you stay within its rules, they'll find a way to help you. If she'd said, 'Things aren't going right for me. I'd like to get away for a bit, perhaps take a group of girls to France this summer . . . ,' why, somebody would quietly have come up with the money to help her get away from that man. But when she insisted on living as she did, their rules made it impossible for them to lift a finger."

In 1970 Springside's headmistress had retired, and Jean had hoped to be named to the post. But when Jean Harris gave up school-teaching for administration, she chose an occupation for which she was not as well suited temperamentally; although she was exceptionally creative, diligent, amusing, and intelligent, she was also high-strung, perfectionistic, and quick to anger. Someone else got the job. "Always a bridesmaid," she quipped. *Put the blame on Mame.*

Another reason she was passed over was her relationship with Tarnower. The previous Christmas, over a third wassail bourbon, a powerful Springside figure had said, "Jean, you will never become the headmistress of this school, or any other, because everybody knows you've been living with that Jew." Mrs. Harris often told people afterward that nothing that had ever happened in all her wonderful times *with* Hi ever endeared him to her as much as this slur, which happened while they were apart.

One day Jean Harris learned, again through the Smith College Vocational Office, that a small girls' day school in Rowayton, Connecticut, was looking for a new head. She jumped at the chance. It did not matter that she had never heard of the Thomas School, that Thomas and the last head had just abruptly parted company, that the school had been turned down for accreditation and was running out of money. If the Thomas Board was willing to give the failing school one last college try, that was good enough. The pay was better, and Jean was obsessed with providing her sons with as much money as she could. Not that she wanted David and Jim to worship money in the manner of Hi's rich friends, but she knew the severe handicap that lack of money imposes. The summer she had expected to marry Tarnower and move to Westchester, she had let both boys' scholarships lapse. It had taken two years to get them back.

David was now in college, Jimmie in boarding school; "uprooting" them was no longer the consideration it had once been. But the most wonderful thing about the new job was that Jean would no longer have to worry each time she left Hi how to contrive to get up to see him again. Rowayton and Purchase were only twenty minutes apart.

Rowayton, Connecticut, is a charming waterside village with several boatyards, two liquor stores, two beauty shops, a drugstore. On a panoramic site just outside of town sits an imposing pile called Rock Ledge. Part English manor house, part Irish castle, it was originally the home of a steel baron; by 1971 it had become the home of the modest Thomas School, and it was not a good fit. It suggested a little girl dressed up in her grandmother's ball gown. Thomas had a distinguished academic history, but by the time Jean arrived, the student body numbered only 115 girls. Like most private schools, especially small, single-sex ones, Thomas had faltered badly through the permissive and difficult 1960s, a disastrous period in American private-school history during which hundreds of schools either merged or shut down altogether.

Not long after Jean moved into the spacious headmistress's suite on the top floor of Rock Ledge, Adeline Penberthy, a Smith College classmate who lives in Rowayton, strolled over to see how she was faring. It was a Sunday, and the Penberthys found the headmistress on a ladder pruning some overgrown rhododendrons. Musing aloud as she worked, Jean said she felt Thomas had been functioning as a kind of expensive baby-sitter for a lot of marginal students, and she had about decided it was necessary to prune the dead wood in the student body in order to encourage new growth. "Jean was only really interested in quality education," Adeline Penberthy remembers. She believed that only if Thomas developed a very tight, academically strong student body could it hope to attract a better class of students. This was not an all-popular idea in a school already hurting for lack of enrollment. "I suppose jealousy and resentment were only natural," says Mrs. Penberthy. "And it didn't help that Jean was a very beautiful, young-looking woman and the school people were rather frumpy and academic."

Peg Kinney, assistant to the headmistress at Thomas, put it this way: "Jean's worst fault was that she was competent, terribly attractive, and knew exactly what she wanted." One thing she wanted to do right away was to institute major medical coverage for the faculty, comprehensive health insurance, and a pension plan. The little school had been drifting along since 1922 with no employee benefits whatever.

Thomas had always called itself "experimental." It taught music by encouraging students to write it and perform it; it taught art and history by encouraging the girls to paint historical events; it prided itself on its high intellectual ideals. Jean was slow to catch the special Thomas flavor, and meanwhile she managed to offend much of "old Thomas" with her hot temper and overhasty decisions. But she always was quick to admit she had been wrong. "Well, I blew that one!" she would announce at a faculty meeting. "Now, where do we go from here?"

"I've felt her wrath, and it was certainly direct," one teacher recalls. "But there was no meanness in it. She was just fed up with incompetence and halfhearted efforts."

Still, Jean's lack of tact was sometimes startling. Her secretary wore a hearing aid, and one day a visitor to the office was startled to hear the headmistress snap, "Darn it, Mary. You get more deaf every day!" For someone in education, Jean had a notably short fuse. Little things made her fly off the handle. She did not react well under pressure, and the pressure at Thomas seemed never to let up. Living as well as working in Rock Ledge made her feel that she was on duty twenty-four hours a day and she lacked the energy to get through it all. During the daytime she worried about the girls, classes, faculty. At night she thought about the mortgage, the building code, the old oil burner, the worn-out sewage system.

Marge Rooney, who taught mathematics at Thomas, and is the wife of TV curmudgeon Andy Rooney, recalls: "Physically, Jean is one of the most tense and intense persons I've ever met. She never walked; it was always closer to a run, and her foot was jiggling all the time." All those who have ever spent time with Jean Harris—schoolmates, hostesses, observers at her trial —speak of her ever-jiggling foot. She sits with her legs crossed, and the foot that is not touching the floor tilts constantly up and down, up and down, like the beam on a tiny oil derrick. Like *Mame,* the foot seems to be a means to discharge inner tension and maintain control.

"She was a great one for assigning blame, and it sometimes created ludicrous situations," recalls a former teacher. Jean's beloved golden retriever had the run of the school. One day a sixth grader was having a birthday and when no one was looking, the dog got into the big cake, which had been left unguarded on a windowsill. When the child found her cake mutilated and ran to the headmistress in tears, Jean's reaction was to summon the entire school into Assembly and deliver an impromptu sermon on the imperative to respect other people's property. But by that time everybody had seen the dog wandering around with marshmallow frosting on her chops.

Another teacher remembers, "I don't think Jean really liked

children. One day we were all upset about something or other and Jean said to me, 'Don't you just *hate* kids?' No, I said, I don't."

This was, of course, a literal-minded teacher talking to a hyperbolic headmistress. Jean Harris clearly adores children. But it is true that most of her years in Grosse Pointe were spent teaching first graders; her master's thesis was based on her work with a group of gifted second graders; at Springside, she was responsible only for girls through the eighth grade. At Thomas she was dealing with teenagers for the first time. And they were all girls. Often at Thomas, and later at Madeira, Jean would thank God that her own children were boys. "I said it to myself a thousand times: thank God these girls aren't my own! I wouldn't know *how* to bring them up."

Furthermore Jean, like many women, did not feel entirely relaxed in an all-female environment. She preferred the companionship of men. Not that they made her feel flirtatious; they made her feel comfortable, whereas being around women made her uneasy. Despite abundant evidence to the contrary, she felt that other women were vaguely "better" than she at conversation, entertaining, cooking, and all the domestic arts, that they were indefinably more "feminine." Jean's sense of not being entirely feminine, or not sufficiently feminine, is always just below the surface of her thoughts. One can imagine it circling, like a great fish beneath the ice. This sense contributes to her persistent feeling of not quite fitting in socially; of not really being pretty; of being different from, and somehow less womanly than, other women; it makes her slightly ill at ease in her primary identity, her womanhood. In one of her letters she tells Tarnower, "I wish I had been born a doormat, or a man."

It always was difficult for Jean to delegate responsibility. One evening just before Parents' Night was to begin, a teacher was surprised to find Jean, in her best dress, on a ladder scrubbing fingerprints off the stairway woodwork. "Of course, we should have *all* been doing it—in a way," she says, reflecting the ambiguity most staffers felt about Jean's rigorous housekeeping efforts.

Certainly the new headmistress had extremely high standards —in housekeeping no less than in manners, morals, and academics. And it was those impossibly high standards that invariably got her into trouble when she had to deal with disciplinary matters. Jean Harris has never quite understood her reputation as a harsh disciplinarian. "You know, I'm really very easygoing, until I put my foot down," she says. "But when I put it down, I put it very hard. I was always referred to as 'bossy old Jean.' I didn't *feel* bossy, but people thought I was."

"She was fairly strict," says Mrs. Alfred Powell, who was head of the Thomas Middle School, "and her temperament might have made her inconsistent in handing out punishments. I think anything slovenly she found abhorrent—whether physical or mental. But slovenliness made her more sorrowful than vindictive, and the trouble was that she had nobody to share those sorrows with. I often felt her sensitivity was more than she could handle on her own. She was addicted to *The New York Times,* and one morning she was reading an editorial about some kind of tax relief bill for senior citizens, and as she began to describe the plight of those old people, she got so emotional tears came to her eyes. They were tears of compassion, but I admit I was made uncomfortable by the *intensity* of her passion."

Jean's intensity led her constantly to question whether she was doing enough. "We've got to do more for these girls!" she repeated over and over. She herself kept up to date on all curricular matters, as well as books and literature. She knew what was going on in every classroom, and was quick to spot incompetence. She knew how to stimulate people to try new things. She was not afraid of old things. Teachers were permitted to return to the classics. She encouraged one teacher to use *Great Expectations* as a text because "it's a feast of words for those girls." She introduced a new history course for eighth graders, "From Subject to Citizen," and offered to teach a course herself on *The New York Times,* but not enough people signed up. She instituted a day on Careers for Women. "She got around and got her girls around. Her energy never flagged." She organized all-school field trips to the Poconos, or to Williamsburg, with stops at Winterthur and the Smithsonian, and when they all got home, utterly worn out, each teacher found a bit of Chinese porcelain from the Smithsonian, and a note from Jean. "Put this where you don't have to dust it often, and think of me."

A former trustee whose daughters were students at Thomas

was bothered by Jean's inconsistency. "She never really listened to what anyone had to say, and she was forever flying off the handle, and going in twenty-seven different directions at once. She had a tendency to twist things, and magnify them out of all proportion. One year our daughter's SAT scores were not the most exciting things in the world. Jean called her into her office and said, 'Your parents are *very upset!*' Obviously, it was Jean who was upset. Fortunately, our daughter knew us well enough to know we loved her regardless of what she did on tests, and we were not overly concerned with SATs. We felt Jean was not capable of handling people. She was very erratic."

Being head of a private school is one of the most punishing occupations imaginable. John K. Shank, a professional adviser to school heads, has described the job this way:

> The average work week is more than 70 hours, and you're on call every hour of every day. Because a house is usually provided, they know where to find you when they want you. The pay is about what a good plumber, a good electrician, or a General Motors assembly line foreman makes—comfortable as long as you keep your tastes fairly modest.
>
> The job sounds permanent, but when you take it you know that you will probably hold it six years at most. . . . What happens when you leave? Only one in three goes on to take a comparable job at another place. . . . [Roughly half the remainder] get fired because those who have the authority to hire and fire (the board of trustees) have lost confidence. If you do make it to retirement in good standing, and the chances are not more than one in ten, you can expect benefits amounting to about half of what a retiring steelworker, postal clerk, or Sears Roebuck salesperson receives.*

Professor Shank notes the "special isolation and anxiety" of the school head. Furthermore, the school head's basic values are wrong for the job. Whereas a senior business executive "is

---

* John K. Shank, "Treating People Right," *Independent School* (NAIS publication), October 1979.

primarily a pragmatist committed to getting the job done and producing results, the school head is primarily an idealist committed to human values and to people. . . ."

The small skirmishes in Jean's life, academic and domestic, went on all week. But the weekend always came. School let out at one o'clock on Fridays, and on those days the carpool mothers waiting in the driveway noted that by about one-thirty the headmistress would come bouncing downstairs nicely dressed, smiling, her hair freshly waved, and hop into a chauffeur-driven blue Cadillac that waited beside the massive, cast bronze doors of Rock Ledge.

The four years Jean lived at Rowayton were the rosy zenith of her love affair with Herman Tarnower. For long periods, she spent almost every weekend at his house. During Spring Break in 1972 they took a second glorious five-week round-the-world tour. This one included a stop in Teheran, a trek through the Khyber Pass, a visit to a rajah's private tiger-hunting camp in Nepal, and stopovers in Katmandu, Burma, Thailand, Hong Kong, and Hawaii. Back at school, Jean made her adventures the basis for many lectures, and the doctor was as invisible in her stories as she had been in his "Dear All" letters. As before, the headmistress was discreet but unashamed of her relationship with Tarnower. She told her assistant, Peg Kinney, about him the first time they met, and several times invited the Kinneys and other faculty members to dine with Tarnower when he came to visit.

In her second year there, teachers noted that Jean was more tense than ever, but they were scarcely surprised. "You know, you have to be an awfully relaxed, cool, together person to do this job at all," says Marge Rooney. "Teaching is difficult enough. But when you're the headmistress too, and the kids, the faculty, the trustees, the alums, and the employees are all at cross-purposes, it's quite natural to feel persecuted. Still, Jean had a dreadful temper. She never hesitated to tell me she thought something was none of my business, even though I had two children in the school and taught there for practically nothing."

April 26, 1973, was Jean Harris's fiftieth birthday. "This is the big one, isn't it, Big Woman?" her older son said on the phone, and he told her that both boys would be coming home to celebrate. That Herman Tarnower did not join them tells much about the nature of the relationship. The doctor did not know it was Jean's birthday. He had never asked her the date, and she had never told him, even though on seven occasions Jean had helped Hi to celebrate his March 18 birthday, arranging elaborate parties from Nepal to Hong Kong to Scarsdale. Jean's reticence was part of a general reluctance to seem too demanding, too possessive, a reluctance to invade his "space," even at considerable loss to herself. The same Japanese-like diffidence on their world tours made Jean wait until Hi was asleep before slipping into the bathroom and washing out his favorite pair of old khaki travel pants. "I didn't want him to think of me as acting 'wifely.' He wouldn't have wanted that," she has said.

Later that summer, Jean visited Colorado for two weeks to take part in an executive seminar at the Aspen Institute, but she spent most of her free time on Purchase Street. One weekend Jean arrived to find the doctor's mother visiting her only son. She was an old woman by then, nearly blind, and lived in Philadelphia with another of Hi's sisters. In a strong Yiddish accent, she asked if the Harrises were a Jewish family.

Tarnower never sought to meet Jean's father, but he did often suggest to Jean that she bring her mother along for dinner, and Jean tried hard to arrange it. Mrs. Struven invariably replied, "I don't think so, dear. Thanks just the same, but I don't believe I'll do that." The certainty of enraging her husband was not worth it.

That fall, Jean stayed home while Herman Tarnower went to China. His companions were Iphigene Sulzberger, then eighty-one, the much-beloved doyenne of the family that owns *The New York Times;* her granddaughter Susan Dryfoos; Chester Ronning, a former China diplomat; his daughter Audrey Topping, wife of Seymour Topping, foreign editor of the *Times;* and Audrey's daughter Susan. The trip was unquestionably the high point of Tarnower's world travels. All the other trips were exotic in the manner available to any American tourist with an unlimited bankroll; the China trip verged on a diplomatic mission, and Tarnower bragged about it ever after. Six years later, when he published his diet book, the doctor sought to use the picture of himself with Chou En-lai on the cover.

At the Thomas School things went bumpily along, declining

slowly from bad to worse. Staff members noticed that Jean was becoming increasingly irritable, that she ate very little during meals, seeming to subsist almost entirely on candy bars. The school nurse wondered aloud if perhaps low blood sugar contributed to her irritability. (Several years later, the Madeira School nurse would raise the same question.) Jean was becoming unpredictable. "You never knew whether to try and see her in the morning or afternoon," says one teacher. People fell into the habit of checking today's mood with her secretary before making an appointment. On several occasions girls were summarily dismissed by the headmistress without prior consultation with their teachers or faculty advisers. When members of the faculty protested, the beleaguered headmistress threatened to quit unless given a vote of confidence.

She began to express her grievances in long, four- or five-page letters, expecting faculty members to reply in kind. She seemed to find face-to-face confrontation increasingly difficult. She was tormented by insomnia. One Saturday night the faculty held a party in the Rock Ledge living room. On Sunday morning Jean came downstairs in a shaking, silent fury and thrust a note into the hand of one of the revelers, saying that because of the noise she had been unable to sleep all night despite the number of sleeping pills she had taken. One teacher was so frightened of Jean's wrath that she hid in a closet.

"Most of the time she was away for the weekend, however, which was a great relief to the rest of us," this woman says. Surely it must have been an even greater relief to the headmistress. Life at school appears to have become acutely uncomfortable for everybody, even though the truth of so many old and petty accusations is impossible now to evaluate.

Jean Harris had a standing hair appointment every week at Patricia's Beauty Salon in Rowayton. "She'd come in here and regularly blow her top," Patricia remembers. "Things weren't going right at the school. She was very unhappy. She felt they didn't really want her in the first place." One day down the street from Patricia's at the Rowayton Pharmacy, a strange incident occurred. Jean stopped in to have a prescription refilled and the druggist refused, saying it was a restricted substance and nonrefillable. Jean became enraged and summoned the town police. Evidently she did not swear out a complaint, since the Rowayton cops have no record of the incident, but Rowayton citizens who were in the drugstore will never forget the scene.

Tenseness, foot-tapping, insomnia, loss of appetite, irritability —not all the changes in the headmistress's increasingly erratic behavior were due to the pressures of her round-the-clock job. Some time early in 1971 Jean Harris had begun taking a powerful drug called Desoxyn in order to combat her growing feelings of fatigue. Desoxyn is a trade name for the fast-acting stimulant known as methamphetamine, and sometimes as Methedrine. The street name is "speed." Every day Jean Harris broke a five-milligram tablet in two and took one half after breakfast, the other half before dinner. The doctor who had recommended this regimen, and who supplied her with the drug for the next decade, was Herman Tarnower.

It is impossible to discuss the next chapter of Jean Harris's life without considering the subtle chemical effect of this drug on her entire personality. Tarnower first prescribed the drug casually after Jean complained of exhaustion, she said later, just as he had given her a painkiller for a bad back and an antibiotic for a bad cold. But Desoxyn is no casual chemical. It is five to ten times stronger than the amphetamines familiar to truckers, students, and others who must stay awake and alert for long periods. It is not just speed but high speed; it hits the central nervous system five to ten times faster than ordinary amphetamines—rather in the manner of cocaine. The effect is temporarily to banish fatigue and depression and enable the user to work long hours. Side effects include irritability, insomnia, suppression of dream sleep, and loss of appetite. (The latter effect makes the drug temporarily useful in weight-loss programs.) The insomnia can be counteracted with sleeping pills, and one danger of amphetamines is that users frequently find themselves bouncing back and forth between "uppers" and "downers," unable to break the cycle. Five milligrams a day, or even ten, is considered just an average or high-average dose to prescribe for a person on a two- or three-week crash diet program. But the cumulative effects of this amount of Desoxyn taken daily for ten years are still largely unmeasured and unknown. Experts in the field of psychopharmacology believe they can be disastrous to an individual's basic personality structure, delicately but incalculably damaging one's inmost sense of "self."

Persons who regularly take a drug such as Desoxyn are called "drug-dependent" rather than "drug-addicted" because the craving is more psychological than simply physical. The amphetamines appeal in particular to dependent, weak-ego personalities because they confer a temporary feeling of strength and independence. But in the long run the drug has a way of subtly *increasing* the sense of dependency because, when it wears off, the person tends to feel, "Without the drug, I am nothing." Thus a drug like Desoxyn is not so important in a pharmacological sense as in a psychodynamic sense; the down side of the drug effect—"I am nothing"—becomes bonded to the personality. The user tends to overlook the fact that she *is* doing her work, drugs or no, and begins to think that without the drug she would no longer be able to function, which is not necessarily so.

Persons who depend on such drugs as Desoxyn will tell you they use them to combat persistent feelings of exhaustion. Although the sufferer does not realize it, this kind of fatigue is usually the result not of physical exertion but of emotional depression. Depressed people feel exhausted because of the psychic battle raging within: the struggle to suppress aggressive or angry or self-deprecatory feelings that they dare not reveal. They have a pounding, ever-present sense of being unable to cope with daily tasks, a chug-chug litany, over and over, not of "I think I can!" but, equally powerful and hypnotic, *"I know I can't!"* But because the drug has a roller-coaster effect—because after every "high" comes the inevitable "low"—the user's sense of exhaustion can itself be an insidious effect of the drug.

Desoxyn not only diminishes the need for sleep. It may also diminish the need for social life. Users tend to be hard-driving individuals anyway, and the drug permits them to work compulsively without the stimulation of other people. Ultimately it tends to isolate a person. When a doctor sees a chronic user, he asks himself, what else does this person do for pleasure? Often he finds that the drug has become a substitute for pleasure.

Finally, the bad news about Desoxyn is also old news. Unlike Valium, whose dangers have become apparent only recently, Desoxyn has been classified as a dangerous drug for many years. Most doctors stopped prescribing it over a decade ago; it belongs back in the Benzedrine inhaler era. Today most hospitals recommend to their residents that they never prescribe it. One conceivable use might be to try it, for a week or ten days at most, for an acutely depressed patient whose doctor is looking for a way to avoid the kind of crude electric-shock therapy that was used to treat Albert Struven.* But even then, it would be used in conjunction with some other, nondangerous drug, one of the standard antidepressants. Desoxyn was always categorically forbidden for long-term use; the likelihood of dependence and the risk of psychosis were considered too great.

Psychopharmacology—the study of the psychological effects of mood- and mind-altering drugs as they interact with the chemistry of the brain—is a relatively new area of medical specialty. An outstanding authority is Ralph N. Wharton, M.D., a physician who is also a psychiatrist, a psychoanalyst, and consultant on psychopharmacology at Columbia–Presbyterian Medical Center, the largest teaching hospital in New York City. "Tarnower, as her doctor, was apparently missing the correct symptoms, the depression," Dr. Wharton says, "and treating the misunderstood symptoms with the wrong drug. The result of her treatment with the wrong drug was that she felt she had a defect *in herself,* rather than that the doctor was giving her the wrong medicine. She misinterpreted her disorder when she said 'I can't live without him,' and 'Hi keeps me alive.' The correct interpretation would be, 'I am ill, and my illness is being masked by a drug he is giving me.' Any doctor who prescribed this drug to this kind of patient for this long, ten years—well, it's *bad practice.* It's atrocious practice. I would condemn it in public, or in court, and I think most physicians would."

Furthermore, the other drugs that Tarnower prescribed for Jean's bad back and insomnia—Nembutal, Plexonal, and Percobarb—are precisely the wrong things to give a patient who is on Desoxyn. Because these drugs are also depressants, they simply compound the problem. "The result," says Dr.

---

* Jean's father's depressive episodes, and the possible suicide of an uncle, would tend to make her especially vulnerable to bouts of clinical depression. Recent studies have shown that genetic susceptibility to depression is cross-sexual, that is, father-daughter or mother-son.

Wharton, "is that his pharmacotherapy produced psychological complications in the patient's already difficult psychological dynamics."

In plainer language, to give a patient like Jean Harris methamphetamine is like applying leeches to someone who is bleeding to death.

9

Callers Anonymous

IN 1974 HERMAN TARNOWER returned from a hunting trip to
Mozambique in time to attend graduation exercises at the
Thomas School. Marge Rooney met the doctor at the dinner
party Jean gave, and found him "quite charming." She recalls
"a very pleasant smile" and a man who said to her, "Hello, my
name is Hi Tarnower, pronounced like Eisenhower." He spoke
of his trip to China with Iphigene Sulzberger and said, "As I
said to Chou En-lai . . ." four times. At graduation exercises
the next day, Jean followed her usual custom of introducing
each girl by name as she handed her her diploma, and taking a
moment to sum up her particular accomplishments for the audience in a witty and affectionate tribute. A charming and stylish stunt, it appeared to be completely ad lib. In fact, as with
almost all her public appearances, Jean had spent days writing,
rewriting, and memorizing her remarks.

That summer was another round of lunch and dinner parties
interspersed with visits to Century. It was the summer of the
nation's discontent with President Nixon, but Herman

Tarnower remained fiercely loyal. When his good friend Seymour Topping ventured his opinion that Nixon would have to resign, his host was outraged. "I can't believe you'd be so stupid, Top, as to say that!"

But Jean Harris had begun to change. Once so meticulous, outspoken, and stylish in her public statements, she now seemed oddly unassertive in her lover's presence. She had always been a passionate Hubert Humphrey Democrat, but this summer she remained silent when the doctor announced his intransigent political position.

In their private conversations, it was Tarnower who was changing. In 1974 Herman Tarnower stopped telling Jean Harris "I love you," and substituted a new credo: "I don't love anyone."

"I don't love anyone, and I don't need anyone." That summer he said it over and over.

On November 6, 1974, a new name appears for the first time in Suzanne Van der Vreken's dinner guest books: "Lynne Pernice." The best-known florist shop in Westchester is Tryforòs & Pernice. The many long-stemmed roses Herman Tarnower had telegraphed to Jean in Philadelphia had been ordered from the shop, and Suzanne had quite naturally confused the name of the demure-looking young guest. She was not Lynne Pernice but Lynne Tryforos, the wife of the florist Nicholas Tryforos, and the mother of two little girls, Laura and Elektra. For many years, Lynne Brundage Tryforos had worked full- or part-time at the Scarsdale Medical Center. Not a nurse but a trained secretary and very capable Girl Friday, she wore a white uniform and helped the doctor with examinations, measured heights and weights, temperatures and blood pressures, did cardiograms, and kept records. Patients and staff knew her to be a pleasant and extremely efficient assistant who was devoted to Dr. Tarnower, nothing more.

There was, of course, much more. Mrs. Tryforos for some years was the much younger "other woman" in Tarnower's life. At Jean Harris's trial the prosecutor would suggest to the jury that it was a sudden decision by Tarnower to abandon Mrs. Harris and in fact marry thirty-seven-year-old Mrs. Tryforos that had precipitated the older woman's homicidal rage. But the prosecutor would offer no proof to back up his speculation, and

Mrs. Tryforos never testified. Nor did she give a single interview, or make any public statement whatever. The information that follows has been assembled from dusty records and the recollections of old acquaintances.

Marjorie Lynne Brundage was born in 1943 in Ossining, New York, a declining Hudson River community whose major industry is servicing New York's notorious Sing Sing prison. Marjorie Lynne attended elementary school in the nearby town of Eastchester, and Scarsdale's Edgemont High School. Schoolmates remember her as one of the more "prudish, cloistered" girls in the class, and some recall that she was "heavily into religion." Her brother, Lee Brundage, was the star athlete on both the basketball and football teams, but despite his eminence, teammates recall that neither one of his parents showed up at the big games.

In her 1961 graduating class, Lynne Brundage was voted the girl "having the most drag with the faculty."

"That was our euphemism for being the biggest brown-noser," says a male classmate. "I know because I was voted her male counterpart"

In 1962 Lynne married Nicholas Tryforos, a handsome Greek American who liked to race his motorcycle on weekends, and otherwise dutifully toiled in his parents' chain of flower shops. Between the births of their daughters, in 1964 and 1968, Lynne sometimes worked part-time for her husband, and sometimes for the Scarsdale Medical Center. She had begun there as a part-time secretary-receptionist right after her graduation from high school, well before she became personal assistant to Dr. Tarnower. When the more intimate relationship between the doctor and his comely assistant commenced is unknown. Court records show that Mr. and Mrs. Tryforos did not separate until September 1975. The following February, Lynne filed for divorce, accusing her husband of leaving the marital home on Grand Boulevard and moving in with another woman. Her weekly salary at the Scarsdale Medical Center was then $123.70, and she asked $400 a month in child support. The marital home, purchased in 1969, had been put in Lynne's name only, as a protection against its ever being seized as an asset by creditors of the ambitious young florist. Now that the couple was getting divorced, it became necessary for Mrs. Tryforos to buy out her husband's interest in the house.

Lynne's schoolmates do not recall how many times her mother was married, but they do say "it was certainly a multiple marriage situation, and not a tranquil home environment she grew up in." Suzanne Van der Vreken used to tell people that Lynne's mother had had six husbands. (At the time of Dr. Tarnower's death, Westchester newspapers reported that Lynne's mother was currently Mrs. William Tirrell.) If this is so, it could well explain the strong attraction Lynne felt to men and women much older than herself, persons who might be seen as parent-substitutes. After Tarnower's death, at sixty-nine, Mrs. Tryforos was escorted frequently by Joseph Cullman III, sixty-eight, and she was engaged for a time to Dr. Eugene Humbert, seventy-two, who had been Tarnower's dentist. Her new women friends included Iphigene Sulzberger, eighty-seven, and several Century widows in their late seventies.

By fall 1974 the Thomas School's financial position had declined to the point where the trustees had to borrow money over their own signatures to pay daily operating expenses, and they began searching for a buyer for Rock Ledge. Just before Thanksgiving, Jean announced a plan to merge with the Low-Heywood School in Stamford, Connecticut. Cries of "Deal!" and "Foul!" immediately arose. Many people were certain to lose their jobs. The choice of Low-Heywood was especially galling to the Thomas loyalists; the school had for years been their arch-rival. The ideal of "quality education" was being abandoned in the interests of Mammon, they were sure, and Jean was identified as the architect of the betrayal, even though sixteen out of eighteen trustees ultimately supported her plan. Recriminations abounded. A small group of loyalists on the Board believed then, and still do, that Jean willfully shut down the school rather than admit her own managerial incompetence.

For her part, Jean says, "The closing was inevitable—and managed to bring out the best in some and the worst in others."

It is worth mentioning here that without the advent of Jean Harris the members of the Thomas faculty might have received no retirement benefits whatever. But when Rock Ledge sold for $300,000 more than the original asking price, Jean persuaded the Board to use the extra money for termination bonuses. Teachers with as much as thirty-three years' tenure might otherwise have faced the prospect of going on welfare. The Thomas School went under in what Jean has characterized as "a year of wall-to-wall trauma." People screamed at one another over the telephone. Others stopped speaking for good. "I've never heard such a blast in my life!" Marge Rooney says of her last conversation with Jean.

Matters came to a head amid the punch and cookies at the annual alumnae-student Christmas party in the living room at Rock Ledge. Jocelyn Moreland, a member of the same family as the school's revered founding mother, Miss Mabel Thomas, and a leader of the loyalist, antimerger faction, noticed that a large oil painting of the school seal had been removed from the great hall. The seal depicts a cloud-covered globe on an octagonal ground, and it is bordered with the singularly opaque Thomas School motto: "To learn and discern of our brother the Clod, our brother the Worm and our brother the God."

Jean was graciously doling out the punch when Mrs. Moreland approached and reminded her that the school seal was the property of the Moreland family. When she had offered it to Mrs. Harris a few years earlier, the headmistress had had it framed and hung in the front hall. If she no longer chose to display it, Mrs. Moreland said frostily, she would like the heirloom returned.

Jean dropped the ladle and raced upstairs. A full half hour later, she reappeared, having discarded her party clothes and also managed somehow to rip the stout canvas out of its frame. She descended the grand staircase dressed in her beloved safari pants, crying openly, the canvas under one arm and her mink jacket over her shoulder. Reaching the bottom, she handed the school seal to Mrs. Moreland, said to Marge Rooney in a not-so-quiet voice, "I cannot wait to get out of this fucking place," and stalked out the door.

Early in March, over Spring Break, Jean and Hi took their third major trip, to Greece, Crete, and Rome. A high point for Tarnower was their visit to the Greek island of Cos, birthplace of Hippocrates, where he picked up a pebble he thereafter kept on his dresser next to the photographs of his parents.

After its final graduation, the Thomas School closed for good, but Jean stayed on for a few months at Rock Ledge. She had received several job offers, but turned them all down. "I knew I wanted to get away for a while from what I had seen in the schools—a kind of falling apart of values, and nobody quite knowing what the rules were anymore," Jean has since said. "I knew that probably where I belonged was teaching. But I would not go back unless I went to a school that was strong enough to have some standards, and did not have to bend with the wind all the time just to keep the place filled." As Jean saw it, a school had to be firm enough to resist the mindless educational peristalsis that pushes kids along from class to class, ready or not.

One day at Hi's house, a friend of his offered Jean a job in New York City. Dan Fraad was president of Allied Maintenance Corporation, a large industrial service organization with 19,000 employees and a wide range of activities. They had contracts to clean office buildings, factories, colleges, airports, Madison Square Garden. They serviced airplanes and airports from JFK to Saudi Arabia, supervised fueling, and looked after major industrial landscaping projects, such as the big IBM headquarters in Westchester. "I have a place right at the heart of my business," Fraad said. "A man or woman could go straight to the top from there." What he needed was someone to write up bids to get contracts, and Jean decided to take the job. She knew she would be the organization's token woman, but she did not mind. As she noted in the employment résumé she kept on file at Smith College, she had also by then been "offered the leadership of two schools, and Dean of another, in addition, of course, to the option of going to Low-Heywood-Thomas.* I chose instead to accept a unique offer to go into business. At a time when women are talking about wanting new and broader opportunities and young girls are being advised (by people who haven't tried it) to tread new paths, it seemed too much of a challenge to turn down." While this was doubtless true, the unpleasant and protracted demise of the Thomas School had left Jean feeling wrung out and sick at heart. She

---

* The present headmistress of Low-Heywood-Thomas has said she thinks Jean did a superb job at Thomas School.

lacked both the vigor and enthusiasm necessary to remain in education. The trauma of the Thomas closing had been most severe on the headmistress. The person who had experienced a "falling apart of values," the person who did not "quite know what the rules were anymore," was Jean Harris. By the time Thomas School closed up, even Jean's strongest supporters on the faculty and staff agreed that she was not, for the moment at least, in good shape to be headmistress of any school.

New York City is an hour's drive from Purchase Street, and Jean much disliked the thought of moving so far away from Hi. She had grown accustomed not only to spending weekends with him; she never left without planning what they would do next time. She kept her evening dresses for Century dances in the downstairs guest-room closet at Hi's house, as well as her sporting gear for their fishing and duck-hunting trips, her resort clothing, and cosmetics. She had become a kind of semiresident chatelaine to the place, careful never to change anything in Herman's home, only to preserve things exactly as he liked them. When necessary, she ordered chairs recaned, bought place mats, replaced a lampshade. She ordered new towels and sheets during the winter white sales, and bought the platters or glassware Suzanne required. It was important to Jean that all her gifts be simple, utilitarian objects that silently and humbly asserted her secure, semiresident, semi-wife-like status. It was important to make clear that she was not a mere girl friend, not a part of what she called "his cuff-link collection." A gift of cuff links from a woman, at least in Herman's world, was an indication that the giver had been happily bedded. Jean's status was of another order.

Rather than move to New York City, Jean made bids on two houses in nearby Greenwich, Connecticut. Tarnower objected strenuously each time. He did not want her to be a commuter, he said. He offered several times to buy her an apartment in New York City. Now it was Jean who objected. She was not a casual in the cuff-link collection, and neither was she Herman's kept woman. She was an independent career woman who paid her own way in the world, and worked to support her children; a woman who happened also to be very much in love with a wealthy man, and who chose to spend as much of her life with him as possible despite the acknowledged impossibility of marriage, and despite the differences in their incomes and ways of life. Every bit of her own earnings went to pay for her boys' education. Although her sons had jobs whenever possible, and their father helped, often she endorsed her salary check directly over to their school or college. But when Tarnower offered to help out, she always refused. When he offered to pay her dental bills, she refused. When he had insisted she keep the ring, she put it in a vault because she could not afford the insurance, until one weekend, before going back home to Philadelphia, when she had simply left it on his dresser. Owning it made her uneasy. She knew that on Tarnower's travels in the Far East it was his custom to buy rings, brooches, necklaces, bracelets, and earrings in wholesale batches for later distribution as it struck his fancy, so she accepted his occasional gifts of other jewelry with mixed and often bitter feelings. Her need to feel independent of Tarnower's largesse was fierce. Her net income was little more than the doctor paid his servants. On their travels abroad, Jean had just enough money to get her hair done and buy a few souvenirs. Herman paid for two sets of tickets and hotel bills, and Jean did not feel compromised in her integrity because she knew that if she did not go with him, someone else would. Someone else always had.

Critical matters in every romance are sexual jealousy and who pays the bills. Sexual jealousy between two independent persons was not acknowledged in Jean's canon. It did not exist. Each was free. "No strings on me." Jean had always known she was not the only woman in Herman Tarnower's life. She did not know how many others he was seeing; nor would she allow herself to care. She visualized her role as rather like that of the Number One wife in a large Oriental household. Secure in her own position, she could ignore all the others, or tolerate them with a thin, cool smile.

Jean rented a small, cheery, tenth-floor, unfurnished apartment in Manhattan's East Sixties, and took up her duties as Manager of Sales Administration for Allied Maintenance. She had stored her extra furniture in Hi's basement. Weekends whenever possible were spent on Purchase Street. While Hi played golf, Jean remained alone by his pool reading, swimming, sunning. Tarnower always met Jean's train on Fridays, and drove her back to the station Sunday nights. But each time she mentioned buying a house nearby, the doctor said, "You already *have* a home here. With me." When she did buy a tiny, unheated cabin in the woods, she thought of the place more as a hideaway for her sons than a residence for herself. Herman Tarnower lent her $8,000 to buy the little cottage a short distance away in Mahopac, on a street called Bullet Hole Road.

One hot Saturday in July 1976, Jean was sunning herself beside Tarnower's big pool when Lynne Tryforos came around the corner, carrying a gallon of paint and followed by her two daughters. The children jumped into the pool, and Lynne began to paint the garden furniture.

After a while, Jean Harris looked up from her book and said, "Does it not seem bizarre to you, Lynne, that you are here painting his furniture while *I* am here?"

It appeared to Jean that Lynne did not understand what the word *bizarre* meant, so she rephrased her question. "Lynne, why in hell are you here?"

"I'm here because I'm allowed to be."

"Not while I'm here, Lynne," Mrs. Harris replied, and Mrs. Tryforos collected her paint and daughters and left.

Late in July, Jean was sitting in her office at Allied Maintenance when she got a call from a man who introduced himself as Bob Myers. He told her he was publisher of *The New Republic* in Washington, and also Chairman of the Board of the Madeira School in Virginia. "We are looking for a new head," he said, "and your name keeps coming up." Myers happened to be in town, and he suggested they meet for a drink. Jean invited him to her apartment. Their chat was pleasant, brief, and noncommittal. Jean was pleased by the inquiry, but did not take it too seriously. She was not sure she wanted to get back into the school world, and very uneasy at the thought of living even farther away from Purchase Street.

During the summer and fall Jean heard that Madeira was making inquiries at the Smith College Vocational Office, where her academic résumé and all her letters of recommendation were on file. Questions were being asked of her old friends in Cleveland and Grosse Pointe, and at the Boston headquarters of the NAIS. One day she received a plane ticket and went down to Washington to meet with the Madeira Search Committee, a group headed by Alice Faulkner, the cool and level-browed Virginia gentlewoman who would succeed Bob Myers as Chairman of the Board. She met with the committee once at the school, and once in the Washington offices of Jim Worsley, Vice-Chairman of the Board. She was asked many questions, but found it hard to remember them afterward. "What would you do about our Tuesday night religion courses?" is one she does recall. She answered that she did not know. She asked the Search Committee how the Madeira Board was set up, and was told that they did not know.

In the fall of 1976, Hi invited Jean to accompany him on a tour of Eastern Europe—Bulgaria, Rumania, Hungary, Poland —the part of the world his parents had come from, and virtually the only section of the planet he had not seen. To compensate for the anticipated discomforts behind the Iron Curtain, they planned to wind up the trip with a gala few days in Paris. Suzanne's record books indicate that on September 15 Mrs. Tryforos was the doctor's dinner guest and remained overnight. On September 16, the doctor and Mrs. Harris left for Europe. In many ways, it was their best trip. They both were very moved by their visit to the Warsaw ghetto memorial. They made a game of studying people's faces in each country and trying to figure out whether Herman looked more Bulgarian, Rumanian, or Polish, and they arrived in Paris in high spirits. When the porter showed them to their elegant suite at the Ritz Hotel, Jean saw a large manila envelope lying on the carpet just inside the door. Tarnower awkwardly tried to hide the letter, and Jean pretended not to notice. It was time to unpack and then dress for dinner. Tarnower took off his gold and malachite cuff links, dropped them on the mantelpiece, and headed toward the bedroom. Jean took off her earrings and pearls and placed them beside the cuff links, which she knew well; Tarnower had worn them for several years. They came from a grateful patient, he always said. But now for the first time Jean saw the underside of the cuff links. Engraved in tiny letters was "All my love, Lynne." And there was a date: February 23, 1974.

For a few moments thereafter persons passing in the corridor outside the closed door of the suite might have heard a woman shouting, and then a tremendous crash of shattered glass, as if an object had been thrown against a mirror. But shortly after, two well-dressed, middle-aged people emerged from the suite and strolled out to dinner. He was tall, lean, and saturnine and the pretty woman on his arm was petite, blonde, and smiling. By the time they returned from dinner, someone in the hotel had swept up the shards of broken glass, and from that moment forward Herman Tarnower and Jean Harris both behaved as if the scene with the cuff links had simply never occurred.

The letter under the door at the Paris Ritz, "thick as a term paper," Jean said later, was by no means the first. Letters had followed Hi and Jean on their travels for years. She recalls a letter waiting for him in Hawaii, in 1972, which Hi had also tried clumsily to hide. When she had asked about it, he said brusquely that his office naturally had to have his itinerary, and this was "just a little note from one of the girls." Four years later, when Jean saw the cuff links and screamed at Hi in Paris, he said in a quiet, controlled voice that he understood why she was angry. He should have known better than to offend her in this way, he added, and he apologized. That having been done, the subject was closed. Jean washed her face and they went out to dinner.

It was a matter of willed forbearance. Either forgive the man or give up the relationship. Jean knew she should walk away, but she could not. It seemed ironic to her that the time had come when it was necessary to become more like Herman Tarnower—more selfish, more egocentric—in order to survive Herman Tarnower. Since she could not do it, from that moment in Paris onward, total forgiveness became the baseline of their relationship. Forgiveness made still loving him possible. For each new humiliation, there was now but a single acceptable response: "But I love him." *Put the blame on Mame.*

The 1976 world tour was their last. When they got home Tarnower told Jean, "I've now seen everything I want to see, and visited every country I want to visit. From now on, any traveling I do is only for hunting or fishing." Thereafter they went together to Palm Beach, Palm Springs, and the Bahamas; they fished in New Brunswick, went after tarpon in Mobile Bay. The high-minded sight-seeing and on-site study of world history was over. "It was playtime from then on," as Jean said.

* * *

The anonymous phone calls had started a year or two before. Sometimes it was a woman's voice, more often a man's. Usually they came late at night, awakening her from sleep. Sometimes the caller graphically and obscenely described Tarnower and another woman in bed. Sometimes he advised Jean to take sex lessons. At other times he told her she was "old and pathetic" and suggested she "roll over and die." Most frequently the man called while Jean and Hi were away on a trip and left a call-back number with Jean's secretary. When Jean came home and returned the call she would get Lynne Tryforos, who in turn would demand that Jean stop harassing her. Sooner or later Lynne would change her phone number. The man would then call Jean again and leave the new call-back number, and the pattern would be repeated. During this hellish period, Mrs. Tryforos's private phone number was changed five times, yet someone always saw to it that Jean got the new number. Occasionally there were obscene letters too, but Jean was unable to produce either telephone message slips or letters at her trial because, as with all her problems, she had turned to Tarnower for help and had mailed the evidence to him as proof of her suffering.

Dr. Tarnower himself was plagued by anonymous calls for eight or ten years, but he refused to become upset. The calls drove Jean wild. In her efforts to get them stopped, and to prove to the skeptical doctor that she was not exaggerating the extent of her harassment, she consulted a Virginia private detective, Jack Swanson, and had numerous conversations with two Virginia phone company employees, a Mrs. Shipman and a Mrs. MacNamara. She was meticulous about sending Tarnower the names and phone numbers of all the individuals from whom she had sought help. Yet he remained oddly aloof, unconcerned. Sometimes he affected not to know what she was talking about. Sometimes he appeared to doubt her. At other times he told her, "Don't get mad; get even." Finally she called Lynne at the office and begged her directly to stop arranging for the calls; Lynne complained to Tarnower that now she was being harassed at work. Tarnower took Lynne's side. He told Jean to stop calling Mrs. Tryforos or she would be forever "banished" from Purchase Street.

Convinced that Lynne was the source of her torment, Jean at

one point started calling Lynne's home number every night at one or two or three in the morning, to demand that she cease her harassment. But Lynne was never home. Her daughters answered, and Jean could hear *The Late, Late Show* playing in the background. More than anything else, it was Lynne's continuous nocturnal absence from home that convinced Mrs. Harris that Mrs. Tryforos was, in her words, a "slut" and a "whore," out every night sleeping with half the men in Scarsdale. Herman Tarnower could have eased her anxiety—and incidentally disabused Jean of her most unfair opinion of Lynne Tryforos—had he told her that his office assistant was in fact spending every night with him. But for some reason he chose never to do so. Ultimately, Tarnower would base his rejection of Jean on her poisonous opinion of Lynne. Yet that opinion at least in part was Herman's own doing. Why did he say nothing? Why did he fail to set right Jean Harris's bile-drenched delusion? Why did he never tell her that Lynne Tryforos was as devoted and faithful in her adoration of the doctor as was Mrs. Harris herself? It is hard not to believe that, painful as the situation was to both women, it was the way the doctor wanted it.

Many observers surmised that Tarnower deliberately encouraged each woman to be jealous of the next, in order to feed his own ego. In fact, he seems to have devised the more subtle game of denigrating each woman to the next. He tells Gerda that Jean is "crazy." He tells Jean that Gerda is "boring." He encourages Jean to think of Lynne as a slut. To Lynne, he evidently portrays Jean as a bothersome old lady.

"Lynne, how can you *stand* this?" a friend asked her a few years before Dr. Tarnower's death.

"You know, Jean was a friend of Hi's long before *I* met him," Mrs. Tryforos replied sweetly if not perhaps quite accurately. "I cannot say to Hi now, 'Herman, you cannot see your old friend.'"

Cruel though it might be, the doctor's game of round-robin disparagement was eminently pragmatic; it tended to discourage jealous scenes and female cat-fighting; it lessened the pressure on Tarnower himself. To keep his servants happy, he doubtless denigrated all his women to the Van der Vrekens evenhandedly.

In her many overwrought letters to Tarnower during these years, Jean sounds less like a jealous woman than a whimpering child, and in them one can sense the gradual overlap and intermingling that must have begun to occur in her distracted mind between her cruel lover, Herman Tarnower, and her cruel father, Albert Struven. "I think I am not basically a coward or a crybaby. . . . But the game was not to mention unpleasant things. [You told me] 'It's your problem' until the chink in the wall got too wide—and then I cried—and you got mad—and I promised to be good—and you said 'You'd better be or I won't let you come back.' "

A few weeks after she wrote this, Tarnower apologized to Jean for accusing her of "bothering" Lynne, and "forgave" her.

It was during this period that Sid Gerhardt, a psychiatric social worker in New Canaan, Connecticut, who had done some counseling at the Thomas School, got a call from Jean Harris. Was he planning to be in New York City soon? No, but if it was something important he would be happy to change his plans. He had very much respected and enjoyed working with Mrs. Harris. "To me, she represented everything I think an educated woman should be," he would say later. But now, on the telephone, she sounded different, troubled, afraid. "She was in great fear of something, like she was almost paranoid," Gerhardt recalls. "But she wouldn't open up, wouldn't tell me what it was, and I never heard from her again."

Despite the mounting pressures of her life, this single telephone call is the one instance in fourteen years when Jean Harris even tried to reach out for professional help. It seems astonishing, and a measure of the totality of her dependency, that the sole person from whom she sought comfort, advice, or surcease was Herman Tarnower. But Herman, as we know, had no use for psychiatry. Save for prescribing some vitamin shots in the late 1970s, to be administered by the school nurse, and his nonstop supply of Desoxyn, the doctor never in their long association showed any professional concern whatever, or even professional awareness of his mistress's gradually increasing emotional disarray.

The plague of anonymous phone calls is one of the true mysteries of the case. Could Jean Harris have invented or hallucinated them? No, her secretary at Madeira has confirmed that Jean often received call-back messages with a 914 (Westchester) area code, usually from a male caller, when she was away traveling with Dr. Tarnower. For seven years, the Van der Vrekens assured Jean that they were certain it was Mrs. Tryforos who was behind the calls. The servants also pointed out to Jean's sons that the caller had to be either Mrs. Tryforos, or a man whom she knew well enough to entrust with her private telephone number. But if this is so, then who besides Jean was calling Lynne Tryforos? Why was it necessary for her to change her private number five times? And who was it who called Dr. Tarnower for nearly a decade? The doctor himself said he thought it might be the thieves who had stolen his gun collection, checking to see if anyone was home, and after a while he ceased bothering to change his private number. Jean thought that probably some of the calls that came to Tarnower's house were from various old girl friends, and that the rest were Lynne's attempts to discomfit Jean. Certainly it is true, as every jealous woman and jilted lover knows, that the blunt instrument which comes easiest to hand is the telephone. With Tarnower, Jean, and Lynne *all* getting calls, it seems possible that more than one brokenhearted lover had taken to soothing his or her pain with the help of Ma Bell.

Between the flare-ups about the letters and phone calls, Jean toiled at Allied Maintenance. The executive life was not very exciting but the salary was $40,000 a year, and she told herself that if one has been lucky enough to teach school, *any* other job will be something of a bore. So she buckled down to writing worldwide bids for industrial cleaning contracts. She was responsible for the refinement and rewriting of the final bid, and coordinating all aspects of the bid from all Allied departments. George Mailloux, a top Allied executive, says, "Jean was a first-class person, and superb at her job. The deadlines made it hectic. Bids have to be in by the hour they're to be opened. Jean was extremely loyal to Allied. She'd stay till ten o'clock at night, and if no one else was around to do it, she'd even bind the proposal herself. The press keeps saying she was a 'socialite.' She was not a socialite. She was a career woman, and I was very sorry to see her go."

Meanwhile, Madeira's investigation of Jean Harris was mov-

ing forward, and for the first time she began to take the offer
seriously, a viewpoint enthusiastically endorsed by her friends.
"Jeannie, it's a great opportunity! Get the hell out of here and
start a new life for yourself," Marge Jacobson urged. Indeed,
Marge had been trying to wean her friend away from Tarnower
for years. But the new pairings that Marge dreamed up never
worked. "Instant take" had congealed into an imperfect but
seemingly permanent bond. Jean was still secretly hoping to
marry Tarnower, Marge believed, even though this clearly was
not possible. "Not," Marge joked, "unless you plan to poison
Henri and Suzanne."

At every dinner party of late the doctor had taken to repeating the same little maxim: the ideal wife for any man was a
woman half his age plus seven years. Since most of his friends
and their wives were in their sixties, the joke managed casually
to insult every guest at the table. Nonetheless, he continued to
repeat it. Jean consulted a plastic surgeon about a face-lift. But
after taking the recommended vitamins and doing the prepara-
tory exercises, she lost the nerve, fearing that the surgery might
make her look "even uglier."

How could a woman like Jean Harris have let her life deterio-
rate so, and why was she powerless to rescue herself? The
Desoxyn was part of it, of course, and so was her own neurotic
nature, and his, and perhaps sheer bad luck. But probably the
fundamental problem was the one she had alluded to when she
described her very deep need to be told—not asked—where
they were going to dinner. She was the boss in every aspect of
her life save in her relationship to Hi—and like many women of
her generation, she did not like being boss. To her the position
was not only uncomfortable; it was also ipso facto unfeminine.
If she must be head of school on the job, and head of family at
home, then in her relationship to her man, she needed to be
mistress, even servant, in order to restore her sense of womanhood. "The biggest attraction Herman Tarnower ever had for
me was that he never asked my opinion on anything!" she
would exult. Her womanhood is what Herman Tarnower
shored up. That is why she could never let go.

* * *

Executive experience was a rare commodity among middle-aged women in the 1970s. Most potential headmistresses had only a classroom background. Thus Jean Harris's years at Allied Maintenance paid off far more handsomely than she could have anticipated, and on December 15, 1976, she was notified by the trustees of the Madeira School that she had been selected as the school's fifth headmistress. Mrs. Harris was unaware of the other factors that governed her selection when she signed the first of the four one-year contracts which the Madeira Board would offer her. She was expected to take command in the fall of 1977, and her salary was to be $25,000 the first year, with $5,000 increments each year her contract was renewed. The school had promised a house on campus, and a new automobile that, she hoped, would get her from Virginia to Tarnower's house in a little more than five hours. Jean was not sure she could sustain her frayed lifeline to Purchase Street, and not sure she could live without it.

Not two weeks later, while she and Hi were making their annual Christmas visit to the Schultes in West Palm Beach, Jean took a car and began driving fast and aimlessly. Many women seek to calm shattered nerves by jumping into automobiles and roaring down the freeways at eighty or ninety miles per hour. Joan Didion and Dory Previn have described this sort of encapsulated panic. A man is more apt to confront his weather directly. A woman rushes off cocooned in glass and steel, twists the radio on full blast, and hurtles herself, foot on the floorboards, through endless afternoon. Jean was afraid to take the Madeira job, and afraid not to. She drove blindly around in the Florida sunlight. *Why not stay here? Have one glorious week here with Hi and never go back! Not ever.* She drove to a sporting-goods store and told the clerk she wanted to buy a gun. Did Jean Harris really intend to kill herself? She did not know what she intended. Some people just get to a point in life when they're used up, she believed. She had brooded idly about suicide for a long time. It had started long ago, back in Grosse Pointe, when she was still married to Jim; now the idea made sense again. She really could not think of another way out. But the clerk asked to see Jean's driver's license, and he said he could sell a gun only to a Florida resident. She thanked him and left the shop and drove back to the Schultes' house.

Ever conscientious, Jean resigned early from Allied Maintenance so she could spend a couple of months visiting East Coast boarding schools in preparation for her new job. The men at the office threw a farewell party in what President Fraad called "The Fancy Room," a facsimile Olde English Tavern, complete with leaded windows and pewter tankards, which he had reassembled inside their corporate headquarters. He filled huge buckets of ice with magnums of champagne, and the firm's vice-presidents—mostly diamond-in-the-rough types who had worked their way up in the toilet-cleaning business—gathered to wish Jean well. She was extremely touched. When they read her their farewell poem, she responded, "Do any of you know the motto of the Madeira School? 'Function in disaster, finish in style'? You've made me feel I can *do* that!"

But the Maintenance men had never heard of the Madeira School, let alone its motto. Jean thanked them for her farewell present, a Gucci bag, and left.

The winter in Detroit that year was exceptionally bitter. Jim Harris, Jean's ex-husband, who since their divorce had remarried, redivorced, and suffered a severe heart attack, was living alone in a two-story house. One day the temperature hit five degrees below zero. Jim had been warned not to smoke, and not even to walk downstairs unaided. That day he lit a cigarette, walked downstairs and on outside, wearing only his pajamas, and had a long, idle chat over the fence with the neighbors next door. The next morning after a second heart attack he was found dead.

At the age of not quite fifty-four, Jean Harris was making preparations to pull up stakes, move to Madeira, and begin a new life. A very important book to her that spring was Gail Sheehy's *Passages*. Having spent her life secretly wondering, "Why did everybody grow up but me?" and then, in her forties, experiencing the breathtaking, roller-coaster emotions that most people go through in adolescence—such at least was Jean's image of herself—a book that charted "the predictable passages of adult life" was a discovery Jean found both "mind-bending" and "soothing." It showed her she was not so different from others as she had thought, and she drew a great sense of security from its predictions of what was going to happen next, especially its promise that one's fifties are the age of "no more bullshit."*

By now, Jean Harris had a clear-eyed picture of what her move to Virginia would mean. She was capable, she had decided, of accepting Lynne's continuing and doubtless increasing presence in the doctor's life, so long as her own access to him was not cut off. Of course geography would cut it down, but geography could be seen as an ally in the conscious "passage" she was about to make. From the very beginning, in Jean's eyes, she and Herman Tarnower had been good friends, intellectual companions, true comrades as well as lovers. Indeed, she considered him her best friend. Even had he not given her repeated assurances—"We'll always be friends, Jean. We'll always be very close"—she knew that so deep a friendship would always endure. Implied if unspoken was the understanding that dear old friends, on special occasions, might continue to be lovers too.

Nonetheless, Jean felt that in certain respects a clean break with Tarnower was in order, and she was therefore uncomfortable about moving so far away while still owing him $8,000 for her house on Bullet Hole Road. The only other asset she had was 1,500 shares of a stock that was worth about $4 a share, and so she insisted the doctor accept it. This wiped out $6,000 of her debt; and he told her to forget about the other $2,000. But Tarnower owned a quantity of the stock himself—they had bought it at the same time, on a tip from a Century friend—and he continued to watch it carefully. When it hit $9, Tarnower sold. Jean was in Virginia by then, and he never mentioned to her that he had come out $5,500 ahead on the deal.

Several times that spring Jean told Hi that she would like to have back her diamond ring, which she had not seen since leaving it on his dresser. "Hi, we're in a whole different part of our lives now. I'm going to a place where I *can* wear it, and I'd like to, because it means a lot to me."

"Okay, I'll get it out of the safe."

---

* Gail Sheehy, *Passages* (New York: E. P. Dutton, 1976), p. 32. "At 50, there is a new warmth and mellowing. Friends become more important than ever, but so does privacy. Since it is so often proclaimed by people past midlife, the motto of this stage might be 'No more bullshit.' "

It was midsummer when Jean again brought up the ring. "Look, I've sold it and I don't care to talk about it," Herman said. She said nothing. *Put the blame on Mame.* The Van der Vrekens told both Jean Harris and her son David that Dr. Tarnower had sold the ring to raise money to buy Lynne's house from her husband during her divorce proceedings. The diamond's value now was $40,000, they claimed.

Jean was due at Madeira on July 1. A few weeks beforehand she began to collect boxes from the corner liquor store. She was a practiced, thrifty packer and did as much of the work as possible herself. She was entirely alone. The new springer spaniel puppy, another gift from the Maintenance men, had made so much noise the landlord complained and David had taken it back temporarily to the house in Mahopac. She arranged for the moving van to stop first at Hi's house and collect the furniture she had stored in his basement. She was packing not just her possessions but packing up herself. The move to Virginia and a whole new career was a rare opportunity for a woman her age, she reminded herself. She flew down to Madeira to pick up her new car, but evidently she had been confused. Barbara Keyser, the retiring headmistress, was getting a new Audi with her retirement bonus; Jean was given an old, 1972 blue and white Chrysler. Jean told Miss Keyser she wanted to meet some of the soon-to-depart seniors so she could find out what they had not liked about the school. Her tactlessness was characteristic, though it is doubtful either headmistress could ever have won the other's admiration. In fact, they loathed one another.

A student defined the difference between them this way: "Everyone respected Miss Keyser. Not everyone loved her as a person. With Mrs. Harris, very few of the girls respected her, but many loved her as a person. The first time we saw her was Father's Day weekend in the spring. Barbara Keyser, you must understand, was a very strong woman and very big. She got up in front of us and said, 'Girls, I'd like to introduce the new headmistress.' And all of a sudden this little lady gets up there, a little *tiny* lady, and puts her glasses on . . . and even with the microphone, you could barely *hear* her. And you could *see* her shaking!"

In early summer Peg Cullman gave a small lunch party. Her

guests were Mr. and Mrs. Alfred Knopf, Jean Harris, of whom she was extremely fond, and Herman Tarnower, her late husband's country doctor. Ten years earlier, as soon as Herman Tarnower met Jean, he had introduced her to Mrs. Cullman. He hoped to win the approval of the distinguished older woman, and he had not been disappointed. "Jean was definitely a cut above anything I'd ever seen him with before," Mrs. Cullman felt. "I had an immediate sense of sharing a social and intellectual background and rapport. She was unlike his other ladies—what I'd call 'determined blondes.' "

Today at lunch, Alfred Knopf, not usually considered a gossipy man, pulled his hostess over to a corner of the terrace. "I don't know what's happening to our friend," he whispered, "but he's behaving ridiculously. He's always with that nurse in his office! It's an open scandal."

"Shh-h-h," said Peg, nodding toward Jean. "It could get back to her."

"She knows all about it!" Knopf snorted.

"You mean, they *both* know?"

"Yes."

"I don't know the nurse. But I cannot imagine Jean putting up with this kind of thing!" said Peg.

"Frankly, none of us can understand why she does it."

"The happiest times of my life I spent with Hy Tarnower," Jean Harris was to write to a friend from prison. "Without feeling the slightest bit morbid I can wish that I were gone and he were alive. I have never met anyone who so appreciated the gift of life as he did. He could be totally self-centered, bitchy, selfish, even cruel by my standards (but not by his) but you would walk a long way to find a more agreeable companion. Selfish people are usually the ones we love the most. They're more interesting, because they do the things *they* want to do. Friends said Hi and I were at a dead end. But it wasn't for me. And it must not have been for him either, or he wouldn't have continued to see me."

All her life, Jean Harris had been blind to her own worth. She *was* a good teacher, a beautiful woman, a warm, devoted, responsible parent, a dutiful daughter, a staunch friend, and a Japanese mistress. But she never knew. Misreading both the outer and the inner reality, she would grow more and more isolated, more and more insecure, more and more helpless, like the Korean baby crying by the roadside. Her husband had once told her she would never be happy because she didn't know what she wanted out of life, and she thought that was probably true. She wanted to be a good girl. To do the right things. To win Daddy's approval. But she wanted most of all *to be wanted;* if she did not have that sense, she did not feel fully alive. And so, as Tarnower began to want her less, and to tell her more and more often that he wanted nobody, needed nobody, she began slowly to die. She died from the inside out, the way a tree does, the heartwood drying out while the bark still stands.

10

Madeira

IN THE YEAR 1977 Herman Tarnower and Jean Harris were both at the height of their professional careers. Had they appeared together on the television program *What's My Line?* and been asked the show's stock question, "Do you perform a service?" each of the lovers could have answered yes. "Yes, I perform a service for the well-to-do."

"I look after their bodies."

"I look after their daughters."

The daughters of Madeira are a special lot. Wellborn, many of them Southern, they come from quiet, old-money families, from Washington's "cave-dweller" society, from the ranks of middle-level government and professional people. Although Madeira's alumnae rolls are sprinkled with glittering names—Rockefeller, Morgan, Loeb, Vanderbilt—these families enroll their daughters because the tone of the school is *not* super-rich. Its girls are not flashy but healthy, somewhat horsey, somewhat intellectual and—compared with most other teenagers—stunningly poised. Madeira views itself as the most private of private schools, and in recent years its normal xenophobia has been intensified by a series of tragic events. Most notably, in 1973, a youngster was savagely molested, tied naked to a tree in the dense woods behind the chapel, and left there to die of exposure. To keep this story out of the headlines required heroic efforts of Madeira's then headmistress, Barbara Keyser. So when Madeira's next headmistress was arrested for murder—a world-class scandal even by the gothic standards of girls' boarding schools—Madeira was nearly as hostile to curious reporters as the CIA in McLean, Virginia, just down the road.

A word about that road. Driving along Georgetown Pike, one looks in vain for a sign, *Madeira School*. There is just a small marker midway in a long white horse fence: *Greenway, Va.* But Greenway does not exist; it is only the postal address of the school. Venturing in through the unguarded gate, one has a sense of rich, rolling greensward and, behind the four-slat fence, five Georgian buildings, six student dorms, seven playing fields, eight tennis courts, and just past the guardhouse and around the next bend, for all one knows, there may very well be nine maids a-milking and ten ladies dancing.

The point is, one does not know. Madeira is reclusive in the extreme. The preservation of its privacy is the self-appointed duty of a group of powerful trustees, graduates, benefactresses —call them the Druids of Madeira—who guard the school with quiet ferocity. A kind of institutional chastity seems at stake.

As a social structure, Madeira bears a certain resemblance to a medieval convent. It is an isolated and prosperous all-female community dedicated to the academic education and moral perfectibility of a group of carefully selected young women of good family, and it is administered by a female hierarchy. (At the time of Jean Harris's arrival there was only one man among the faculty.) One difference between a convent and the school is that, in the former, the lines of authority were clear and understood by all members of the community. Such was not the case at Madeira. During her two and a half years of stewardship Jean spent much of her energy meeting regularly with members of Student Government to devise and codify all rules affecting student life. That no such overarching code existed was due at least in part to the very personal way this particular school had evolved. It was founded in 1906 by an ardent Washington intellectual, socialist, and bluestocking named Lucy Madeira, a woman so fine-minded and idealistic that she often expressed her hope that one day genuine state-supported public education, with classes no larger than fifteen students, would make an "economic royalist" institution such as her beloved Madeira an unnecessary anachronism.

The female passion to be economically independent of men at all costs was responsible for Lucy Madeira's career in education, just as it was much later for Jean Harris. In the economic chaos that followed the Civil War, Lucy's mother, a Southern gentlewoman, had been forced to open a Washington boarding-house. After putting herself through Vassar College and teaching school for a few years, Lucy determined to open a school of her own so that she and a seriously ailing sister should not be burdens upon the men of her family. The Madeira School has had high academic rank since it opened in a Washington brownstone. By 1929 the nation's capital had begun to change from a sleepy Southern town into a bustling big city, not thought to be the ideal environment in which to raise adolescent girls. Through the generosity of two of her greatest admirers, the financier Eugene Meyer and his wife, Agnes, Lucy Madeira eventually was able to move her school to a magnificent 400-acre hunk of Meyer-owned virgin woodland along the Potomac, although not before the Meyer family had also led the drive to raise $300,000 to erect the school buildings. Another Eugene Meyer property was *The Washington Post*, today part of a family-owned communications empire that includes *Newsweek* and several radio and TV stations. Its empress is the Meyers' daughter, Katharine Graham, frequently described as the most powerful woman in America. Mrs. Graham is, naturally, a Madeira graduate and benefactress, but she is not overly involved in school affairs.

Why do girls' boarding schools exist? The fact of someone like Katharine Graham suggests an answer. Boys' schools in the United States were founded in response to the need to prepare young men for the ministry. Hence Groton, St. Paul's, and such. Girls' schools came about when a heroic founding headmistress like Lucy Madeira encountered a wealthy and enlightened father like Eugene Meyer, a man determined to do as well by his daughters as his sons, but also determined to keep the sexes safely apart. (Not that the Meyer sons, being Jews, would have been available to staff the Protestant clergy. The urge to equal excellence in education was the spur.)

In 1917, at the age of forty, Lucy Madeira had married David LaForest Wing, a widower with two children. But she remained steadily on the job as headmistress of her school until her retirement at eighty-three, and as a socialist who did not believe in the profit motive, she never paid herself more than a $5,000 annual salary. Lucy Madeira belonged to the same great tradition of spirited, vital, quirky, passionate founding headmistresses as Emma Willard of Troy, Ethel Walker of Simsbury, Sarah Porter of Farmington, the three Quaker Shipley sisters of Bryn Mawr, the two Masters sisters of Dobbs Ferry, Mabel Thomas of Rowayton, and dozens of others who someday, one hopes, will receive from historians the attention they deserve. To the girls of good family whose education was entrusted to one of them, the strict, beloved, and deeply respected headmistress became a powerful, lifelong presence. It was more likely Miss Porter, Miss Shipley, or Miss Madeira than gentle Mummy who set the standards of behavior which the young woman would endeavor to live by, and pass on to her own daughters. Women today in their seventies have navigated entire lifetimes adhering to standards and principles enunciated to them by Lucy Madeira when they were fourteen. "Be calm at the center of your being," she would urge. *Festina Lente*—make haste slowly—were the words she chose as her school's official motto. But her most famous exhortation was the bewildering yet bracing "Function in disaster, finish in style!" Thousands of women have seen themselves through the pains of childbirth, divorce, misfortune, and ruin by silently repeating Miss Madeira's gnomic incantation. Even today when one of these women negotiates a difficult passage particularly well, though now she is a grandmother many times over, she still thinks to herself, "*She* would like the way I am carrying this off! Miss Madeira would be proud."

Lucy Madeira believed in a hard-core classical curriculum: Latin, history, English, mathematics. Her girls got into the best colleges—Vassar, Smith, Wellesley, Bryn Mawr—married well, and sent their daughters back to Madeira. Until uniforms were abolished a decade ago, each girl was required to wear a mannish white cotton shirt and necktie and a woolen jumper (navy, green, or rust, choice optional) under a matching blazer. The jumper top was attached to bloomer bottoms; except during athletics, these were covered by a matching, button-on skirt. The costume had fourteen buttons, and a girl who needed to go to the bathroom had to take it all off. *Festina Lente,* sewn onto the breast pocket of the blazer, then seemed particularly appropriate. School dances were held in the gymnasium with a live, all-male orchestra, but no boys. The girls wore their uniforms and danced with one another.

Lucy Madeira held Sunday night Bible classes in her home, The Land, and constantly reminded her girls of their "obligation to society." In their senior year she gave them some personal advice. Always read aloud to your children, especially Dickens, and be sure each child has his own room; privacy is a birthright. She told her girls to save sexual intercourse for marriage "because it's so wonderful," and explained that the poorer classes have so many children "because it's their only form of recreation."

To understand the choice of Jean Harris as Madeira's fifth headmistress, one needs to know a bit about her predecessors. When Lucy Madeira finally retired, Miss Allegra Maynard, for years her devoted assistant, took over the reins, but only provisionally, until a permanent replacement could be found. She had always said she would never even attempt to fill Miss Madeira's shoes, nor did she wish to get old and die in office. Today Miss Maynard lives in secluded retirement in Dedham, Massachusetts, but keeps in close touch with her old girls. Not long ago she told one of them she thought Jean Harris had been doing an excellent job as headmistress.

Miss Maynard stepped aside briefly for a Miss Smith. When it became apparent that she would not work out, Miss Maynard returned temporarily until Barbara Keyser could be found. Miss Keyser, nicknamed by the girls "B.K." and "The Beak," served as headmistress for the twelve years before Jean Harris. Her cropped gray hair and rough-and-ready manner were in sharp contrast to the gentle airs of her predecessors. She spoke in a basso profundo voice, ran the school with an iron hand, made up her own rules, and led the fierce fight to keep Madeira from going coeducational. Going coed (and becoming only a day school) could have solved Madeira's severe economic problems, whereas remaining a single-sex boarding school (with some day students) ensured that tuition would continue to go up, and increased the risk that Madeira might soon become chiefly a playpen for the problem children of the rich. But Madeira traditionalists maintained that, no matter the difficulties, it was essential to have a place where "girls could become persons." This transition could take place, they insisted, only in a setting where girls did not have to compete with boys, be distracted by boys, or be at the mercy of boys. Thanks in great part to Barbara Keyser, tradition won out over coeducation, but with unforeseen results. As the better boys' schools themselves went coeducational, they attracted the livelier female applicants, and Madeira wound up with fewer adventurous-minded, independent students, and a lot more Southern girls.

In retrospect, perhaps Madeira should have gone coed in the early seventies. But Barbara Keyser's firm leadership in support of the status quo won her the respect of the Board. Male trustees were particularly impressed. "Barbara Keyser, that's my kind of woman!" they used to say. "Lots of backbone, lots of spunk. Wonder why she never married?"

"The Beak was clean, clever, hard, and intellectually very acute. A real tyrant—but what a *good* tyrant!" says one faculty member whom she appointed. "The girls hated her, yet she gave the faculty free rein to hang ourselves—which any teacher must respect. But there was a lot of fear on campus. She ruled by fear."

"She *was* a model, but a very harsh one. She had the toughest exterior of anyone I've ever dealt with," says one former student, speaking for many. But some girls grew to like and trust her. One tenth grader came to the headmistress in tears. "I detest this school! I am lonely. I want an Easter basket."

"Why don't you make Easter baskets for the whole school? Probably many girls here miss their Easter baskets." So saying, Keyser herself went out and bought hundreds of eggs, dye, baskets, jelly beans, and stayed up all night like a big, gruff Easter Bunny helping out her homesick little girls.

Miss Keyser's behavior was sometimes quixotic. A student moved by conscience to turn in an entire busload of girls for smoking pot recalls that the headmistress told her, "You must know about this because you are the pusher." A senior was told she would not be permitted to graduate because she was late turning in a paper. To spare her and her parents embarrassment, it was agreed by a faculty committee to let the girl go through the motions and receive a fake diploma. Miss Keyser then told the young woman she thought her "hypocritical" to take part in the ceremony under these conditions, and when the moment came, The Beak handed her not a rolled-up piece of blank paper, but a flat-folded piece—thereby making her "hypocrisy" apparent to all.

Hypocrisy is a favorite boarding-school topic; the word is on every tongue on both sides of the desk, and it may be that a judicious amount of hypocrisy is the necessary oil that enables such a place to function. The schools serve worldly and fraying families as holding pens and staging areas for their still-tender young, so perhaps the hypocrisy is built-in. The casual visitor seems to detect a subtle hierarchy among both girls and adults, a caste system quite possibly as rigid as that of the Hindus, but all hidden, unwritten. The tone of the place is helplessness cloaked in heartiness; a miasma of female abandonment seems to pervade these green lawns and lush woods.

When, after twelve years, the strain of the job finally began to tell on Barbara Keyser, the Druids were sympathetic and scarcely surprised. Her beloved sister Virginia, who had worked at the school as Director of Development, had died of cancer after a long illness; Miss Keyser herself was worn out and in poor health. It was time to go. She notified the Board of her decision, and strongly recommended as her successor a dear colleague whom no one else thought would do at all. So a Search Committee was named, and a full-scale hunt was on. Jean Harris was one of about a hundred candidates considered; about two dozen were interviewed personally, some several times. In the end, there was a power struggle, and Mrs. Harris was pushed through by a group of arch-Druids who steamrollered all opposition.

On balance, there is no doubt that Jean Harris left the Madeira School in far better shape than she found it. Enrollment was up. Inquiries were up. Annual giving was up. Faculty salaries were up forty percent. To a great degree, structure and discipline had returned to campus life. Still, one must wonder how, out of one hundred candidates, the Search Committee settled on this tense, frail, unhappy woman who had been something of a controversial figure in both her previous jobs. (Not that controversial persons are ipso facto bad, but they are more likely to be creative and mercurial than dull and safe, and creative and mercurial is not what Madeira was looking for.) What it seems to come down to is that Jean Harris looked the part. She had the gracious, ladylike image that the Druids thought would attract the kind of students, and donors, the school needed. She was worldly. "If I were to have a dinner party with Henry Kissinger among my guests, Jean's the woman I'd seat next to him."

But more than anything, Jean was perceived as the antithesis of Barbara Keyser. In the words of one top staff member, "They concentrated on what they *didn't* want, rather than what they did. They were hasty. They were unprofessional. They wanted no public controversy." They held but two formal meetings; the heavy politicking took place late at night on the telephone. The atmosphere was that of a sorority rush session. The advice of the very people who knew the school's needs best— the faculty—was disregarded. Some members of the specially appointed Faculty Advisory Committee considered Jean a lightweight in comparison to other candidates; her academic résumé seemed "thin"; and, perhaps divining her principles from her modish appearance, they feared that she would lead Madeira back in a "finishing-school" direction. But they were not permitted to read their written report to the Board. The Madeira alumnae who had known and taught alongside Jean Harris at Springside and Grosse Pointe were never interviewed. Rowayton's opinion of Jean Harris was not checked out. Suddenly Jean's selection was a fait accompli. A formal vote was taken, it was formally unanimous, and the new headmistress, who had quietly been brought back to Virginia and told to wait in an adjoining room, was now brought before the assembled twenty-person Board and officially congratulated. Good girl!

Commenting today on Jean's selection, a disaffected Druid who is herself a former teacher says, "You must understand the mentality of the private-school Board. To them, a headmistress is an employee. They really want a kind of low-paid, super-

governess-in-residence.* Jean Harris was picked at the last minute over other, better-qualified candidates who happened to be
married, because people thought that Jean, as a single woman,
would give more time to the school. Private-school boards look
for people with no dependents, and nothing else to fall back on;
people without full lives, people who *cannot* walk away. Teachers in public schools are much more healthy mentally; teachers
in private schools tend to be emotionally deprived. You cannot
take a bright, with-it woman like Jean Harris and leave her
alone out there to be bled to death."

The headmistress is seen as a surrogate mother figure by hundreds of stranded girls and lonely faculty women. Many girls,
deep in the throes of the adolescent I-hate-Mummy crisis, turn
to the head as a substitute, and the psychic drain on her can be
considerable. "When a person of Jean Harris's nature—a warm
and giving person who *needs* to give of herself, to prove her own
worth—takes that kind of job, she winds up torturing herself by
giving herself away in spoonfuls. If you are warm and compassionate, yet also weak in self-esteem, and all these young girls
are saying, 'You are my mother. *I need you,*' well, you feed on
that, and at the same time, you are being bled to death by it."

Like any headmistress in those years, Jean sometimes found
herself having to deal with girls who were drunk, pregnant,
stoned, suicidal, severely ill and injured, or facing arrest for
stealing, check-forging, and other serious crimes. One evening
less than a month after she took office, for example, a wretched
youngster showed up on her doorstep, weeping and talking of
suicide. For two years, every Saturday morning, the girl had
ridden the Madeira shopping bus to the mall at Tysons Corner.
But instead of going shopping with the other girls, she had gone
to a motel and met a man who flew down from Scarsdale. She
had first met him on a family vacation with her parents when
she was fourteen. He had been at the same Caribbean resort,
with his wife and children. Now, after two years, it was suddenly over. The girl did not want to talk to a psychiatrist, and

---

* After Jean cracked up, one member of the Search Committee seriously suggested, "Next time I think we should go to England and find a nice little couple.
The English expect so much less—and they cost less, too."

she certainly did not want to talk to her parents. She just
wanted to die.

"How did Mrs. Harris talk you out of it?" the girl later was
asked.

"She spent hours and hours talking to me. She said I was
really just a little girl. She said I hadn't *really* been in love any
more than he had. She told me over and over that I was just
being used, and finally she made me believe it."

Despite the pressures, Jean Harris in her first year at Madeira
was holding her professional life together reasonably well. But
privately, the war with Lynne Tryforos was heating up. Lynne
complained to the doctor that she was now getting anonymous
phone calls during working hours. Tarnower in turn accused
Jean of harassing Lynne at the office, and again he punished her
with "banishment."

Office of the Headmistress, Nov. 1977

Dear Herman,
    I know in such a warm familiar way the everyday pat-
tern of your life it seems odd that you have absolutely no
conception of mine. In the past 5 weeks I have spoken at
a large reception in my honor in Phila., Chicago, N.Y.,
Boston & Greenwich and then raced home to mind the
store.
    Friday I had dinner with the head of the Nat'l Gallery.
Saturday I went to a small dinner party at Polly
Gugenheims with the Ambassador to S. Africa; Sunday I
had lunch with our new Ambassador to Indonesia, one of
our fathers and Sunday night I had dinner with John
Haynes and his kids.
    My workday begins at 8:00 A.M. & lasts until I drop. I
rarely stop for lunch—every responsible member of my
staff is as new as I am and looks to me for leadership;
long-range planning, a new Calendar for the school year
1978–79, and a report to the Board get squeezed between
interviewing people to replace head of publications who
has leukemia and telling a girl her mother has had a
massive stroke. My last appointment last night was at

9:30 P.M. with a father flying in from the Philippines etc.
etc.—

Yet somehow a man whose judgement I have always
considered pretty sound is able to be persuaded that in
the middle of this kind of day, this kind of life style I stop
and ring up a little receptionist in Scarsdale, NY. Why in
the name of heaven would I call—and what in the name
of God would we talk about?—

You're right that I have talked about her—that sort of
exorcised the sleazy element of the whole thing and
seemed to demean you less. The greatest frustration for
me has been feeling that Lynn demeaned you publicly
and made you seem less the man you are. I guess I'm
beginning to realize now that I am away from the very
personal harassment of almost 2 years of phone calls in
the night, and the frustration of watching you be subjected to the same harassment that she simply isn't important enough to change your public image much one
way or another. I think she is for you a marvelous para-
digm of your favorite myth about women—that they're
2nd class, and that integrity or the lack of it and intelligence or the lack of it aren't relevant in women, only in
men from whom one has high standards and high expectations. The truth is, dear Herman Tarnower, you really
don't like women at all. That being the case I'm much
your best candidate for a good androgynous relationship
—Darby and Joan, who used to be Jack and Jill!—

As for Lynn, I will never mention her again. I only ask
in return that you never equate us or ever again suppose
that I can or could or would operate at her level. It has
been an ugly interlude in an otherwise deep and wonderful friendship.

Since the moment I met you I have gone on making
my own life but somehow the part with you was the only
real part—the rest was just treading water—being a good
girl and doing what I must until I could do the one thing
I wanted to do which was be with you. I go on making
my own life and by and large it's as interesting as the
next, more so I suppose—but that doesn't replace the
knowledge that somewhere on the other end of a phone,

or a plane ride, or a damned long drive you are sitting there alive, well, self-contained, bright, interesting, quite smug about how well you have planned your life, aggravating, remarkably cruel at times, unbelievably kind at others. And nothing and no one can replace the gladness I feel that you are there.

I would like to see you and be with you when I can for as long as we both are alive.

Jean—

Once Jean moved to Virginia, the time she spent with Tarnower dropped off sharply. According to the housekeeper's records, Jean spent only sixty-three nights in Purchase in 1977, forty-nine nights in 1978, and twenty-six nights in 1979.* Around Westchester, the doctor was seen socially more and more with Lynne, but he still continued to invite Jean as his guest on the ritual holiday visits to Tarnower's fanciest friends. Even if he had spent the night before and would spend the night after with Mrs. Tryforos, it was always Mrs. Harris whom the doctor brought to the Schultes' in West Palm Beach for Christmas or New Year's, and to the John Loebs' estate at Lyford Cay in the Bahamas for Thanksgiving, traveling back and forth on one of the Loebs' own jets. Mrs. Loeb is an outspoken woman— "I always call a spade a shovel"—and more than once she took her guest aside for a bit of stern talk.

"Jean, why are you doing this to yourself? You have an unbelievably good job at Madeira, so why don't you *undo?* How can you bear it? Don't you *know* that the minute you leave, Lynne is in that bed? They probably don't even change the sheets!"

Mrs. Harris looked at Mrs. Loeb and repeated her stock answer. "But I love him," she said.

It would not have occurred to Mrs. Loeb to give this sort of advice to Lynne Tryforos. "She is not my favorite person," Mrs. Loeb once said of her. "She is not my unfavorite either. She is

---

* Suzanne testified during the trial that her 1978 and 1979 records might be incomplete because the Van der Vrekens took a few weeks' vacation in each of those years and went home to Europe. (The servants had no regular vacation. They were expected to be on duty whenever the doctor was in residence, and they appear to have had no quarrel with this arrangement.)

simply a person who does not matter in my mind." But back in Westchester, other friends of Mrs. Tryforos *were* giving her similar advice: walk away from this humiliating triangle, at least until the doctor can make up his mind. Alas, Mrs. Tryforos appeared to be just as hooked on Herman as Mrs. Harris was. One hostess entertained both women often. "He was nuts for Jean, and he was nuts for Lynne too," she says. "And Lynne has this father thing, just the way Jean did. After all, her mother was married several times. Lynne also had the Great White Father–doctor syndrome very bad. She thought her job was the greatest thing on earth; she was God's right-hand lady. And she *was* a great nurse for him! One night Arthur Schulte fell down our basement steps, and she'd flown out to the car and was back with her black bag before we even noticed she was gone! I think Lynne would have drunk cyanide on the rocks if Hi had asked her. She'd lie down and let him trample her from her chin to her pussy, it that's what he wanted. One time I said to her, 'Lynne, why don't you walk out on this guy?' She looked at me as if I'd just hit her a *klop* in the mouth.

" 'Oh my God, I love him so!' she said."

When Jean returned from Lyford Cay in 1977, she talked obsessively about a young couple who had come to visit the Loebs. The girl had worn a dress made of pierced white-eyelet embroidery, and no underwear. The dress seemed tangible proof of the unraveling of young America's morals. Jean mentioned the eyelet dress in public speeches on at least four occasions. It was one of those dog-with-a-bone symbols she got hold of from time to time and could not seem to drop. The word *integrity* was another. She used it so frequently that behind her back a few girls began to call her "Integrity Jean." Surely these obsessive words and images were clues to Jean's own interior distress, but at the time they passed unnoticed. After Tarnower's death, many friends were asked if they had any inkling Mrs. Harris might have been cracking up or suicidal. Not really, they said. Yes, she was tense. But Jean had always been tense. With Tarnower's friends as with her Madeira colleagues, Jean was able to put up an excellent front. "I think there are probably many women who spend their lives crying themselves to sleep," she says, "and get up and are very jolly and funny the next day. You just don't talk about it, that's all."

* * *

By 1977, Herman Tarnower had upped Jean Harris's daily Desoxyn from five to sometimes seven and a half milligrams. Federal law requires that dangerous drugs be dispensed by the druggist only to the person named on the prescription blank, and Tarnower was not licensed to practice medicine outside of New York State. Thus when Jean moved to Virginia, it was necessary to devise a new system to ensure delivery. Dr. Tarnower took to writing out prescriptions for Desoxyn in the name either of Lynne Tryforos or of his personal secretary. They were then filled by a Westchester druggist, and the tablets were handed directly to Jean Harris by Tarnower when they met, or else mailed to her from the offices of the Scarsdale Medical Group.

In her first year in Virginia, Jean's home life was comfortable. Madeira provided a personal aide, Mrs. Penn, who did everything from arranging flowers to chaperoning girls to driving to the airport to laying out the headmistress's clothes, and she once remarked, "I think I know how it feels to be a good wife."

"And I know what it feels like to have one," Jean replied. Had this paragon not retired, school life might have been easier for the headmistress, though scarcely less lonely. Once again in Virginia, as in Grosse Pointe and Philadelphia, Jean was misreading social currents and temperatures, often turning down invitations she should have accepted, and ignoring invitations from people whom she did not consider "important." Alas, her notion of "importance" was based on the Washington gossip columns, scarcely a measure of Old Virginia society. Jean's social naiveté was astounding. Her insensitivity earned her implacable enemies she never even knew about. She would snub people who she thought "couldn't possibly be important," then wonder why she was never asked back. "She wouldn't take the time to find out who a person was," one observer says. "Then, when she was told that he *was* important, she'd say, 'Why didn't somebody *tell* me!'" Her trouble appears to have arisen from a fatal combination of ignorance—which, as Miss Infallible, she could not admit—and her regrettable tendency to make snap judgments. Always the outsider, she had not even felt comfortable with her husband's Grosse Pointe friends. She had *no* social grounding, and when she took up with Tarnower, she also took on many of his social values. One cannot imagine less appropriate conditioning for the new headmistress of a very WASPy and markedly Southern girls' boarding school. People thought Jean Harris a snob when she was in fact a *naif;* a chicly dressed but unknowing bumpkin in a low-heeled, horsey, prideful Southern world.

An unimaginably powerful locus in that world is Miss Mildred Gaines, Madeira's legendary, eighty-year-old riding mistress who retired only in 1978. Craggy and six feet tall, with a face like a windblown rooster, Miss Gaines is an antique equestrian statue come to life. What is the mystique of girls and horses, she is asked? "No mystique," she hoots. "Give a girl a horse and it makes them forget boys."

Visiting this heroic relic at her Warrenton, Virginia, horse farm-home is like calling on the Commendatore in *Don Giovanni* and being offered a cucumber sandwich. She can still shoe a horse, drive a tractor, or pour tea for two hundred guests. Mildred Gaines is not an admirer of Jean Harris. But she also says, "No single person, man or woman, can handle the pressures on a head of school. You cannot just go home alone and brood. You have *got* to have someone there to talk things over with." If the visitor wants to hear about the party she gave for the new headmistress, Miss Gaines will oblige. "Right after she got here she began saying, 'I need help. I don't know anybody.' We heard she was having a very lonely time, so I said I'd give a party. I asked all the alums I knew." Although Miss Gaines is too much the Virginia gentlewoman to say it, she also asked every person of wealth and influence in the county. "This house and porch were *full.* And she didn't even show up! Just a day before, she called me and said her mother was ill and she wasn't coming. She was going to Florida."

Half a hundred people thronged Miss Gaines's veranda, sipping her famous iced mint tea and nibbling delicately at her cucumber sandwiches. "Where *is* she?" the guests all asked.

"She's in Florida . . . *they say."* The hostess waggled a dubious eyebrow.

"Well, these were not *my* friends!" Miss Gaines continues her story with a snort. "They were all people for *her."*

"Maybe her mother really did have a heart attack," the visitor suggests.*

Mildred Gaines sniffs again. *"He* called her to go to the Bahamas!"

A social gaffe of such proportions would be hard to live down, and Jean never did. When the headmistress left Madeira almost three years later, the gentlewomen of Virginia telephoned one another to say, "God finally took care of it."

"What do you mean?"

"He got rid of Jean."

"Well, that was the *first* thing she did against me," Miss Gaines continues. "The second was, she took another's word against mine when a horse broke its leg. Of course, with her temper, you never knew *what* was going to happen. You didn't know if she was going to tell you *you* were a liar, or maybe not even know what you'd said to her. The trouble dealing with Jean Harris was that she'd just blow up."

Miss Gaines is only one of several staffers who went to Madeira's Board and said, "That woman is crazy!" When she was asked why, she cited "her sudden ups and downs, her violent likes and dislikes." She told them that Mrs. Harris was apt to burst into tears unpredictably, lose control, "and have to beat it back to her house. Sometimes she'd fire kids for no reason at all. Yes, she was intelligent, but she'd lose her train of thought." Soon, Miss Mildred Gaines was gently asked to retire. With all its eggs in the Harris basket, the Board could not have enjoyed hearing such tales.

When Jean arrived in Purchase for the Christmas holidays, she took her best blue nightgown out of "her" closet in Hi's dressing room. It was the one she had bought and worn over Thanksgiving. Now the skirt was splashed with orange splotches; it looked as if someone had thrown a bottle of Mercurochrome at it. She believed Lynne was the culprit. Without saying a word to anyone, she threw it away, took $40 from one of the extra wallets hidden in Tarnower's cathedral ceiling, where she knew he always kept a goodly amount of spare cash, and marched back to Saks, where the same blue nightdresses

---

* In fact, she did.

still hung on the rack. She bought herself an identical replacement that she still has today.

Back at school, on Valentine's Day, Jean received an unsigned valentine covered with typewritten obscenities. Did she investigate the matter herself? Alas, no. She sent it to Tarnower with a note wondering if he thought the typewriter could be traced? One can imagine the groan with which the busy doctor tossed the latest "evidence" of Jean's long-run torment into his wastebasket.

On March 18, 1978, Herman Tarnower was sixty-eight years old. His grateful patient Dan Comfort gave the party at his Briarcliff mansion, and the doctor's companion was Lynne Tryforos. Jean Harris was aware that she and Tarnower were drifting farther and farther apart. But she remained honestly unaware of the true situation in Purchase; she did not and probably could not accept the increasingly snug installation of Lynne in her shoes, puss in her boots.

Not that Jean Harris lacked insight into the psychological dynamics of their relationship; she simply felt powerless to alter them, or to walk away. After another of their quarrels, she would write:

> Perhaps a man who hated his mother and a woman who hated her father were bound to have an uphill climb. You've spent a lifetime, quite unconsciously I'm sure, trying to pay her back by being very hard on the women who've really loved you. I've spent a lifetime, quite consciously I'm sure, looking for a man who isn't like my father. Obviously you learned a long time ago that there's something of your mother in every woman. While I'm not as qualified to generalize as you, I'm afraid there's something of my father in every man. It was always *his* house, it was always his rules, and it was always "take it or leave it."
>
> I don't know whether I love you Hi, because I don't really know what love is. It certainly isn't the simplistic thing I once thought it was. And I know that the line between whatever-it-is and masochism is sometimes finely drawn.
>
> If love is wanting to be with you, to build on a founda-

tion of great happiness, to give and share warmth and understanding, and pleasure (and some displeasure) then there is a great deal of love left in me.

As for being a "great" woman Hi, unlike Malvolio I neither aspire to greatness, nor wish to have it thrust upon me. Right now I simply aspire to avoiding "door-matness." It's something I could never wear well. And even if I could, you already have one full-time, live-in door mat. I hope it isn't your style to aspire to two.

11

Tender Little Ladies

RUNNING A BOARDING SCHOOL is a far more demanding task than presiding over a day school. When Jean Harris took over the reins, the Madeira community numbered more than one hundred adults and three hundred and twenty students of whom two thirds were full-time boarders; the remainder were day students or girls who lived close enough to go home on weekends. For boarders, tuition plus extras came to nearly $10,000 a year. Girls lived mostly two to a room, in the original Georgian-style, ivy-covered brick dormitories named North, South, East, West, Old Dorm, and New Dorm, from which drab names one may infer that in the recent past none of Madeira's well-heeled alumnae has been flamboyantly generous. Madeira owns thirty buildings in all—including a new chapel; a new two-million-dollar indoor riding ring, the largest in the East; and a new science building that cost $750,000, was the first solar-heated structure in the state of Virginia, and leaks badly. The new headmistress swiftly discovered that the leaky science building, while troublesome, was the least of her wor-

ries. She was astonished to learn that so prestigious a school as
Madeira had never been properly accredited. The faculty was
poorly paid and poorly organized, the rules for student behavior
were unclear, and the administrative structure was next to nil.
There was no funded maintenance for the lovely, fifty-year-old
buildings, and the building endowment was at least ten years
behind the times. Finally, Madeira had very few adults living on
campus; after classes and on weekends, the girls were virtually
unsupervised.

Madeira was a place that seemed lonely even to adults. An
alumna who is also a member of the Corporation says, "I never
went back there for a meeting that I *didn't* feel lonely." One
student says, "You're living in a forest. There are a few light
patches, but it *feels* like a forest. It's awful to be put in that
dark, brooding place." And finally, a recent graduate: "It feels
haunted, very removed from life, and oppressive in its homoge-
neity of sex and class. So rarefied and distilled an atmosphere
gave you an intensified longing for family, yet it was so very
much *not* a family."

Madeira once had genuine, live-in housemothers, but by the
time Jean arrived, the "House Mother" in each dorm was actually a student elected by her peers, which meant that out of
school hours the boarding girls had virtually no contact with
adults. Jean's determination to change this setup did not endear
her to the staff. "Either you live in a dorm and save your
money," says one senior staff member, "or you live in your own
house and save your sanity." She goes on to describe "wonderful faculty parties. 'Group gropes,' we call 'em. Jean was absolutely super at skits and limerick contests." Hearing this, one
shudders at the sustained heartiness it must take an adult to
endure the boarding-school life, especially if one is a single person.

One of Jean's first new rules was that the four faculty families
who occupied the four rent-free on-campus houses must open
their homes to students on evenings and weekends. In two of
the six dorms, she carved out small faculty apartments; and she
required all adults who lived on campus to eat in the student
dining room at least three nights a week.

In the past, Madeira had been run largely by custom, whim,
and unwritten fiat. In her first months as the new headmistress

Jean, with others' help, wrote a new faculty handbook and a new student handbook, defined the various areas of staff responsibility, and wrote out job descriptions.

Miss Keyser had preferred a rubber-stamp Board. Mrs. Harris needed a working Board to help her in the many changes she thought overdue. Dismayed by the suave, mannerly tone of the Board meetings—"an hour and a half of polite talk, and half an hour of sherry"—she expanded the quarterly meetings from two hours to two days, and told the members to come in rough clothes so she could walk them around the campus and "show them their school. They didn't know the place." She urged them to borrow money for desperately needed faculty housing and repairs before some alert *Washington Post* reporter made front-page headlines out of certain substandard living conditions.

But Madeira's most serious problem when Jean arrived was lack of proper accreditation. The IRS already was looking askance at the tax exemptions of unaccredited schools, and many large corporations that offer accredited schools matching educational grants were prohibited from doing so in Madeira's case. In her first month she was dismayed to receive a polite note from the Chase Manhattan Bank saying it was unable to match a hundred-dollar parent grant; it made no difference that two grandchildren of the bank's president, David Rockefeller, were Madeira students that year.

Madeira's rival schools across the Potomac, National Cathedral School and Holton-Arms, were accredited to the Middle States Association of Schools, to which Madeira was geographically ineligible. The Southern Association of Schools had standards that—incredibly—Madeira could not meet. They demanded "certified" teachers, for example, which meant teachers who had taken various Mickey Mouse courses dear to the heart of the Virginia State Board of Education. Many members of Madeira's excellent faculty, people with degrees from Harvard, Princeton, and the Sorbonne, were not eligible. The State of Virginia also demanded that a proper school year encompass at least 180 class days, and Madeira girls attended classes for only 123 days. Jean promptly cut Christmas vacation from six weeks to three, and made other calendar changes not likely to endear her to either students or faculty. But the real problem was Madeira's vaunted Co-Curriculum program, under which the girls spend only four days a week in class. Every Wednesday they are bused to Washington, and each student works as an unpaid helper in some government or congressional office. Barbara Keyser had created the Co-Curriculum, and her original idea had been to get the girls out of the ivory tower and introduce them to the sort of high-minded volunteerism that, for many of their mothers, has become their life's work. But the State of Virginia felt that the program lacked sufficient academic value, and the new headmistress tended to agree. Madeira seniors were working as gofers for senators and congressmen, but they had no notion of what the Constitution says. Rather than scrap the program, Mrs. Harris added various academic requirements. Then the headmistress got a letter from an irate mother reporting that Madeira sophomores were spending Wednesdays in Georgetown having long, alcoholic lunches. Jean's reaction illustrates her disciplinary style. She immediately called all the girls together and pointed out that the Co-Curriculum was based on trust. She asked the culprits to step forward and confess. "And I'm telling you that, if you *are* one of those girls, I'm going to suspend you. Mere confession will not be enough to wipe the slate clean."

Half a dozen girls came to Jean's house that evening and turned themselves in. "They were proud of themselves for 'coming clean,' " Jean later told a friend. "The one who said nothing I think wished later that she had been honest. I didn't punish her. She punished herself." Once again Jean Harris was mistakenly assuming that others lived by a moral code as strict as her own. To Jean, simply knowing one has lied and cheated, and having to live with that knowledge, is a truly terrible punishment. This may be part of the legacy of her Prussian-style upbringing. Her father used to ring a dinner bell at mealtimes; children not washed and in their places were not fed. This sort of treatment makes certain children into rebels for life, but others emerge from such a childhood with an unusually rigid moral code; indeed, a psychologist who examined Mrs. Harris at length after her arrest found that she had "an almost Biblical sense of right and wrong."

When the mothers heard that the headmistress was demanding self-incrimination, they objected that her system made the honest girls suffer and let the guilty go unpunished. Jean replied that she was comfortable with her decision and thought the kids understood her much better than their mothers did. But how can one be sure? Here is a student talking:

> Mrs. Harris came to Madeira in my sophomore year. She called me and a friend into her office. "Well, I've heard rumors that you girls have been smoking pot and drinking alcohol in your rooms. Is this true?" I said no, but it was perfectly true. She let us go. As time went on, she kept cracking down more and more. I got called to her office again for being caught off campus after hours. I denied it and she said, "I don't believe you." She started going on her own ideas rather than listening to the girls. She started forming her own opinions and judgments. She started taking everything personally.

Fashions in discipline have changed greatly since Lucy Madeira's day. In the late twenties Barbara Colbron, the recently retired headmistress of the Spence School in New York City, was Madeira's President of Student Government, and met weekly with Lucy Madeira. "The main difference between then and now is that the girls' primary loyalty used to be to the school. Now it is to one another," Miss Colbron says. "Also, they had real house *mothers* in those days, not kids playing mother. It makes all the difference."

Miss Madeira's method for dealing with scandal, crime, or rumor never varied. She stood up in front of the whole school and said: "Girls, these are the facts." But by the time Jean Harris arrived, this straight-talking tradition was long gone. A previous headmistress had hired private detectives to hide in the basement to catch pot-smokers. Jean believed that a comprehensive written and published code of conduct was essential. Otherwise, students not only lacked the necessary guidelines; rebellious or simply adventurous girls were put in the unfair position of "playing Russian roulette all the time." Even in her third year, still hell-bent on this project, which she viewed as critical to the operation of any institution, Mrs. Harris continued to meet regularly with the leaders of Student Government.

"We weren't trying to 'revise' the rules," she told a friend later. "We were simply trying to write down what they were."

The moral climate which Mrs. Harris characterized as a game of "Russian roulette" disturbed many serious educators. Asked to rate Madeira in comparison with other schools, a top staff member (recently departed) has said, "Academically I would place it in the top ten percent, maybe the top five. But in terms of any philosophical or moral training the girls received, I would certainly not rate it highly. Our graduates could get into Harvard, Yale, and Princeton and do the class work very well, but there are other aspects to education. Considering the values I want my own children to have when they come out of school, I would *never* send them to Madeira. I'm afraid they would emerge lacking all sense of compassion, of brotherhood, and any sensitivity to those less fortunate than they."

All the foregoing notwithstanding, Jean Harris in her first year at Madeira was deemed so impressive that at the end of Spring Term the Board of Trustees threw a big dinner in her honor. The entire Madeira community turned out, and the dining room could not hold all the guests. "She gave a knockout speech," recalls a former Madeira English teacher. "Everyone thought—at last! She's so charming, so intelligent, so feminine, and yet so femin*ist*. At last we've got the right headmistress!"

All her life, Jean Harris has been a controversial personality. Because she is quick-witted, quick-tempered, and outspoken, and also perhaps because she is pretty and always carefully turned out, she makes a striking first impression, which tends to polarize people. In any given group, thirty or forty percent see her as an uncommonly interesting and appealing woman, and the others experience a range of emotions from mild dislike to hatred. Very few people are neutral about Jean Harris. At Madeira, complaints about the new headmistress had begun the moment she took office. Those who did not like her said she was rude, bad-tempered, unqualified, and unstable. The Board refused to listen. When the complaints escalated, the Board turned a deaf ear. They had made their choice and that was that. Although most observers considered that Jean was doing a good job under extremely difficult circumstances, the minority complaints about Jean Harris never let up.

Her detractors—all individuals of some experience and responsibility—say now that nothing Jean might do could ever surprise them. They say that she had what amounted to a multiple personality. "Sometimes she was a very beautiful woman, her face so smooth she looked as if she'd just had a good face-lift. At other times she looked like a haggard, skinny old woman, all hunched over; she would age twenty years and her face got all wrinkled up. [One might imagine that this is an impressionable schoolgirl speaking; it is in fact a highly placed member of the Madeira administration whom the headmistress later fired.] And then there was the third personality, the one who tried to look like a preppie, swore like a drunken sailor, put her hair in pigtails, and wore knee socks.

"Sometimes she had 'spells.' I can describe these quite accurately. She would completely lose her temper, her language got pretty awful, and she would rush out of the room and go back to her house and take a bath to calm down. Sometimes the spells took the form of writing, and she would write wild letters to trustees or faculty members which you had to try to stop her from mailing. And yet, if she suddenly had to function again in the midst of a spell—say a stranger suddenly came in—she was instantly able to pull herself together.

"Anything could set her off, it needn't be a major crisis. A girl leaving the school grounds without permission, or a girl failing to go to class. She didn't really like the girls. She was nervous about them. You could upset her very easily, and not necessarily by talking back to her or opposing her. If you cried, that too could upset her. Any little thing could upset her. Making announcements in the dining room in the wrong way could upset her. Trash on the school grounds upset her. Orange peels upset her so much that she once banned oranges from the campus. Short skirts upset her. No bras upset her. . . . Of the full-blown kind of spells, I saw perhaps a dozen in two and a half years. She had them in front of the students, in front of the faculty, in front of the Board, and with the parents."

Madeira's dining room could drive Jean wild. "It was not a pleasant, ladylike place," says one school official. Girls occasionally threw food. They sang rowdy songs. "Hark the herald angels shout. Three more days till we get out." They flipped butter onto the ceiling. "Jean couldn't stand it. First she stood up and shouted at them. 'You girls make me sick! You make me so sick I can't eat here! You are disgusting, terrible, horrible creatures!' Her outbursts were awfully humiliating to the girls, really heaped with withering scorn, and these were youngsters only fifteen years old. Finally she gave up eating there. She didn't understand the difference between horseplay and meanness. Most of all, she never decided what she wanted the school to be—whether she wanted a finishing-school image, or whether she wanted the girls to be 'just like men.' 'Find a job and stick to it!' she used to say. She'd complain that girls should be less 'like women' and more 'like men.' The difference, she said, was that 'women make lists and plan. Men pick up the phone and get things done.' "

A senior staff member says, "Jean's lack of understanding of women, all women, turned out to be really total. She told me one time, 'I never had a woman friend,' and she was very puzzled by close women friends. The very thing Madeira gave me —that special ability to make friends with women—is what Jean Harris lacked. She assumed deep friendships between women were lesbian."

There is a certain kind of woman prevalent in the world of private schools, not just Madeira, with whom Jean Harris seems constitutionally unable to get along. She is the wellborn gentlewoman, often a graduate of the institution she now serves, who for reasons of propinquity and economic necessity has taken a school job and, without ever having taken time out for proper training, has risen in the administrative hierarchy to a position she is not quite competent to handle. Jean Harris is impatient and uncharitable with such persons, and they became her enemies in every school. As an old Springside buddy, Ellie Casey, puts it, "Jean didn't belong with the tender little ladies. She was really in the wrong line of work. She was too dynamic, too bright, to put up with what you have to put up with. She really belonged at the Harvard Business School."

Some sense of the professional and social responsibilities of a headmistress can be gleaned from a lengthy job description that Jean Harris wrote for the Madeira Board midway in her third year:

. . . My regularly scheduled meetings are these:
  1. I take Monday chapel every week.

2. I meet at my house each morning at 8:30 with Carol Potts. (This was started because it proved the only way to have an uninterrupted one-half hour a day together.)

3. I meet each Monday morning with the two Deans, the Chairman of the Board, Business Manager, the Head of Development . . . and the Head of the Co-Curriculum.

4. I meet daily with the Deans. . . .

5. I meet every Tuesday morning with the Director of Development, the head of publications, the Alumnae Secretary and usually the Director of Admissions.

6. I meet every other week with the entire faculty at a Wednesday faculty meeting.

7. I teach an hour class of 15 freshmen every Wednesday.

8. I meet once a week with the Executive Committee of the Student Government, and at any other time that a case of suspension or expulsion comes up. (Last week, sadly enough, ten girls had to be suspended, two seniors for plagiarism and eight sophomores for drinking beer at lunch on their Co-Curriculum jobs. This type of thing is extremely time consuming because it means calls and letters home, individual talks with each of the girls, etc.)

9. I have a monthly dinner at my house with the entire Student Government. I have also had a number of extra meetings with the Student Council this fall because we are trying to write by-laws or a charter for the Student Council, something which has not existed in many years. . . .

10. I meet with the faculty individually whenever they ask for an appointment; I try to remember to have lunch with them several times a week. I have a long talk with each of them individually at contract time in February, and have a talk with them in the spring after they have filled out their self-evaluations. I attend occasional Department meetings. . . .

11. I have a luncheon for faculty at the beginning of the school year, and cocktails and dinner for faculty and staff at the beginning of Christmas vacation, and a cocktail and dinner party at the end of school in summer.

12. For the past two years I have also entertained the faculty before we surprised the girls with a faculty play or skit, both of which I took part in, one of which I helped write.

13. As a member of the Admissions Committee I meet on a regular basis to discuss applicants starting some time late in January. Our first long meeting was a five-hour meeting. . . .

14. I attend Alumnae functions on campus. . . .

15. . . . I have each year a special dinner party for members of Spectator . . . similar meetings with the student and faculty members of Gate . . . similar meetings with the Education Committee of the Student Council and the Food Committee.

16. I entertain in some small way (lunch, tea) almost all speakers who come to campus . . . something over 15 overnight guests so far this year.

17. I have been meeting for at least half an hour with each member of the senior class . . . to see if there is any way I can help them in their college preparations. . . .

18. I have coffee at The Hill in the fall for all local mothers of the freshmen and sophomores, and another for the junior and senior mothers.

19. I meet with the Board four times per year and am a member ex-officio of all committees of the Board, and attend most of them.

A regular part of my duties which I consider very important is reading every girl's report card before it goes out, and writing personal comments. . . . Report cards go out five times a year. . . .

The coming of the 75th anniversary of the school . . .

. . . Faculty illnesses . . . two operations, one miscarriage, two serious infections, one pneumonia, and, happily, one baby. I have also spent a great deal of time with some psychological problems that the girls have had, including two deep depressions, one alcoholic, and one tragic case of anorexia nervosa. . . .

I have told the Infirmary that whenever there is any kind of serious accident at any time of the day or night, particularly in the night, that I want to be the one to take the student to the emergency room at the hospital and stay with her. I have done this on five different occasions during the first trimester. . . .

Thanks to our very successful annual giving program, the writing of letters, which I do in the evenings, while a very gratifying job, is also a very time consuming job. Between 5 and 10 percent of the letters are handwritten by me, and another 35 percent have handwritten notes added. . . .

By February and March, a good deal of time, including Saturdays and Sundays, is taken up in reviewing resumés and interviewing candidates for next year's faculty. . . . Seven replacements mean *hours* of search and interview time. . . .

And so on for nine tightly packed pages, including such chores as buying material for six chairs and reupholstering them herself—"It was summer relaxation"—and trying regularly to read the *Washington Post, New York Times, Wall Street Journal,* magazines, NAIS materials, "current literature on what is or is not legal today in school administration—and even, as a special treat, some books!"

A more tedious, grueling, punishing, exhausting schedule is difficult to imagine. Reading it, one can only marvel that the headmistress did not collapse under its weight long before she did.

12

Leibarzt Into Literary Lion

ONE OF THE GREAT, as yet uncharted tidal movements in our national life is the relationship of mass diet-book sales to changes in American eating habits. Twenty-five years ago you could not give diet books away. Today's best-seller lists always include three or four fancy formulae for losing weight. The surge in diet-book sales waddles hand in hand with America's growing passion for junk food. The sales curve of the all-time best-selling Dr. Atkins diet—still the one to shoot at—parallels the rise of the fast-food franchisers. By now, takeout food has taken over. Colonel Sanders and Arthur Treacher have replaced Horn & Hardart, and more Americans are employed by Mc-Donald's than by U.S. Steel.

The book that bids fair to shoot down Dr. Atkins is *The Complete Scarsdale Medical Diet.* It all began on a Sunday in April 1978, when a beauty article in *The New York Times Sunday Magazine* mentioned that it was but "six weeks to bikini season . . . and the beautiful people of Scarsdale are now the skinny people of Scarsdale," thanks to a new diet developed by a Dr. Herman Tarnower, of Scarsdale. "A vice president of Bloomingdale's . . . lost 20 pounds in 14 days and claims he was never hungry and never tired."

The so-called Scarsdale Diet was really the same old one-page instruction sheet that Tarnower had handed out to over-weight heart patients for years in order to minimize the risk of heart attacks. To avoid writing out the same no-nonsense rules over and over again—lean meat and fish, lots of fruit and vege-tables, no fats, few carbohydrates, low salt, no alcohol—Tarnower had had it mimeographed. Nonetheless, such is the book world's lust for best-sellers that before nightfall that Sun-day, a half-dozen people had called Tarnower to suggest he write a book. Jean Harris, quietly doing the crossword puzzle by the fireplace, was instantly wary of the perils of schlock publishing, and fearful lest her eminent cardiologist be debased into a vulgar "diet doc." Much later, in prison, she would re-mark to a friend, "Why do they want to read about me? My life was not eventful until I was part of a terrible, tragic night when Hi died. And he was eventful because he wrote a crappy book that a lot of people bought. He *had* a good diet, and he gave it away for nineteen years. I thought that was super. But when he started selling it, well I didn't think that was too grand."

One who saw the sales potential was Oscar Dystel, a slow-moving, fast-thinking, ursine man who had been a patient of the Scarsdale Medical Group for some years, and was the longtime president of Bantam Books. Dystel was sure he knew the right way to market the book: contract it to Bantam, but ensure saturation sales by first auctioning the hardcover rights. He also knew just the man to do the actual writing. Dystel's old buddy Samm Sinclair Baker is natty, elfin, and sixtyish, a onetime Madison Avenue advertising writer who used to turn out punchy copy for rose catalogues and books that tell how to grow enormous vegetables with miracle chemicals. He made his breakthrough by shifting from advice on growing giant toma-toes to growing better human beings, and had piled up a devas-tating track record: twenty-seven self-help books that motivated millions to do everything from calisthenics to fighting acne. His five diet books with Dr. Irving Stillman* had sold over fifteen million copies. But success had not come easily. Sixteen publishers had rejected Samm's first diet book. Since then Samm had formulated his own strict rules for success: the diet has to work, the diet has to be easy to understand, and the book has to express hope in its very first sentence and continue to motivate the reader all the way through. He also had firm rules for coauthorship, based on his twelve previous collaborations. "We work fifty-fifty. My name has to be as big as his, because he has to respect me as much as I respect him. If we trust each other, that's all we need, and if we don't trust each other, it's no good anyway."

Tarnower was himself uneasy about going commercial, and sought advice from such good friends in the publishing world as Alfred Knopf, Arthur Schulte's son Tony, who is a vice-president of Random House, and several others. They advised him to forget it. Mrs. Arthur Schulte, once a professional nutritionist, told the doctor he was "in way over his head." Tarnower was hurt. He had spent hours listening to these people's problems; he had hoped for the same courtesy. Quickly absorbing the harsh truth that when it comes to altruism, the most exalted of publishers cannot compare with the most indifferent of physicians, Tarnower decided to go with Dystel and Baker. Rawson, Wade, a small, husband-and-wife hardcover house that had done extremely well with self-help publishing, including the Dr. Atkins diet and Dr. David Reuben's everything-you-always-wanted-to-know-about-sex, et cetera, books, undertook to get out the $7.95 hardcover edition of Tarnower's diet, and work began with frantic speed. Esther Margolis, Bantam's brilliant manager of marketing, knew that the great sales month for diet books is January, right after the Christmas eating binge, and already it was June.

Expanding a single page into an entire book in only three months' time became the professional challenge of Samm Sinclair Baker's career. An old hand by now at expando-journalism, he approached the problem with the panache of a master

---

* *The Doctor's Quick Weight Loss Diet, The Doctor's Quick Inches-off Diet, The Doctor's Quick Weight Loss Diet Cookbook, The Doctor's Quick Teen-age Diet,* and *Doctor Stillman's 14-Day Shape-up Program.*

pastry chef advancing on a bowl of egg whites. Had not the great Dr. Stillman himself said, "I give Samm a sentence, he gives me a chapter"?

Although doctor-written books are notoriously difficult to publish, Eleanor and Kennett Rawson were confident, and their confidence was not misplaced. *The Complete Scarsdale Medical Diet,* published in January 1979, lasted forty-nine weeks on *The New York Times* hardcover best-seller list, thirty-one of them as Number One, and sold 711,100 copies. The Bantam paperback, published a year later, would remain on the list eighty weeks (the previous record for nonfiction was a mere fifty-two weeks), forty of them as Number One. Almost overnight, Herman Tarnower's strict and rigid diet—exactly the same foods every Tuesday, every Wednesday, and so on through the week, with "six walnut halves" recommended to break the monotony—had made him the era's most successful packager of self-disgust. Like many an author before him, he was selling millions of books by causing Americans to become dissatisfied with themselves. As of October 31, 1981, there were 5,309,000 copies of Tarnower and Baker's book in print, and it is still selling. Smart publishing and promotion, aided by the unexpected publicity boost from Mrs. Harris, have made *The Complete Scarsdale Medical Diet* the longest-running nonfiction book on Bantam's list, and given it the greatest continuing impact of any work in diet-book history.

"Let me give you the lowdown on diet-book writing," Samm Baker recently told a visitor to the stately waterfront home overlooking Long Island Sound that twenty-seven self-help books have bought. "There has to be a liking between coauthors, and I *liked* Hi right away. He was one of the finest men, one of the ablest men, one of the most brilliant minds I ever worked with. When people say he was a hard man, a tough man, I point to this inscription." He carefully opened the cover of a first edition of their *oeuvre: For Natalie and Samm, Warm, gentle, sensitive friends who have been great collaborators, Hi.* "Now I maintain that only a basically warm, gentle, sensitive man can recognize those qualities in others.

"The first thing he said to me was, 'Why should I write a book?' I told him he could make a lot of money and help millions of people around the world at the same time."

The hard-working little motivator had pushed just the right button. But Herman Tarnower was a cautious man. Having met Samm, he wanted to check out his wife, and so Mr. and Mrs. Baker were invited, for the first and only time, to one of Tarnower's famous dinner parties. The other guests were the Arthur Schultes, Joseph Cullman III and his first wife, Sue, and Jean Harris. When the Bakers got home that night, Samm told his wife he had liked everybody but the outspoken little blonde woman. "I'll give it to you in two words," said the great expander, on occasion a fine diminisher. *"Better than.* Those two words, I thought, were her measure of everything. To use an expression from my boyhood, she acted as if her ass was cake."

Baker's present recollection may be colored by the fact that, during the breakneck course of his work, he learned that not only was Jean Harris contemptuous of diet books and the people who wrote them; at one point she had completely rewritten his entire manuscript herself. He never actually saw Jean again. Having once checked the Bakers out, Tarnower saw nothing further to be gained by inviting them back to dinner. Samm was just as happy. The dinner party had made him uncomfortable. "Why? Because I don't like the smell of money."

Long before they had signed a contract, the two men had shaken hands and begun work. Samm had already constructed his magic first sentence. When he talks about it, he still glows pink in admiration of its perfection:

I, personally, explain the Scarsdale Medical Diet's phenomenal popularity in two words: *"It works."* A slim, trim lady said to me recently, "Your diet is beautifully simple, and the results are simply beautiful." I just say, "It works."

The book's solid-gold title was a group effort. Tarnower said many times over that he was sure it was *his* word—*medical*—that made all the difference. Dystel thinks the Miracle-Gro word is *Scarsdale.* "Scarsdale is a name like Beverly Hills or Grosse Pointe. Not everybody recognizes it, but people of influence *do.* In the jargon of merchandising, that's called 'trading down from a powerful brand name.' " *Complete* is also considered an extremely potent word, implying as it does that somewhere shysters are peddling a less-than-complete version. Certain feminists and tea-leaf readers of the social matrix such as the writer Judith Rossner believe the box-office magic of the title resides in a single syllable: *scar*. "It connotes damage, and anything which subtly conveys a sense of defeat, or injury, is per se attractive to many women."

The collaborators' work pattern was simple. Tarnower talked, Samm took notes, wrote them up, and returned them to the doctor for revisions. Usually they met at the doctor's office. Baker found Tarnower's house gloomy, "like a men's club. Not my kind of place. But in the office, oh, was he a presence! Just pure strength. He wears a white coat and sits in a chair as if he were part of the chair. I've rarely seen a man so sure of what he was. Yet he was gracious, soft-spoken, old-worldly. I don't think I ever heard him even say 'Damn.' "

Dystel's confidence in Samm had not been misplaced. How did the great expander inflate one page into a whole book? He recycled the same recipes under different headings: the Scarsdale Medical Diet, the Scarsdale Gourmet Diet, Keep-Trim Diet, Money-Saver Diet, Vegetarian Diet, and International Diet. He padded with charts, case histories, poesy, weight tables, and a "medical appendix." He name-dropped. He answered questions nobody would ask—"Is there any special kind of grapefruit you recommend for the Scarsdale Medical Diet?" He pumped up all his text into a kind of prose Styrofoam: "Smell and taste can be fully appreciated only by thoroughly chewing each bite of food before swallowing. The true enjoyment is gone once the food leaves the mouth. Chew, chew, chew."

One day at the office, Samm asked to see some of Tarnower's medical writings. "He buzzed, and a very attractive, tall, slim young woman walked in. He said, 'Lynne, this is Samm Baker.'

"She turned out to be just marvelous!" Baker says. "My experience as the coauthor of twelve books on medical subjects had taught me that if the doctor's right-hand person is intelligent, smart, nice, and eager, I can work twice as fast."

Baker found Lynne helpful, gracious, and unassuming, and he was appalled at the media image of her that later emerged. "She's very well educated, as opposed to her image as a dumb little blonde, and perceptive, bright, and sunny." The Bakers are Jewish, and Lynne Tryforos and Natalie Baker spent some time working out a section of kosher Scarsdale Diet recipes, an idea Tarnower later vetoed. Samm once exclaimed, "You're so bright, Lynne!"

"That's because I have some Jewish blood in my background," she proudly replied. The news would have surprised her schoolmates. Back at Edgemont High School, her brother Lee Brundage had courted a Jewish girl until the romance was broken up by her parents because his family was not Jewish.

While Samm and Tarnower worked on the book, Jean Harris was busy composing a farewell message to the graduating seniors. As so often in her public remarks, the headmistress might have been addressing her private self.

My Dear Seniors,
  I have often talked with you about those useful study skills and good manners that we hope you have woven into the fabric of your lives during your years at Madeira. But it occurs to me I have seldom mentioned that most important ingredient of all, a stout and loving heart. . . . Hard work, good intentions, politeness, even genius are not substitutes for it. . . . Keep it polished and constantly put it to the test.

                                        Fondly,
                                        JEAN HARRIS

No one needed a stout and loving heart more than Jean Harris that summer as the true relationship among Herman Tarnower, Lynne Tryforos, and herself grew more and more apparent to all. But the advent of the diet book also gave Jean a new role in the doctor's life. Every time they spoke on the phone, he complained about the way the book was going. She vowed to become his silent partner, dedicated to keeping this crassly commercial project on as high a literary level as the material would allow. For the first time, she was going to be able to be as helpful to the doctor professionally as the very efficient Mrs. Tryforos.

In that same fevered summer of 1978, Jean asked the doctor to return all of her letters. She might not have done so had she not noticed one weekend that the hated "term paper" from Lynne, first glimpsed on the floor of the Paris Ritz, was now stacked along with her own letters in the capacious headboard cabinet behind the doctor's bed. (Tarnower also kept a stack of surgical masks in his headboard, for reasons no one has ever explained.)

Sometime in the middle of that summer, Jean again began calling Lynne Tryforos, goaded by a new outbreak of anonymous telephone calls. Again she was threatened with "banishment." After weeks of frantic pleading, she at last heard Tarnower say he believed her repeated denials that it was she who was harassing Lynne—but then he banished her anyway, and for two whole weeks! Her next letter sounds a new and pathetically childlike note:

> Dear Hi,
>
> Your casual call cancelling a weekend with you that I have spent a summer of work looking forward to—like light at the end of a dark tunnel—is the kind of punishment I have not earned. It was deliberately cruel. . . .
>
> . . . I am grateful Hi for so much, but what I am most grateful for for all my life is the time I have with you. I am being punished in ways I don't understand, Hi—please don't *you* punish me any more. Life is so short, Hi. You say it yourself—Help me to be with you when I can. . . .

Work on the diet book was going ahead full tilt, Tarnower and Baker writing and rewriting, and Suzanne Van der Vreken herself writing and testing each one of the recipes. The staff at Rawson, Wade found their new author hostile, suspicious, and difficult to work with at first. "But once he got to trust us, things changed," says Eleanor Rawson. "I found him a very decisive person, meticulous about returning telephone calls. He also made decisions on the spot and stuck with them. And you always knew where you were with Herman Tarnower. He was a man of great consistency."

But the Rawsons deliberately avoided dining at Tarnower's house, and instead sent underlings to Purchase to handle editorial chores. It was an assignment they came to dread. "You'd

have to spend an entire evening looking at his scrapbook and
hearing about all the awards he'd received," says one young
woman. "Then came the descriptions of his hunting expedi-
tions, and you'd have to admire all the trophies on the wall. The
food was ghastly—not distinguished, just fancy, and the doctor
had no small talk. He never smiled. He had no wit. He had no
subject matter but Dr. Tarnower. To him, money equaled class.
He constantly talked about how much things cost, how much
land people had, how much money. He would speak of his
friends as 'my friend Joe Cullman, Chairman of the Board of
Philip Morris,' or 'my friend John Loeb, president of Loeb
Rhoades.' Once he even said, 'My friend, Chou En-lai.'

"Mrs. Tryforos was always there. She literally walked behind
him. She served him hand and foot. You would watch him both
lapping it up, and at the same time entirely ignoring the fact
that she was doing it. It was disgusting. It made me feel debased
as a female."

Before Jean's latest "banishment," Tarnower had talked a lot
to her about the book, and after she was forgiven and arrived in
mid-August for a two-week holiday, she found the doctor very
upset. "More than I had ever seen him before," she would tell
the jury. "Hi was wonderfully in control of his life and of everything he did, but this had gotten out of hand . . . and he was
very unhappy with some of the writing that had been done."

Jean set up a card table in the breakfast area adjacent to the
front door, and for the next two weeks she worked on the
manuscript day and night, ripping it apart and rewriting whole
sections in her own hand, and watching with workmanly pleasure as the manuscript expanded, like "The Blob," from the
card table to the dining room until finally it was spread out all
over the living-room floor. At the stove, Suzanne perfected her
recipes for dishes coyly dubbed by the antic coauthors Baked
Chicken Breasts Herman, Spinach Delight à la Lynne, Mustard
Sauce Henri, Borscht Suzanne, Baked Apple Oscar, and
Chicken Bake Samm. Samm and his wife, Natalie (she of Cold
Poached Fish Natalia fame), were hard at work in Mamaro-
neck; and out at their home in Long Island, the Rawsons were
working at such breakneck pace that some weekends they never
got out of their bathrobes. Jean became so engrossed in her
work, she did not even object when Hi went out to a birthday

dinner for his dentist, Dr. Eugene Humbert, and brought Lynne along as his date, while Henri served Jean a hamburger on her card table. Later she would write to Tarnower:

> Working together with you for a few days, doing something that really helped you for the first time in 11 years, ranks as high on the list of good memories as all those very happy trips. I was so caught up in it and so honestly happy to be a useful part of the book, I actually felt quite at peace working on it Monday night while you went out to a dinner party. . . .

The authorship of the final Scarsdale Diet manuscript nonetheless remains in dispute. Prominently displayed during Jean's trial was a large liver-colored portfolio containing a page-by-page comparison of Samm Baker's manuscript, Jean Harris's rewrite, and the published version. Defense lawyers said it would prove Jean's primary authorship, but the judge refused to let the jury see the evidence, on grounds that the contents of the portfolio had already been described to them by Mrs. Harris. Today for reasons known to themselves, her lawyers refuse to make the portfolio available.

One Monday morning at their regular get-together, Tarnower said shyly, "Samm, I've done some revising. See what you think."

Samm looked at the opening page. "This is terrible!" he exclaimed. Someone had cut his crucial first sentence.

"Maybe that paragraph is not just right, Samm . . . maybe it's too pushy."

"That first paragraph has to stay, or we have no book!" Samm declared. "Hi, I just can't understand this stuff coming from you. You are so *straightforward*. This doesn't even sound like you. It's 'Look how clever I am!' *cutesy* stuff. It looks like a teacher correcting a kid's paper."

"Okay, Samm, ignore it. Do what you want." Herman shrugged and, as always when confrontation threatened, he turned away.

The publishers are not positive who wrote the final version, by then a well-homogenized editorial product, but Kennett

Rawson says, "It had Samm Sinclair Baker's earmarks all over it. I have published others of his books and I know his style." Jean Harris has told Marge Jacobson that after she tore apart, rewrote, and reassembled the manuscript, she and Hi went on another trip, and she believes that during this period Samm Baker must have revised much of it back along his original lines. A reliable source who examined the contents of the liver-colored portfolio during the trial says that it did contain almost the entire manuscript in Jean Harris's handwriting, and that large sections of the printed book were indeed taken word for word from her handwritten manuscript.

Because of the extreme crash program under which the final book was produced, everybody pitched in, including Lynne Tryforos. With the doctor's magnum opus and reputation at stake, jealousies between his women evidently could be set aside for the higher good; manuscript pages in Jean's handwriting were later corrected and clarified for the typist by Lynne Tryforos. If the women were getting along for the time being, others were not. The fights had started even before Tarnower's contract was finally signed, in August. The Rawsons very much wanted some science in the book, to lend a whiff of authority. Tarnower resisted. "He wanted to be very, very simplistic," says Kennett Rawson. The reason was that Tarnower had no idea why his diet worked. He had done no double-blind experiments. Nor has any other best-selling diet doc, Rawson says. "It's all based on clinical observation. None of 'em know why their thing works."

Other, more serious fights concerned the many hands *not* in the pot, namely Tarnower's six fellow practitioners at the Scarsdale Medical Group. They were threatening a lawsuit, arguing that the diet had been developed at the Group, and therefore Tarnower's obligation to share his income with them included any revenues from the diet. Tarnower toyed with the idea of taking a year's leave of absence and working only out of his house; perhaps that way he could shelter his earnings from the communal pie. He claimed the book was done on his own time, that the diet was *his,* and that having given it away free for so many years, he was now entitled to cash in. He had another meeting with his colleagues and "we both gave a little," he told

Jean. "They made some concessions, and so did I.* But I'm not going to give them one cent of my book royalties. They all pay less rent than they should anyhow." (Recently Dan Comfort had told Tarnower that he should be collecting three times the present rent.) Although a suit was avoided, not all of Tarnower's partners were mollified, and this was the principal reason that several had stopped speaking to him at the time of his death.

By Labor Day, Jean had finished her work on the manuscript, elated at having been truly useful to her lover at last. When he then offered to pay her $2,000 for her labors, she angrily refused and left for Virginia. The lady who came to dinner that night was Lynne Tryforos.

Mrs. Harris had been back at Madeira two days when she received a curt, handwritten memo:

> Dear Jean,
>   For reasons that I cannot explain, it is imperative that I make all book disbursements at this time.
>   I am enclosing a check for $4,000 that I hope you will accept.
>
>   Love,
>   Hi

Unsure whether to accept the money, uncertain of its legal implications—was her labor of love being "bought off"? Could Herman be thinking that she, like his doctor-partners, might anticipate a share of his royalties?—she sought advice from Leslie Jacobson. The lawyer said he could not possibly discuss the matter with her because, as a close friend of both parties, he had a conflict of interest.

Jean decided to keep the check, but the following weekend she wrote Tarnower a long letter explaining her hurt feelings.

> . . . when you offered me $2,000 "because it's conve-
> nient for me this way—I don't have to tell you why—and

* Tarnower had agreed that the right to publish a sequel, a kind of "Son of Scarsdale Diet," was vested in his fellow doctors.

next year maybe I'll give you $2000 more—but that's at
my discretion, I don't have to if I don't want to. I don't
owe it to you" your voice sounded as if you were offering
a little tip to a $2.00 whore. It was cold and utterly con-
temptuous.

I don't want a pound of flesh, Hi. I was quite happy to
settle for "Thank you." I still am. If the book's successful
I hope you may decide on another trip, somewhere, anywhere, together. . . .

You have said to me a hundred times "I never ask
anything of you . . . I never ask anything of anyone."
But my dear it isn't true. For starters you ask every
woman to be as incapable of love as you are. That's like
asking her to be a parameceum, or a woodcock, or some
damn thing she can't.

The letter goes on to tell him that, this year, her opening
address to the faculty concerned the qualities a woman needs in
order to survive in today's world. "Then I wondered how a
woman like me, who lacks many of these qualities, could convey them to young women." Her speech sounded a warning
against something she called *The Anointment Syndrome.* "Men
work for power; women work for praise. In her heart of hearts
most women think that sooner or later hands will be placed
gently on her head and a deep voice will say, 'You have been a
good girl . . .'" Her letter adds, "I guess on Monday I was
expecting anointment—not a tip—and my idea of anointment
from you, my dear, is just a pleasant drive in the country.
That's all I bargained for. . . . There are big months ahead Hi
—please know I'm in the cheering section—not lined up for a
piece of the action."

It is clear that by the fall of 1978, Jean Harris's feelings
toward Herman Tarnower already had begun to wobble errati-
cally from adoration and childlike dependency to resentment
and back again. The wobble would continue long after his
death, with Jean trying to rehabilitate Tarnower's image even
after she was convicted of his murder. "At that time so many
people were trying to stick their hands in Hi's pockets, he mistakenly thought I was one of them," she recently told a prison
visitor. "He saw that Samm Sinclair Baker had a very generous

deal—fifty percent! The men at the clinic wanted a share. Suzanne Van der Vreken—who had written *all* the recipes— wasn't getting anything and wanted something. When Hi sent me that check he was saying, 'I want to close all my books because I'm just giving it away too fast.' " At the time, no one could possibly guess what the little diet book would earn. In fact, authors' royalties to date are over three million dollars.

When the book *did* become a runaway best-seller, Mrs. Harris once diffidently suggested to Tarnower that he might like to make a small contribution to Madeira.

"Why the hell should I give anything to Madeira?"

"Okay, Herm. I'm sorry I asked."

At the beginning of the 1978 fall term, Ann Kinzie, Jean's old friend from Grosse Pointe, paid the headmistress a visit. They toured the campus and Jean greeted many girls by name and spoke to Ann with enthusiasm about what she had been able to accomplish. The Co-Curriculum was working better; the dining room was a more seemly place, and the faculty was eating with the girls, at least on occasion. "Last year at graduation," Jean said, "I found myself shaking hands with a lot of girls and thinking, 'I don't really know enough about you.' " This year she was making a particular effort at least to know the seniors, and had been inviting them to her house in the evenings in small groups to chat and cook dinner together. Her current project was to remodel the library, remove the cell-like study cubicles, and replace them with comfortable sofas, lamps, tables, perhaps even a fireplace. "It's a privilege and pleasure to have a library, and it should not be a place of punishment," she said, explaining that, formerly, students who broke rules on weekdays were ordered to the library to study on Saturday mornings.

Back at The Hill, Ann Kinzie remarked, "Gosh, Jean, I look out of my window and see nothing here but trees, trees, and more trees! Your house is really way out at the edge of things."

Jean's two dogs made her feel quite safe, she said, even though her house was indeed remote, and a few years ago a girl had been found murdered in these very woods. "As a matter of fact," she added, "some of the trustees think I should have more protection. They've told me I ought to buy a gun."

In October Jean Harris drove to Irving's Gun Shop in the Tysons Corner shopping mall and said she wanted a gun "for self-protection." The salesman recommended a Smith & Wesson Model 10, and Jean filled out the necessary "layaway" form that, under Virginia law, holds the weapon until a police check can be made. Jean failed to collect her purchase, but several weeks later she returned, asked to look at the gun again, and also to examine another, smaller gun she saw in the case. This was a .32 caliber Harrington & Richardson Model 732, a much lighter weapon. Men consider it a "ladies' gun" and a "dumb" gun, and the salesman did not recommend it. But after hefting the weight and clicking the triggers of each, Jean chose the one that was easier to handle and filled out new forms, the old ones having lapsed. On November 20, 1978, the salesman notified Mrs. Harris to come in and pick up her purchase.

"Self-protection" was indeed on Jean's mind, but what she feared was not rapists in the woods. It was her own secret sense of growing desolation. Jean Harris's lifelong posture, if not her conviction, had been that she could take care of her own problems. Not one of her old friends can remember Jean's asking them for help. She was the superwoman who could raise the boys, run the school, stay up all night, paint the walls, be surrogate mother to 300 girls—whatever had to be done, she had always been able to handle it. But now she was frightened by the kind of exhaustion she felt, and her attendant sense of helplessness, despite the daily Desoxyn. Whenever Tarnower told her he didn't need anybody, she had always longed to reply, "Herman, I don't either." Now that she owned a gun, she could. Jean told the jury she thought of her gun as a "security blanket. . . . I felt if I couldn't function anymore, I could handle it, and I didn't have to worry as much about becoming helpless."

Why a gun, people wondered afterward? In the popular imagination, suicide by gunshot is the masculine mode; women take pills, or put their head in the oven. But Jean told a friend, "A gun was the one way I knew I wouldn't mess it up. I could have got a lot of sleeping pills, but I couldn't be sure how many it would take to make it work."

Guns don't kill people. People kill people. So runs the nutty and deadly slogan of the National Rifle Association. If there were any truth to this glib rubbish, Herman Tarnower would be alive today. The doctor is dead because, on her third try at buying a gun, a sick and distraught woman happened to be in the right state with the right credentials, and the one instrument of death that is always reliable became hers for the wave of a credit card.

November 1978 brightened for Jean Harris with the prospect of the traditional Thanksgiving flight with the Loebs down to Lyford Cay. Shopping last year in Remin's, the Westchester discount store where she bought most of her clothes, she had come across a lovely lemon-yellow silk dress, expensive even when marked down to half-price, but quite outrageously becoming. Since she was a perfect size eight, the dress required no alteration, and she had brought the box back to Purchase Street and left it in the downstairs guest closet, the place where she stored the clothes that she needed only with Tarnower. She had intended to wear the dress on her next trip south, but in the flurry of packing to leave, she forgot all about it.

By the time Jean and Hi returned from their week in the Bahamas, the first copies of Tarnower's book had arrived. The Acknowledgments page began, "We are grateful to Jean Harris for her splendid assistance in the research and writing of this book." Natalie Baker, Suzanne Van der Vreken, Lynne Tryforos, Oscar Dystel, Mr. and Mrs. Rawson, and the twenty-nine girls and one man of the Medical Center staff also were thanked by name, though the names of the doctors they worked for were not mentioned. When Samm Baker had first seen the salute to Jean Harris, in manuscript, he was astounded. "So far as I know, she did nothing on the book," he says today. But when Baker had called Tarnower to voice his objections, the doctor had cut him short.

"Samm, please leave it just as it is," he had said in what Baker thought "a very cold tone of voice." More gently, he added, "I like to make people feel good. And I want to make *her* feel good."

Early in December Gerda Stedman was waiting in her car at a Scarsdale stop sign when a truck slammed her from the rear and pushed her face into the windshield. Extensive plastic surgery would be required. Mrs. Stedman in recent years had become something of a recluse, living alone except for her servants and occasional guests, part of the time in her secluded Westchester home, part of the time on her private island. Now she was brought to White Plains Hospital, and soon learned that her nose had been broken in four places, and her eyes, mouth, and cheeks badly cut. One of her first hospital visitors was Herman Tarnower. He had come immediately when he heard of the accident, not even bothering to change into his white coat. She had not seen him in nearly nine years, and she could barely see him now, peering out through eye-slits in a massive surgical dressing that made her head look like a heavily bandaged football. But she thought he looked thin and drawn and, well, *old.* She noted that he still had the old fur hat she had given him fifteen years ago, and the same overcoat, its fraying cuffs now faced with velvet.

Although they talked but briefly, Tarnower did not seem happy. When she inquired, he would say only, "Gerda, I am into something that I can't get out of."

When she got home from the hospital several weeks later, Mrs. Stedman sent her butler down to the wine cellar for a case of her late husband's very special Mouton Rothschild '59, now nearly priceless. She knew how Herman had come to appreciate good wine, and she *was* very grateful for his concern. On Christmas Eve she had the local taxi deliver the wine to the house on Purchase Street, and within moments Tarnower was on the telephone. He, too, had a very special gift. Could he pass by her house just long enough to drop it off?

Herman's gift was a copy of the just published *The Complete Scarsdale Medical Diet,* inscribed "For Gerda—A woman with great style who can only be faulted by her great generosity. Hi."

The doctor had arranged to interrupt his book promotion chores over the Christmas holidays for the usual visit with Jean to the Schultes' in West Palm Beach. Jean arrived in Purchase a few days before they were to head south. Starting to pack, she noticed the forgotten dress box from Remin's. She opened it and saw that the thin yellow silk was no longer swathed in layers of white tissue paper; it had been wadded up into a ball. When she shook it out, she saw that the dress had been smeared with excrement. In horror, she threw it away and said nothing.

The important thing was not to provoke a fight that might spoil the precious vacation ahead. *Put the blame on Mame.*

Earlier that year, while she and Hi had been visiting Palm Springs, Jean had spotted in a gift shop what she thought was the all-time champion Herman Tarnower Christmas present—a framed drawing of a marionette with the legend, "No strings on me." She gave it to him now, just before they flew off to Florida, and he was so pleased he immediately hung the little picture in his bedroom, right beside the portraits of his parents.

By February his book had hit the best-seller list, and it was clear that a publishing phenomenon was at hand. A hearty, $25,000 advertising and publicity budget assured a rich profusion of personal appearances, TV interviews, and other hoopla, and despite some initial reserve, the self-described "country doctor" soon showed great enthusiasm and not a little skill. As a celebrity author, Herman Tarnower was a natural. His ego, his white coat, his measured manner, his air of absolute authority all were perfect for the role. *Leibarzt* into literary lion was for Tarnower a transition as inevitable, and as interesting to watch, as polliwog into frog. He did not miss a trick. When someone reported to him that the Queen of England was on the Scarsdale Diet, he immediately dispatched a polite letter of thanks to Buckingham Palace. Late one night at a Manhattan literary soiree, the writer Peter Maas looked across the smoke-hazed room and spotted a tall and lovely blonde in a green dress.

"Who are you?" he asked.

"I work for the Scarsdale Medical Clinic."

A saturnine older man immediately glided to the woman's elbow. "Who are *you?*"

"My name is Peter Maas."

"Well, she works for *me.*"

"Hi," said the woman, "that was unnecessarily cruel."

When Gerda Stedman had seen Tarnower in the hospital, he had told her that in February he expected to be cruising in the Caribbean with his friend I. W. "Tubby" Burnham, of Drexel Burnham. If the party got near her island, he would call. She was alone on the veranda when the phone rang. "Gerda, we're in Tortola! We'll be there in half an hour."

No *may I?,* no *would it be convenient?* That had never been his style.

"Good! Come to lunch," she said. "How many are you?"

"Six. Why don't you bring it to the boat?"

Half an hour later the yacht appeared, and Mrs. Stedman made her way down the steep, flowering hillside, followed by two servants carrying picnic hampers of homemade patés, salads, and cakes. On board were five people more or less Tarnower's age, all fit, lean, and deeply tanned, and one scarcely half as old.

"Gerda, this is Lynne Tryforos."

Mrs. Stedman remembers a docile, respectful, pretty woman who wore her blonde hair knotted into an elaborate French twist, a coiffure identical to the one Gerda herself had once worn. When Gerda remarked that the bread recipe in the diet book was wrong, Lynne ran for a pencil and, secretarylike, took down the corrected version. After lunch, Lynne strolled on the beach alone, seeming forlornly out of place among these freckled, suntanned senior citizens. Tarnower took Gerda on a tour of the boat and pointed out the small cabin he and Lynne shared.

"You know, Hi, you are funny. How did you know I'd recognize your voice when you called? I haven't heard from you since you gave me the book."

"But you did," he said.

In lieu of a yachting cap, Tarnower sported a little German cap initialed with the insignia of a Munich beer hall, a souvenir of a recent hunting trip in Bavaria, he said. Could Herman Tarnower possibly be unaware that he, a Jew, was larking around the Caribbean wearing the house cap of Adolf Hitler's favorite beer hall? Mrs. Stedman did not ask. She was not sure she cared to hear his answer.

Tarnower and Lynne Tryforos returned from the Caribbean in time to plunge into a round of parties and personal appearances designed to hype the sales of his book, and celebrate its instant best-sellerdom. But when the Jacobsons gave their friend a private book party at their Manhattan apartment, Tarnower escorted Jean Harris. He knew how the Jacobsons felt. Every time he asked them to Purchase to dinner, Marge would say, "Is Jeannie up this weekend?" and if the answer was no, she always said, "Hi, do me a favor. Ask me when Jeannie's up."

Jean was quiet and withdrawn at the party, "sweet-looking, but certainly no longer beautiful," another guest recalls. "As for Hi, he had become totally arrogant, and intensely dislikable. Suddenly he was an expert on every aspect of book publishing —all on the basis of one book, which was a non-book, that he didn't even write. The entire conversation was about how to arrange still more publicity to help maintain the book's Number One position."

Part of Jean's evident depression was indeed due to the book's success. She disapproved of Herman's being involved with a diet book for the same reason she did his involvement with Lynne. Both, she said, "denigrated" a great doctor. "Lynne was corrupting because she told him he was God all the time," Mrs. Harris recently told a friend. "She called him 'Super Doctor!' She left little love notes and 'Super Doc' buttons all over the house! When I found them, I threw them in the pond. She called him 'Chair!' I guess she meant *cheri.* The book corrupted Hi too, and I tried very hard to keep him from writing it. Because what is he called today? He's 'The Diet Doc.' Herman was a superb internist and cardiologist, and to be known as 'The Diet Doc'—I think that's a hell of a comedown!"

13

Embrangled Triangle

HOW DOES ONE DIAGRAM the three-way relationship among
Jean Harris, Herman Tarnower, and Lynne Tryforos? Certainly
Tarnower's was not the conventional "Captain's Paradise." The
women knew each other. A minimal effort was made by the
servants, and sometimes by the doctor, to hide one woman's
belongings when the other was expected. The purpose, however,
was not to protect the women's sensibilities but the doctor's, to
shield him from "scenes." The shield was not impregnable; both
of the Van der Vrekens, and many other witnesses, have spoken
of tears, screams, telephone harangues, flying ashtrays, dinner
parties interrupted, threats of suicide—none of it very surprising, given the basic untenable, intolerable situation. If it was no
Captain's Paradise, neither was it conventional "two-timing,"
to use a quaint term for the moment when that Paradise becomes purgatory. "Two-timing" implies that one of the women,
at least, is unaware. Lynne always understood the situation entirely, and the self-induced know-nothingism of Mrs. Harris
could no longer be sustained after the Paris confrontation. But

even when she thought she knew all, and forgave, and loved her prince "anyhow"—even then, she did not know all. Undeceived, she was still deceived.

What did Herman Tarnower think he was doing? He handled every other aspect of his life masterfully; why did he run his love life in so untidy and mutually degrading a manner? The question caused endless speculation among his friends, many of whom had taken to speaking knowingly of "the weekday girl" and "the weekend girl." The situation generated an everflowing stream of coarse public joking about the doctor's virility that he affected not to hear.

Whatever the nature of the doctor's feelings for his young office assistant, and they seem to have grown increasingly tender, he appears to have preferred to maintain a situation that created maximal opportunities for inflicting humiliation and pain upon both women. But was pain and humiliation a conscious objective? Most observers did not think so. Some thought Herman loved Jean too much to be unkind to her, or unkind *enough* to banish her for good. Dr. Allen Tanney, his oldest friend, says, "I think Hi always had a great deal of feeling for Jean, and that he was genuinely loath to hurt her." Others thought Tarnower simply did not know how to get out of his embrangled triangle; they believed he was horrified by the possible consequences of imposing a complete break: a public scandal was likely, and suicide a real possibility. Some noted that Lynne was actually playing the role of devoted slave, which Jean may have felt herself to be, but was too ambivalent, or perhaps too dependent or too much "a lady," to act out. Tarnower did not really believe Jean loved him, they thought, because he saw insufficient evidence. She may in fact have subtly undercut his power by refusing fully to submit to it—scorning his money, his ring, his largesse. In his eyes, she may have appeared to sacrifice little and receive much. Perhaps he saw no evidence of her sacrifice and her suffering because she took such pains to conceal it from him. Friends who knew both women often describe Jean as "brittle" or "tense," and they comment on how "easy" Lynne was with the doctor, on how skillfully, instinctively, she seemed to know how to "handle" this difficult man. Others thought the doctor so lacking in empathy that, despite the escalating conflict between Jean and Lynne, he was

truly unaware of the depth of either woman's feelings, or of the
pain he was inflicting. And some, worldly as the Moroccan
limousine driver, understood the enjoyment it can afford a vain
and aging man to watch two attractive, desirable women fight
over him tooth and claw. They thought it simply turned him
on.

By his sixty-ninth birthday, March 18, 1979, Herman
Tarnower had succeeded in making every one of his dear
friends and grateful patients willy-nilly accomplices to his own
rococo private life, and they arranged for his birthday to be
celebrated elaborately but serially. On Friday the sixteenth, the
Comforts threw a big, black-tie party at their Briarcliff Manor
estate for Herman and Lynne. On Saturday, Jean arrived in
Purchase from Madeira. The Comforts' party was not mentioned. On Sunday, Jean and Tarnower flew to Nassau for another birthday party, this one with the Loebs. They remained in
the Bahamas for a week, returning the following Sunday. It was
not until midmorning Monday that Jean Harris went to the
downstairs guest-room closet. She opened the door and
screamed. Every one of her garments had been slashed, ripped,
and torn. Some had their sleeves pulled out, others were in
shreds from collar to hem. She shouted for Suzanne to come
and look, and turned away, feeling sick. Suzanne told Jean (and
she would tell the jury the same thing at the trial) that no one
but she and Henri had been in the house the entire week, but
that yesterday Henri had been out working in the garden and
had happened to look up in time to see Lynne Tryforos slip in
through the front door. Then Suzanne pointed to a blue suede
jacket hanging in the closet. It belonged to Mrs. Tryforos, she
said, and it too had been slashed. Suzanne promised to report
the vandalism to the doctor as soon as he returned from his
office. Jean begged her just to throw away the destroyed clothing and say nothing.

"But I *have* to tell him, Madame!"

"Please! We have had a very happy holiday, and I don't want
it ended this way." Jean said she was going back to school
Wednesday and would leave a note on Tarnower's pillow then.
She did not want to destroy their last two days together with

"worrying about these clothes." Later she told her trial jury, "I didn't discuss it with him at all." *Put the blame on Mame.*

Three weeks later, Tarnower took Lynne Tryforos on a fishing holiday in the Florida Keys.

By 1979, the headmistress was in a situation to crack the composure of an archbishop and, under the strain of her personal life and the pressures of her job, she was beginning slowly to turn back into the very model of a flighty, rebellious adolescent. When a jealous faculty member complained to the Board, inaccurately, that Mrs. Harris had been leaving the campus untended on weekends, and the headmistress was confronted with this preposterous accusation, she reacted like a girl caught smoking in the bathroom. She hedged, she fudged, she swore, she wept. Thereafter she began to behave, in relation to the Board, more and more like a distraught schoolgirl and less and less like a headmistress.

Adding to the Romper Room atmosphere were the nicknames. "Everybody down at that place is called Kiki, Sukie, DeeDee, Poopsie, Muffie," Jean once exclaimed. "I was the only one that was just plain Jean." Faculty meetings sounded like an agitated aviary. As Alumnae Secretary, Sukie Hodgsdon Smith worked closely with the headmistress and saw the deepening schoolgirl hysteria. Discussion that began calmly tended to disintegrate into shouting matches as Jean brought up and rehashed irrelevant sins of the past. "The problems in that big office at the end of the corridor were just too much," Sukie says, "and it got so you couldn't find her when you needed her. She'd be running around the basement saying it was much too dirty, which it *was,* or she was in the kitchen seeing to pots and pans, or back at her house soaking in a hot bath because she got so cold all the time. She was very frail, and ate hardly anything. Her temper was getting worse. One day Maxine, a secretary, fell into my office shaking, literally *fleeing.* 'Mrs. Harris has just had another temper tantrum and I'm terrified!' she gasped. Some letter had been done wrong, and she'd absolutely torn strips off Maxine! Often in my office I'd hear shouting down in the business manager's office; then a door slam and footsteps. You're trying not to hear, you know, but your ears are on stalks. A headmistress just doesn't behave that way—and yet you couldn't help but feel fond of her. I remember once she came in, shut the door, and said, 'Sukie, how do you manage your life as a single woman living in Washington?' Then she said, 'It's really difficult having men friends when you're our age. I'm very lucky to have a gentleman friend who will take me everyplace, but unfortunately he won't marry me.'

"She was very upset that the Board had not entertained her more. Barbara Keyser used to complain of the same neglect. Jean was a sad, lonesome, pathetic woman. She needed to be hugged. I wanted very much to know her better, but she was so cold, she froze me out. One time she told me that there could never be an old-girl network among females because there was no warmth in women's feelings toward one another. Any head of a girls' school who says that is really in the wrong place."

By 1979 it was clear to all that Madeira's fund-raising efforts were at least a decade behind other comparable schools', and the immediate need was to raise ten million dollars. Russell R. Browning Associates, professional school consultants, were hired by the Board to conduct interviews with potential heavy givers to find out how the school was currently rated. The confidential Browning Report, dated May 1979, was a shocker. One director said Jean Harris was the most controversial head of school in the nation. A parent said, "Mrs. Harris doesn't care what she says, and isn't careful to whom she says it." A "friend" mentioned that Mrs. Harris's inability to handle disciplinary situations had moved several sets of Madeira parents to try to dissuade prospective new families from applying. Another director said, "The headmistress is probably not irrational, but she acts as if she were." There were favorable comments too, but the general tenor of the remarks led Mr. Browning to recommend that the Board "get rid of Jean Harris immediately" and put in an interim head until they could conduct another, proper search.

The Board was stunned, took an immediate vote, and decided to ignore Mr. Browning's drastic recommendation and destroy all copies of his report. But the headmistress managed to send a copy to the NAIS for review, and they proclaimed it entirely unprofessional. Nonetheless, whatever remained of her self-confidence was now entirely shattered, and only now did she learn that she had never been the unanimous choice of the Board.

Coming at this time, the news devastated her. She felt gulled, flimflammed. When the Thomas School had gone under, Jean Harris had felt "professionally wiped out." The Browning Report did her in a second time. "I couldn't any longer feel I was going to finish my professional life at Madeira, and I didn't have the strength to go look for another situation. When I came home in the evening, the lovely house they gave me, The Hill, didn't feel the same anymore. I knew from that moment that I was just *camping out.*"

Automatically, if not realistically, she turned for approval back to Hi. She accepted his next casual invitation to Purchase, to the big Century spring dance, even though she knew it meant buying an expensive plane ticket for only a brief weekend. After the Browning fiasco, she thirsted for the sort of reassurance only Herman could give.

"Hell, they'll never fire you," Tarnower said when she told him the story. "They're too lazy to look for another head."

Jean had worn her good diamond and pearl earrings to the dance, but on Sunday as she was packing to leave, she thought she might lose them on the airplane, and impulsively she left them behind, in the ashtray on Tarnower's dresser. When next she returned to Purchase, some weeks or months later, the earrings were gone, and she never saw them again. Nor did she ever mention the loss. She did not know how to bring up the matter without making it sound like an accusation of theft, and since she had never before lost anything in the house, she preferred to keep silent now. The household air already was thick with acrimony; a perhaps baseless cry of "jewel thief" would have been furiously resented by master, servants, and guests alike.

By summer, Herman Tarnower had begun to lose patience with Jean's increasingly overwrought phone calls. He instructed his servants no longer to permit her to destroy the tranquil perfection of his dinner hour. If she called while the doctor was at table, they were to say he was not at home. He scarcely seemed the same Herman Tarnower these days. The "caring" doctor had metamorphosed into the latest guru of the talk shows, America's national god of lean, and he was enjoying his new role immensely. For the first time in his on-the-make life, Herman Tarnower was unabashedly allowing himself to have fun. He loved the television appearances at which, on occasion, Jean sat quietly off-camera, "a middle-aged geisha," according to one observer. But Jean was less and less around. Rich and famous, no longer needing Jean Harris to confer respectability, Tarnower could now be seen anywhere with his worshipful little *tsatskeleh* on his arm. He could afford to become still more imperious. Henceforth, he announced, he would accept travel invitations only from hosts who sent their private plane.

Lynne was thrilled by her beloved's new acclaim. A guest invited to a Purchase dinner after a quail-shoot reported that Lynne assisted Suzanne in serving the feast, herself carrying the heavy platter of birds around the table, and when she came to the doctor's place, she sank to her knees and held the platter up over her head in the manner of a Grecian cupbearer. On other occasions, if Hi and Lynne preferred to give up the gourmet pose and send out for pizza—why, that was all right too. It was this rich and late-blooming enjoyment of life, from which Jean was excluded, that left her, in her own words, "old and bitter and sick."

Submissive, adoring, and very efficient, Lynne had by now become a full-time handmaiden. "She literally worshiped the ground he walked on," John Loeb told a friend. "All she really cared about was *his* well-being, and I think she was very good for Hi. She really loved him."

Her devotion was so entire some of Tarnower's friends were embarrassed to be around the pair. Lynne seemed to have no friends. Tarnower was her whole life. She ran his office, prepared and served his Scarsdale Diet lunches, cosseted and attended his patients. At his home she was housekeeper-hostess, playmate, and bedmate, unless Tarnower wished to sleep alone, on which occasions she apparently crept uncomplainingly home to her daughters in her bungalow nearby. Suzanne, who has seen Lynne's home, reported, "It had hardly any furniture, very bare and modest. Dr. Tarnower took her out from her misery."

A close shooting buddy of Hi's reports that Lynne was a natural marksman. "The first time he brought her along, I pointed to a wounded chukar in a tree, handed her my gun, and said: 'Shoot it! Take a bead on it, and kill it.' She put the gun up to her eye, fired off the first shot of her life, and it was perfect! Now she's a crack shot. She's got a *fantastic* eye. It opened up a whole new world for Hi when he found they could go shooting together."

An aspect of Lynne's adoration was her dogged determination to organize the bachelor doctor's home life as efficiently as she had his office. She inscribed Herman's name in all his books, including the many that Jean had given him. She even went through the scrapbooks of Jean's and Hi's world travels and captioned all the photographs. She left love notes on Hi's telephone pads. She salted his private quarters with homemade badges that said "Super Doc."

Each time Jean came to visit for a weekend, her first task was to exorcise Lynne's presence. She threw the Super Doc badges in the pond, and tore the drawings of hearts and flowers off the phone pads. If Suzanne had slipped up in her housekeeping, as she often did, Jean also dropped Lynne's lingerie down the laundry chute, removed her cosmetics and douche equipment from the guest bathroom, and got rid of her hated pink electric curlers, which she usually stowed in Herman's car trunk. She had done these things ever since Paris. A swift quarter hour of remedial housekeeping, and all was the same as before.

By July, Tarnower's book had been Number One for twenty weeks and he was beginning to think about a sequel. Having slain the great American dragon of overweight, he was ready to take on the twin dragon of aging. There would *be* no more aging; he would decree it. Such being the case, what did he need with a fading and unhappy schoolmistress? He upped the Desoxyn to a steady seven and a half milligrams and hoped for the best.

Jean hung on. That summer she went to the Century show, which featured a parody tribute to Herman's book. Two pregnant girls, one fat, one thin, sing, to the tune of "Officer Krupke," "Hey, Doctor Tarnower, she was a cow. But she's on your diet now!" Wild applause.

Afterward Jean and Marge Jacobson met in the powder room. "Goddammit, Jean. I'm so mad you didn't marry Hi that first summer!"

"In retrospect, it really was not a good idea, Marge. Hi really doesn't like children." But the old refrain was pitifully out of date. The "children" were now twenty-eight and twenty-six.

In August, Jean returned to the Middle West to give a speech at her old school, Laurel, and visit her old friends at their lakeside summer homes. "She never stopped talking," Do Johnson recalls. "But her only two subjects were Madeira and Hi. She talked about Lynne, and she knew she was losing Hi. She didn't know how she could live without him. She was strung taut as a wire and spent hours alone on the beach. That helped her, she said."

Her speech at Laurel once again reflected the excruciating concerns of her own heart.

> The first step in teaching integrity . . . is to come to terms with your own integrity, your own standards of personal wholeness. It's a tough thing you're wrestling with right now; be sure that as you work your way through it you do not confuse hand-wringing and anxious self-scrutiny with critical self-examination. You must determine first what your own values are and how much you actually value them; what set of rules or morals you will live by in order to achieve them. In that interplay between what you value and how you achieve it, you become a person of integrity or a person without integrity.

September 1979 marked a renewal of activity in Purchase after the summer doldrums. Unbeknownst to Jean, Suzanne and Henri Van der Vreken had a private phone installed in their bedroom. Heretofore there had been only one line into the house, with four extensions—one in the living room, one in the downstairs guest room where the Van der Vrekens slept, a wall phone in the kitchen, and a phone upstairs in Tarnower's bedroom, on the shelf between the twin beds. The house had no true intercom system, but a large white button next to Tarnower's bedside phone sounded a loud buzzer in the kitchen. A servant could then pick up the wall phone extension and converse with the doctor above the humming of the telephone dial tone.

In September, four of Herman Tarnower's dearest friends approached him with a proposition. Three were grateful patients Dan Comfort, John Loeb, and Arthur Schulte. The fourth man was Hi's most frequent golfing, fishing, and hunting partner, Joseph Cullman III. The year 1980 would see not only the thirtieth anniversary of the founding of the Westchester Heart Association, to which Dr. Tarnower had given so much for so long, but also the doctor's seventieth birthday. His friends wanted to mark the occasion with a formal testimonial banquet, and some sort of philanthropic recognition of his achievements. The Westchester County Medical Center lacked a cardiovascular research lab, and Tarnower's tycoon friends thought that creating one might be a suitable tribute. "We knew there was four thousand square feet available, and we could get the nuts and bolts," said Dan Comfort, who served as the banquet committee's informal chairman. "We would have to raise between $250,000 and $400,000 for doctors and staff."

The prospective honoree appeared to Comfort to demur. "At first Dr. Hi was very reluctant. Dr. Hi was a very retiring person, you see, and the limelight didn't appeal to him," Comfort said later. But evidently Tarnower was persuadable, because a fund-raising committee was named, and Comfort, Loeb, Schulte, Cullman, the staff of the Westchester Heart Association, and Lynne Tryforos all spent a good deal of their time that fall and winter planning and selling tables for the big affair, which was to be held on April 19, at the Scarsdale Country Club. The entire Westchester social and medical establishment could be expected to turn out, and in addition to Tarnower's own remarks, there would be speeches by Dr. Frank Spencer, the eminent heart surgeon who had operated on Dan Comfort, and Dr. Howard Rusk of New York University's Rusk Institute in Manhattan.

On September 18, less than two weeks after the opening of Madeira, a tragic incident occurred. The Brazen Hussies was a secret society whose members did everything from hanging toilet seats in the trees to smoking pot in the basement. Occasionally they vandalized school property, but most of their pranks were harmless. This time the Hussies were shampooing the hair of some new girls when a foreign student, perhaps unable to read English labels, poured caustic toilet-bowl cleaner over their heads. One girl's face was severely burned. Jean drove her to the hospital, learned that eventually plastic surgery would be required, and struggled to keep the story out of the Washington papers. To quell baseless rumors, she sent a full account of the incident to all parents the next day. The injured girl went home temporarily to recover, and a lawsuit was filed; when she returned to Madeira she became the headmistress's special pet and protegée. Jean often invited her to visit at The Hill, and seemed to be trying personally to make it up to her for her injury and pain. Doubtless she was also comfort and company to Jean in what was becoming an increasingly bleak personal life. Suzanne's record books indicate that Mrs. Harris spent but two weekends with Tarnower that fall, although their big Thanksgiving and New Year's holidays together took place on schedule.

October 12 was Mothers' Day at Madeira, and again the headmistress's speech was preoccupied with integrity. She also told her audience that, to keep the girls out of the bars, she had decided temporarily to rule all of Georgetown off limits. At this, the assembled parents leaped to their feet and tendered the headmistress a standing ovation.

Jean Harris received other, stronger indications of renewed support that fall. After the devastating Browning Report of last May, she had told the Board, "There is no way you can raise $10 million if this is your opinion of yourself, of the school, and of me. Get me three people who know the difference between a good school and a bad school, and I'll let them have the run of the place, talk to everybody, see all the books. I want an honest report for once in the seventy-five-year history of this school." Her remark may have sounded overwrought, but it was based on sound professional experience. A good prep school submits itself to just this kind of periodic objective peer review every eight to ten years. Madeira—in part reflecting its Southern heritage—had never sought outside evaluation.

In mid-October, a three-man team of professionals, all of them former school heads,* visited Madeira for three days and personally examined every aspect of campus life. They turned

---

* The late Carl Andrews, Jr., their leader, was the former head of New York City's Collegiate School; Gerald N. LaGrange was chairman of the board of NAIS and formerly with Rye Country Day School; and Frank Miller, a director of NAIS, had been head of the Hackley School.

in a glowing report. "Our considered judgment about the administration of the Madeira School can be simply expressed. We feel it is properly organized, responsible and effective. . . . We are impressed with what the Headmistress has accomplished in her two years at the school, especially in the administrative area. . . . [she] keeps an appropriate oversight of her administrative associates and their work, meets regularly with them, and appears to be readily accessible. . . . We commend Madeira's administration for its high quality, effectiveness and smooth functioning. . . ."

"Whitewash!" cried some members of the Board. But most of them backed Jean. She had, after all, gotten the school properly accredited by then; she also had improved the administrative structure, improved the staff, the curriculum, and the physical plant, raised faculty and administrative salaries, bettered the college admissions record, and codified the rules of student behavior and administrative practices. But alas, in her current state, the fact of these accomplishments, and the fact that the majority of the Board supported her in her efforts, were no longer enough. "I knew by then that I didn't belong there," she would say later, "and that it was just a matter of time before I left."

Jean and Hi flew to Lyford Cay over Thanksgiving, and at lunch one day Jean mocked his diet book in front of the Loebs' other guests. Later, John Loeb asked her to "please lay off." Tarnower was getting so much pleasure from his book Loeb thought her raillery unfair. She was also being "unreasonably possessive," the financier said.

In December Jean Harris made several highly emotional phone calls to Dan Comfort. She had heard that Hi had invited Lynne to the Heart Association banquet. This was intolerable, totally unacceptable. It amounted to public humiliation, indeed, public dethronement, and Jean would not allow it to happen. That banquet was going to be the most important occasion of Herman Tarnower's life, and she intended to be the woman beside him, no matter what. Jean remembers only one phone call, but she knows she became extremely agitated. "He saved *your* life, Dan . . . he destroyed mine!" she cried. Comfort says Jean found the prospect of not sitting beside Hi "just unbelievably upsetting. I should have realized then that she wasn't herself. It wasn't at all like her."

The dinner became one of her obsessions. "Did I talk to her *once?* We talked on many occasions. Jean felt badly when I wouldn't call her back after we had had a half-hour conversation on the subject. You couldn't cope with her. She was crying, and she wouldn't let it alone. You know, Dr. Hi's real friends were *men,* and none of us knew what to do with an hysterical woman. Also, Dr. Hi was our great friend, and we felt that he should be able to bring whoever he wished to the party we were throwing in his honor."

The pre-Christmas letter the Kinzies received from Jean was the most upbeat communication she had ever sent them. Her description of the schoolgirls weaving wreaths and singing carols made Madeira sound like a Walt Disney campus. What on earth could the headmistress have been thinking as she posted her Christmas cards and letters, and prepared once again to join her lover for the holidays in West Palm Beach? Certainly she knew they were drifting farther and farther apart, that a bachelor who never traveled alone, and who lusted to be known for the best table in Westchester, needed a hostess ever at his side. She knew that this hostess was now Lynne, and that Lynne shared his bed. She knew that becoming a national celebrity had diminished the role of *any* other person in his life. She knew all this, but instead of facing it, she refused to think about it. Instead, she lived more and more with the old Hi, the Hi of Bahrain and Katmandu, the Hi who had told her he loved her and given her a big diamond ring. She read and reread the dry old letters, squeezing out droplets of feeling. She used the memory of the past to help her endure the present. Over and over she told herself: *Herman Tarnower is the strongest, most wonderfully selfish person I know. If he did not want to see me, he would send me away—and except to punish me, he never, ever has.*

One can try to imagine what that last Christmas together must have been like; Jean Harris does not discuss it. The Schultes later told friends that most of the time Herman Tarnower pointedly ignored Jean. Why, then, did he bring her along? Did he pity her? Did he fear her? Did he dread the consequence of a final rejection? Or did he still have some sentimental regard for her? Perhaps it was a bit of each. As for the headmistress, that Christmas she found another clever and even more obsequious way to acknowledge the Tarnower canon, "no strings on me." She composed a sardonic parody of that same poem she and Dodie Lewis had read aloud with their children long ago on their perfect Christmas Eve in Grosse Pointe, and when she wrote it out in red ink, tied it up with red ribbons, and read it out to everybody on Christmas Eve, Vivian and Arthur laughed aloud, and Hi enjoyed it so much he asked Jean to make him a second copy.

But the poem is pathetic, not funny—an abject fantasy in which each of the others is presented with the perfect gift and Jean Harris gets nothing. The tone throughout is bitter and mocking, yet never quite overtly so; the writer dares not risk displeasure at this court where she plays the fool.

> *'Twas the night before Christmas, and in part of the house*
> *Arthur was snuggling with Vivian, his spouse.*
> *In the guest room lay Herman who, trying to sleep,*
> *Was counting the broads in his life—'stead of sheep!*
> *On Hilda, on Sigrid, on Jinx and Raquel;*
> *Brunhilde, Veronica, Gretel, Michele;*
> *Now Tanya, Rapunzel, Electra, Adele;*
> *Now Suzie, Anita—keep trucking, Giselle.*
> *There were ingenues, Dashers, Dancers and Vixens,*
> *I believe there was even one cupid—one Blitzen!*
> *He lay there remembering, with a smile broad and deep*
> *Till he ran out of names, and he fell fast asleep.*
> *(Let me mention, my darling, if this muse were inclined*
> *Toward unseemly thoughts, or an off-color mind,*
> *It wouldn't be easy to keep this thing refined!)*
> *But 'tis the time to be jolly—and very upbeat—*
> *And for now, that's not hard, because Herman's asleep!*
> *Beside him lay Jeannie, headmistress, by Jiminy—*
> *Who was waiting for Santa to come down the chimney . . .*
> *. . . Then all of a sudden, there arose such a clatter,*
> *Herm woke from his sleep to see what was the matter.*
> *And with Jeannie obediently three paces back,*
> *They tiptoed to the living room to watch Nick unpack . . .*
> *"Now let's see—there's Herman—with Tarnower for a monika*

It seems to me he got his best stuff for Chanukah . . .
But here's one little thing that I know he will use.
If his evenings are lonely, he'll have no excuse.
Here's some brand new phone numbers in a brand new black
book
(I'm not quite the innocent gent that I look!)
This book holds the key, and the hope, and the promise,
Of a whole bunch of fun with some new Red Hot
Mommas." . . .
And the warmth that they felt—say, the heart really melts.
This Santa Claus feeling is just—something else!

> With that Santa Claus feeling,
> JEAN, 1979

By 1980, the game had worn down the players. Tarnower was nearly seventy and showing his age. He was getting deaf, stingy, and ever more selfish. He seemed to some no longer to care how he lived; the old pretensions were slipping. His close friends by now were all old men, scared of dying although not yet, thanks to the doctor's attentions, tired of living. Once they had helped make him rich, through stock-market tips and other business advice. Now Tarnower's fading but still feisty nabobs had come to need him as much as he once needed them. These patriarchs and their various women were not necessarily close friends of one another; as they got older, animosities and petty jealousies grew. More and more it was Herman Tarnower who held them all together. As for his women, certainly by 1980 Jean Harris was cracked within, although grimly hanging onto her all-but-capsized ship. Lynne Tryforos seemed to be playing a careful, quiet, waiting game. But the game went inexorably on.

During Hi's Christmas vacation with Jean at the Schultes', he received at least one letter and one telegram from Lynne; Jean affected to ignore both. But on the morning of New Year's Day, while they were eating breakfast on the Schultes' terrace, the butler brought in *The New York Times.* Right on the front page, in tiny type at the bottom of a column, it said, *"Happy New Year Hi T. Love Always Lynne. Advt."* Jean felt her entire holiday shatter. Now she felt publicly mocked before the whole world.

"Jesus, I hope none of my friends see it!" Tarnower exclaimed.

"I'm your friend, Hi, and I see it," is what Jean wanted to say. Instead she resorted to her characteristic sarcasm. "Herm, why don't you suggest she use the Goodyear Blimp next year? I think it's available."

In February, Jean's older son David was planning to marry Kathleen White. In an excess of ill-temper grandfather Struven had refused to have any part of the wedding, and angrily declined to lend David money for the honeymoon. Tarnower was genuinely fond of Jean's sons. He had always encouraged them to swim and play tennis at his house when they were growing up, and on the whole, he got on well with the boys. Indeed, Tarnower had been instrumental in helping David secure his present good job in the trust department of a Manhattan bank. When Hi and Jean returned to Purchase, he seemed happy to assist her in making her son's wedding arrangements.

The paperback edition of *The Complete Scarsdale Medical Diet* was published January 3, and its coauthor plunged into a renewed round of book promotion. He also spoke to his lawyer about a new will to accommodate the anticipated flood of literary revenues.

That Jean Harris was very tightly wound up during this period is increasingly evident from her actions over the next weeks. But those few at Madeira who noticed her obvious emotional distress elected to look the other way. At the January Board meeting, Jean's contract was routinely renewed for another year, and she received the agreed-on $5,000 annual raise. But on the day the meeting ended, Jean told her secretary she "felt like packing a bag and getting the hell out of here." She had spoken the same words to Marge Rooney at Thomas five years before.

Also in January, she had a long discussion with the Student Council about the resurgence on campus of drugs and alcohol, and she followed this up with a stern and somewhat rambling letter to parents, inviting them to reply with candor. One father sent back a response he termed "hard-boiled," criticizing Jean's prior lack of firm discipline. The headmistress scribbled a stinging reply. ". . . Your choice of adjectives is most inappropriate. Your letter is not 'hard-boiled.' It is presumptuous, gratuitously rude, uninformed and not in any way constructive. . . ."

When she read in the *Wall Street Journal* that a book reviewer, discussing "bad, dirty novels," had lumped Smith College and Madeira School into a list of items that included Vail, Biarritz, eating at Elaine's, Cheryl Tiegs, Studio 54, Perrier water, silk pajamas, "and every other imaginable potsherd of the *nouveaux riches,*" Jean fired off a response quivering with moral outrage and bordering on the incoherent. These letters could be taken as signals of an imminent breakdown, but plenty of other letters she wrote that month seem like the entirely normal brisk and cheery correspondence of a boarding-school headmistress. Overall, Jean's letters in January and February suggest a woman in a ferocious struggle to stay in control of herself. Yet when challenged, she lashes out.

Jean's own memory of her last days at Madeira is clear. Recently she told a friend, "I reached a point where I didn't really give a bloody damn if those kids tore the school apart, smoked pot, shot heroin, and threw their garbage in the middle of the living room. I just couldn't tell them not to do it anymore. Not and know the Board was sitting back making odds on how long it would take before I fell apart. By that time, all of me that went to Washington was burnt out and used up."

Reminded that many people thought her a very good headmistress, she said, "I *was* a good headmistress, a damned good one. But I wasn't strong enough to go on being one." Long ago, at Springside, Jean had once made a declaration to her own headmistress: "Look, I don't have the answer to the pot question. I don't understand it any more than anybody else does. From now on, these questions are going to be shifted to *you,* and I'm going to concentrate on getting back and becoming an educator again, not a cop, and not a drug official."

Eleven years later, now a headmistress herself, Jean was forced to reverse her position. "Because, you see, as headmistress you *are* a drug official," she would say later. *"And* you play the go-between with Mummy and Daddy. *And* the heavy. *And* a dirty dog. And all the kids say, 'Mrs. Harris, why do you have to get involved in everything we do?' And I'd think, 'Gee, I'd like to know myself—because I really don't like it.'

"My last letter to anybody at Madeira went to a very dear friend of the school who had written me asking for a copy of my talk on integrity. I said, 'I hope the immorality of this school has now bottomed out, and there is no place to go but up. Because a National Merit Scholar without any conscience is no scholar at all!' And I realized that I had changed my ideas completely in the past eleven years of what it is an educator has to do. By the time I left Madeira, I had finally knuckled under and decided that the only thing you can do when you're in charge of a school is to try to keep them from lying, stealing, and cheating *before* you teach them to read and write. I just knew, as I was writing that last letter, that teaching kids standards and morals, if they don't have them, is an educator's first job."

On January 21, the same day that Jean signed her pot-and-alcohol letter to the parents, Herman Tarnower signed the revised last will and testament he had asked his lawyer to prepare. The document offers as accurate a map as one will find of the doctor's current feelings toward important persons in his life. The will begins with his wish to be cremated and sprinkled on his pond. He makes conditional bequests of $25,000 each to six grandnieces and nephews to pay for their college education, and $20,000 each to the two daughters of Lynne Tryforos for the same purpose. The Van der Vrekens are promised $2,000 apiece for each year in Tarnower's employ. (The will refers to the servants as "chauffeur" and "wife," although in court they would describe themselves as "estate manager" and "house manager.") Tarnower's fellow doctors are granted the right to rent or buy the Scarsdale Medical Center from Tarnower's estate. He leaves his house and grounds to his sister, Billie. Then, after a few personal bequests, he leaves the residue of his estate to his nieces and nephews. The personal bequests include $220,000 to Jean Harris, $200,000 to Lynne Tryforos, and $10,000 to Gerda Stedman. At his death, Herman Tarnower's net worth was estimated at $5,000,000.

Does his will indicate that Tarnower was planning to marry

Lynne Tryforos, as the prosecutor would claim during Jean Harris's trial? Or does it suggest the opposite? Mrs. Harris would claim the doctor told her otherwise; Mrs. Tryforos never took the stand. After the trial, Jean told a friend that she and Tarnower often discussed marriage in their last years together. "He would bring it up in the car. As we were driving someplace, he'd say, 'Jean, it's better we didn't marry. We've been happier this way. I married my profession.' I'd say, 'But I keep hearing about Lynne.' And he'd say, 'Jesus Christ, Jean, you of all people should know better! What am I going to do with a woman with two kids? What the hell do *I* want marriage for?' "

Was Mrs. Harris telling the truth? One does not know, but the will Tarnower signed seven weeks before his death indicates that his affections were divided equally between his two women, which in turn seems to imply that he had not the slightest intention of marrying either one of them.

In January, the doctor had increased Jean's Desoxyn to ten milligrams. The headmistress was preoccupied with putting her personal affairs in order. She gathered her furniture together in one place; gradually, it had become scattered all over campus as she lent various items to the infirmary, faculty houses, and dorms. She updated the status of her beneficiaries in her retirement fund. She brought her insurance papers up to date, and she worked on her pet project, the reorganization of the Madeira library. A Board member remembers inviting Jean to lunch in Washington at around this time to meet a distinguished librarian. On her way to the headmistress's office, the hostess ran into the woman whom Jean had appointed Academic Dean. "I'm so glad you're taking Jean out to lunch. Boy, she *really* needs a break!"

But at lunch, Jean was very tense and literally ate nothing. The librarian thought she had a very good grasp of what needed to be done, but when the headmistress got out of the car back at school, the hostess and librarian turned to one another and each said the same thing. "My God, I've never seen such a nervous person in my life!"

Sometime that month Jean Harris received another anonymous letter. Enclosed in a Scarsdale Medical Group envelope was a photostatic copy of what appeared to be two pages of Tarnower's new will. Jean Harris's name had been scratched out as beneficiary, and the name of Lynne Tryforos substituted, seemingly in the doctor's handwriting. As usual, she mailed the "incriminating evidence" back to Tarnower.

On Sunday, February 10, Henri drove to the airport to meet the doctor and Mrs. Tryforos. They had spent the past ten days visiting Joseph Cullman III and his divorced second wife, Joan, at their Jamaica estate. On Wednesday Jean got into her old Chrysler and drove up to Purchase to spend a four-day weekend and preside over the wedding of her elder son. It was a joyous and tender time despite the fact that, within two hours of Jean's arrival, the telephone rang and when Suzanne picked it up, there was only silence.

"My God, is that still going on?" Jean exclaimed.

"All the time, Madame. But especially when you come." As in the past, Suzanne and Henri both said they were sure the caller was Lynne Tryforos.

Tarnower was a charming host to the young people. During the various festivities, he almost literally replaced Jean's father. He read a special bridal toast to Kathleen at the elegant prenuptial dinner for fourteen guests that Suzanne prepared, and as a memento of the occasion he presented each of the young women in the wedding party with an autographed copy of his paperback best-seller. The next day Jean learned from her son that Tarnower had slipped a thousand-dollar check into his pocket as a wedding gift. Driving back from the church with Tarnower, Jean thanked him, and she happened to mention that she was furious with her younger son, Jimmie, for losing his father's gold watch. The doctor said Gerda Stedman had once given him a very fine gold watch, worth at least $2,000, and Jimmie could have it if Jean would spend the money to get it repaired.

"No one could accuse you of being a sentimental man, Herman."

"You know, Jean, it was better we didn't get married," he said once more. "I don't ever want to worry about what retirement home your mother is in, and I didn't want you to worry about where mine was. I don't want to watch you die of cancer, and I don't want you to play nursemaid to me. . . ."

On Sunday morning, before she left Purchase, the headmistress and the doctor tenderly made love, and she presented him with the gold caduceus she had bought in Virginia as her own wedding gift to the only man she had ever truly loved. Shortly before noon, she drove away down the long, driveway feeling loved, needed, and "replenished." The manuscript of the first section of Tarnower's new book was in her suitcase. He had asked her to look it over with her schoolteacher's eye. The title was "How to Live Longer and Enjoy Life More." Before they parted that last, lovely morning, Hi and Jean had even resolved the big problem of the Heart Association banquet. Lynne would have to be there; after all, she worked for the Heart Association. But somehow Jean Harris felt reassured that on the most important night of Herman Tarnower's life, he very much wanted her at his side.

Purchase Street is heavily wooded and bordered with large, stone-walled estates. A quarter-mile down the road at the Westchester Community Center stands a lone pay telephone. Impulsively, Jean pulled up and dialed Dan Comfort's house in Briarcliff.

"We just had a gloriously happy weekend, Dan, and Hi wants *me* to be there! So no more need to worry, Dan. It's fixed. All is well."

14

Four Bullets

IN LATE FEBRUARY 1980 Jean Harris was getting ready for a
ten-day fundraising and recruiting swing through the Far West,
San Diego to Seattle, including a stop in Colorado Springs for
the annual meeting of the National Association of Headmistresses. Such trips are a grueling sequence of lunches, speeches,
meetings, and slide shows as tightly scheduled as a presidential
campaign. In her last chapel speech before leaving, Jean gave
the girls a glowing description of David's wedding and reiter-
ated her belief that, for everybody, marriage was "still the best
way." She forced herself to revise and return the manuscript of
Hi's new book before she left town. Her covering letter,
scratched out and rewritten several times, is a sacher torte of
double messages of love and jealousy.

Dear Hi,

    T.S. Eliot I ain't, but this may hang together a bit
better. I don't know where you go from Chapter Two.
My secretary thinks I have gone bananas. I did a bit of

cutting and pasting at the crocodile testicle bit. She is a
loyal, unquestioning employee up to a point—not the
point of your "loyal, unquestioning employee"!—but
then the 'perks' aren't the same either.

You were wonderfully kind and generous to do all that
you did for David and Kathleen—and me, my enigmatic
friend. I wish—same old wish—there were many more
ways I could do things for you. It just wasn't in the cards
for me to fix the cottage cheese at noon and run errands.
—I wish you didn't feel socially obligated to the person
who does.

If it's any help, tho, darling, I can find you someone
who would be thrilled to give the same 24 hour door to
door services and take shorthand too!

I'm sure it has never occurred to you—because you
would never be able to think of men and women as equals
—but the truth is darling if one of the few women you do
admire—say Audrey [Topping] or Ronnie Rothschild, or
Elizabeth McCormick [a college president and former
nun] or Iphigene were to adopt the male equivalent of
Lynne as lover and richly rewarded "boy Friday" you
wouldn't ask them back to dinner the second time—

Not only are you the man I have loved for 14 years—I
think you are unconstitutional!

All my love and gratitude,
JEAN

When Jean Harris reorganized the Madeira administration,
she had appointed two seconds-in-command, Jean Gizriel,
Dean of Students, and "Kiki" Johnson, Academic Dean. Both
are capable women, but scarcely the sort of persons likely to be
sensitive to Jean's private stress. Miss Gizriel is a hearty, 170-
pound Californian whose adult life had been devoted chiefly to
teaching physical education in girls' schools. Mrs. Johnson, a
Madeira graduate, met her future husband on the school lawn
on her graduation day, married him right after Vassar and
Princeton respectively, and had three children by the time she
was twenty-five. "He was, and has been, the only love of my
life," she says, "so I find it rather hard to relate to a woman

whose life history includes a divorce. And a love affair. That's walking in someone's moccasins I've never known." Mrs. Johnson accompanied Jean Harris on part of the western tour, and later reported, "We ate dinner together, occupied the same room, talked about our children as well as school. I had no sense whatever that she might be at the edge of a crack-up. I found her a very cool lady." One may wonder what it cost the headmistress to give this impression.

Sunday, March 2, found Jean in San Francisco and so bone-weary she had to cancel most of her appointments. Even the Desoxyn was insufficient to erase her overwhelming feeling of sickening fatigue. She spent the day in bed at the San Francisco Club grinding out long handwritten thank-you notes—the bane of any headmistress's life, and the spoor that marks her travels. She also wrote to her mother describing Tarnower's warm, fatherly behavior at David and Kathleen's wedding, and announcing, "This morning I have decided to put out feelers for another kind of job. I really haven't the physical strength for this one, and it's lonely as hell to boot."

Jean Gizriel was waiting at the Washington airport Wednesday afternoon. "There's an awful lot of talk about pot parties in South Dorm," she warned on the drive back to school. The headmistress was not surprised. That particular dormitory had been a trouble spot for drugs and alcohol all year.

"I'll have a talk with the House Mother," Jean said.

"I wouldn't do that. They say she's involved herself. They say half the Student Council's involved."

"Then I guess we'll have to look."

The headmistress considered room searches distasteful but occasionally necessary, part of the school's legal responsibility to act *in loco parentis*. Every Madeira girl at the time of her enrollment signs a form saying she knows that having drugs on campus is forbidden and makes her subject to expulsion. Thursday afternoon, when all the girls were at a movie, Jean sent Giz and an assistant to search South Dorm. While she waited, she telephoned Dr. Tarnower. She had been attempting to reach him since yesterday to report that she was completely out of Desoxyn. He promised to send more, and brusquely asked about some missing books. Jean interpreted the simple inquiry as an accusation of stealing, made by the very person to whom she had freely given everything. Next, Tarnower told her she would not be beside him at the Heart Association banquet after all. They had worked out a compromise. She was to sit at the Comforts' table; Lynne would be with the Cullmans. No women would be at the head table. To Jean, this was no compromise; rather, she saw it as a public demonstration that Lynne was now in fact her equal.

Too stunned to talk, not daring to cry, she said she'd call back, and hung up the phone. It rang again almost immediately. Giz had hit pay dirt. "Come over here and see for yourself!" she cried.

In a suite of rooms occupied by four of Madeira's outstanding senior girls, the searchers had found a small amount of marijuana seeds and stems, and some bongs (various paraphernalia to enhance the pleasure of smoking), hidden in a bureau drawer; many more bongs were stashed at the bottom of the bathroom laundry hamper. They brought all the evidence back to Jean's house, and Giz went to the auditorium to round up the girls and staff. Tomorrow was Friday, March 7, the last day of classes before Spring Break, and it was important to clear up the matter before the students went home, rather than let it fester over the holidays. Directly after dinner, said Giz, every Student Council member and faculty member who lived on campus would be expected to assemble in the headmistress's living room.

Giz then escorted the culprits to The Hill, and Jean asked for an explanation. The girls maintained that they kept only bongs on campus; the marijuana was stashed where they smoked it, at the nearby home of one of their grandmothers. Jean thought them insufferably rude and told them so. But what truly appalled her was the discovery of *who* the miscreants were—not just anybody, but the topmost leaders of the school. All of them were on the Student Council, one was South Dorm's own House Mother, one was actually head of the Student Judiciary —and now all four were revealed as utter hypocrites! Since the beginning of her reign as headmistress, Jean had been meeting regularly with these very girls to hammer out a charter for the Student Council, and all the time that they had been pretending to codify the rules, they had in fact been breaking them. Jean felt betrayed on a personal level that had nothing to do with marijuana. This was a breach of faith by the entire student body.

The long meeting lasted until 11:30 P.M., and the four girls stuck to their story: no pot on campus, not ever, even though Giz and the other teacher testified that their entire suite of rooms smelled of marijuana. Jean chaired the meeting, saying little, but insisting that everyone present speak out frankly. "It got pretty rough," says one girl. "Some kids said, 'If you're not expelled for this, what *do* you have to do to get thrown out of this place?' " Older girls took the attitude, *everybody's doing it;* the younger ones believed that rules meant what they said. Jean sided with the youngsters and told them they had the most courage.

By the time the vote for expulsion was taken and found to be unanimous, if not heartfelt, and the four girls were sent to call their parents, it was too late to call Tarnower. Jean did not sleep at all that night. She knew she would have to deal with the parents herself the next day. She does not recall speaking in chapel Friday morning, although she later received a letter from a young teacher saying her talk had been so powerful she was herself inspired to become the head of a school one day. "When we find people among us of the wrong type, we are obliged to weed them out for the good of all," Jean had said, adding that the student leaders had proven themselves so hypocritical that the girls "should seriously consider not having a Student Government next year."

The headmistress spent the next two days in face-to-face confrontation with various parents. The mother and father of one of the girls, one already on school probation after being accused of shoplifting in Georgetown, said the activity for which she was being expelled was not their daughter's fault; she was "in with a bad lot of girls." The mother whose own mother had harbored the marijuana accused Jean of "Hitler tactics" and said, "If I had known you ran this school with your own Gestapo, I would never have sent my daughter here," quite forgetting that she had chosen Madeira *because* of its strict reputation. Not all the parents were churlish. "I know I shouldn't have done it!" the third girl sobbed. Her parents said they hoped their daughter had learned something from her mistake, and then they watched student and headmistress, equally high-minded, stand weeping with their arms around each other. "Can't my daughter take the rap for all the girls?" said the fourth father, who was also a trustee. "She was House Mother, after all, so she had the ultimate responsibility."

"No," Jean said, "I have the ultimate responsibility. All four must be punished alike."

Throughout Friday a student backlash built up against the drumhead justice of the night before, and it culminated in a spontaneous rally that afternoon to reinstate the Madeira Four. The mass meeting ended with a blanket indictment of the administration for its harsh behavior, and with a massed shout, "We love you, Keri! Kelly! Kathy! Nina!" the impassioned girls poured down the chapel steps and into the Oval. Two members of the faculty were strolling past.

"You . . . fucking . . . hypocrites!" the rally's chief orator screamed out at the pair of teachers just as one set of parents drove up to reclaim their disgraced daughter. The screamer was brought to the headmistress's house, and Mrs. Harris administered a furious tongue-lashing. *"How dare you* speak that way to people who work for slave wages, breaking their backs to give you ingrates a decent education!" That the girl was the granddaughter of Madeira's most powerful Druid added brimstone to Jean's tirade. When it ended, Kiki Johnson escorted the shaken girl outside.

"It's the word *hypocrite* she can't stand," whispered the Academic Dean. "If only you'd called them fucking assholes, she wouldn't have minded so much."

Friday was Jean's third day off Desoxyn. Even after a short period of habituation, abrupt methamphetamine withdrawal produces feelings of fatigue, depression, lassitude, melancholy, agitation, helplessness, self-doubt, and inability to cope. The full effect of the sudden absence of the drug after such prolonged use as Jean Harris had experienced is unknown. Doctors say such studies have been considered too cruel to perform, so there are no data.

Late Friday afternoon, one of the deans reported to Jean that full ashtrays and empty liquor bottles had been found stashed under the bed of another respected senior. "You deal with it," the headmistress said. "I can't handle anything more."

All day Friday, Saturday, and Sunday, and late into the

nights, Jean Harris attempted to telephone Herman Tarnower. She did not understand what was happening to her; she just knew she was coming unglued. But her doctor was unavailable. Each time she called, Henri said he was out. He had in fact taken Lynne to "21" on Friday night for the birthday party of "Bunny" Lasker, former president of the New York Stock Exchange. Saturday night they attended another formal New York gala. Many of his Century Club cronies were present on both occasions. It was the last time they would see him alive. Saturday and Sunday Lynne Tryforos was Herman Tarnower's house guest, and he had told his servants he did not wish to be disturbed by needless phone calls. He and Lynne were planning another shooting trip in a few days, and over the weekend she laid out their shooting clothes and paraphernalia on the long dressing-room window ledge.

The weekend passed for Jean in a blur of sleepless disorder, agitation, and panic. "I find it very hard to describe that weekend," she would tell the jury. "I don't have a language to describe it in. . . . I remember very distinctly Saturday morning going in and out of my bedroom several times. I wanted to clean it up, but I didn't know how. I couldn't decide where anything goes. I didn't know which pile of paper went where. Just hanging up a dress seemed to involve more decisions than I could cope with." Although she did not realize it then, her mental state had begun the downward slide from turmoil to agitation to disorganization that finally would reach its nadir on that fateful Monday evening in total dissociation.

Because she could not get through to Tarnower by telephone, she began that Saturday to write him a very long, rambling letter that listed her grievances and sought to diagram her pain. It was written randomly in her odd free moments during the next two hectic days and near-sleepless nights.

Hi:

I will send this by registered mail only because so many of my letters seem not to reach you—or at least they are never acknowledged so I presume they didn't arrive.

I am distraught as I write this—your phone call to tell me you preferred the company of a vicious, adulterous psychotic was topped by a call from the Dean of Students ten minutes later and has kept me awake for almost 36 hours. I had to expel four seniors just two months from graduation and suspend others. What I say will ramble but it will be the truth—and I have to do something besides shriek with pain.

Let me say first that I will be with you on the 19th of April because it is right that I should be. To accuse me of calling Dan to beg for an invitation is all the more invidious since it is indeed what Lynne does all the time. I am told this repeatedly. "She keeps calling and fawning over us. It drives us crazy."

I have and never would do this—you seem to be able to expiate Lynne's sins by dumping them on me. I knew of the honor being bestowed on you before I was ever asked to speak at Columbia on the 18th.

Frankly, I thought you were waiting for Dan's invitation to surprise me—false modesty or something. I called Dan to tell him I wanted to send a contribution to be part of those honoring you and I assured him I would be there.

He said, "Lee and I want you at our table." I thanked him and assured him I would be there—"even if that slut comes—indeed I don't care if she pops naked out of a cake with her tits frosted with chocolate."

Dan laughed and said, "And you should be there and we want you with us."

I haven't played the slave for you. I would never have committed adultery for you—but I have added a dimension to your life and given you pleasure and dignity, as you have me.

As Jackie says, "Hi was always such a marvelous snob. What happened?"

I suppose my check to Dan falls into the "signing of masochistic love" department. Having just, not four weeks before, received a copy of your will with my name vigorously scratched out, and Lynne's name in your handwriting written in three places, leaving her a quarter of a million dollars and her children $25,000 apiece—and the boys and me nothing.

It is the sort of thing I have grown almost accustomed to from Lynn—that you didn't respond to my note when I returned it leaves me wondering if you send *[sic]* it together. It isn't your style—but then Lynn has changed your style. Is it the culmination of 14 years of broken promises, Hi—I hope not—"I want to buy you a whole new wardrobe, darling." "I want to get your teeth fixed at my expense, darling." "My home is your home, darling." "Welcome home darling." "The ring is yours forever darling. If you leave it with me now, I will leave it to you in my will." "You have of course been well taken care of in my will, darling." "Let me buy an apartment with you in New York darling." It didn't matter all that much, really—all I ever asked for was to be with you—and when I left you to know when we would see each other again so there was something in life to look forward to. Now you are taking that away from me too and I am unable to cope—I can hear you saying, "Look, Jean—it's your problem. I don't want to hear about it."

I have watched you grow rich in the years we have been together, and I have watched me go through moments when I was almost destitute.

I have twice borrowed fifty cents from Henri to make two of the payments on the Garden State Parkway during these five years you casually left me on my hands and knees in Philadelphia.

And now—almost ten years later—now that a thieving slut has the run of your home you accuse me of stealing money and books, and calling your friend to beg for an invitation.

The many things your whore does openly and obviously (to your friends and your SERVANTS! Sadly not to you) you now have the cruelty to accuse me of.

My father-in-law left me a library of over 5,000 books. I have given away in the past ten years more books than you own. I have thanked you most sincerely and gratefully for books you have given me.

Ninety percent of them have been given to a school library and on at least four different occasions I have asked you if you wouldn't like a letter on school stationery that you could use as a tax deduction.

Each time you have airily refused and now, for God's sake, you accuse me of stealing your books. It borders on libel.

Any time you wish to examine my home or the school library you are certainly welcome to do so—a surprise raid might be most convincing for you.

Twice I have taken money from your wallet—each time to pay for sick damage done to my property by your psychotic whore.

I don't have the money to afford a sick playmate—you do. She took a brand new nightgown that I paid $40.00 for and covered it with bright orange stains. You paid to replace it—and since you had already made it clear you simply didn't care about the obscene phone calls she made it was obviously pointless to tell you about the nightgown.

The second thing you paid for (I never replaced it) was a yellow silk dress. I bought it to wear at Lyford Cay several years ago.

Unfortunately, I forgot to pack it because it was new and still in a box in the downstairs closet. When I returned it was still in the box, rolled up, not folded now, and smeared and vile with feces.

I told you once it was something "brown and sticky." It was, quite simply, Herman Tarnower, human shit!

I decided, and rightly so, that this was your expense, not mine. As for stealing from you, the day I put my ring on your dresser my income before taxes was $12,000 per year.

I had two children in private school. They had been on a fairly sizable scholarship until I told the school I wouldn't need it because 'we were moving to Scarsdale. It was two years before we got it back.

That more than anything else is the reason David went to Penn State instead of the University of Pa. He loathed every minute of it, and there is no question that it changed his life.

That you should feel justified and comfortable suggesting that I steal from you is something I have no adjective to describe.

I desperately needed money all those years. I couldn't have sold that ring. It was tangible proof of your love and it meant more to me than life itself.

That you sold it the summer your adulterous slut finally got her divorce and needed money is a kind of sick, cynical act that left me old and bitter and sick.

Your only comment when you told me you had sold it (and less than two months before you had assured you would get it from the safe so I could wear it again) was "Look, if you're going to make a fuss about it you can't come here anymore. I don't need to have anyone spoil my weekend."

Too bad Somerset Maugham didn't get hold of us before he died. He could have come up with something to top the Magnificent Obsession.

You have never once suggested that you would meet me in Virginia at your expense, and so seeing you has been at my expense—and if you lived in California I would borrow money to come there too if you would let me.

All my conversations are my nickel, not yours—and obviously rightly so because it is I, not you, who needs to hear your voice.

I have indeed grown poor loving you, while a self-serving ignorant slut has grown very rich—and yet you accuse me of stealing from you. How in the name of Christ does that make sense?

I have, and most proudly so—and with an occasional "Right On" from Lee and others ripped up or destroyed anything I saw that your slut had touched and written her cutsie name on—including several books that I gave you and she had the tasteless, unmitigated gall to write in.

I have refrained from throwing away the cheap little book of epigrams lying on your bed one day so I would be absolutely sure to see it with a paper clip on the page about how an old man should have a young wife.

It made me feel like a piece of old discarded garbage—

but at least it solved for me what had been a mystery—
what had suddenly possessed you to start your tasteless
diatribe at dinner parties about how everyman *[sic]*
should have a wife half his age and seven years.

Since you never mentioned it to anyone under 65, it
made the wives at the table feel about as attractive and
wanted as I did.

Tasteless behavior is the only kind Lynn knows—
though to her credit she is clever and devious enough to
hide it at times. Unfortunately, it seems to be catching.

The things I know, or profess to know about Lynn—
except for what I have experienced first hand I have been
told by your friends and your servants, mostly the latter
—I was interested to hear from Vivian and Arthur's next
door neighbor in Florida. I don't remember her name
though I'm sure Lynn does.

"I took her to lunch she seemed so pathetic" that you
sat at table while I was there and discussed Lynn and her
"wonderful family—brother a Ph.D."

I can't imagine going out to dinner with you and telling my dinner partner how grand another lover is.

I told the woman to ask you somtime why if her family
is so fine, Lynn decided to sell her kids to the highest
bidder and make you and your family the guardian of her
children if she should die before they do.

It must go down as a "first" for a splendid family to
do.

My phone tells me this—that "mysterious" caller—I
hope to God you don't know who it is! Who pays him?

When my clothes were ripped to shreds Suzanne said,
"Madame, there is only one person who could have done
it. You must tell him."

In my masochistic way I tried to down play it in my
note to you, although in all honesty I thought it was so
obvious you would know who did it. Instead you ignored
it and went happily off to Florida with the perpetrator.
Suzanne told me—and I think would say so in court.

1. The clothes were not torn when she went into the
closet to find something of Henri's on "Wednesday or
Thursday" while we were away.

2. On the Sunday morning before we came home Henri and Suzanne both saw Lynn drive hurriedly up to your house. They were outside and she did not see them. They saw her go in but not out.

3. Lynn knew you were coming home that evening and that she would see you by 8:00 the next morning. What business did she have at your home that morning?

4. When I discovered the clothes destroyed Suzanne was sitting in the dining room at the wooden table right next to the door. I said, "My God—Suzanne come look!" and she was right there.

When I called your slut to talk to her about it and see what she was going to do about it she said "You cut them up yourself and blamed it on me."

That was the first time it occurred to me they had been "cut" not ripped. Only someone with a thoroughly warped mind would decide that a woman with no money would ruin about one-third of her wardrobe for kicks.

Suzanne still believes Lynn did it and I most certainly do too. I think there is enough evidence to prove it in court!

The stealing of my jewelry I can't prove at all—I just know I left some things in the white ash tray on your dresser, as I have for many years. When I thought of it later and called, Lynn answered the phone.

When I called again and asked Suzanne to take them and put them away they were gone. I only hope if she hocked them you got something nice as a "gift"—Maybe I gave you some gold cuff links after all and didn't know it. I don't for one instant think Henri or Suzanne took them.

I had never called Lynn at the office anonymously as you accused me that grim November day in 1977. I had in fact called her at the office before I left and said, since I did not have her number and could not get it I would call her at the office everytime I got an anonymous phone call if she did not immediately stop them.

Within two weeks my "mysterious" caller told me her number. I have had it ever since then. Every single time she changes it I get it.

And yet though I was the one being wronged, you refused to let me come see you that month because a lying slut had told you I was calling her. The thought of it had never crossed my mind. Her voice is vomitous to me.

The next month I called her virtually every single night only because of your rotten accusation while she sat simperingly by letting you make it.

Not once did Lynn answer the phone. At one, two, or three in the morning it was her children who answered, very quickly, TV playing.

Where does mumsie spend her nights. That she "totally neglects her children" is something Henri and Suzanne have told me. That you admire her for it is sad.

"Stupid" is certainly not the word for Lynn. In that I was totally wrong. "Dishonest, ignorant and tasteless" but God knows not stupid.

It would have been heartbreaking for me to have to see less and less of you even if it had been a decent woman who took my place.

Going through the hell of the past few years has been bearable only because you were still there and I could be with you whenever I could get away from work, which seemed to be less and less.

To be jeered at, and called "old and pathetic" made me seriously consider borrowing $5,000 just before I left New York and telling a doctor to make me young again —to do anything but make me not feel like discarded trash—I lost my nerve because there was always the chance I'd end up uglier than before.

You have been what you very carefully set out to be, Hi —the most important thing in my life, the most important human being in my life and that will never change.

You keep me in control by threatening me with banishment—an easy threat which you know I couldn't live with and so I stay home alone while you make love to someone who has almost totally destroyed me.

I have been publicly humiliated again and again but not on the 19th of April. It is the apex of your career and

I believe I have earned the right to watch it—if only from a dark corner near the kitchen.

If you wish to insist that Lee and Dan invite Lynn, so be it—whatever they may tell you they tell me and others that they dislike being with her.

Dan whispers it to me each time we meet "Why weren't you here? Lee hates it when it's Lynn."

I always thought that taking me out of your will would be the final threat. On that I believed you would be completely honest. I have every intention of dying before you do, but sweet Jesus, darling, I didn't think you would ever be dishonest about that.

The gulf between us seems wide on the phone but the moment I see you it's as though we had been together forever.

You were so absolutely perfect over David's wedding and I will always be grateful.

I wish 14 years of making love to one another and sharing so much happiness had left enough of a mark that you couldn't have casually scratched my name out of a will and written in Lynn's instead.

But for God's sake don't translate that into begging for money. I would far rather be saved the trial of living without you than have the option of living with your money.

Give her all the money she wants, Hi—but give me time with you and the privilege of sharing with you April 19th—There were a lot of ways to have money—I very consciously picked working hard, supporting myself, and being with you.

Please, darling—don't tell me now it was all for nothing.

She has you every single moment in March—for Christ's sake give me April—T.S. Eliot said it's the cruelest month. Don't let it be, Hi.

I want to spend every minute of it with you on weekends. In all these years you've never spent my birthday with me—There aren't a lot left—it goes so quickly.

I give you my word if you just aren't cruel I won't

make you wretched. I never did until you were cruel—
and then I just wasn't ready for it.

Sometime on Saturday, in between scribbling paragraphs of
her letter, Jean Harris began to write her will. She quickly hid it
when some students walked in unexpectedly, then couldn't find
it, and on Monday began a new will. She does not recall Sunday
morning, nor much of Sunday evening.

At ten minutes to seven in the morning on Monday, March
10, one of the servants saw Lynne Tryforos leave the doctor's
house. Not long thereafter, Herman Tarnower headed for his
office, which is where Jean Harris finally got through to him
after trying for four days straight. It was 9:59 A.M., according
to phone company records, and the call lasted six minutes. The
main reason she was calling, Mrs. Harris would say later, was
to ask him not to read the eleven-page letter she had just put in
the mail on the way to her own office. "My role with Hi was
. . . to be good company and not to be a whiner. And it was a
very whiney letter," she told the jury, which was rather like
calling the Book of Revelations "a very downbeat yarn."

The headmistress turned to her morning mail. One little letter was from Jean's special pet, the girl disfigured in the Brazen
Hussies incident. In a round, childish hand with tiny circles
dotting the *i*'s, and a smiling cartoon for a signature, the youngster had written, ". . . this isn't a 'hate' letter at all. I just feel
that you are not handling the situation correctly. . . ." She
went on to say that lots of people at Madeira smoked pot, and
everybody knew it. Therefore it had been "hypocritical" of the
headmistress to punish only four girls for something one hundred girls did. To Jean Harris, hypocrisy was the very antithesis
of integrity—and so, with this faint feather-dusting of criticism,
Miss Infallible finally crumpled.

"It sort of put a box on my life," Jean Harris would tell the
jury. She had called in two seasoned teachers and, in tones of
rising distress, she had read them the letter aloud. "They did
not think it was so bad. I thought it was the end of the world.
. . . I overreacted, I realize now. But I couldn't really function
from then on."

What triggers a decision to take one's life? Very often when an individual feels forced to make a choice, and each alternative seems equally impossible, she makes the other choice, death. To be called a "hypocrite" by her favorite child was proof to Jean, in her frazzled state, that the last of her support systems had now been knocked out from under her. Her family, her lover, her "new life" at Madeira, her peers, the Druids, and finally the girls themselves—one by one they had all abandoned her. The little letter was the last straw, the "triggering event," Jean said: thereafter, suicide seemed her only choice.

"Hi, it's been a bad few weeks," Jean Harris recalls saying when she finally got through to Dr. Tarnower for the second time that day, back at his home at 5:16 P.M. on Monday afternoon. "I'd like to come up and talk to you for a few minutes."

"Debbie's coming to dinner," he said. Debbie Schwartz Raizes, his sister Billie's daughter, was his favorite niece. No need for him to mention that Lynne Tryforos was expected too.

"She always leaves early. And I wouldn't get there before ten-thirty."

"It would be more convenient if you came tomorrow."

"But I can't talk to you tomorrow. Please, Hi. Just this once, let *me* say when."

"Suit yourself," he replied.

Jean felt as good as she always did when she turned off Purchase Street and saw her headlights picking up the long curve of his driveway. . . . *I won't stay too long . . . won't let him know what I'm going to do . . . won't let him spoil my resolve* . . . The house at the end of the driveway was dark. The rain had let up slightly. She was surprised not to see any lights, but perhaps he had left the door ajar. She parked in front of the steep, short flight of steps and was starting up them when she remembered the white daisies someone had left in her car. He might like those. She went back, opened the door on the passenger's side, and when she reached in for the flowers her hand touched her pocketbook. She picked them up together. The sliding glass front door was locked, so she went around through the garage, as everybody did. The light switch was right beside Tarnower's blue Cadillac. She climbed the narrow spiral staircase with treads like the blades of an old wooden ceiling fan.

The ground floor of the house was dark, and quiet except for the sound of the rain.

"Hi," she called softly up the next flight of spiral stairs. "Hi?"

No reply, so she started up, the pocketbook under her arm, the flowers in her hand. She is left-handed, and she steadied herself with her left hand on the coiling iron banister. It was pitch-dark, but she could hear him begin to stir. His bed was the one nearer the stairs, and she walked carefully around it, feeling her way until she found the narrow, eighteen-inch aisle between the beds and sat down on "her" bed. She felt for the tricky, three-way light switch that illuminated first his bed, next the shelf with the phone, and finally her bed. She clicked the switch once and his little reading light went on. The rest of the room remained in shadow. He was just waking up, rubbing his eyes.

"Hi, I thought you would leave a lamp in the window. It's black as pitch out there!"

"Jesus, Jean, it's the middle of the night!" The electric clock on the shelf over his head, next to his glasses, said almost ten-forty.

"It's not really that late, and I'm not going to stay very long. I just came to talk with you for a while."

"Well, I'm not going to talk to anybody in the middle of the night!" and he rolled onto his left side, facing her, one pastel-flowered pillow under his head, the other clutched to his chest. "I don't feel like talking in the middle of the night." He shut his eyes.

She sat for a moment, waiting for his eyes to open again, knowing he was used to middle of the night phone calls, knowing how quickly he could awaken and dress and race out. But this night he did not stir. She waited.

Finally, "I brought you some flowers."

No reply.

"Have you written any more on the book?"

"Jesus, Jean. Shut up and go to bed."

"I can't go to bed, dear. I'm not going to stay that long. I'm just going to be here a little while." No answer. She waited. He lay motionless. "Won't you really talk to me for just a little while?" Still no reply from the figure in blue pajamas clutching his pillow, eyes closed.

She sat waiting, unsure what to do next, not wanting to leave, not believing he was asleep, and certain that if he was, he would wake up at any moment, shove the other pillow behind his head, and say with a smile, "You're some kind of nut, Jean, to drive five hours in the middle of the night just to *talk!* But . . . what do you want to talk about?"

She sat a while longer, and then she said, "I left a shawl here, and I want to be sure Kathleen has it. So I'll just go get it." She had left the black shawl on "her" side of the dressing room.

She got up, leaving her things on the bed, flowers near the pillow, pocketbook toward the foot, and walked around back into the dressing area behind the huge, fretwork headboard. She turned on the lights and pulled open a drawer. The black shawl was underneath some other things—gloves, handkerchiefs, lingerie—and she took them all out and came back around to the front side of the headboard. She saw he was still lying with his eyes shut, and she placed the shawl in the center of her bed with the other things on top. He was surely wide awake now but obviously annoyed at her intrusion. She turned and went back to "her" bathroom, at the east end of the dressing area, and flipped on the bathroom light.

A strange greenish-blue satin negligee embroidered with bright flowers glimmered on the hook. Strange gold slippers with curled-up Turkish toes glittered on the floor. On the shelf, the familiar box of pink electric curlers. Strange jewelry in a box on the sink. She snatched at the negligee, stormed around the corner of the headboard, yelling, flung the loathsome thing on the floor, and rushed back into the bathroom. She was hurt, frustrated, enraged. She knew to whom these things belonged. The script wasn't working out as she had planned. She had looked forward to a few quiet minutes together, to feeling "safe" one more time; that wasn't happening. She grabbed the curlers, yelled, flung them through the open door. *Crash* of broken glass. She had thrown it in the direction opposite to where he lay sleeping, and had broken the dressing-room window. But he was not sleeping. As she rounded the end of the headboard this time, still yelling, he was standing there in the shadows, and he smacked her hard across the mouth. She retreated to the bathroom and blindly snatched up the jewelry box. *Crash!* Her own big cosmetic mirror shattered. She dashed back around the headboard, and he struck her hard in the mouth a second time. He was very angry. She sank down onto the edge of her bed, defeated. The tender plans she had made in Virginia were not happening. Now she just wanted to die. She pulled her hair back behind her ears with either hand and raised her face to him and closed her eyes.

"Hit me again, Hi. Make it hard enough to kill me."

She waited, wondering how much it would hurt. She heard him walk away.

"Get out of here. You're crazy," he said.

It was very quiet. She could hear the rain on the deck outside the sliding glass doors. There was nothing to do now but leave. She stood up and walked toward the foot of her bed. She would go down to the pond. But when she picked up her pocketbook and felt the weight of the gun, she thought, "What difference does that make now?" She was facing southeast toward the sliding glass doors and her back was to him as she unzipped the leather bag and grasped the gun in her left hand.

"Never mind, Hi. I'll do it myself," she said, and she raised the gun to her temple.

He sprang at her from behind and as he knocked her hand downward and away from her head she heard the gun explode. "Jesus Christ! Look what you've done!" he shouted. Turning, she saw the blood and the small, neat bullet hole in the web of flesh at the base of his right thumb.

They stood staring at each other for a moment, then without a word he turned and walked away and disappeared around his end of the massive headboard. She could hear the water running in his bathroom. She began to follow him, then realized she had not seen him carry the gun to the bathroom; it still must be somewhere in the room. If she found it fast enough she could get everything over with before he could return and stop her.

The gun was nowhere visible on the floor or on the twelve-foot square green-flecked rug beneath the beds. She got down on her hands and knees between the beds and saw the gun way under her own bed, almost touching the headboard. She reached in and got it with her left hand, and she had just sat back down on her heels, facing the telephone now, and started to raise it to her head again when suddenly her upper arm was clamped hard from behind in an iron grip. The pain forced her to drop the gun, and he picked it up. She had not heard him coming, and thought later that he must have dived at her right across the foot of his bed.

Now he sat on the edge of his bed facing her. He held the gun in his injured right hand, which he had wrapped in a wet towel. At one point he set it down on the bed beside his right hand. With his left hand he pushed the big white buzzer several times, the one that summoned the servants. She had swiveled around, still on her knees, and now knelt in front of him, panicky that at any moment the Van der Vrekens might come running upstairs in response to the buzzer.

"Hi, please give me the gun! Give me the gun, or shoot me yourself, *but for Christ's sake let me die.*"

Tarnower looked down at her. "Jesus, Jean, you're crazy!" he said. "Get out of here!"

With his left hand the doctor picked up his phone to speak to his servants, whom he expected to respond to his buzzing.

To this point, Jean's recollection of the sequence of events seems to her clear, precise, entire. Hereafter, many details remain precise, but there are holes, gaps, inexplicable lacunae. When she reruns this next part of the film in the movie of her memory, it is as if certain frames have been snipped out and the film respliced. She knows that she and Dr. Tarnower engaged in a furious and close struggle over the gun—bruises on her eye and upper lip and a huge discoloration on her upper left arm are evidence—but what follows is every single bit about that struggle which she can now remember. It is the "respliced struggle film" in its entirety. Because the splice-marks are invisible, she cannot tell exactly where within the sequence the missing frames must once have been—the frames that would show the firing of the two fatal shots.

Nor does she know at what point the patchy memory—or patchy amnesia—ends.

Such amnesia is extremely common, psychiatrists agree, when an individual experiences the sudden onslaught of severe emotional stress. Brain function is essentially electrochemical, and when this type of amnesia occurs, it is as if the overwhelming emotional experience temporarily blows all the fuses. Thereafter the body acts "automatically," but separated from all one's rational and critical faculties, and even one's self-awareness. Although many individuals are known to have undergone such an emotional "blowout," or "overload"—it probably happens most frequently under battlefield conditions—one hallmark of the phenomenon is that invariably it is a once-in-a-lifetime experience.

In Jean Harris's case, psychiatrists later would theorize, the sudden emotional stress brought on by a concatenation of Tarnower's physical assault, his utter rejection, and his total unresponsiveness to her appeal for help—none of which had fully happened ever before—was compounded by the physical stress caused by prolonged lack of sleep, lack of food, and lack of her accustomed amphetamines. "The great horror of realizing that she was serious about suicide, and *still* he does nothing to stop her, or even to soothe her—that must really have flipped her," one of the doctors who later examined her has said. "She may not have fully, wholeheartedly wanted him to stop her suicide . . . but surely she wanted him to *want to* stop her."

Jean saw the gun was now on the doctor's lap. She put her hand on his knees to pull herself up from her kneeling position on the floor. When she had pulled herself up sufficiently to get her feet under her and gain her balance, though not yet enough to be standing erect, she grabbed with her left hand and got hold of the gun, her finger on the trigger. Immediately he dropped the phone and used his left hand to grip Jean's left wrist hard. She was pulling back away from him, trying to get free of his grip, in a kind of tug-of-war over the gun, and then she felt the pressure momentarily let up, and suddenly she fell back across her own bed and he lunged forward on top of her. He seemed to be trying to tackle her. She saw a flash of his hands coming toward her and felt them close around her waist. Now they were in a prone or not-quite prone clinch, he on top, and she felt something hard poking into her lower abdomen. It must be the muzzle of the gun, she thought, which was still in her left hand. Consciously, deliberately, she squeezed the trigger. Another very loud explosion. *My God, that didn't hurt at all!* she thought. *I should have done it a long time ago!* Then he fell back off her body, and she jumped up and ran. She needed to get far enough away from him to shoot herself in the head before he could catch her again.

She ran around to the other side of his bed until she was at about the same latitude as the massive headboard, midway between the staircase and his bathroom, facing in his direction. He remained between the beds, seemingly on his knees now. She was not positive about that. The important thing was that he had stopped chasing her. She stood still, took a very deep breath, raised the gun to her temple, and pulled the trigger.

Click!

Startled, she lowered the gun and looked at it. She had been careful to load it fully down in Virginia precisely to avoid playing Russian roulette. Still looking at the weapon in her hand, she pulled the trigger again. *Boom!* So she put it back to her head, and now she shot and shot and shot and shot, and the gun went *click, click, click, click.* Either the gun was not working, or it was empty. She grew panicky. She had to find more bullets and get them into it and be dead before Suzanne and Henri came pounding up the stairs. She remembered putting extra bullets in her jacket pocket while she was loading the gun in Virginia. But where was the jacket? She did not remember taking it off. She raced around the shadowy room and finally found it lying on the floor next to the TV set, over at the far end of the sliding glass doors, on "her" side of the bedroom. She ran into her well-lit bathroom and shook the fur jacket upside down. Bullets and coins bounced onto the tiles. She swung open the cylinder and clawed at the spent cartridges, trying to push or pull them out with her fingertips. They would not move. She had no ice pick. Frantically she banged the weapon against the bathtub, hoping to jar them loose. On the third try the gun flew out of her hand. She picked it up from the tub and saw the cylinder had broken free. She tried to force it back into place and, still jamming and shoving at the cylinder, she returned to the bedroom in time to see him dropping the telephone receiver and attempting to pull himself up from his knees onto her bed. She ran to the phone. The line was dead. Not even a dial tone. She jiggled the cradle but nothing happened.

"Hi, it's broken. I think it's dead."

"You're probably right," he said.

You're probably right—the last words she would hear him utter. With her help, he got onto his own bed and she helped him to lie back across the blue velour blanket. His arms were stretched out wide, and his color was poor. He looked exhausted, she thought, as she hurried down the spiral staircase, starting to be aware he was injured, rushing now for help. The dining-room lights were on now, and she could hear Suzanne in there talking. But the front door and steps were dark.

"Somebody turn on the goddamn lights! I'm going for help!" She fumbled at the panel of door switches. Lights blazed and she ran into the rain and jumped in her car and streaked out the driveway, racing for the pay phone at the Westchester Community Center a quarter-mile away.

Through the rain she could see the dim glow of the phone booth light, but just as she began to turn into the parking lot, a police car with flashing lights bore down on her from the direction of Anderson Hill Road. She made a U-turn and headed back toward the house, the police car following. Both cars pulled up and she jumped out and ran over to the policeman.

"Hurry up! Hurry up! He's been shot!"

They ran up the steps. Henri Van der Vreken stood at the top, silhouetted against the glass door, screaming, "She's the one! She did it! She's the one!"

Suzanne, Jean Harris, and the policeman ran upstairs to the bedroom. Herman Tarnower was now on his knees between the two beds, slumped against the white telephone, its bloody receiver dangling down. With Suzanne's help, the police officer gently laid the wounded man down on his back between the beds. Though the room was but dimly lit, the officer could see enough to send him dashing downstairs for emergency oxygen. Kneeling beside him, Suzanne took the doctor's hand and spoke to him gently.

Lying across the foot of his bed on her stomach, Jean Harris caressed his face. "Oh, Hi, why didn't you kill me?" she said.

The doctor seemed unable to talk. Moments earlier he had spoken perfectly clearly. Mrs. Harris looked at the bloody telephone. After she left, the doctor must have got off the bed and tried once more to call for help. She was clear about that. She was less clear and would remain unclear about how many times Tarnower had been shot. She would not really know what happened to him until months later, when she read the autopsy surgeon's report. Louis Roh, M.D., said that four bullets had penetrated the doctor's body. One had entered high on the right anterior chest wall, nicked the collarbone, severed the big sub-clavian vein, and dropped into the chest cavity. Another bullet had entered the top of the rear right shoulder and ripped straight downward and slightly back to frontward, breaking three ribs, piercing the diaphragm, and lodging in the right kidney. Massive internal bleeding from these wounds was the cause of death. A third bullet had gone almost completely through the doctor's right arm, above the elbow, shattering the bone. Then there was the bullet hole through his palm.

Police officers soon swarmed the scene and Jean Harris freely admitted that she had done the shooting. She led them out to her car where the gun lay on the front seat. Then they returned to the foyer. She told the police that she had come there in-tending to kill herself, and she gave them the note in her purse listing her next of kin. Other notes were at her home in Vir-ginia, she said. She refused medical attention for the bruise near her eye, and for the swelling purple-red mark on her upper lip where the doctor had struck her.

"Who had control of the gun?" asked Detective Arthur Siciliano of the Harrison Police Department.

"I don't know."

"Who owned the gun?"

"It's mine."

"Who did the shooting? Do you recall holding the gun?"

"I recall holding the gun and shooting him in the hand," she said, and she began to weep.

Upstairs, the cops had finally succeeded in strapping the doc-tor onto a flexible stretcher, and now they lowered him head-first down the circular stairway shaft. The job took five men. Just as Jean was begging police for permission to see him, the stretcher was carried past her. His face was exposed and his right arm flopped crazily. Jean Harris fainted in Detective Siciliano's arms.

Later the detective would repeat other statements the suspect made to him, statements that Jean Harris did not remember making. "She told me she had driven up from Virginia with the hope of being killed by Dr. Tarnower. She then hesitated a second and said, 'He wanted to live, I wanted to die.' She hesitated. She said, 'I've been through so much hell with him. I loved him very much. He slept with every woman he could, and I'd *had it!*' and she motioned in this fashion," said the detective, pushing both hands downward and away from himself.

"The policemen were all very kind to me that night," Jean Harris later told a friend. "There wasn't anyone who pushed me around in the least. In fact, they *couldn't* have been nicer! They kept saying, 'Do you want a doctor?' and I said no. They said, 'Do you want a lawyer?' and I said no. But when they said, 'All right, we're going to take you to the police station,' I said, 'You mean you're going to *arrest* me!' This was how dumb I was. When they said 'Yes,' that's when I said, 'Then I want a lawyer.' "

Marge and Leslie Jacobson were asleep in their Manhattan apartment when the telephone rang. Marge answered and a man identified himself as a member of the Harrison Police Department and asked for Leslie. "There's a young woman up here who's in very deep trouble."

Leslie picked up the phone and could hear Henri Van der Vreken shouting in the background, "Mr. Jacobson, Mrs. Harris has shot the doctor!"

"What! Put Mrs. Harris on the phone!"

"Leslie," she said. "I think I've killed Hi."

"Do not utter another word," he commanded. He was on his way. While they dressed he told Marge to call William Riegelman, a member of his firm who lives in White Plains, and have him get over to the police station immediately. A slim corporate lawyer in his late sixties, Riegelman is the son of one of the firm's original founders, and he has worked there ever since his graduation from law school in 1938. Like his father, Riegelman is a lifelong member of Century, and as it happened, his locker was next to Tarnower's. He had known the doctor twenty years.

Riegelman arrived at the tiny Harrison Police Station just as Jean Harris was being booked for aggravated assault. He saw a woman with a bad bruise on her lip, and another near her right eye. She wore a blood-smeared white blouse. It was 11:55 P.M. Three minutes later a call came in from St. Agnes Hospital. The desk sergeant told Riegelman that Herman Tarnower had been pronounced dead, and he was changing the charge against his client to murder. Jean Harris crumpled sobbing in the lawyer's arms.

The Jacobsons arrived an hour later. Jean told Leslie about all the notes she had left in her house in Virginia, and the certified letter she had posted to Tarnower that morning. He hurried to call Alice Faulkner, Chairman of the Madeira Board, and told her to get over to Jean's house and recover as many documents as possible before the police arrived. He awakened a lawyer in his Washington office and arranged to collect the documents and fly them to New York. Jacobson spent the entire night on the telephone, orchestrating the recovery of as much documentary evidence as possible of his client's intentions, and negotiating, unsuccessfully, for her release on bail.

Marge called her godson, David Harris, and told him to come down to the police station; his mother had been involved in a bad accident. She allowed him to assume it was an auto accident "because I didn't want him to come there not alive." She awakened Mary Margaret Lynch, Jean's eldest sister, in Cleveland. "There's been a terrible accident. A gun went off. Hi is dead, and Leslie thinks someone from the family should be here." Jacobson did not want to take sole responsibility for choosing a trial lawyer to handle Jean's defense. He told Riegelman to have his wife, Roz, pack a bag and bring Jean some clean clothes. As the police later discovered, Jean had blood on her blouse, skirt, belt, shoes, bra, and hair. It was five in the morning before the Jacobsons left the Harrison Police Station.

The police and the District Attorney's staff spent the night scrambling for evidence. To obtain the necessary search warrant from a sleepy Virginia judge, they assured him Mrs. Harris was in custody and had "confessed" to the crime. While Jean was being booked as a murder suspect, a kindly police matron permitted her to wash out her blood-smeared white nylon blouse. Wearing only her short fur jacket over her bra, the suspect was escorted to the police station jail. Every time they started to close the door to her cell, Jean Harris screamed uncontrollably. Finally they agreed to leave the door open, providing a fellow prisoner was willing to sit up and keep watch from a chair in the corridor. Minnie Jones got busted once a week for shoplifting; the guards knew and trusted her. Mrs. Harris spent her first night in jail curled in a fetal position, watched over by the benevolent booster of three polyester pantsuits.

The next morning in the Greenway, Virginia, post office, in the basement of Madeira's main building, a clerk placed a small brown-paper package in the headmistress's mailbox. It bore the label of the Scarsdale Medical Group, and inside were two full vials of Desoxyn. The package was addressed to Jean Harris, but the prescription was made out in the name of one of Herman Tarnower's female office assistants.

III

After

15

"It Could Happen to Anyone!"

SHORTLY AFTER MIDNIGHT ON March 11, 1980, Lynne Tryforos was awakened by a telephone call from Billie Schwartz. "There's been a terrible accident," she said.

Mrs. Tryforos spent much of the next twenty-four hours on the telephone. It was two o'clock when she awakened Vivian and Arthur Schulte and told them their dearest friend had been murdered. When she hung up, Schulte said, "If he's dead, why couldn't she have waited until morning?"

At 6:46 A.M. the private line rang at the bedside of Mrs. John Loeb. "This is Lynne," said the voice, and told her the news. Half an hour later the phone rang again. The news was now on the radio, Lynne said, and she suggested it might be easier on Mr. Loeb if he heard it first from his wife.

"Punch" Sulzberger, publisher of *The New York Times,* and his sister Judy wanted to break the news to their elderly mother before she read it on the front page of the family newspaper. Judy was elected to make the call to Iphigene.

"Mother, something terrible has happened. But it's *not* the children. They're fine, and we're all fine."

"Yes, yes. What is it?"

"It's Hi, Mother. He's dead."

"What do you mean, dead?"

"He's been shot, Mother. Murdered. Jean Harris did it."

There was a very long pause, and then Mrs. Sulzberger said, "Murdered! I've never known anyone who was murdered before."

Within hours, the dreadful news had saturated all of Herman's world. Joseph Cullman III was yachting off the China coast with his first wife, Sue, when he got the cablegram. Peg Cullman was at her winter home in Barbados and got a call from her late husband's city doctor. "I didn't want you to hear it on the radio, but Hi's been shot and they're holding Jean Harris."

"Oh, my God, it's finally happened."

Gerda Stedman had learned of Tarnower's death on the seven o'clock radio news from Puerto Rico. In midmorning her island telephone rang: "Mrs. Stedman, this is Lynne Tryforos. Do you remember me? I met you on the boat with Hi?"

"Of course I remember you."

"And you've heard?"

"Yes."

"Then I just want to let you know that you are mentioned in his will. He left you ten thousand dollars."

When Leslie Jacobson and his partners asked for the name of the best criminal defense lawyer in White Plains, everybody mentioned Joel Martin Aurnou, a short, smart, badger-shaped, cigar-chomping courthouse regular, forty-nine years old, who had briefly been a county judge and was active in local Democratic politics. Aurnou had got his first call from Jacobson in the early morning hours of March 11. At the jail he met a sobbing woman who could say only that she didn't care what happened to her, and didn't want a defense. She had a big bruise on her lip and a seven-inch purple discoloration on her upper left arm. Aurnou spent the day arranging medical attention and bail, interviewing his tearful client as best he could, and fending off the reporters who had descended on Westchester like a flock of starlings. It looked like the case of a lifetime; he wanted to proceed with care. "Listen, fellas, you gotta understand my client!" he barked, stalling for time until he could understand her better himself. "She's very much a lady!"

That morning Naomi Richey, Marge's mother, got through on the telephone to Al Struven in Florida. The old man was in a rage. "This thing is going to break up the family!" he shouted. "It's going to cost me a million dollars!"

By Wednesday, bail was set at $40,000. Jean's father declined to contribute. The money was put up by Jean's brother, Captain Robert Struven, USN, who had flown in from California, and by her two sisters, who had arrived from Cleveland. Virginia had been married for some years to a well-to-do businessman, Fred McLaughlin, and Mary Margaret had long been the wife of Danny Lynch, an Irish Catholic who had done well in the trucking business.

Late Wednesday the Jacobsons called Jean and her family together at the Riegelmans' house to advise them of their legal options; the spouses and the Riegelmans waited in another room. Jean looked numb and shrunken. Marge spoke first. "Jean, everybody's here now, and we can't do anything for Hi, so let's do the best for you we can."

Leslie explained the situation. His presentation lasted over an hour. Aurnou had been everybody's middle-of-the-night recommendation as defense counsel, he said, but they were not compelled to stick with him for the long haul. "There are other options. For example, we might get Racehorse Haynes, from Texas, though you have to consider that he's a Southerner with a Southern accent, and the likelihood of having a number of blacks on a White Plains jury is great." He mentioned Melvin Belli and F. Lee Bailey, and said the trouble with both was not only that they are expensive; the client is guilty in so many of their cases that their mere presence in a courtroom telegraphs guilt to a jury. He mentioned Edward Bennett Williams, but said he was very expensive, and also not a local man. "This is your decision," he told the family. "You must make it together."

No one spoke. Finally, Jean said, "I don't really care whether I live or not, and I've got very little money, maybe twenty-five thousand dollars in cash, plus my Chinese porcelains [twelve or fourteen pieces of Lowestoft that turned out not to be worth much], so I don't want an expensive lawyer."

No one else said a word. Marge was astonished when nobody said thank you to Leslie, nobody said, "Thank God you're here." No one said, "Whom do *you* recommend that we choose?" No one asked, "How much money will it take?" Nobody even said, "Jean, for God's sake stop worrying about the money!" In the dead silence it grew clear that Joel Aurnou, who had already agreed to take the case for Jean's $25,000, was thenceforth the man in charge.

"Dr. Herman Tarnower exists no more," the rabbi intoned at the funeral on Thursday. "His life's song was broken off halfway." The tall, gray woman, her rouged face ravaged by grief, was Billie Schwartz, leaning on the arm of her husband, Jack. The black-coated blonde in a black scarf who had slipped in the side door was Lynne Tryforos. The rabbi compared the dead man to Albert Einstein.

In the end, science lost out to orthodoxy, and despite his wish to be cremated, Herman Tarnower was buried in the ground in Mount Hope Cemetery in the traditional Jewish manner. Among the four hundred mourners at the temple had been David and James Harris, representing their mother. The day before, Joel Aurnou had received a call from another Westchester attorney, Roger Sirlin, who said he represented the estate of Herman Tarnower, and also the Schwartzes, Mrs. Tryforos, and the Van der Vrekens. Sirlin told Aurnou that, to avoid any possible hysterical outburst, his clients thought it best that Aurnou's client not attend the funeral, despite her wish to do so, and Aurnou had agreed. Three days after the killing, emotional fires in Scarsdale again were banked, the lid was on, and the laws of God and man appeared firmly back in control.

"Are they *allowed* to do that?"

Press photographers swarm over the tiny Harrison town courtroom. A telephoto lens pokes up at her over the back of the judge's empty chair. Three more cameras stare in through a crack in the doorway behind the bench. "Are they allowed?" she repeats, incredulous, annoyed.

Aurnou ignores the question. "How *are* you, Jean?" he says

gravely. The hand he places across her shoulders holds a dead cigar.

"Not good," she says, turning her head just slightly, chin in hand, to peek at still more rows of reporters on the benches behind her. In profile she looks no more than thirty. Her complexion is fine and transparent; a blue vein beats in her cheek. The lovely face turns further, and—is it a mustache? a birthmark?—something indigo blue and the size of a nickel tattoos the right side of her downy upper lip.

Bang of gavel, swirl of robes, and on Friday, March 14, four days after Herman Tarnower's death, the preliminary hearing in the case of the People of the State of New York against Jean S. Harris is under way. Patrolman Daniel O'Sullivan, sallow, wearing a windbreaker, climbs into the witness box. Mrs. Harris stares at him intently while he focuses his own gaze on the airspace above her neat blonde head. "Inside the front door I saw a white female standing. She stated to myself and Detective Siciliano that Dr. Tarnower had been shot, and was in the bedroom upstairs. Detective Siciliano asked who shot him, and Mrs. Harris stated, 'I shot him. I did it.' Detective Siciliano then advised Mrs. Harris of her rights."

Without taking her eyes off the witness, Mrs. Harris extends her hand to her lawyer for a pencil, like a surgeon requesting a clamp.

"Detective Siciliano asked where the weapon was. She stated it was in her car. . . . She stated that Dr. Tarnower and herself had an argument and a fight in Dr. Tarnower's bedroom. . . . She further stated that Dr. Tarnower had pushed her away and told her, 'Get out of here, you are crazy!' . . . She stated the struggle then resumed and that several shots were fired. . . . Detective Siciliano asked her who pulled the trigger. . . . She stated she didn't know."

It is time to cross-examine. Her lawyer stands up. "Officer, did my client say to you in words or in substance that she had asked the doctor to kill her, because she wanted to die?"

"Yes."

"Did she tell you she had no intention of going back to Virginia alive?"

"Yes." At each question O'Sullivan regards the microphone like a trout eyeing a hook, then snaps off his reply.

"Did she tell you specifically that she did not even know who pulled the trigger?"

"Yes."

Snow blows in through an open transom. The defendant trembles. She wears a lightweight coat, expensive shoes. She draws the lawyer's ski parka over her knees. A brief recess is called. The judge and lawyers withdraw, and the room falls silent. Snow melts in puddles on the floor. The defendant sits hunched and trembling, her back to the courtroom, guarded by two beefy investigators who flank the defense table like a pair of library lions.

A tall, thin woman in the front row leans forward. "Mrs. Harris, may I talk to you? I went to Madeira."

"No questions, lady!" growls one of the lions. The woman sits back.

Five minutes later Jean Harris suddenly swivels fully around. *"Did you really go to Madeira?"*

"Yes. I'm Lally Weymouth. Kay Graham's daughter."

If Jean Harris has never heard of Mrs. Weymouth, at that moment a reporter for *The Village Voice,* she certainly knows her mother, even though Jean did not assume command of Madeira until long after both Mrs. Graham and her daughter had walked under the ribboned graduation archways of white roses and moved on out into the grubbier world of journalism. The headmistress is appalled to have to face any Madeira graduate, let alone this one, at so grotesque a moment. She is about to be charged with murder. That she knows she is innocent of intentional homicide does nothing to alleviate her overwhelming despair. Her ruin is entire, ludicrous in its totality. She has not only failed at her own suicide, she has managed in the process to kill the one person she most loved. Adding to her intense feelings of personal grief and guilt is a sickening sense of shame at the notoriety she has brought on the school. The sudden apparition behind her now of the granddaughter of the Founding Father of the institution she feels she has so vilely betrayed seems to Mrs. Harris almost surreal in its horror. She stares at the blank notebook lying open on Mrs. Weymouth's well-dressed lap.

"Madeira doesn't need *this!*" is all the headmistress can think to say. She wants to melt into the floor and disappear like the snow puddles at her feet.

But Mrs. Harris has not reckoned with the flawless Madeira training of the woman with whom she speaks. *"Keep calm at the center of your being." "Function in disaster, finish in style!"* And so, when Mrs. Harris turns around and, looking stricken, says, "Madeira doesn't need *this!*" Mrs. Weymouth smiles back brightly and replies reassuringly, "Don't be silly, Mrs. Harris. It could happen to anyone!"

It is this essential Madeira tone of voice—mindless, mannerly, and *wrong*—that colors everything that is to follow: hearings, trial, imprisonment.

Bang of gavel; the hearing resumes. Seated around the prosecution table, the men of the Westchester County District Attorney's office strive to look professionally grave. These are men accustomed to a heavy, monotonous diet of assaults, burglaries, dope busts, and drunk driving offenses. Now they tingle with anticipation at the prospect of handling a world-class crime of passion complete with celebrity victim and high-society defendant. Socko headlines guaranteed. The case is not a whodunit but a whydunit, and the DA's men are confident they know the why. Jealousy, pure and simple. Open-and-shut case. Discarded mistress, having lost her man to a younger woman, decides, "If I can't have him, nobody can," and in said frame of mind, marches into her faithless lover's bedroom and pumps four bullets into his sleeping body. Throughout these lengthy courtroom proceedings, the men at the prosecution table wear the carefully straight faces of car salesmen at the point of sale.

Joel Aurnou and his several assistants are arguing that Dr. Tarnower's death was an accidental homicide that occurred during a struggle over a gun. It cannot be "murder," he tells the court, because murder is by definition intentional, and there is no way anyone can prove that Jean Harris intended to kill her lover.

"All I need to prove intent," the chief prosecutor had boasted to a reporter during the recess, "is Herman Tarnower's body and four bullet holes."

After three hours of argument and evidence, the judge rules that some sort of felony has been committed. Whether it was

murder, manslaughter in either the first or the second degree, or
criminally negligent homicide—all of which are felonies—is not
his business to decide. The judge's ruling gives the DA a green
light to take his claim of second-degree murder to the Grand
Jury.

The day after the hearing, Saturday, found Jean Harris increasingly unable to cooperate with her lawyer. She insisted she
wanted only to die; life without Tarnower was not worth living.
She had now decided that *none* of her savings should be used
for her defense, she declared, because that would only deprive
her sons of their rightful inheritance. Her tearfulness, agitation,
and talk of suicide had increased markedly. Psychiatrists were
summoned; they agreed she was severely disturbed and required
hospitalization. There followed several difficult hours, with Jean
refusing to accept the idea of a psychiatric hospital, saying she
was not crazy, and the whole idea was just a lawyers' ruse to
earn her public sympathy. If everyone hated her, she argued,
she would be able to die sooner. Meanwhile, the doctors were
trying to find a Westchester psychiatric hospital that would accept Jean Harris as a patient. (The terms of her bail required
that she not leave the county without court permission.) This
was not easy. One hospital was fearful of the attendant publicity; another would not accept her without major medical insurance, which she could not prove that Madeira provided. Finally
she was admitted to the psychiatric ward of United Hospital in
Port Chester and placed under the care of its chief psychiatrist,
Abraham Halpern, M.D. Here she was diagnosed as being in an
acute suicidal depression with transient psychotic features, and
placed in a special room where she could be kept under twenty-
four-hour suicide watch.

According to the official psychiatrists' handbook,* a diagnosis of "depression" requires at least four of the following symptoms: poor appetite and unintentional weight loss; insomnia;
psychomotor agitation; loss of interest in life; decreased sex
drive; loss of energy and sense of fatigue; feelings of self-re-
proach; feelings of worthlessness; inappropriate feelings of guilt;
inability to concentrate; bizarre behavior; and recurrent suicidal

---

* *The Diagnostic and Statistical Manual of Mental Disorders, Third Edition.*

ideation. At this point, Jean Harris had them all. She remained in the hospital ten days, and was treated with sedatives and tranquilizers and simple psychotherapy. Gradually she got over the idea that she had been "tricked" into signing voluntary admission papers, and accepted the idea that her doctors, lawyers, and family were in fact trying to help her. But she still cried bitterly and almost continually for Herman Tarnower, and for the disgrace she had brought upon Madeira. She saw no difference between an accidental killing and an intentional one, she said; Tarnower was just as dead either way, and her own life was over. She told a fellow patient that the reason she had not committed suicide at her home in Virginia was because she could not bear the thought of future generations of Madeira girls strolling past the house and pointing out, "That's where the crazy headmistress killed herself." Also, she said, she had wanted to go "home" to die.

Each time she saw or talked to Joel Aurnou she reminded him of the promise she had extracted at their first meeting, that he would never do or say anything in the course of her defense that would in any way besmirch the good name of Herman Tarnower or of the Madeira School.

Gradually, painfully, and unwillingly Jean Harris began to understand for the first time that she had been seriously depressed for many, many years, and that for the past decade her chronic depression had to a degree been masked by the drug she was taking. When she occasionally asked Dr. Halpern for Desoxyn, saying it was the only way she could get through a meeting with her son, or her lawyer, without crying the entire time, he gave her some five-milligram tablets which she took one half at a time. She would continue this procedure when she felt the need throughout the pretrial period, and during the trial itself. Halpern had let himself be guided by the Hippocratic Oath: *Physician, first do no harm.* "Due to the situation," he said later, "her already immeasurable confidence in the treating physician [Tarnower] was now even greater because of her guilt that she had caused his demise." Only *his* drug helped her, Jean insisted. "To insist otherwise, at that point, would have been too risky," Halpern believed.*

---

* In prison, the state psychiatrists had the time, which Halpern did not, to switch her over gradually to a maintenance dose of one of the appropriate drugs for

After ten days in United Hospital Jean Harris was discharged as still severely depressed but, the psychotic manifestations having lifted, it was agreed she would continue with intensive psychotherapy on an outpatient basis. Although Halpern and Aurnou had been able to keep Jean's whereabouts a secret from the press, the lurid story of the headmistress and the "Diet Doc" had become worldwide front-page news; it even was carried on the front page of the fastidious *New York Times.* Much of the coverage was dead wrong,* and in her last days in the hospital, Jean had begun to talk about the great importance of counteracting the purple cloud of lies, distortions, and speculation daily appearing in print by "getting out the truth." This new determination seemed to her doctors a strong positive sign that she now accepted the inevitability of a trial, and that her will to live had begun to return.

The day before she checked out of the hospital, Mrs. Harris telephoned Suzanne and tried without success to learn the name of the cemetery where Herman Tarnower had been buried. The Van der Vrekens had been told by counsel to give her no information.

On March 25, the same day she was released from the hospital, Jean Harris was indicted for the murder of Herman Tarnower. She had not appeared before the Grand Jury herself, nor had she been advised of her right to do so. Such an appearance would have been somewhat unusual, but Halpern had suggested the tactic to Aurnou, offering to back up her appearance with his own testimony as to his patient's extreme emotional disturbance at the time of the crime. He knew from his own experience that sometimes in such cases an indictment can be avoided. He reminded Aurnou of the case once presented to a Syracuse Grand Jury of a mother who had become despondent and killed her newborn infant. There was obviously no criminal intent, it was explained, an argument that the Grand Jury accepted. But this was no obscure young woman in Syracuse. It

---

chronic depression, Elavil, and to wait for the usual early side effects, which disappear after a few months, to pass.

* Sometimes it was hilarious. The *New York Post,* having dug up some facts, but not many, about Tarnower's activities in recent years, reported that in 1973 he had been romantically linked with an Oriental beauty named Zhou Enlai.

was "The Headmistress and the Scarsdale Diet Doc," and the DA's men were panting like bloodhounds. Aurnou reminded Halpern that it was his job to devise the legal strategy; the psychiatrist could handle the emotional aspects.

In an impromptu press conference after the indictment, Aurnou was able to give reporters their first accurate picture of his client's intentions on the fatal night. Originally he, like the reporters, had believed police reports that Mrs. Harris had gone to Tarnower's house in order to ask him to kill her. But this story had been based on a misunderstanding by one of the arresting officers. Now that Aurnou had had an opportunity to discuss the matter with his client, he understood that "the real purpose of her visit was to try to get the doctor to convince her not to go ahead with plans to kill herself."

Aurnou also announced the defense strategy from which he would never waver. "I'm going for broke," he told reporters. To convict his client of murder, the prosecutor would have to prove that Jean Harris intended to kill Herman Tarnower. Aurnou was convinced he could not do it. Hence he would not seek any lesser charges or give the jury any compromise outs. "We're not looking for a lesser offense. We're looking for acquittal," he said. For the same reason, he would not consider an insanity plea, which might lead to an indefinite commitment to a mental hospital. (The lawyer did not mention another factor that ruled out an insanity plea: Dr. Halpern, who was continuing to treat Mrs. Harris, and who was expected to testify in her behalf, would have pulled out of the case. Halpern is one of the nation's most vocal and articulate opponents of the insanity plea. Anytime another madman takes a shot at a politician or a rock star, the soft-spoken psychiatrist turns up on the evening news explaining why the insanity plea has no place in a court of law.)

Aurnou needed to keep Dr. Halpern on his team. A very real defense problem was that their client was still deeply depressed, had scant wish to live, and didn't really care what the jury decided. As long as this was so, they could not prepare her for or sustain her through the rigors of a jury trial. The psychiatrist came up with a way to strengthen her motivation to "get out the truth." He and Aurnou reminded her that winning an acquittal was the only way to clear the family name. Otherwise

David and Jimmie would be known as the sons of a murderess. To strengthen her involvement, she also was told she herself would be the captain of the defense team.

These tactics were psychologically sound, but they would prove strategically disastrous. They may indeed have kept her alive during the pretrial months. But once the trial was under way, there was no question that Mrs. Harris's active, not to say fevered, participation in her own defense—calling the shots, interrupting the judge, sassing the prosecutor, sneering at witnesses, holding impromptu press conferences—made her lawyers' task immeasurably more difficult, and had a most unfortunate effect on the jury. Things got worse when she took the witness stand herself. Aurnou had always known he would be taking a calculated risk in calling her. "She could come across as smart-ass and bitchy," he had predicted accurately to a friend that spring. "But she was the only one who was there," he added, "so I may need her to tell the jury what really happened in that room."

The decision as to whether Jean herself should testify did not have to be made until the trial was under way and the prosecutor had presented his case. Other strategic defense decisions were far more urgent. Foremost among them was the matter of how to handle the long, rambling document Jean had mailed to Tarnower that last morning, the so-called Scarsdale Letter. Thanks to some exceptionally fleet-footed and brainy legal maneuvering, one of Aurnou's partners had recovered the Letter from the Harrison Post Office one jump ahead of the men from the DA's office, and so far the little defense lawyer still had the Letter in his possession. For months before the trial, Aurnou carried it everywhere in his inside breast pocket, proudly displaying the bulging envelope to visiting reporters. But he was not sure he could keep it out of the prosecution's hands indefinitely (in fact, the DA's escalating court appeals to obtain the Letter as evidence would continue until the trial was half over), and he was not even sure that he wanted to. He thought that if the Letter were properly presented to a jury that had been suitably prepared to understand it, it might do his client a great deal of good. The prosecution thought, and hoped, that the Letter contained death threats, or some other indication of Jean's hostile intentions on the weekend before the crime.

Aurnou knew it did not. Further, he believed that the Letter might help him overcome his greatest handicap in mounting an effective defense: the restrictions Jean had laid down against saying anything critical of Madeira or Herman Tarnower.

Not just Aurnou, but his several legal assistants, and his mostly invisible masters, Jacobson and Riegelman, were all of the same opinion, and Dr. Halpern tended to agree. Properly introduced, the Letter would help Jean more than hurt her. It painted such an ugly, evil picture of Herman Tarnower, they reasoned, that it could only create sympathy for Jean. It also showed her confused state of mind; the Letter was unsigned, and its pages had been stuffed into the envelope in random order. Moreover, it seemed unlikely she had any intention of killing Tarnower Monday night if she first mailed him a letter she knew he could not receive until Tuesday or Wednesday morning. And distraught though the Letter was, it certainly contained no threats of any kind.

While one of the foregoing is incorrect, it turned out to be largely irrelevant. The Letter screams with jealousy and jangles with vulgarity. Its author sounds like a dangerously angry woman. A "lady" would seem incapable of writing such a diatribe. How could the defense lawyers possibly have been so blind to the Letter's many negative aspects? In fact, the impact on the jury of the Scarsdale Letter was devastating. Had everything else gone right for the defense, the Letter alone might have done Jean in.

The one person who consistently fought to suppress the Letter was Jean Harris. "I will not let that Letter be made public headlines," she repeatedly told her lawyers, her doctors, her sons, anyone who would listen. "It was not written for the great unwashed American public. It's just too awful for Hi, for me, and for Lynne too, if she's not going to be able to get up and answer it." But the people in charge would not listen.

March 26, the day after her indictment, Jean Harris was back in court to be arraigned and plead not guilty. The following day she learned for the first time that she was indeed a beneficiary in her lover's will, just as he had always promised, phony photostats notwithstanding. But she also learned that she could not claim Tarnower's $220,000 legacy if she were convicted of his murder.

Lynne Tryforos spent the ensuing weeks replying in flowery terms to hundreds of condolence letters. After his death Tarnower's friends had decided to cancel the banquet but go ahead with the fund-raising for the cardiovascular laboratory as a memorial to the slain physician. Mrs. Tryforos told friends that her involvement in this work was "a lifeline." She carried on with her job at the Scarsdale Medical Group, another "lifeline," now assisting Gary Raizes, M.D., who is married to Billie Schwartz's daughter. Otherwise Lynne remained in semiseclusion and unavailable to the press.

That spring and summer Lynne took to coming to Century almost every weekend, alone, taking a golf lesson, and afterward looking for a game. Two widows in their late sixties played with her once, "and she was adorable!" one later exclaimed. "She sent us flowers afterwards to thank us, and said she had the most wonderful time."

Soon Mrs. Schulte and Mrs. Sulzberger were inviting Lynne to lunch, and Joe Cullman III and John Loeb, Jr., were escorting her to dinner. Century was rallying round. For a while, Lynne's most frequent escort was the man who had been Herman Tarnower's dentist, Dr. Eugene Humbert, seventy-two, and rumor had it that they were engaged. Later, during the trial of Jean Harris, a startled desk man at the *New York Post* would get a telephone call from Iphigene Sulzberger. She asked him if the *Post* could not find a way to print some nice pro-Lynne stories, to counteract the "atrocious bad taste" of the Scarsdale Letter.

Within a week of the crime, Alice Watson Faulkner, Chairman of the Madeira Board of Directors, had sent a letter to school alumnae and friends saying that Kiki Johnson had been appointed acting headmistress, and that the school was resolutely carrying on. But because the former headmistress had been charged with homicide, "we are in no position to comment."

The truth of the matter was that the Druids were not talking because nobody could think what to say. Clearly their little headmistress had cracked up in spectacular fashion. Overnight, the Victorian standards of character, mannerliness, stoicism, modesty, and self-restraint that Madeira had struggled to inculcate in its daughters for seventy-five years had been flouted by the supposed embodiment of those standards, the headmistress herself.

The Druids had never been unanimous in their support of Jean Harris, and the minority that had always questioned her suitability now felt smugly vindicated. Not surprisingly, those who had supported her were far more upset. Jean Harris had seemed so much one of their own kind. She was Madeira's first headmistress who had also been married, and had borne and raised children. In the words of one damp-eyed and heart-broken Druid, "Jean had known the full experience of womanhood. What is so awful is," and here the lovely voice caught in her throat, "this woman could have been one of us!"*

One of us. When one heard those words, one knew one heard truth. Whatever she was, Jean Harris was no psychopath, no dingbat; she was not even Ophelia or Crazy Jane. She was a woman like themselves, of their generation and general background, very much a lady, to whom something dreadful had happened, or had perhaps been happening for a long time. What the Druids sensed, however dimly, was sisterhood, and it appears to have scared hell out of them.

The resolve to remain silent produced some bizarre confrontations between Druids and reporters. "As a lifetime teacher of literature," said one beloved old English teacher—it was she, in fact, who had left the gift of daisies in Jean Harris's automobile on the fatal day—"as a lifetime teacher of literature, I have learned to distrust writers. They have a regrettable tendency to burst into print."

"But so much error has been published that . . ."

The teacher was not accustomed to being talked back to. "My dear, I am simply not going to sit in judgment on another person," she said, quite unaware that she just had.

This judgment of silence from her peers was, to Jean Harris, the most painful part of her ordeal, after the loss of Tarnower

---

* On December 17, 1980, after a six-month search, Madeira announced the appointment of a permanent new head to replace Jean Harris: Charles McKinley Saltzman III. So much for the full experience of womanhood.

himself. For the Druids not only turned their backs to the world; they turned their backs on Jean. What is more, Madeira never abandoned its stiff-upper-lip, no-comment stance, not even privately to Jean Harris herself. Their silence seemed the louder because of the tremendous outpouring of sympathetic phone calls and letters that Jean received from all over the world. Teachers, students, parents, and grandparents from the four schools where she had taught; her own classmates from Smith and Laurel; neighbors, friends, and strangers all wrote. Sometimes it seemed that Jean's entire past life had risen up and taken pen in hand. But from the twenty Madeira trustees, the people she "worked for," the people who had sought her out, signed her up, and to whom she felt *professionally responsible,* from those twenty avatars of graciousness the headmistress would receive no phone calls, and but three notes, one a *pro forma* letter no more spontaneous than a child's letter from summer camp. From the others, silence. After she was tried and convicted and sent to prison, the official silence from Greenway became total. It was as if the school's fifth headmistress had simply never existed. As exemplars of Christian charity, the Druids would seem to be somewhat lacking. They functioned in disaster, but scarcely finished in style.

The girls were more generous. A day or two after the killing, the seventeen-year-old student body president told a reporter, "Mrs. Harris is a fine woman and a fine headmistress, and no matter what happens I will always believe in her." The senior class already had dedicated their yearbook to their headmistress. When they returned from Spring Break, they were offered a chance to rescind their dedication, but chose instead to reaffirm it. A number of girls wrote Mrs. Harris notes of sympathy and condolence, and some continue to correspond with her in prison, including two of the four she "expelled." In fact, all four girls did graduate after all. Although Kiki Johnson had been a part of and a supporter of the disciplinary proceedings, once she became acting head of the school, with hopes of a permanent appointment, she switched and told the Board she had been "appalled" by the expulsions.

What worried her most, Mrs. Johnson told a visitor to her office a few weeks later, was not Madeira. It was the *students.* Her brow creased sharply. The acting head was a cheerful, hearty, bespectacled woman wearing a yellow bandanna knotted around her throat. "Our girls have been *appalled* by the publicity," she said. "What *I* dread most is the possibility of reading about us in *True Detective*. But the words that really appalled our girls were being called 'posh' and 'snob.' Because they know this school is open to all . . . providing they can swing the tariff. Heh heh." And here the acting headmistress gave a slow, saurian smile.

The visitor inquired about the pot-smoking incident. The smile dried up. "Nobody smoked pot. There was no pot on campus. Nobody was expelled. The girls went home for a while, but all four girls are back, and all four will graduate."

On Easter Sunday, four weeks after the killing, *The New York Times Book Review* reported that, after twelve weeks on its bestseller list, mostly in the Number Three spot, Tarnower's book had leaped back into the Number One position, and Bantam had hastily gone back to press for another 200,000 copies, making a total of 1,400,000 in print.

In June, the company that issued her disability insurance found Jean Harris to be totally disabled, at least through the end of 1980. Insurance company physicians diagnosed her as suffering from a "major affective disorder (DSM II 296.0) with subjective symptoms of severe depression, insomnia and agitation." Her mental-nervous impairment was considered to be in Class 5, which is the most severe level, and one examiner wrote that "in the period immediately preceding cessation of work she was no longer capable of using good judgment in making important decisions."

While she was hospitalized, Dr. Halpern had routinely ordered a standard battery of psychological tests. The clinical psychologist who administered them, Dr. Eileen Bloomingdale, eventually submitted a report to the defense that she thought might be helpful to Joel Aurnou in understanding his client's emotional state. Dr. Bloomingdale concluded that Herman Tarnower had become a kind of "father-lover" for Jean, a "good father" who provided the kind of holding, touching, stroking, and approval she had never had from her own father. The report speaks of Jean's "lifelong feeling of loneliness, emptiness, inferiority and inadequacy," and says that "Dr. Tarnower's relationship was vital to her own sense of being a significant person, indeed, her sense of existence as a person at all.

"Mrs. Harris had lived, I believe, for some time in a state of truncated emotional existence, perhaps a kind of partial death." On the night of March 10, Dr. Bloomingdale adds, Jean's resolve to commit suicide was blocked by her primary indecisiveness. "The part of her that wished to die needed the executioner within her to be willing to do the job." But her own internal executioner was not willing; that was why she had turned to Tarnower and begged, "Hit me again, Hi. Hit me hard enough to kill me," Dr. Bloomingdale believed.

"In my opinion," her report concludes, "she had no intent whatsoever, at any time, to kill her lover-father. She needed him to be the life-line to keep her internal executioner from agreeing to consummate the act of suicide."

In plainer language, Dr. Bloomingdale was saying that she believed that Dr. Tarnower had indeed fought to keep Jean alive, fought to prevent her suicide, and that part of the reason Jean had driven five hours to see him that night was in the desperate hope that he *would* try to talk her out of it. Unfortunately, the jury would never get to hear from Dr. Bloomingdale, nor from Dr. Halpern, nor from the notably independent-minded psychoanalyst John Baer Train, M.D., who had also examined Jean Harris and like the other two was waiting to testify.

Spring and summer passed for Jean Harris in a surreal blur of anguish and absurdity. She felt zombiefied by grief. She was certain no psychiatrist could possibly help her. She grew to dislike Dr. Halpern, who had begun to remind her of her former husband. "Jim always knew when you had the curse," she told a friend, "so that's when he put the knife in." (The "knife" had been a mild suggestion by Halpern that perhaps she *had* been a bit strict with the girls. But "Miss Infallible" was dominant in Jean's personality these days, and she could not bear even the lightest criticism.) She continued her therapy sessions only to continue getting the drugs Halpern prescribed. None of his substitutes for Desoxyn was any good, she thought, but she was willing to swallow anything the doctor offered, providing he also gave her something else to combat the shattering insomnia at night.

During the day she consulted with her lawyer, got her hair done, and dutifully answered hundreds of letters from friends and strangers alike. She lived with a kindly woman, a stranger who had offered to share her large Scarsdale home after reading that the terms of Jean's bail required she reside in Westchester County until trial. The woman's husband had had a crippling stroke; Herman Tarnower had been his doctor. Jean Harris was not an easy houseguest. Her grandmotherly hostess was shocked by the headmistress's vocabulary—"Mercy, I've never *heard* such language!" she would say later—and bewildered by her sudden spurts of manic energy. Frequently she encountered her guest vigorously washing the car, hoeing the lettuce, bathing the dog. Yet she complained bitterly and constantly of exhaustion. Furthermore, as the court date approached, Jean seemed to become less and less aware of what her hostess politely describes as "the realities of daily living." She would forget to lock the door at night, or leave the teakettle on until the bottom burned out, or tie up the telephone for an hour without realizing it, or let the bathtub run over. "She was just so *distracted.* I think she was overcome not just by grief but by utter bewilderment at the pickle she was in. Here she was going on trial for murder, and she kept saying, 'I have *no recollection* of any but that first bullet!'"

The other thing her hostess remembers was that her guest was "so adorable looking! So fine-boned. And in her underwear, just so pretty and darling. *Adorable!* Yet she never preened. I don't think I once saw her look in the mirror."

Seeing friends and going to church brought Jean no comfort. At times her exhaustion was crippling. She had never known what was the matter with her before, never thought of herself as ill. Now she painstakingly read Maggie Scarf's comprehensive new book on female depression, experiencing shocks of recognition on almost every page.

Sometimes Jean drove aimlessly around Westchester, not knowing what she was looking for, not admitting it, until finally one day she found herself at the cemetery where Herman Tarnower is buried, and rolled up the car windows, and screamed and screamed and screamed.

"I cry over Hi. I sit by his grave," Jean told a friend that summer. "And then I think: is this a form of self-indulgence? Am I *enjoying* this? And was what I felt for Hi self-indulgent too, or was it worth having? And I ask myself, if you're really in love with someone, and he finds himself a little lollipop, a little tootsie roll, and that's what he wants—what do you say? 'Darling, if that's what you want, go your way and be happy'? Or do you fight? Or do you sit there and wring your hands and say, 'How can this wonderful man be so dumb?' Which is what I did. I thought I was handling it rather elegantly by being very cleverly snide and sort of Noël Cowardish about Lynne. But he . . . he . . . you know, it just didn't bother him! He didn't seem to hear me.

"It's so egotistical, really, to think you're better than somebody else. And yet . . . and yet there *she* is, pure as the driven snow. And here *I* am indicted for murder. So who's the good girl and who's the bad girl? I don't know."

In June, Lynne Tryforos told a friend that she was feeling so blue, so entirely empty, that impulsively she had decided to visit Hi's gravesite. It was raining. As she approached, she looked down the green avenue and was startled to see a woman kneeling on the grave. Lynne continued forward, the other woman rose to leave, and the two figures passed each other without speaking.

Several visits later they finally did speak. By then, Lynne had planted the grave with pink and white petunias. "Now you've made even his grave cheap!" Jean heard herself burst out and, turning away, bitterly regretted her remark, knowing that Lynne was in mourning too.

A year later, in June 1981, Mrs. Tryforos turned up at her twentieth high school graduation reunion clad in black from head to toe. Since she spoke scarcely a word, "stayed within herself," and attended only the initial class get-together in Michael's Bar, skipping both the class picnic and the dance that followed, her classmates concluded that Lynne's sole purpose in attending had been to "make a formal appearance as a mourning woman."

As the summer of 1980 drew on, Marge Jacobson grew increasingly worried about Jean Harris's emotional state. She telephoned Mildred Struven in Florida to say she thought her daughter needed moral support, and her parents ought to pay her a visit. When they didn't, she knew it was because "Mildred just couldn't buck Al."

Al Struven died suddenly of a heart attack at the end of July. Jean got court permission to go to Florida to attend the funeral, and she helped her eighty-four-year-old mother pack up and move back to Shaker Heights.

During the summer the blooming media coverage of the Harris-Tarnower affair continued apace. By now everybody was into the act, from the *Harvard Lampoon* to *Good Housekeeping*. Joel Aurnou's behavior with the press was not reassuring. He told a reporter from *Ms. Magazine* that his client was "a classic victim . . . a one-man woman hopelessly in love with a cad." Aurnou further explained that women are always fascinated by men with interesting careers, money, and success—he had experienced some of the same thing himself. "We're different from you, you know. Guys just like to fuck," he said. This unpleasant but revealing interview, coupled with the information from Jean Harris herself that Aurnou had told a reporter in her presence that she stayed with Tarnower "because he was her entrée into high society," suggested to some observers that Joel Aurnou found it somewhat more natural to identify with the victim than with his client.

Attorney friends of Jean Harris, wise in the ways of the world, advised her to make certain hard-headed preparations for her coming ordeal: plead insanity, put her money in trust so as to interpose a shield between herself and possibly rapacious lawyers, and begin to change her public image, to dress less like a chic divorcée and more like a penitent frump. Jean rejected all this advice out-of-hand. "I'm certainly not going to put on Peter Pan collars or any other nonsense," she huffed. "I still believe in my simplistic way that it's just going to be a matter of me and the jury. Either they're going to believe me or not believe me. Frankly, I don't think they will. The whole thing sounds too crazy. But I don't think there's any way anybody can *trick* anybody into deciding I'm guilty or innocent."

By the end of June, Suzanne Van der Vrecken was having a show of her flower paintings at the Purchase Library, and Henri had earned his degree in landscape gardening. At Billie Schwartz's request, they were continuing to look after the

Tarnower estate. Two days after the crime, a judge had refused to issue an order permitting the defense to inspect the scene, on grounds that he had no power ". . . to order inspection of property which is not in possession or control of the People," and Aurnou had failed to appeal his ruling.

One day in her golf locker at Century Marge Jacobson found an elaborate needlepoint pillow she had once made for Hi and decorated with his well-known themes: leopard-skin border, caduceus, golf clubs, insignia of his gourmet society, and so on. A note from Lynne Tryforos said, "We're breaking up the house and I thought you would want to have this." Mrs. Jacobson gave the memento to Jean Harris.

Mrs. Schwartz had offered her brother's modest collection of African sculpture to Gerda Stedman, along with two huge mounted heads of African Cape buffalo. "You're the only person who is not trying to take things," she said.

By the end of July, the two shaggy buffalo heads lay staring dumbly upward from the cement floor of Mrs. Stedman's garage. Mrs. Schwartz had sold the Tarnower place lock, stock, and barrel to a stockbroker and his family for $475,000. The new owners asked Henri Van der Vrecken to stay on and look after things.

On August 19, Jean Harris, accompanied by her lawyer, finally was able to revisit the scene of the crime. When Jean saw that the volumes of Herodotus, Gibbon, and Plutarch were still in place over the doctor's bed, she again dissolved in tears. That Herman's books had been left behind because nobody understood that they had been his most prized treasures seemed to her ineffably sad. Aurnou was more concerned with all that was gone. The cops had taken the bloody bedding, the jewelry, the curlers and clothing and the telephone as evidence. It would have been helpful to find Jean Harris's fingerprints on the phone, to prove her statement that she had tried to call for help before rushing out to the pay phone. But not even Tarnower's prints were left. The only prints on the phone were those of the Harrison police chief, and the only prints on the gun those of his chief of detectives.

The Van der Vreckens had rolled up and thrown away the blood-spattered carpeting from beneath the beds, after receiving police permission to do so, and the new owners had replaced

Tarnower's skimpy single beds with more comfortable three-quarter-sized ones. Aurnou had always known that the only way he could prove Jean's story of the fight over the gun was with hard physical evidence, the mute but powerful testimony of blood-spatter patterns and bullet holes. But much of that evidence had been obliterated or contaminated by clumsy, amateurish police work as fourteen cops and crime lab personnel traipsed through the crime scene that night and in the following days.

A mighty expert in crime-scene reconstruction would be needed. Fortunately, a mighty expert was near at hand and available for hire. Professor Herbert Leon MacDonell is very well known in criminal justice circles, having been called in on the Robert Kennedy and Martin Luther King assassinations, the Joanne Little murder trial, the Peter Reilly murder case, the Joanne Chesimard case, and the police raid on Chicago Black Panther headquarters,* as well as hundreds of lesser-known homicides, worldwide. Indeed, MacDonell is so good at his job that only one day after Joel Aurnou lugged an armful of evidence up to the professor's private crime lab in Corning, New York, and signed him up to work for the defense, the professor got a call from the DA's office asking if he was available to work for their side. The DA would attempt to deny this during the trial, but MacDonell, an exceedingly thorough man, has a tape recording of the call.

Herb MacDonell will work for either side, prosecution or defense. Should his subsequent inspection of the crime scene turn up facts at variance with his client's story, his ethics require him silently to renounce the assignment and to remain silent unless subpoenaed by the other side. Fortunately in the Harris case there was no such embarrassment. Indeed, on September 26, when the professor and his client first met and visited the Tarnower bedroom, and Jean Harris reenacted everything that had happened, MacDonell was amazed at the completeness and accuracy of her recall. "Everything she told me was confirmed by the physical evidence. Nothing she told

---

* An event that the professor proved decisively to have been not a "shoot-out" but a "shoot-in."

me was inconsistent with the evidence," he said later. But she could not remember the two fatal shots.

During the summer it had been announced that the chief prosecutor in the case would be Assistant District Attorney George Bolen, thirty-four, a tall, slender, boyish yet serious-looking lawyer from Long Island. Since graduating from the University of Virginia Law School in 1971, he had accumulated a great deal of prosecutorial experience, working for three years in Manhattan under its famed DA, Frank Hogan, before coming to Westchester. He estimated that in Westchester he had tried twenty to thirty cases—robbery, rape, sodomy, vehicular death, and perjury against police officers—and won most of them, including three murder cases. The trial judge would be Russell R. Leggett, forty-nine, a large, square-faced, athletic-looking man, raised in the Bronx. A political conservative who had worked his way through St. John's University Law School at night, Leggett became a very effective trial lawyer. A few years earlier, his breezy, informal manner had helped him get elected county judge.

Pretrial hearings begin October 6, jury selection three weeks later. Sitting in the deserted courtroom, sunlight streaming in through the tall windows behind the empty jury box, and waiting for the drama to begin is like watching the opening moments of *Our Town*. First, a bare, empty stage. Now a deputy sheriff comes in, switches on the lights in the spare, undistinguished modern courtroom, sets out pitchers of water and paper cups, hooks up microphones for the lawyers, witnesses, and the judge, who sits on a high bench under letters that spell IN GOD WE TRUST. The judge's clerk enters and takes her position beneath his veneered escarpment. One by one the members of the press straggle in and fill their front-row benches. The room is very quiet. Telephones offstage purr gently. One hears coughing in the wings, the hum of air conditioning. The smell of w-a-i-t-i-n-g hangs in the air. Two breathless young clerks, one male, one female, rush in with armfuls of briefs and briefcases. The sheriff's deputy returns with a little glass of water for the judge. The court reporter sets his stenotype machine on its terrierlike stand between his knees. Jean Harris appears wearing a tortoiseshell hairband, creamy tweeds, pale silk blouse, horn-rimmed half-glasses, sling pumps. Briskly she shrugs off her coat, drapes it over the back of her chair, adjusts her spectacles, shakes open "The News of the Week in Review" section. The lawyer squats behind her on bearlike haunches, chatting softly. When the deputy approaches, Aurnou greets the young man warmly and introduces his client. Jean stands up and gives the cop a firm handshake. Very well-mannered crime is soon to be judged in this room.

The most important part of any trial, according to criminal lawyers, is also the dullest to watch. Jury selection in the Harris case involves a special panel of 750 candidates. Slowly the lawyers grind through their voir-dire. A mysterious, mustachioed young man has appeared at the defense table, scribbling notes on a pad. Press and prosecution fail to learn the identity of the person assisting Aurnou in the selection of the jury. He is Phil Jordan, a professional psychic, who is also a college hypnosis instructor and an Episcopal seminarian. Jordan sees an aura around every living thing, including prospective jurors. Blue or green indicates emotional calm and well-being; anxious persons have a red aura that in moments of unusual frustration he observes to pulsate. Aurnou does not always heed Jordan's whispered advice, and later he confesses that the main purpose of his mystery assistant was to upset prosecutor Bolen.

Aurnou asks prospective jurors whether they have any strong aversions to guns? Strong personal feelings that suicide is cowardly, or a sin? Strong feelings about the use of "controlled substances"? The case may involve testimony regarding an adult relationship of long standing that crossed religious lines and did not include a marriage certificate, he says. "Any problems with that?"

Mrs. Harris has not been eating or sleeping well and has lost weight. The fashionable tweed skirts now have to be tied onto her body with belts, like sail lashed to a mast. She has developed a nervous tremor, her foot wiggles nonstop, and out of the courtroom she cannot stop talking. She tells friends she expects to be convicted because she doesn't think the jurors will believe her story. Nonetheless her composure holds up well during the lengthy voir-dire except for the moment in chambers when a prospective woman juror remarks, "It occured to me that she must have loved him very much." This gets Mrs. Harris sob-

bing uncontrollably for the remainder of the day. She is too
tightly wound, too defended, to tolerate sympathy directly.
Concern must be couched in a joke, or some derogatory inver-
sion, to be bearable.

"You are about to join an elite group," says the Honorable
Russell R. Leggett, smiling as the final juror at last is seated.
Tall, tan, and friendly, he seems more host than judge. The
group she joins, twelve jurors and four alternates, are middle-
class and middle-aged. *Kojak* fans. *Reader's Digest* fanciers.
More bowlers among them than bridge players. Of the twelve,
eight are women, and three of the women and one man are
black. The foreman is a bus mechanic, and the other men are a
middle-aged systems analyst, a youngish black social studies
teacher, and a silver-haired retired school administrator. The
three black women are a widowed keypunch operator, an anti-
poverty worker, and a part-time chambermaid. The white
women are a special education teacher, a housewife married to
a Brooks Brothers receiving manager, a reading teacher who is
married to a retired cabinetmaker, a cabdriver's wife who sells
Avon Products, and a part-time cardiac therapy nurse married
to a food company executive. Jean Harris has watched their
selection carefully and made notes on a yellow pad. Seen from
the back, seated at her table, leaning forward, tapered fingers
along her firm jawline, the defendant looks slim, chic, girlish, as
if she should be fluttering at the bow of a Chris Craft jaunting
through the harbor. There is some delay. The jurors are dismissed; Aurnou has disappeared. The TV sketch artists occupy
the empty jury box, working fast with blurry fingers. Jean Harris is twirling her horn-rims gaily by one earpiece; her legs are
crossed and one foot pumps up and down, up and down. The
glasses flip pertly back and forth in little arcs, like tiny windshield wipers. Finally Judge Leggett reappears and says court is
to adjourn for the day.

Outside on the sunshiny courthouse plaza, the defendant
walks briskly away between her lawyers, and one of the trailing
reporters shouts out, "Hey, Jean! You're looking great!"

She turns, and with a shock one sees the face of an old

woman with harsh, dark lines between and underneath the eyes. "No compliments, please. They make her cry," Aurnou scowls.

"Yes, I'm not programmed for that," she says bitterly. Tomorrow morning, Friday, November 21, her trial will finally begin.

16

Woman in an Empty Chair

IT IS OF COURSE a public circussing. Hundreds of reporters and photographers bopping around the bleak municipal spaces of the Westchester County Courthouse. Miles of film. Oceans of ink. Carnival time in medialand, another public burning. The press plays it as a *crime passionel,* and the coverage is a lot sprightlier than the trial itself, a proceeding undistinguished in every aspect save length, sixteen weeks from jury selection to verdict. The players are from central casting: a small-town lawyer with the biggest case of his lifetime, an uptight young prosecutor in steel-rimmed glasses, a folksy and politically correct judge, a long parade of faltering witnesses, a defendant who looks like Constance Bennett, and for a jury, a double row of Archie and Edith Bunkers, a third of them black.

Billie Schwartz refers to it as "Herman's trial," and she and her husband and one or both of their daughters are in daily attendance. "It's the least I can do for my brother," she says. The Tarnower women dress themselves for court in the pelts of rare jungle cats: ocelot paws, sable-collared leopard. One sees them in their furs smoking and chatting with reporters and thinks: Uncle Hi has been shooting again.

On Day One, Mrs. Harris wears a Chanel-style suit of unflattering mustard hue and an expensive-looking mauve silk blouse that looks vaguely ecclesiastical. George Bolen rises to begin his opening statement. "Judge Leggett, Mr. Lalla [Tom Lalla, the assistant prosecutor], Mr. Aurnou, Mrs. Harris, and ladies and gentlemen of the jury." Jean Harris looks up at him as if waiting to be hit. Bolen reads the indictment. Mrs. Harris is charged with Murder in the Second Degree, Criminal Possession of a Weapon in the Second Degree, and the Third Degree. "The events we will be concerned with here took place some eight and a half months ago in the residence and home of Dr. Herman Tarnower." At the mention of his name, a shadow of pain crosses Constance Bennett's face. "March 18 would have been Herman Tarnower's seventieth birthday. He was in remarkably good health for a man of his age." Constance Bennett gulps hard. "As of March 10, 1980, Dr. Tarnower had been seeing two women. One was a Mrs. Lynne Tryforos . . . he had been seeing her for several years." The blonde head stops looking at him, turns toward the wall. March 10 was "a normal Monday" and the dinner guests left at about 8:30 and "that was the last time either of them saw Dr. Tarnower." The defendant's eyes close.

"Several hundred miles away . . . Jean Harris placed keys into the ignition of one of her school automobiles . . ." Jean Harris starts to cry. Her crying is unpleasant to watch. Her face reddens and contorts in total silence. Perhaps that is why some observers will write that she failed to cry. She cries almost daily, but recovers quickly. She takes notes briskly, studies transcripts, looks cool, impatient, and bossy. Today her handsome brother sits behind her on the front-row bench, wearing his navy captain's uniform. Later we shall see her sisters, cheerful matrons in sweaters and plaid skirts. David Harris has Byronic chestnut hair and wears a banker's blue serge; Kathleen, his wife, is dimpled, dark, and luscious. Jimmie Harris looks like Tom Sawyer in the Marine Corps. Not all these people will be there every day. On many days the front-row family pew is unoccupied.

By the time Bolen finishes describing Tarnower's disordered bedroom and the difficulty of getting the dying man down the spiral stairs, it sounds very bad for Mrs. Harris. But now Joel Aurnou rises to say that what happened did not happen in the *way* that the prosecutor described it, and that this case "will be a classic example of the American system of justice and the meaning of reasonable doubt." Jean Harris, listening, flushed, her mauve-silk-lined jacket open, judging her lawyer in action for the first time, looks almost sensual. Aurnou promises the jurors his evidence will show them that "a woman is capable of having her own life, her own career, her own feelings, her own emotions independent of a man . . . will show them how she felt about herself, her fears about aging, her depression about work, the end of her role as an active mother . . ." Mrs. Harris puts on sunglasses to hide new tears. She wraps her long arms around her body, hugging and rocking herself. "The answers to the elements that count in this case lie within the mind of Jean Harris." The jury foreman, the bus mechanic, stares into space like Rodin's *Thinker.*

As for Mr. Bolen's assertion that the motive "was a love triangle—I am not going to waste any time with that . . ." On the night of March 10, when Jean talked freely to the police "and answered their questions—Who shot him? Where is the gun?—truthfully, the name of Lynne Tryforos . . . never came up. Somebody added that later." The police had "tunnel vision" that night. It made them leap to the wrong conclusions. If Suzanne recognized Mrs. Harris's voice when she first picked up the phone after Dr. Tarnower buzzed, as she now claims, why is it the police came to the house in response to a report of "burglary in progress"? Bolen's suggestion that Jean fled the scene is also "totally false." And finally, in peroration: "There came a time on that night when both Jean and Dr. Tarnower struggled over the gun, when both Jean and Dr. Tarnower fought over her life—and both of them lost. He lost his life in what we will show you was a tragic accident, and she was left with a life she no longer wanted to live."

The first witness for the prosecution is a police sergeant at the women's jail. Save for the ominous Van der Vrekens, nearly all the prosecution witnesses will be cops or technicians of death. Exhibits appear—a worn fur jacket, women's panties in a plastic bag, lace handkerchief, pantyhose, another pair of pantyhose, a live bullet, brassiere in a plastic bag. A small bloodstain was found on the bra under her left arm; that section of cloth has been scissored out. The live bullet was found in jail the next morning, tied in a corner of Mrs. Harris's handkerchief.

That evening in Aurnou's office, Jean says, "Now you know why your mother always told you to wear clean underwear." The pace has been antlike. The lawyer says George Bolen has been stalling deliberately.

On November 24, Day Two, we get a gun salesman who speaks in a soft Virginia accent. "She looked at the gun as if it were a strange object. To me, I felt she was unknowledgeable about handling handguns."

The uptight prosecutor hopelessly tangles his syntax, as in this question:

Q. Back in October and November of '78, sir, to your knowledge, was there any in-house procedures promulgated by either yourself or someone immediately superior to you with respect to the procedures to be done with respect to acquainting any prospective purchaser of firearms, with the operation, maintenance and care and general safety of any handgun, whether it be a gun, or any type of weapon?

Suzanne Van der Vreken, shapely in a tight-fitting brown knit dress, wears tall boots, horn-rimmed glasses. A huge pectoral cross rides high on her bosom. She has a face of heart-shaped petulance framed in white-blonde bouffant hair, and her heavily accented speech is often unintelligible. When she speaks of "Dr. Tarnower," making it sound like "turnover," her voice trembles with devotion. She knows Mrs. Harris well, since long before she moved to "Konna-*tee*-koot." Jean stares stonily at the witness. Suzanne does not look at her.

"Then Mrs. Harris start to speak about Lynne Tryforos, and she used some words, not very nice, about that lady. .. . . She

said, 'I will make their life miserable. I will sue them.' "* Court
adjourns, and the press crowds up to the rail, asking Bolen,
"Did she say *sue* or *shoot?*"

"I don't really know *what* she said," the prosecutor admits,
and on that murky note the day ends.

The next morning the housekeeper describes two calls from
Mrs. Harris on March 10. "The first call she seem very angry.
The second call it seem to me she was crying." Mrs. Harris has
become agitated, is whispering to her attorney, shaking her
head. It is clear she thinks Suzanne is lying. Indeed, phone
records prove that Jean's first call to Tarnower was made to his
office, not his house.

Suzanne says that on the night of March 10 the guests left
right after dinner. She served the doctor his nightly laxative in
applesauce, and at about nine o'clock he retired. She was in her
room painting and watching TV when, shortly before eleven
o'clock, she was startled to hear his buzzer. She went to the
kitchen and picked up the phone, heard yelling, then a shot,
and recognized Mrs. Harris's voice. Later, during the police
interrogation at the house, Suzanne was in her bathroom when
Mrs. Harris passed by and paused to glance at herself in the
bathroom mirror. She fingered her lip and said, "Oh, he beat
me. He used to beat me a lot." Jean Harris half smiles.

"Did you *ever* see the doctor hit or beat Mrs. Harris?" the
prosecutor asks.

"Never!" says the housekeeper, her chin quivering.

Suzanne identifies a box of electric curlers found at the scene
as belonging to Mrs. Tryforos, then adds, "I lent it to her."
Jean's smile widens. Whenever the defendant thinks Suzanne is
lying, she smiles.

By the end of the first week, Jean believes she understands
the prosecution's strategy: it is based on the expectation that
she intends to lie. Prosecutors always expect defendants to lie.
In anticipation of this, the Van der Vrekens have been led to lie
repeatedly in the pretrial hearings, she tells a friend, and the
small deceptions are continuing. The box of curlers in evidence

---

* What Suzanne must have overheard, the lawyers will finally figure out, was
some discussion between Harris and Tarnower regarding the likelihood of his
doctor-partners' filing suit over the proceeds of the diet book.

is yellow, for example, whereas Lynne's familiar hated curlers were pink.

When Jean Harris believes a witness is lying, she not only smiles; sometimes she snorts and hoots audibly, and her lawyer must put a restraining hand on her shoulder.

Holding up a black nightgown, the prosecutor asks Suzanne if she has ever seen it before. Yes. "On Mrs. Harris's dresser. In her drawer. In his drawer. On her drawer. Excuse me."

Joel Aurnou moves to strike the answer as incomprehensible.

A trial lawyer needs a towering ego. Perhaps that is why so many are snappy dressers. Joel Aurnou alternates two favorite getups: ultraconservative blue pinstripes, worn with a detachable-collar shirt to suggest an English barrister, and a set of baggy Irish tweeds. Heavy gold cuff links and a watch chain adangle with seals, fobs, and a Phi Beta Kappa key are worn with either ensemble. Outdoors, a Tyrolean ski hat or a Russian beaver hides his scabby tonsure. In moments of tension, the lawyer picks his bald spot until it bleeds. From time to time his client reaches out and pats his shoulder to make him stop.

Aurnou rises to cross-examine. The anonymous phone calls to Tarnower's house came only when Jean Harris was visiting, Suzanne says. Aurnou also brings out that whereas Suzanne told Bolen she saw Jean look into the bathroom mirror and say, "Oh, he beat me. He used to beat me a lot," in the pretrial hearing she had said she heard only, "Oh my God, he hit me!" Seeing the witness squirm, Mrs. Harris looks pleased.

"How am I going to know who the liar is? We've *got* to find out who he is!" she continually insists to Aurnou offstage. She cannot accept the fallibility of memory; if a witness remembers something one way on one occasion, and a different way the next time, or if two witnesses remember the same event slightly differently, then one has to be a liar, and must be identified and nailed.

Jean is convinced the prosecutor is unfairly out to get her. When he says, "Your Honor, may we please go on and discuss something that's relevant to this murder trial?" she snaps, "Thank you very much!" and this time Aurnou's young assistant quickly puts a hand on her shoulder. Some days she seems very agitated and cracked. When the detective who had told the Grand Jury she "seemed sincere" on the night of March 10 now says she "could have been acting," Jean cannot restrain herself and protests aloud. The judge calls a recess, but it is too late. "Shut up! If you say that again I'll—" the reporters hear her threaten one of Aurnou's young assistants before snatching up her coat and stalking out a rear door behind the judge's bench. She reappears in the corridor, pretrial transcript in trembling hand, and rushes over to a knot of reporters, announcing she has decided "to take my case directly to the people."

The first appealing witness for the prosecution is Debbie Raizes, daughter of Billie Schwartz and wife of Dr. Gary Raizes, the youngest man in the Scarsdale Medical Group. Debbie and Lynne Tryforos had been the doctor's dinner guests that night, and Lynne had brought a homemade cake to surprise Suzanne on her birthday. When she describes Uncle Hi's champagne toast, Debbie's bereavement is unmistakable, and not lost on the jury.

What must the jury think of the rest of them? Joel Aurnou is brainy, pudgy, and increasingly rumpled as the trial progresses. George Bolen is stork-legged, truculent, and tense. Jean Harris comes across as vivacious and a bit dotty. She frequently nibbles chocolate at the defense table, sometimes in the presence of the jury. She seems oblivious of the jury. She appears tormented, but exhibits no histrionic repentance, no obvious remorse, no apparent sense of personal responsibility for Tarnower's death. George Bolen will point this out to the jury, and Marge Jacobson will feel guilty for taking off with Leslie on an Egyptian holiday right after her own testimony, not sticking around to give moral support or follow through on her instructions to Jean. "In that courtroom, you gotta come through as the sweet schoolmarm you are." Such is certainly not the impression she projects. She seems to be playing the role Aurnou and Halpern have devised for her with more gusto than necessary, and the Della Street posture is disturbingly inconsistent with her tearfulness at other moments.

The police surgeon on call that night says he arrived just as Dr. Tarnower was being wheeled into the ambulance. He saw a man whose right arm was "totally disarticulated," and who was unconscious and in shock. The police call that had summoned him said only that a man had been shot, nothing more specific.

A well-done cross-examination is an act of *pointillism*. Under the flashing tattoo needles of a skilled cross-examiner, an elegant, just-drawn butterfly may be transformed into a coiling dragon, or a dripping dagger made to rebloom as a rose. As Aurnou cross-examines the police surgeon the jury learns that, unlike other trauma victims, persons who have been shot in the chest should immediately be picked up and rushed to the nearest hospital emergency room. Only there are drastic lifesaving measures possible. The chest may be opened at once, says the witness, who turns out himself to be certified in thoracic (chest) surgery. "They are not really living at that point, or feeling pain," and if the emergency-room surgeon can see the bullet hole in the heart, or in a major blood vessel, he can hold it together manually, and clamp and stitch to stop the vital leakage. Very often the victim survives. Had anyone that night realized the severity of Herman Tarnower's injuries, had anyone rushed him immediately to St. Agnes Hospital, instead of allowing him to lie for twenty minutes or more on his bedroom floor and then slowly lowering him down the stairs, such drastic procedures could probably have saved his life. The surgeon who rode with him in the ambulance has seen it many times. Getting there only seven minutes sooner might have made the vital difference, he says. The tragic irony was that the two fatal bullet holes, one in front, one in back, lined up so perfectly that it appeared to everyone, doctors and medics as well as the cops, that Tarnower had sustained a single, superficial flesh wound clean through the shoulder, an illusion strengthened by the fact that there was surprisingly little external bleeding.

By the time he was wheeled into the emergency room, nearly an hour after he was shot, Herman Tarnowner had no vital signs. There were a number of reasons for this. Police dispatchers had great difficulty understanding anything the Van der Vrekens were saying, including Tarnower's name and the address of the house. The cops had great difficulty getting the dying doctor out of his bedroom, and the village ambulance was primitively equipped, lacking any intravenous fluids. Herman Tarnower bled to death; probably he expired in the ambulance. It was only after he was dead that anyone who saw him that night realized that the injured man had sustained even a single potentially fatal bullet wound, let alone two of them. The bleeding from these wounds was mostly internal. In the course of trying to restart Dr. Tarnower's heart in the emergency room, 1500 cc's of blood were removed from his right chest, the surgeon testifies, and another 1500 cc's of partially clotted blood were removed from the same area at autopsy. Here, as in various pretrial statements, both Van der Vrekens will describe a man drenched in blood. But the doctor says that the pajama top was not very bloody until they got to the emergency room and certain drastic procedures were begun.

According to the defense, the "tragic accident" that caused Tarnower's death was the police failure to comprehend what had happened to him, and their consequent failure to rush him immediately to the hospital.

But on redirect examination, Bolen elicits very damaging information from his man: police consider a hand wound in which the bullet track is front-to-back a "classic defense wound." Angry muttering by the defendant can be heard. The prosecutor is suggesting that Jean bore down on her sleeping victim Frankie-and-Johnny style, gun blazing, and that the doctor put out his hand in an automatic, futile effort to protect himself.

The next witness, an eye doctor, says that without his glasses Tarnower could read only the top letter on an eye chart. Yet he never put on his glasses that night. Again the implication is a surprise attack by Mrs. Harris. Aurnou attempts to minimize this testimony by saying that he himself is equally nearsighted, and yet without his glasses—here he dramatically removes his gold-rimmed spectacles—he can see, can walk, can even distinguish one juror from the next. "Blue blouse, purple blouse, tie with stripes," he calls out, walking confidently along the jury rail. Several jurors laugh aloud. They enjoy the humiliation of the witness.

Mr. Drummond, the police serologist, has found a trail of bloodstains leading into Dr. Tarnower's bathroom and back out again, as well as stains on the sink, towels, wastebasket, telephone shelf, carpet, and bedding, and more blood on Jean Harris's blouse, bra, hair, belt, and shoes—a Grand Guignol extravaganza.

Henri Van der Vreken wears a striped silk shirt, hacking jacket, supercilious sneer. He looks like a deck steward. "When you got up to the bedroom, what if anything did you see?" Bolen asks.

"What I see there was Dr. Tarnower lying off his knees, blood coming from his back." The Belgian accent is nearly the equal of Suzanne's.

"Oh, Henri!" Jean exclaims, shaking her head in disapproval.

Later, he testifies, he was sitting on the end of the bed in his room when Mrs. Harris telephoned Leslie Jacobson on the Van der Vrekens' private line, but "I didn't pay attention to what Mrs. Harris was saying."

"Oh, Henri!" she whispers again.

When it comes time to cross-examine, Jean moves her chair so as to face him head-on, in a direct posture of confrontation. But the chauffeur never looks at her. Aurnou's questions are blunt, and in the man's curt answers one senses gathering fury. Did you hear Mrs. Harris say, Hi, why didn't you kill me? No. See her touch the doctor's face with her hand? No. She didn't do it, or you don't recall? I didn't pay attention *at all* to what Mrs. Harris was doing or saying. Up to that point, what had *you* done to help the doctor? (Gallic shrug.) What could *I* do to help the doctor?

Henri has testified that Mrs. Harris had asked him, "Who was here for dinner?" at which point the butler had asked police to have Mrs. Harris removed from the house. Aurnou wants to know when this conversation took place. During her interrogation by Detective Siciliano. So you have strong feelings about Mrs. Harris? "It's not a question of feelings, Mr. Aurnou. You don't have any feelings at all when you are in the presence of such . . . immoral . . . *murder.*" His gust of scorn sweeps the courtroom.

"So you'd made up your mind already?"

Leaning forward and speaking carefully. "I was in the house."

"But were you in the *room?*" Aurnou shouts.

Shouting back, "I will tell you something—" but Judge Leggett cuts him off. Jean has observed the trial's first major confrontation with madonnalike calm.

Louis Roh, M.D., a graduate of Seoul National University in Korea and now a deputy medical examiner of Westchester County, has a serene olive of a face, neat brown suit, black glasses. The man does not lack experience. In the New York City Medical Examiner's office he personally performed seven hundred autopsies, and participated in ten thousand, of which three thousand involved gunshot wounds. Since coming to Westchester he has participated in another ten thousand autopsies. He looks to be in his early forties; one wonders when he finds time to eat. Dr. Roh's exploration of Dr. Tarnower's body is now described in meticulous detail. The cause of death is bullet wounds. The mechanism of death is hemorrhage, or hemothorax. Roh has found a total of five wounds, four wound tracks, and three bullets. (He counts the entry and exit wounds in the hand as two.) He estimates that Tarnower went into intractable (irreversible) shock within five to ten minutes of receiving his chest injuries. But the most devastating part of his testimony, arrived at after interrogation by Mr. Bolen so bumbling that Mr. Aurnou has to help him phrase his questions, is his opinion that "the one bullet that caused the wound to the hand is the one that caused the wound in the right anterior chest wall." The medical examiner is supporting the prosecution contention that Jean Harris shot the helpless man in bed as he vainly raised his hand to ward off attack. Dr. Roh bases his opinion on two facts: one, the hand and chest wounds can be lined up properly. Two, when the bullet struck Tarnower's body and dropped into the chest cavity, after hitting the collarbone and severing the big vein, it did not have much force. Dr. Roh believes that as the bullet passed through the hand it lost its normal spiraling, rifling action and just "tumbled in." Jean's eyes close for a long beat.

After lunch, George Bolen asks his witness the "medical definition of the term, 'back'?" and it is clear we are about to deal with the matter of the "shot in the back." Bolen unveils a plaster human torso that had been wrapped in a black garbage bag. It looks like a well-worn dummy from the Police Academy; its brown hair is coming off, its right shoulder looks nibbled on. Billie Schwartz walks out. Dr. Roh indicates the site of the rear shoulder wound, and says it could have been sustained with the doctor's body in a number of positions, including "if the person is lying down on the bed and the person holding a gun is stooped over [him]." A soft moan is heard from the defense table. But there is worse to come. In Dr. Roh's opinion, Dr.

Tarnower's wounds are not consistent with a struggle over a gun between a left-handed woman, five feet four inches tall and one hundred and ten pounds, and a one-hundred-and-seventy-five-pound, five-foot-ten-inch, right-handed male. He is bothered both by the number of wounds and their location. If such a struggle *had* occurred, says this very experienced witness, he would expect to see wounds mainly in the front part of the doctor's body, "chest and abdomen," all at very close range. Jean Harris's face is masklike.

Aurnou is able to raise some doubts about this testimony. He forces the admission that originally Dr. Roh noted in his autopsy report, and told the Grand Jury, that four bullets had struck Dr. Tarnower, not three. Sometime over the summer, after a conversation with his boss, he has changed his opinion to accommodate the "defensive wound" hypothesis.

As spectators leave the courtroom that Friday, piling into the elevator with the homeward-bound jury, it is shocking to see that, despite the judge's daily admonishment not to discuss the case, and completely to ignore the TV and press coverage, every juror carries the day's newspaper. But in the reams of newspaper coverage, there is no mention of the crucial behind-the-scenes defense struggle that has been taking place over the possible use of psychiatric testimony. Three defense doctors who have examined Jean Harris are unanimous in their conviction that she did not murder Herman Tarnower. They are aware that Fried, Frank, Harris, Shriver and Jacobson has researched the question of whether psychiatric testimony on the issue of intent is admissible in a noninsanity case, and they know that Aurnou has received a twenty-one-page confidential brief concluding that such testimony is admissible. The question is how, and indeed *whether*, it is tactically wise to set their opinions before the jury.

Jean Harris knows that if the defense introduces psychiatric testimony, the prosecution is entitled to do the same. If Doctors Train, Halpern, and Bloomingdale testify for her, not only do all their notes and records become available to the prosecution; the prosecution is entitled to have the defendant examined by its own psychiatrists, and to put these experts on the stand. Jean Harris does not want to go through this. She believes that if Bolen has been able to induce his medical examiner, Dr. Roh, to change his medical opinion six times, including the switch from four bullets to three, he will be equally successful in manipulating his psychiatric experts to support the prosecution's case. She will see these experts only if her lawyers insist. But that will never happen; Aurnou will rest his case without submitting the brief to the judge.

The People wind up their case with a ballistics expert who is on the stand for nearly two days. Afterward he sums up for reporters a scenario the jury never got to hear: "She pops him once [through the upraised right hand and into the chest]. She pops him again in a hurry. [The first shot has made him fall forward, which accounts for the second bullet's traveling straight downward after it enters the victim's rear shoulder.] Now he walks to the bathroom to see what the damage is. Realizing he's in deep trouble, he goes back to the phone and, as he is calling for help, she lets him have it in the arm."

Bolen had not asked him to be so specific in front of the jury. The prosecutor seems to have thought that the plain fact of four bullets was his best evidence. He did not want to dilute its impact on the jury by inviting his witness to draw conclusions as to how they got there.

The last bit of prosecution evidence the jurors see is a species of courtroom Magritte. What appears at first to be an eight-by-ten-inch photograph of a wintry beach stippled by the wind, with one carefully placed black rock like the Zen rock gardens of Japan, turns out on closer inspection to be an extreme close-up of an old man's upper arm, its crepey, sagging flesh pocked by a single black bullet hole.

By the start of the defense case, the jury has grown flat and set-looking, congealed like Jell-O into attitudes of suspended disbelief. We see a newly belligerent George Bolen, alert and aggressive in cross-examination, his syntax much improved. Aurnou puts on a brief parade of character witnesses from Grosse Pointe, Madeira, and the NAIS to testify to Jean Harris's reputation for "veracity" and "peaceability." Bow-tied, pink-cheeked, silver-haired, they resemble elderly preppies, and they seem to turn off these jurors.

From the beginning, each side has complained that the other side is withholding evidence. It now turns out that the prosecution has failed to turn over to the defense, failed even to print, 206 photographs of the crime scene. The unprinted pictures are essentially duplicates, the People claim. The defense demands a mistrial, which the judge denies, but he does order a one-week recess over Christmas, to enable the defense to study the new evidence.

During this period, Henri Van der Vreken resurfaces in the press. In October, after three months on the job, Henri has been sacked by the new owners of the Tarnower house and taken to court, accused of stealing a garden tractor and other items, and improperly billing his new employers for $10,000 in goods and services. The complaint had also labeled Henri "insolent, incompetent and dishonest." This week Henri has filed a $2 million countersuit, claiming that he was fired because he had rebuffed sexual advances made by the wife of his new employer.*

When the trial resumes, the defense calls two arch-Druids to the stand. Nancy Baxter Skallerup, tall, limping, and seventy-ish, is known behind her back as "Our Lady Madeira." She is a past president of the trustees, a former teacher, a next-door neighbor, and a longtime patroness. Both her daughters attended Madeira, and her granddaughter, a senior, was the ringleader of the anti-Harris counterreformation. Mrs. Skallerup and Board Chairman Alice Watson Faulkner, who follows her to the stand, are the Madeira officials who went to the headmistress's house in the early hours of March 11 and inventoried the various notes before turning everything over to Jean's lawyers. Here now under subpoena to establish the chain of custody of the notes, they mask their unease with opaque hauteur.

These are the first witnesses Jean Harris does not look in the face. She appears frightened and guilt-stricken. Asked when she has seen Mrs. Harris since March 8, Mrs. Skallerup replies, "I have not seen Mrs. Harris, nor had any communication with Mrs. Harris." She is excused, and hobbles down the aisle and out of the courtroom without a glance at the defendant.

She is succeeded by a cool, assured woman with gray-

---

* This charge, it will turn out, is based on a sarcastic remark by the exasperated woman, fed up with the gardener's lack of initiative: "Henri, do I have to change your diapers for you?" Henri's attorney claims that his English is so poor that he construed this as a sexual invitation.

streaked dark hair drawn back smoothly, wearing a garnet-
colored suit and boots. Mrs. Faulkner beams a practiced, receiv-
ing-line smile at the judge, the jury, each of the lawyers, and
finally Mrs. Harris, turning her head like a lighthouse beacon.
She is asked to describe the headmistress's duties. During her
lengthy recital Mrs. Harris hangs her head like a disgraced
schoolgirl. One wonders what the jury makes of Mrs.
Faulkner's testimony, what their picture is of Jean's world? In
the corridor, during a recess, one of the courthouse regulars, a
grandmotherly trial buff who is here every day, buttonholes a
reporter and says, "Tell me. Confidentially. This school they
keep talking about. Is that place a high school or a college?"

Mrs. Faulkner tells the jury she entered Jean's house at six-
forty-five in the morning, found the letters by the door, and
"saw one with my name on the front." Jean has turned bright
pink with choked-back tears. The letter is produced and passed
to the jurors who read it slowly, two by two. This is a turning
point in the trial; they are hearing the defendant's story for the
first time.

Alice—
    I'm sorry. Please for Christ's sake don't open the place
again until you have adults and policemen and keepers
on every floor. God knows what they're doing.
    And next time choose a head the board wants and sup-
ports. Don't let some poor fool work like hell for two
years before she knows she wasn't ever wanted in the first
place. There are so many enemies and so few friends. I
was a person and nobody ever knew.

The letter is unsigned. A companion document is signed
twice: "I want to be immediately CREMATED AND THROWN
AWAY."

Aurnou leads Mrs. Faulkner through the letter sentence by
sentence. She affects not to understand its meaning except in the
most general way. She is patrician and ladylike. Throughout
this testimony, Jean Harris sits like a bird in a windstorm, hun-
kered down and trembling. She is sobbing, her body shakes, her
fists are clenched in the struggle for control, and her jiggling
foot at last is still.

Professor Herbert Leon MacDonell's testimony will be crucial. On the stand, the tall, bearded forensic scientist proves
himself a man of high, cool intellect and basalt ego. During his
four days of testimony, the scientific and intellectual level of
this inquiry takes a great leap upward. Jean Harris looks
smaller, older; she seems sad and subdued. The hairband is
gone. Perhaps she has been heavily tranquilized to get through
this testimony. The professor speaks knowingly of velocities,
trajectories, and splatter patterns. By measuring the angle of the
bullet hole through the glass door, and tracing a ricochet mark
he found on the deck, he has been able to establish by geometric
projection back into the room the zone within which the gun
must have been when it was fired. Needless to say, this works
out to be just where Jean Harris has said she and Tarnower
were standing when she first raised the gun to her head, and he
tried to disarm her and got shot through the hand. The professor's two schematic diagrams of this are shown to the jury.

While studying the 206 extra photographs, the professor has
made a remarkable discovery. If the bullet went through Tarnower's hand in the manner Jean had described, the blood
would spray in certain specific patterns and parabolas, which
would tend to confirm her story. In examining the new close-up
photos of the door frame, he spotted dark specks that could be
human blood. He has since returned to the house and tested the
specks;* they *are* blood, and "Blood is a fluid which behaves
according to the laws of physics. The molecules tend to hold
together unless the surface tension is broken." This property
allows a water bug to walk on water, or a needle to float—and
perhaps a lady to go free. The professor explains that the high
energy of a gunshot divides the blood into a very fine spray,
almost a mist, *but a measurable mist,* and MacDonell has discovered on the door frame a "directional bloodstain," an oval
droplet 1/25th of an inch in diameter, which again confirms
Harris's story of where she and Tarnower were standing when
the first shot was fired.

During this testimony the faces at the defense table wear a
helpless, naked look. MacDonell is the plow horse that must

---

* The broken glass has been replaced, but the new glass was set in the old door
frame.

pull the entire weight of the defense. In the house, the professor
had also found very small bloodstains in the bathtub. They are
just the right size to have been caused by striking a gun full of
fresh blood against the hard enamel. MacDonell explains how
the gun came to be filled with blood while Tarnower held it in
his wounded hand as they sat and talked. He traces the doctor's
walk to his bathroom, noting that photographs of the bloodstains on the carpet "are consistent with arterial gushing. Arterial gushing results when an artery is severed, due to the rhyth-
mic pulsation of the heart as it goes from systolic to diastolic.
. . . It gushes out in a very recognizable pattern which is essentially a splash . . . remarkable how far the human body
can project blood."*

MacDonell seems to demolish Dr. Roh's testimony. If
Tarnower had been lying in bed and raised his hand to ward off
the bullet in "a classic defense posture," his face and entire
pajama sleeve would have been covered with a very fine spray of
blood; he has read the autopsy report and examined the sleeve,
and such is not the case. After lunch, we are treated to a demonstration of MacDonell's expertise with firearms. By examining the primer in the base of the spent cartridges under low-
power magnification, the professor can tell whether the firing
pin has struck the primer once, or more than once. (If the firing
pin is only slightly off-center, as it was in this gun, subsequent
strikes make the first tiny dent appear less distinct; they add a
kind of ghost image to the initial strike. MacDonell explains
how.) Since he found four shells double-struck, and one single-
struck, he has been able to calculate the precise sequence of the
five shots fired from the six-cylinder weapon: *bang, bang, bang,
bang, click, bang, click, click, click, click.* The first *click* occurred when Mrs. Harris put the gun to her temple and pulled
the trigger; the final *bang* was the bullet that went *Boom!* and
tore into the headboard.

But the most stunning demonstration of the professor's skills
comes the next day, when the prosecutor taunts him into exam-

---

* Indeed, the photograph we are shown later of the dotted line blood trail to the
bathroom looks much more like what the professor is describing than the result of
the prosecution's theory: that Tarnower walked to the bathroom and back after
sustaining the two mortal chest wounds.

ining the bloody bedsheets. "Go ahead! We're not holding anything back," Bolen blusters. "Would you like to see them now?" MacDonell spends one hour alone, over lunch, with evidence he had never seen before. Court resumes and the witness, assisted by a deputy sheriff, unfurls the pink, blue, and yellow flowered sheets and drapes them full-length across the front of the jury box. Indicating with the chemist's spatula he invariably carries in his breast pocket, alongside the other tools of his trade, a powerful pencil microscope and flashlight, the professor identifies swipe patterns, wipe patterns, splashes, drips, and spatters, each with its own meaning. Here is a stain made from close contact with a bloody object, here a stain that has been diluted with water, possibly a transfer pattern. Could it be the gun? He lays his own gun across it—a perfect fit! The jury leans forward, fascinated. Jean Harris and Billie Schwartz are staring into their laps. Here is the mark of a bloody finger, or perhaps thumb. This small stain could be from contact with the bloody tip of a nose, or a finger, but it could not be an ear, thumb, or elbow.

The professor removes his suit coat and puts on Tarnower's blood-caked pajama top. Billie Schwartz leaves the room. The pajamas yield more evidence of the struggle: there is a bullet hole in the rear right shoulder, but none in the loose flap of shoulder lining beneath it. A struggle must have pulled the pajamas taut and the flap askew. He shows the jury the clean portions of the right sleeve, which prove the prosecution's "defensive wound" theory impossible. The watermark on the bedsheet is exactly where Tarnower's wounded right hand would have rested if he and Jean had been sitting as she said. The water came from the wet towel with which Tarnower had wrapped his hand after going into his bathroom.

MacDonell has given the jury an actual map of the mayhem, printed in blood on the doctor's bedsheets. "Would you like to see them now?" Bolen had taunted. He will regret the question for the rest of his lawyerly life.

MacDonell's grasp of physical evidence has revealed him to be a modern, real-life Sherlock Holmes. He has shown the jury where Harris and Tarnower must have been standing at the time of the first shot, and the last shot, and how they individually moved about the room, and over the bedsheets. He even

knows the sequence of shots. He can describe just about everything that happened in the bedroom that night "to a reasonable
degree of scientific certainty"—except for the two fatal shots.
He *believes* these shots were numbers two and three, and that
they could have occurred only during the close tug-of-war over
the gun, when Harris and Tarnower were on opposite beds,
knee to knee. In the professor's reconstruction of events, the
fourth bullet, when she thought she felt the muzzle in her abdomen and "consciously fired at myself," was the one which in
fact broke Tarnower's arm. The pain of that injury would have
rendered him helpless thereafter. But since Jean has no memory
of the two fatal shots, this part of MacDonell's theory can only
be called expert conjecture.

"In an acute psychotic explosion of emotion, which is what
happened to Jean, amnesia is very common," Dr. Train, the
psychoanalyst, has told a reporter. "In the army, they used to
call it shell shock." Unfortunately, he never got to tell it to the
jury. Later, in Bolen's cross-examination of the defendant, he
will be able to use to devastating effect her uncertainty over the
manner in which the vital wounds were sustained.

Now Bolen comes up with a left-field surprise that will
change the nature of this trial. It will result in a protracted duel
of expert witnesses—eight skin pathologists in all—that will
take up much of the remaining weeks of testimony. The steady
stream of technical jargon will so distract the defense and be-
numb the jury that the defense will lose its focus, and the jury
will write off all the experts—MacDonell, alas, included—and
rely on naked instinct.

Over the week's recess, Bolen had happened to chat with one
of the defense pathologists, and learned that if a bullet had in
fact passed through Dr. Tarnower's hand before entering his
chest, one possibly could find minuscule fragments of hand tissue in the chest wound. They might not be too difficult to identify because, under a microscope, the skin of the palm has a
distinctive, five-layer structure that occurs nowhere else in the
body except the sole of the foot. Accordingly, Bolen had ordered Dr. Roh to look again, and if necessary to prepare new
slides from his blocks of frozen tissue. Not so surprisingly, Roh
has found what he was ordered to find, and he is back on the
stand to describe it to the jury: three microscopic fragments of

foreign matter in the chest wound that *could be,* although they are not necessarily, palmar tissue. Under cross-examination he acknowledges that they could also be fragments of collarbone, or cartilage, or cotton fibers from Tarnower's pajamas, or some substance unknown. To knock down this testimony now requires a veritable pathologists' parade, and by the time Aurnou finally is satisfied that he has convinced the jury that the three tiny fragments could be anything at all, it no longer matters.

Jean is now saying privately that she thinks Aurnou should have rested his case after Bolen put on an inadequate prosecution. The defense witnesses are only helping to convict her in the jury's eyes, she believes. She has begun to think about prison. "The thought of being caged puts a kind of fear in me that I can't describe," she tells a friend. "I would go absolutely stark, raving mad in twenty-four hours, and then the state can support a nice, screaming, screeching old lady for the next twenty-five years. I think it was lost from the start. I don't think anybody gave a damn right from the beginning about what happened. They had a corpse with four bullet holes, and that was the beginning and the end of this case. Joel is fantastic. But he is so *up,* I don't think he's being realistic. I think he's on a losing proposition. I'm so tired of it, and so horrified by it. I really don't *care* anymore." Various doctors have been urging her to take various sedatives or tranquilizers. She is obviously overwrought and her agitation is hampering her defense, but she says their drugs are no good.

Bolen has recalled Dr. Roh once more and is asking him whether it would be anatomically possible to have sustained the arm wound in a variety of positions. Aurnou considers the line of questioning off the wall. He is so annoyed he snarls, "Is it also anatomically possible he could have sustained it while sitting on the toilet?"

"Joel! How *could* you?" Jean gasps.

Jean Harris's sudden appearance on the witness stand takes everybody by surprise. She speaks in a dull voice and wears dark glasses. The cords in her neck stand out sharply. She does not look at the jury. It takes less than four minutes to cover the first forty-three years of her life. As soon as Aurnou asks the date of the party at which she met Herman Tarnower, she is crying again. When Aurnou offers Tarnower's letters as evidence of his love, Bolen objects that they are irrelevant, remote in time, immaterial, and hearsay. These words make Mrs. Harris grit her teeth in pain. "He wanted to marry me," she says, and several jurors grin. She describes receiving and returning his diamond ring. "Being married didn't mean that much to me. It was seeing Hi that mattered. So I wrote him a letter . . . finally and said, 'You really have to stop thinking it's so bad that you're not married.' . . . He felt upset for me." Two women jurors laugh. Two others look at their watches. The judge calls for a recess.

Jean tells the story of their romance, their travels, her discovery of the cuff links in the Paris Ritz. "Did you continue to travel with the doctor on that occasion?"

"Yeh-heh-heh-heh-hes!" Now she is laughing at herself, laughing so hard she can scarcely get the word out.

When Aurnou reads aloud her letter, "I don't want a pound of flesh, Hi," she weeps bitterly. Buying the gun made her feel "safer," she says. Some jurors cease looking at her.

She will be on the stand eight days. "For me, it was the easiest part of the trial," she will say later, "because it wasn't having to sit there and listen to other people say things." By the second day, her early nervousness is gone, but her testimony is punctuated with inappropriate grins and smirks, and one gets an impression of barely controlled hysteria. She holds together through the Christmas poem, finding the marijuana and punishing the four girls, and asking Hi to send more Desoxyn. But when Aurnou asks her to describe to the jury how she felt that weekend, physically and emotionally, she crumples. "I told you, Joel, I really don't have the words. I . . . couldn't . . . function." Her face is a mask of tragedy, mouth open, uttering a silent scream.

Then the moment passes, and we are on to the writing of the Scarsdale Letter. As soon as she mailed it Monday morning, she was sorry. On the phone she told Tarnower, "When it comes, throw it away. Don't bother to read it . . . and then we talked about a number of things. He asked me to be there the first weekend in April, and the last thing he talked to me about that morning was whom we should ask for dinner when I came."

Aurnou now tries to get from Jean what he could not get from Alice Faulkner: what did she mean by the last line of her note of resignation, "I was a person and no one ever knew." The subject is very difficult for her to speak about, and it develops into one of the trial's most emotional moments. She already is crying heavily when Aurnou asks:

Q. On March 10, 1980—Jean, look at me, please. When you wrote the words, "I was a person and no one ever knew," tell the jury what you meant.

A. [sobbing] I don't know. I think it had something to do with being a woman who had worked for a long time, and had done the things a man does to support a family, but [sob] still a woman. I always felt that when I was in Westchester I was a woman in a pretty dress and went to a dinner party with Dr. Tarnower, and in Washington I was a woman in a pretty dress and the headmistress. But I wasn't sure who I was . . . and it didn't seem to matter.

Q. It mattered to you, didn't it?

A. I was a person sitting in an empty chair, Joel. I can't describe it anymore. [Floods of tears.]

Judge Leggett calls a short recess. By this time Joel Aurnou himself is weeping. "I can't stand to do it. I feel like a torturer," he tells a reporter in the corridor. He knows that he is dealing with the very core of Jean's pain, her self-image as a "woman in an empty chair." This is what Dr. Bloomingdale was trying to describe when she spoke of Jean's "truncated emotional existence . . . a kind of partial death," and when she wrote that Jean's relationship with Dr. Tarnower "was vital to . . . her sense of existence as a person at all." It is the heart of the thing that bound her to Tarnower and made it impossible ever to leave him. When Jean Harris looked into the mirror of her own life, she saw a distorted figure, as if in a fun-house mirror, a humiliated, prideless creature on its hands and knees. But even that craven image was preferable to seeing no reflection at all; better than having to acknowledge the nonexistence of the woman in the empty chair.

Jean Harris's detailed account of the shooting of Herman

Tarnower is set before the jury in an orderly manner, unmarred by emotional breakdown. No surface guilt, no tears. Most interesting is her fierce loyalty to the dead man. Every time Joel Aurnou tries to defend her, she tries to defend Herman Tarnower. Had he ever struck her before? "No, indeed. He never had. But then I had never come to his house and thrown something before, either." Did you ever intend anywhere along that trip, or before or during or right up to the moment you got there, for Hi to kill you? "No, I certainly did not, and I am happy to finally be able to say it. It wouldn't have made any sense to get in a car and think I would drive there and hand a man like Hi a gun and ask him to kill me with it. He spent his life saving people's lives. Besides which, *I wouldn't have done that to him.*"*

Having said that, she tells the jury that she went to her bathroom and smashed her own aging image in her own cosmetic mirror, the weapon being a box of Lynne Tryforos's jewelry.

Moments later:

Q. And here was the doctor, he smacked you twice in the face—
A. But he didn't know what I was going to do, Joel!

She is surely not an easy client. Her denial of aggression is total. Did you ever that night intend to shoot or kill Dr. Tarnower? "No, I didn't. The most violent thing I did was throw a box of curlers, and I didn't throw them at him. I never for a moment wanted to hurt Hi, never in fourteen years. And certainly not that night."

Before leaving to get help, she has assisted him back onto his blue blanket and, "I looked at his face, and he looked at me. And I guess we were both in a state of shock, wondering how—how something that ugly and sad could have happened between two people who didn't argue even, except over the use of the subjunctive, and I ran downstairs."

Would have. Could have. Should have. For Jean Harris, the night of March 10 will exist forever in the subjunctive mood.

In the corridor, Billie Schwartz is shaking with rage. "No

---

* Italics mine.

way she could drive six hours! Why didn't she kill herself at Madeira? He was too kind to her! He got both boys jobs. He kept telling her, 'Make a new life.' Imagine if she'd come to the hospital that night, imagine *that* scene! She wanted to, you know. She was always making scenes. That wasn't the first time she'd driven up there. I tell you, she was determined to destroy him!"

Next morning Mrs. Harris's voice is almost inaudible. Perhaps this is why Aurnou asks if she is taking any medication at present. Yes, she says, before Bolen is able to object. Reviewing the sequence of shots, she confirms that after the hand wound, the next shot she can recall was the time she thought she was deliberately shooting herself in the abdomen.

Her suicide attempt "wasn't meant to be a big last act . . . a grandstand play, but it sort of sounds that way . . ."

"If you felt so strongly about dying then," says Aurnou, "why haven't you done anything to kill yourself since?"

"Objection to that," says Bolen.

"Sustained."

An awful silence follows, as Jean tries to compel her anguished features to smile before saying, "I didn't think *you* would be the one to ask that."

Since it was a question he knew the jury would want to hear answered, Aurnou later explained, he had preferred they hear it from him.

The lawyer reviews Jean's various statements to the cops before and after she was taken to the police station. Not long after her arrival there, Dr. Roth, the police surgeon, had walked in. "How is he? Can I see him? Can I go to the hospital?" Jean had begged.

"And what did Sergeant Carney finally tell you?"

"He said, 'Oh, he passed on.' " Her red, anguished face might be a Francis Bacon portrait. "Some dumb expression! *Passing on!*"

Aurnou is approaching the end of his direct examination. He knows, although the jury and spectators do not, that they will hear the Scarsdale Letter. The matter has finally been settled this morning in chambers. The lawyer's final questions reaffirm that his client is not a jealous woman. "Mrs. Harris, what were your feelings concerning the relationship that you knew of between Dr. Tarnower and Mrs. Tryforos?"

"Actually, I thought it denigrated Hi. But then I thought the book did too. So maybe I was wrong." She is slurring her words.

"Did your feelings concerning the relationship between Dr. Tarnower and Lynne Tryforos have *anything at all* to do with your being in Purchase, New York, on March 10, 1980?"

"No, they didn't. I think it depressed me to see Hi be less than I thought he was. But that could have been part of my depression. But it certainly had nothing to do with my feelings about Hi. I had feelings about myself and my own integrity."

It is Friday afternoon when George Bolen's cross-examination very gently begins. Did Dr. Tarnower always wear glasses? On fishing trips, for example? "He wore them for safety." She smiles. "Because of the way I cast. He also wore them because he tied a lot of . . . you know . . ." she breaks off, unable to think of the word for "flies." She appears somewhat stoned. Terrified of cross-examination, she has overmedicated herself. Bolen has assembled a group of pictures of Tarnower wearing his glasses in various situations that Jean is asked to identify. "This is just a childish exercise," she says.

"Mrs. Harris, please don't comment," says the judge.

She is asked about her statement that she did not know how to unload her gun. Did the salesman give her no instructions? Bolen seems incredulous.

A. Mr. Bolen, he may have told me everything there was to know about the gun. But there was only one purpose for buying the gun, and that was for killing myself. And I wasn't the slightest bit interested about the gun except filling up the gun with bullets to shoot myself, so I could simply shoot myself. I didn't know what he told me, and I didn't listen, and I didn't ask. The only thing I asked him was, how do you put a bullet in this gun?

Her answer is needlessly snippy and irritable. It is followed almost immediately by questions about the Scarsdale Letter. As soon as Jean herself testified to writing it over the weekend, and mailing it the day of the crime, the Letter had become the "best evidence" of her state of mind, and Bolen was entitled to ask for it on cross-examination. When he does, Aurnou crows, "I just happen to have it with me, Your Honor!" and with a flourish bestows the prize upon the eager prosecutor.

Until now, the Scarsdale Letter has been the case's wild card, meaning whatever anyone wants it to mean. To the men in charge of Jean's defense, it is evidence of Jean's suffering and abuse, and of Tarnower's cruelty. By putting it into the case, they seem to be saying to the jury, "She didn't mean to kill him . . . but he deserved it." But to one of the women lawyers who worked on her case, "The Letter was every woman's ultimate nightmare of humiliation come true. It was the ultimate exposure, the ultimate violation of her modesty and reserve." To militant feminists throughout the country who heretofore had admired and even lionized Mrs. Harris as a much-abused female, a sort of "battered mistress" who had finally decided to stand up and fight, the Letter would come as a bitter letdown, exposing its author as the least liberated of women. Judge Leggett finally decides that the Letter is a "two-edged sword." This is why he lets it into the case. But the prosecution's view of the Letter will turn out to be the most accurate. That view is succinctly expressed in a brief filed by the District Attorney after the verdict, opposing Jean's motion to appeal her murder conviction: ". . . unlike the usual case where the criminal defendant's [state of mind] remains somewhat obscure . . . [this jury] actually possessed an X-ray of Mrs. Harris's state of mind. . . . Her scorn for Doctor Tarnower had been memorialized by her own hand. The letter . . . crude in its language and sophomoric in its execution, was devastating in its impact. . . . by it, the [jury] learned that Jean Harris was a liar, and that the roots of her hatred for Doctor Herman Tarnower ran to the marrow."

Leggett has admitted the Letter on a Friday. The jury will not get to hear it until Wednesday. But the prosecution reads it over the weekend, and all Bolen's questions on Monday and Tuesday highlight the defendant's high-mindedness, her air of being different from, and somehow better than, other people. It is a carefully orchestrated prelude to the Scarsdale Letter, de-

signed to make Jean's denial of jealousy look even more preposterous than it already does.

"In 1975 you were aware of the fact that Dr. Tarnower was
seeing socially Lynne Tryforos?"

"No. I was told by Henri and Suzanne that *they* saw her
socially. I didn't know the doctor saw her socially."

After moving to Madeira, was she aware that Dr. Tarnower
was seeing Mrs. Tryforos? "It's very difficult to give you an
answer to that, Mr. Bolen, because of the stories I was hearing.
I dried Suzanne's eyes twice when she came to me in tears
about Lynne trying to seduce Henri."

Does she know if Tarnower was also seeing other women? "I
don't have any idea. I was given to believe so by Henri but I
don't know."

During the weeks she spent at the doctor's house working on
his diet manuscript, was she at all upset that Tarnower was
seeing Mrs. Tryforos? "Yes. As I said before, I thought it denigrated Hi . . . I think this whole conversation denigrates Hi—
and I hate it!" *Tock!* In her agitation, she has clipped the microphone with her chin.

"You were very concerned about the doctor's reputation?"

"I was indeed, and this thing is tearing me apart." Her face
cracks. Seeing her weep is like watching ice break up on a pond.

On the Sunday after David's wedding, did she and Hi discuss
their relationship? Her answer astonishes. "Yes. Hi made love
to me that morning, and we had a lovely conversation about
our relationship . . ." The headmistress smiles boldly, even vo-
luptuously.

"Mrs. Harris . . . that Sunday, before you left the doctor's
home, isn't it a fact that the doctor told you that he no longer
wanted to see you?"

"No, Mr. Bolen, it isn't."

"And isn't it a fact that he suggested that you stay in Washington . . . ?"

"I can't believe who would do this, and would muddy up his
life in such a dirty way. I think this is just a travesty, I really
do! . . ."

Twice Bolen asks what she can recall of her Monday morning
call to Tarnower. Mainly, it was to ask him to tear up the Letter
she had just mailed. She did most of the talking. He finally said

he had to hang up; he had a patient waiting. Did the Letter have anything to do with her relationship to the doctor? "It had a lot to do with my very deep affection for him, yes." Anything to do with another woman? "Yes, but more with my own integrity in being touched by the other woman than by the other woman herself."

The cat-and-mouse game goes on. "But that Letter was replete with reference to Lynne Tryforos."

She calls his bluff. "Yes. Shall we read it here?"

"Would you like that?" he taunts.

No, because it would expose Hi "in a way that I hope he isn't exposed," and herself and Lynne as well. But she isn't afraid, and rather than play games, she would prefer to have it out.

Jean's denial of jealousy is not easy to credit. Yes, she knows Tarnower and Lynne were away together on holiday just before David's wedding but, "George, it's so many years—you are really not going to get me that upset about it." Her smile as she says this is positively saintly. But she has hooked her arms together around the back of the witness chair and looks like a woman tied to a stake.

Please tell the jury *how* Lynne Tryforos "denigrated" Dr. Tarnower? No, that is much too private. Besides, "it's based on very many ugly stories told me by the Van der Vrekens." Having since heard the Van der Vrekens' testimony in this courtroom, she now thinks some of their previous stories may also have been untrue.

Really? You say the Van der Vrekens perjured themselves here? Yes, repeatedly. Is that also true of Officer McKenna, the first man on the scene? Yes. Really? Tell us how Officer McKenna perjured himself, Mrs. Harris?

He told the jury he found Tarnower on his knees, blood pouring from wounds in his front and back; Suzanne said the same. But in his police report, written on the night of the crime, McKenna said the doctor was lying on his back, and he mentioned only one wound, in the chest. He did not mention blood at all, and in fact there is no blood visible on the carpet in the spot where Dr. Tarnower was found. Jean seems to be speaking here in her capacity as "captain of the defense team," but she has little understanding and no capacity for courtroom debate. She has got herself caught now in a fencing duel that at times becomes a slugging match. Yet she is still struggling to be a lady, and she is making a mess of things. Suzanne did not mention any blood in her written report either, and she told the Grand Jury Tarnower's pajamas "looked okay." But she told this jury they were soaked in blood. "I think that's perjury." The jurors listen attentively.

Jean admits she knew that this year on his birthday Dr. Tarnower was planning to be away with Lynne Tryforos.

"So you were upset about that?'

"I was sorry. I wasn't upset."

Bolen is seeking to provoke her feelings of superiority, her sensibility to class, and the strange distinctions she made. "Who he slept with was one thing. But this was a man who read Herodotus for fun. This was my picture of Hi."

"What did you think of Lynne Tryforos?"

"I think she denigrated Hi, and she gave me a great deal of trouble with my own integrity."

"You felt she did not have the education you had?"

"It wasn't a matter of education, Mr. Bolen. It was a question of—"

"Breeding?"

"Perhaps just common sense and taste."

"Lynne Tryforos had no taste?"

"I didn't say that. You did."

"Well, did Lynne Tryforos have taste?"

"I think you have to judge people's taste by some of the things they do. I think writing to a man for eight years, when he is traveling with another woman, is rather tasteless."

One wonders what she thinks of a woman who travels for eight years with a man despite the fact that he is getting love letters from another woman? The answer, of course, is that Jean is in love, and love has no taste.

"Isn't it a fact that [in their conversation of Thursday, March 6] he told you he was taking Lynne Tryforos to that dinner, and he did *not* want you to be there . . . a fact that you had called and begged an invitation . . . a fact that he told you he preferred the company of Lynne Tryforos . . . ?" No, no, and no. "You *knew* you were not going to that meeting with Dr. Tarnower."

"Going with Hi was not the important thing. Being there to

honor him was the most important thing." But she turned to Hi after the episode with the four students because "I always ran to Hi when the ice started to crack, and it was really cracking that weekend."

"You told us a little while ago that at this point you were entering some kind of depressed state. Is that correct?"

"I had been there for many, many, many years." She has begun to cry again. "But I hadn't realized it. . . . From the time I was a young woman, the only prayer I ever prayed was, Just give me the strength to get through this day, one day at a time." Her face is red. "I always said I was fine. [Gasp] I always got through the day. [Gasp] . . . But by that weekend, I couldn't get through any more days." She crumples, seems to dissolve, come all apart without moving or uttering a sound. The judge calls for a recess.

As a part of his cross-examination, Bolen shows the defendant many photographs of the crime scene. Things she remembers clearly have changed position, shape, or color in the photographs. Lynne's negligee was greenish-blue satin with silk embroidery; the police photograph shows a black, flower-printed robe on the floor. She saw gold slippers with turned-up Turkish toes; the pictures show flat black slippers. She remembers a different brand and color of electric curlers. She remembers a box of Lynne's "jewelry"; the pictures show only a cheap metallic watch bracelet without its watch, and a high school ring. Either Jean is hallucinating, or lying, or else, after the crime, all of Lynne's possessions have been removed surreptitiously, and others substituted. These matters are not resolved.

Bolen has returned to the subject of Lynne Tryforos. How did Jean refer to her in that last letter? "Well, let me see. I referred to her as what I had experienced her to be. . . . Dishonest . . . adulterous . . . a whore . . ."

"Didn't you refer to her as *your* whore? Your *psychotic* whore? . . . Didn't you use the word *slut?*"

Jean turns to the bench. "How long do we go on this way, Mr. Leggett? This is not what I understood we were going to do . . ."

"Mrs. Harris, the district attorney is entitled to question you in regard to the Letter, and that is what he is doing. . . . I will

just remind you once more that Mr. Aurnou is your attorney.
. . . He will pose objections when he sees fit."

Mr. Aurnou is silent, unreadable, his back to the room.
Seemingly she's on her own, and her performance is disastrous.
"A whore is a whore is a whore," she says next. No, that is not
a term she customarily uses, but "being touched by something
like this made me struggle very deeply with my own integrity. I
couldn't bring myself to walk away, and I couldn't bring myself
to come to terms with it." What she is trying to describe is her
own passion. But she cannot explain what she does not understand. She has been deluding herself for fourteen years. Absurd
to expect her to be "truthful" now, when she no longer knows
what truth is. She is floundering helplessly, and when Bolen
suggests, "Those were very strong terms to use, aren't they?"
Jean Harris blurts out a response that will help destroy her.

"They are. They are very out of character for me to use. But
it's not like me to rub up against people like Lynne Tryforos."

"It's not like you to rub up against people like Lynne Tryforos? Because she didn't have the background you had? Because
she didn't have the social breeding you had?" Because she so-
cialized with the servants? Bolen has brought out an element of
snobbery that will cling to her ever after, and seriously damage
her in the jury's regard.

When Jean Harris climbed the stairs to her lover's bedroom
with a loaded gun in her purse and a bunch of daises in her
hand, what was in her mind? Did she intend to kill him, or to
kill herself? That is the question the jury is here to decide. But
when she now blurts out the answer to it, no one even notices.
"When you went back the second time and picked up the curlers and threw those, what if anything was going through your
mind at that point?"

"I don't know. I guess mostly what was going through my
mind was the hope that Hi would sit up and say, 'Come on in
and sit down and talk a while,' or 'Go put the teakettle on and
we'll talk a while, and then I'm going to go to bed.'" This is
quite clearly a woman desperately hoping to be talked out of
that which she has threatened to do. But instead of the kind
word, the gentle hand, the cup of tea, she hears, "Get out of
here! You're crazy!" What happened after that is what the jury
must decide.

For six days they have been wondering about the Letter. Now that the moment has come, Aurnou makes a great show of extracting the document from his breast pocket and handing it over to the representative of the People, asserting piously, "Your Honor, *we* would not have read this Letter in public. Despite the fact that it helps Mrs. Harris."

Standing directly in front of the jury box, Bolen reads the entire Letter aloud. Its contents and tone are stunning in their vulgarity. Judge Leggett closes his eyes and turns his face away from the jury so his expression cannot be read. The jurors avoid looking at Mrs. Harris, who is staring into her lap, but their own faces betray confusion and shock. By the time the reading ends, one juror has tears on her cheeks.

Jean Harris had once threatened to kill herself if this Letter were read aloud. Now that it's over, the psychic relief must be immense. She becomes an excellent witness, accurate and composed, for most of the remainder of the afternoon.

But the day ends in a sudden staccato hail of fierce accusations and outraged denial. "Mrs. Harris, on March 10, 1980, did Dr. Tarnower tell you that he had proposed marriage to Lynne Tryforos?"

"No. Did he tell you, Mr. Bolen?"

"Mrs. Harris, isn't it a fact that Dr. Tarnower had told you he preferred Lynne Tryforos over you? . . . Isn't it a fact that during the morning telephone conversation with you, he told you that you had *lied?*"

"No!"

". . . He told you that you *cheated?*"

"No!" She breaks into tears.

". . . He told you you were going to inherit $240,000?"

"No. He didn't."

"Isn't it a fact that he told you, and I quote, 'Goddammit, Jean, I want you to stop bothering me!' "

"No, he didn't! How long can this go on—forever?"

"Isn't it a fact, Mrs. Harris, that on March 10, 1980, you intended to kill Dr. Tarnower, and then kill yourself, because if you couldn't have Dr. Tarnower, no one would? Yes or no, Mrs. Harris?"

"No, Mr. Bolen!"

The prosecutor has no further questions. The courtroom audience breaks into spontaneous applause for the defendant's staunch behavior under fire. In the corridor outside, deputy sheriffs hold back the crowds as the jury is marched to a private elevator. One has a sense of a troop of cavalry passing, much snuffling and blowing, clatter, steam, and jangling. Twelve jurors and four alternates, and nearly everyone still carries a folded newspaper under his or her arm. To imagine that they do not read them despite the judge's daily admonishments now seems absurd.

Mrs. Harris looks exhausted the next morning. She arrives at the courthouse leaning on the arm of William Riegelman, the senior lawyer who lately has become a daily presence at the defense table. On redirect examination, Aurnou cleans up ragged bits of testimony about the crime, the anonymous phone calls, Madeira. His efforts to reintroduce Jean's love letters in order to show the character and depth of the long relationship are no more successful the second time around. The matter of the drugs is barely touched upon in front of the jury. In chambers, the wrangling had been fierce and protracted. Aurnou wants to tell the jury that, despite his subpoenas, approximately forty-three Desoxyn prescriptions to Mrs. Harris, some made out in the names of Tarnower's employees at the Scarsdale Medical Group, have unaccountably disappeared from the Group's records. The ubiquitous lawyer Sirlin is fighting tooth and nail to keep his clients out of this, and Bolen is determined as a woodpecker to crack through the shield of medical privilege that still surrounds the defendant, protecting all her medical and psychiatric records. In compromise, Aurnou downplays his client's ten-year drug use, briefly putting on a pair of drug experts, psychiatrists, who testify that the amount of Desoxyn Jean took could be termed a "high average" dose—correct but very far from complete information. Earlier, in cross-examination, Bolen had pummeled Jean with questions designed to protray her as a drug addict, and Aurnou had objected vehemently to questions about her "physical dependency." As for Jean, she would acknowledge only that she took what her doctor prescribed. "I didn't think about it. If he prescribed it, it must be right."

By this point, everyone is somewhat strung out. The court reporter's hands are shaking. Aurnou takes Jean back over the

Letter. "You said, 'I have to do something besides shriek with pain.' *Were* you in pain? When you said, 'All I ever asked for was to be with you,' was *that* true? When you said you couldn't have sold the ring, was *that* true?"

She has begun to sob and gurgle uncontrollably. "Yes, but do we *have* to do it again, Joel? *Please!*" She cries helplessly, like a small child.

Aurnou persists. "Let me ask you this, Jean. You said in here, 'Too bad Somerset Maugham didn't get hold of us before he died. He would have come up with something to top Magnificent Obsession.' "

"Yes," she interrupts, gulping for air, trying to talk. "I know Somerset Maugham didn't write *Magnificent Obsession!* But I didn't like to think of it as human bondage. . . . Please, let's have a break." She covers her face with her hands and her shoulders heave with sobbing.

It is Jean's most tearful moment of the trial. Much later she would explain this particular outburst to a prison visitor. The previous day, a writer had approached her and Aurnou in the courthouse lobby and pointed out that Maugham was not the author of *Magnificent Obsession.* Jean had said she always forgot the words *human bondage,* and had burst into tears. "And the next day the son of a bitch asks me the same question on the stand! I felt like Charlie McCarthy. To have to say it on the stand the second time was absolutely awful. It seemed dishonest to be asked the same question twice, when he already knew what the answer was. God, I just hated that! I really didn't know he was going to do it, and I was so upset when he did because I thought it made me—" She stopped, struggling for control. "It made *me* a kind of dirty word. . . . I wasn't crying about Hi then. I was crying about what had happened [more sobbing] to the truth."

Monday morning, February 9. Jean Harris is back in her place at the defense table, pert in a neat blue suit, frequently glancing back over her shoulder at the courtroom doors. A middle-aged woman enters, closely guarded by three men who clearly are plainclothes policemen. The People's first rebuttal witness, Mrs. Juanita Edwards, is a dead ringer for Margaret Dumont, eternal dowager of Marx Brothers movies. She has snapping, black button eyes and a tiny, pursed mouth out of which she can hardly wait to spill the beans. George Bolen gets swiftly to the point: Mrs. Edwards is a longtime patient of Herman Tarnower. On the morning of March 10 she was sitting on a table in his examining room and the doctor was checking her pulse when the phone rang. He picked it up and said, "I'll take this call in my office." Then he excused himself, closing the door behind him.

It was a wall phone, and when the doctor placed the receiver on a small bracket beside the phone, it did not sever the connection. Presently Mrs. Edwards was aware of muffled voices coming through the receiver. She heard a man's voice, "very loud and angry," which she recognized as Dr. Tarnower's. "Goddammit, Jean, I want you to stop bothering me!" he shouted. Next came more muffled voices, one "louder in timbre" than the other, which "would have indicated a woman's voice." Then she heard Tarnower again. "You've lied and you've cheated!" followed by more muffled talk, and finally Tarnower again: "Well, you're going to inherit $240,000!" Now Mrs. Edwards heard a click. Dr. Tarnower returned to the examining room, hung up the phone, and without comment resumed his examination.

Mrs. Edwards had gone to the police as soon as she heard of Tarnower's death. But the defense did not hear her story until this past weekend. Aurnou angrily accuses the prosecution of "sandbagging," unfairly holding back Mrs. Edwards's testimony until its rebuttal case, for maximum devastating effect. The District Attorney's office replies that had not Jean Harris herself testified about the call, even mentioning the "waiting patient," Mrs. Edwards would have had nothing to rebut.

Aurnou hacks away at Mrs. Edwards's testimony, reminding her, and the jury, that Lynne Tryforos was also present in the doctor's office that morning. "Are you aware," he thunders, "that the only person or family that inherits $240,000 from the doctor's will is *Mrs. Tryforos!*" This ploy would be more effective if the actual figure *$240,000* appeared in the Tarnower will. Mr. Aurnou has arrived at it by adding to Lynne's $200,000 bequest the two conditional $20,000 legacies to her daughters. Jean Harris was left $220,000, but at this point the likelihood of her ever receiving it appears more remote than ever. There is no reason to doubt that Mrs. Edwards has told the truth as she remembered it. But does this mean that Jean consciously lied when she said Tarnower had *not* told her to stop bothering him; had not accused her of lying and cheating and so on? Not at all. The relationship of these lovers is clearly such that, if Tarnower says one nice thing in the course of a conversation—invites her to visit him in April, for example—it obliterates any nasty things he may also have said. Words of affection from him are so precious that, when she gets them, all else is forgotten. She has already, in effect, "forgotten" the cuff links, the "term paper," the obscene calls and letters, the traces of all the other women, particularly Lynne, the cut-up clothing, the "banishments," the ad in the *Times*. One more hostile phone call would seem easy enough to bury, especially if it contained a nugget as big as a weekend.

The remainder of the trial is a surreal slide show. Behind the scenes, Jean is begging Aurnou to call Lynne Tryforos to the stand. He refuses, saying, "A, she'd lie, and B, she could hurt you."

"For such a dumb woman, Lynne is being very clever," says Jean.

Instead of Tryforos, we get yet another rerun of Dr. Roh, who now says he can confirm that the three odd, microscopic fragments in the chest wound are "either from the palmar surface of the hand or the sole of the feet."

This sends Aurnou into a frenzy of shouting cross-examination. Unless he can shake Roh's testimony, his case is lost. As Aurnou grows noisier, Dr. Roh becomes more soft-spoken and inscrutable, and the defense attorney must badger and batter the witness to force him to admit that his question has only three possible responses: either it *is*, it *isn't*, or *I don't know*. And the traditional euphemism for *I don't know* in the jargon of a pathology report is *consistent with but not diagnostic of*. "Correct?"

A very long pause. Then, "Correct."

The interrogation goes on and on, Aurnou demanding highly technical answers and refusing to settle for layman's language. His questions leave the jury ever farther behind. Assisting Aurnou in this critical interrogation is the star defense pathologist, A. Bernard Ackerman, M.D. Ackerman is an original, an enormous chap in an expensive suit and aviator goggles whose

knowledge of dermatopathology, his life's work, is encyclopedic, and whose self-assurance is awesome. The jury already
knows him as a dazzling lecturer from his earlier testimony in
the defense case. No question but that Joel Aurnou has made
himself into an expert skin pathologist in preparation for this
mighty duel. But his newly acquired expertise and his lawyerly
ego are a fatal combination. Aurnou is telling this jury far more
about skin pathology than they care to know. The prosecution
is equally aware of the jury's befuddlement; in fact, they dis-
cretly seek to encourage it. Bolen's strategy is so to bamboozle
the jury that they will accept without analyzing his own far-out,
and entirely unproven, claim that Jean shot the doctor as he lay
helpless in bed. So Bolen puts on still another skin pathologist,
Martin Brownstein, M.D., to back up Dr. Roh, whereupon
Aurnou puts Ackerman back on to battle the new man to his
knees, fighting as the champion of pure science against the applied science of police department Philistines.

After a final slide show for the glassy-eyed jury, Aurnou sums
up. "Then, in your opinion, you can make a definitive diagnosis?"

Ackerman: "My diagnosis is unequivocal. All three fragments come from tissue *other than* the skin of Dr. Tarnower."

Cross-examining, Bolen is unwise enough to ask, "If these
fragments didn't come from the hand—what are they?"

"Mr. Bolen, I couldn't care less. I was brought here to answer the question: did those fragments come from the palm?
And the answer is no. And where they come from makes not a
jot of difference to me—the brain or the rectum! . . . I tell my
students, 'Don't speculate!' And I'm telling you the same. I
can't say with one hundred percent certainty what they are. But
I *can* say with one hundred percent certainty what they are *not*.
. . . And I can only think, how ironic that the motto of Harvard—"

"Sustained!" barks the judge before the witness can utter the
word *"Veritas."* After a final fulmination of irrelevancy, the exhausted voice of Joel Aurnou says suddenly, "At this time,
Your Honor, the defense rests."

It is 5:29 P.M. on Thursday, February 12. Thirteen interminable days will pass before the jury renders its verdict. During this
time the lawyers will give their summations, and Judge Leggett

will charge the jury on the law. Although the jury does not know this, first-degree manslaughter has been omitted from the usual list of down-charges at the insistence of the defense, over the objections of the prosecution. "Don't compromise!" Aurnou exhorts the jury in summation, and later, in the discussion of charges with Leggett and Bolen in chambers, he remains adamant about forcing the jury to choose between intentional murder and the nonintent charge of second-degree manslaughter (reckless endangerment), or the still lesser charge of criminally negligent homicide. And he persuades Judge Leggett that only these findings—or total acquittal—are supportable by the evidence. Aurnou feels supremely confident that, with Ackerman's help, he has proven his client not guilty of any of the charges against her.

The jury deliberates eight full days. Three times they send out notes to the judge. They ask to have portions of the defendant's cross-examination reread, and to have the judge explain to them again the legal meanings of "intent," "reasonable doubt," the absence of "controlled substances" at the time of the killing, and the difference between direct and circumstantial evidence. Each time they reenter the courtroom, the rest of the players also must reassemble. Jean is waiting out the verdict in seclusion, and on these occasions she comes to the courthouse entirely alone, unescorted by lawyers or friends, and parks her car in the subterranean garage. The sight of the former headmistress, trench-coated, flat-heeled, satchel in hand, gliding all alone up the courthouse escalator in the pummeling flashes of sixty or seventy photographers, moving along the justice assembly line as if on a stockyards meat rack, offers an image of staunchness that is unforgettable.

"Guilty . . . Guilty . . . Guilty . . . Guilty . . ." Judge Leggett has received their verdict and is now polling the jury. They have found her guilty on all counts. Expressionless, Jean Harris removes her glasses. Two deputies stand by to remand her to the jail at Valhalla to await sentencing on March 20. On that date, the entire cast of characters except the jury reassembles in the courtroom for the last time and, sounding apologetic, Judge Leggett prepares to sentence Jean Struven Harris to the minimum term the law permits him to impose: fifteen years-to-life in prison, without possibility of parole before fifteen years.

From the trial transcript of March 20, 1981, page 9729:

> THE COURT: Mrs. Harris, do you care to be heard before
> I impose sentence?
> THE DEFENDANT [standing up]: Yes, I do.
> THE COURT: Okay.
> THE DEFENDANT: I want to say that I did not murder
> Dr. Herman Tarnower, that I loved him very much,
> and I never wished him ill, and I am innocent as I stand
> here. For you or for Mr. Bolen to arrange my life so
> that I will be in a cage for the rest of it, and that every
> time I walk outside I will have iron around my wrists
> [holding up her hands, as if in handcuffs] is not justice.
> It is a travesty of justice.
>
> The people in the jury were told, "Mr. Bolen will
> prove to you beyond a reasonable doubt that Mrs. Harris intended to kill Dr. Tarnower." In their many statements—and a number of them decided to become public figures now, and they have written for the newspaper, and they have been on television shows, and they have been on radio shows—in every single statement they have said, in essence: "Mrs. Harris took the stand and did not prove to us she was innocent, and therefore we find her guilty."
>
> In the ten thousand pages of testimony that have been taken here, there isn't a page, there isn't a paragraph, and there isn't a sentence in which anyone suggests, in which the prosecution suggests how I was guilty of intentionally hurting Dr. Tarnower. And certainly for him [Mr. Bolen] to suggest that he cannot adequately articulate how people feel the loss—that is really gratuitous. Because he certainly doesn't have to explain it to me.
>
> No one in the world feels that loss more than I do. I am not guilty, your Honor.
>
> [Members of the audience applauded.]
> THE COURT: Thank you, Mrs. Harris.

17

Travesties

IF JEAN HARRIS'S LAWYERS had won an acquittal, this would have been the place to congratulate them. But not long into the trial, a dull feeling had set in: this isn't working. What made the defense go so awry? In retrospect, it is evident that fateful errors were made, and that most of the principals were operating in accordance with hidden agendas.

First, the errors. They fall into eight categories: (1) Failure to understand the client, and to make her behavior comprehensible to the jury. (2) Failure to present a believable defense. (3) Failure to offer the jury the "mercy" option—first-degree manslaughter. (4) Failure to appreciate the impact of the Scarsdale Letter. (5) Apparent failure to demand an adequate fee to cover the work that had to be done. (6) Failures in the preparation of the defendant to testify. (7) Failure promptly to seek access to the scene of the crime. (8) Failure to resist the malign effects of the media spotlight.

Before taking up these items one by one, a couple of general comments: Jean Harris has been much criticized for hampering her own defense, and Joel Aurnou has been called incompetent. The first statement has some truth to it, but not the second. Aurnou is more than competent. Many lawyers and judges who work with him daily consider him one of the two or three best criminal trial attorneys they have seen in action. They say, too, that Aurnou was "literally broken" by the Harris case. Furthermore, as we shall see, Aurnou was operating under crippling restraints, not all of them imposed by his client.

1. Failure to understand the client, and to make her behavior comprehensible to the jury. Juries in criminal cases are routinely admonished to forgo sympathy: "You must not let sympathy or compassion for the defendant influence your verdict." Defense lawyers know, however, that of all ritual instructions intoned by the judge, this one is the least heeded. They know that jurors will find a way to acquit a defendant who wins their sympathy; that the key to sympathy is understanding. To acquit, a jury requires a clear picture of the defendant's motive and state of mind, and of the life history that led up to the fatal event. The lawyer's task is to create the bridge of understanding between his client and the jury, and to do this well he must, in the fullest sense, first understand his client.

None of Jean Harris's lawyers understood her. They knew she *was* a lady, but they had little awareness of what that entails; how "being a lady" conditions the human being who plays the role. They did not, for example, understand that Jean's seeming lack of remorse, which George Bolen was able to exploit to skillfully before the jury, reflected her early training. A lady does not show emotion in public. Also, a lady does not compromise, hence Jean's aversion to plea bargaining. "If you're guilty, copping a plea is a gift," she said one day after she had been in prison thirteen months. "But if you're innocent—!" She threw up her hands. That suggested a level of hypocrisy beyond her comprehension. The term "plea bargaining" has a special, eccentric meaning to Jean Harris. She does not perceive it as a mutual accommodation to oil the cumbersome, costly, overtaxed machinery of justice. To her, "plea bargaining" means but one thing: telling a lie in order to receive a lighter punishment. To have claimed that she was temporarily insane, or, worse, to have acknowledged that she may—however tentatively, or even unconsciously—have intended to hurt or harm

Dr. Tarnower, would have constituted "plea bargaining," and hence been unacceptable, no matter the consequences.

Jean Harris had the idealized misconception of the criminal justice system prevalent among innocents who have never been brushed by its ragged skirts: that it is rational, and that its constitutional safeguards work automatically to protect the innocent. Her lack of "street smarts" was awesome. She really believed that the sole way out of the jam she was in was to tell the jury the truth and hope they believed her.

It is the lawyer's responsibility in a criminal case to make the defendant fully cognizant of her peril. He must also make her understand that the legal system is imperfect, a tattered, treacherous lacework of loopholes; that you don't ever bet on its working the way it is supposed to; that you never leave anything to chance, and never close any options. But Aurnou never succeeded in disabusing Jean of her Alice in Wonderland notions, which tragically affected crucial tactical decisions on his part as well as hers.

Aurnou also did not understand the true meaning to his client of Herman Tarnower's death. He did not understand that Jean not only was swept by terrible feelings of grief and guilt; she experienced the loss of Tarnower as a kind of "amputation." Her focus afterward was not on defending what remained of her "self." It was on defending her romance. Jean Harris really wanted two acquittals, one of them for Herman Tarnower.

In his opening statement, Joel Aurnou had told the jury, "The answers to the elements that count in this case lie within the mind of Jean Harris." He was quite right, but he never put on any witnesses to explain her mind, and she could not explain it herself. Not just her bizarre behavior on the night of March 10, but her entire history had to be carefully interpreted to the jury by experts in the vagaries of human behavior, that is to say, by the psychiatric professionals who had examined and treated her.

Trial lawyers give a great deal of thought to the order in which witnesses are called, the point being to wind up one's own part of the case with the most effective witnesses, the most telling testimony. The aim is to present an integrated whole, carefully crafted, orchestrated for maximum effect. Most often it is the defendant herself who testifies last. But if "state of mind" or "intent" is at issue, the expert psychiatric witness occupies the climactic closing spot.

In this trial, the defendant's testimony backfired. After three days of direct testimony, four of lacerating cross-examination, and then a day of redirect examination by Aurnou that appeared to courtroom observers to be the most painful part of the whole ordeal, Jean Harris's entire performance was obviously in desperate need of shoring up by the expert psychiatric professionals who were there, waiting in the wings for the call that never came. Instead, Aurnou suddenly announced, "the defense rests," and slumped in his chair. The night before, he had held a long strategy conference with Dr. Halpern, reviewing the testimony he intended to elicit from him the following day.

Later, Aurnou described his seemingly quixotic decision to rest as a "judgment call." Believing he had won the war of the skin pathologists, he thought he had won his case. He was asked about published reports that psychiatric testimony had been dropped at his client's insistence. Not so, said Aurnou. "We decided against it for a number of reasons. All Jean's medical records would have been opened up. It would have meant exposing her to the People's psychiatrists—and of course we knew who they were. Whereas I had scientific evidence so strong that I possibly could have rested after MacDonell."

Aurnou might also have said that he feels comfortable dealing with physical evidence, his forte, and less so with the ways of the human heart. George Bolen's introduction of the "defensive wound" hypothesis had been effective not because it made sense scientifically, but because it was just the sort of flashy lure to distract the attention of a physical-evidence specialist like Aurnou, and cause him to forget the first premise of trial strategy: never allow your opponent to stake out the issues on which guilt or innocence turns.

Aurnou has scant regard for psychiatry or psychiatrists. "Pay those guys enough, and they'll say anything. They don't work with real facts, you see. So if you feel your physical evidence is strong, shrinks can only detract from that strength. And teams of counter-shrinks tend to cancel each other out."

The risks of a psychiatric defense are well known. It can sound more like an *apologia* than a valid defense. It does subject the client to brutal exposure and cross-examination. Psychiatry and law do not mesh well. But in this case, Dr. Halpern was scarcely a hired gun. No outsider, he would have had what lawyers deem the inestimable advantage of testifying as the defendant's treating physician, having examined her only days after the shooting and, for months after, served as her therapist. Furthermore, he is considered a great witness.* "Abe Halpern is the best psychiatrist I've ever seen on the stand. He has unimpeachable credibility," says Richard Candee, a young Westchester trial lawyer who has successfully defended six murder cases, and whom Aurnou called on for expert advice in handling what lawyers call "an extreme emotional disturbance case" shortly after taking on Jean Harris. "Halpern could have eaten Bolen up," Candee says.

Jean Harris was never enthusiastic about the prospect of psychiatric testimony, but she would have gone along with whatever her lawyers advised. She was if anything a too-compliant client. In her eyes, Aurnou, Riegelman, and Jacobson swiftly came to share the mantle of total authority and absolute wisdom once worn by Herman Tarnower. Although Jean had come to dislike Dr. Halpern, she had no such reservations about the white-haired, fatherly looking psychoanalyst, John Train.

Had he been called to testify, Dr. Train would have told the jury that, in his opinion, Jean Harris was psychotic on March 10, 1980, and that her extreme reluctance to plead insanity (the plea he himself had favored) was itself an aspect of her psychosis. He believed she was suffering from a psychotic depression of "several years' duration," and that the Desoxyn had aggravated her condition. In his firm opinion, her deterioration had begun back in 1967 with her decision to ignore her own sense of right and wrong, and stick with Tarnower despite the impossibility of marriage.

He would have told the jury that he considered Jean Harris incapable of committing murder. "Sure, she was a woman scorned," he said after the trial. "But she was a person who

---

* Since 1981 Dr. Halpern has served as president-elect and president of the American Academy of Psychiatry and the Law.

only could express anger verbally. That kind of woman kills *herself,* never somebody else."

Dr. Train would have liked to offer the jury his psychoanalytic interpretation of Jean's lifelong struggle with her father. "When her father rejected her, she thought that made *her* nothing. She needed obsessively to prove her worth. She became an overachiever. As a schoolgirl, she became a superstar to get from the educational system what she could not get from her father, i.e., approval. In that sense, the school becomes a mirror of self. In the next stage of development, the opposite sex becomes the mirror of self. Then she does a bizarre thing and picks a lover like Tarnower, someone with no empathy. Herman Tarnower fit the childhood needs of Jean Harris at the expense of the needs of the mature woman, Jean Harris. Finally she became a woman who was using all her adult energy and skills to assuage the longings of the deprived child within her."

2. *Failure to present a believable defense.* Jean Harris got what lawyers call a "tragic accident" defense. It is axiomatic among lawyers that as soon as you have more than one bullet wound, the "tragic accident" defense becomes difficult, if not untenable. To claim that four "tragic accidents" occurred in Tarnower's bedroom sounds preposterous, fantastic; it is unbelievable *even if true.*

It is also axiomatic that you cannot put on a defense at odds with the overall appearance of your case. The crucial Scarsdale Letter portrayed an enraged, jealous woman. This needed to be faced and squarely dealt with, not papered over. The Letter reduced Jean's insistence that she was not jealous to absurdity. Her testimony that before the shooting began she had thrown around Lynne's intimate belongings heightened the impression of a woman not just jealous but consumed by jealousy. The disclosure of the defendant's drug dependency without comprehensive expert testimony as to its major medical and psychological consequences made her expulsion of students for marijuana offenses appear to be an act of blatant hypocrisy.

There were other ways in which the defense seemed to lack credibility. The little gun, which Jean testified she did not know how to cock, had a fourteen-pound pull-pressure. Four shots with *that* seemed hard to square with "accident."

In his summation, George Bolen offered a highly fanciful murder scenario that ignored the evidence presented by both sides. He had Jean first shoot Tarnower in bed, *then* throw Lynne's things around, and then rush out of the house, trying to escape. But by that time the failure to present a believable defense had become so grievous that the failure to present a believable prosecution scarcely seemed to matter.

One reason Jean Harris was not a believable witness was that she no longer knew what truth was. She had kept herself alive for fourteen years with increasing doses of self-deception. Even before, looking way back to her early, uncanny ability to romanticize her nemesis, Struvie, in her essay "The Man I Took For Granted," one can see that Jean Harris has had lifelong conditioning in the suppression of unbearably painful truths, and in the denial of angry feelings. When she tried to explain herself to the jury, she could give them only the same fake explanations she had been feeding herself all along. They, being clear-eyed, rejected them.

Her lawyers' failure to deal with Jean's own psychological defense mechanisms was critical. Maybe the client could not admit jealousy, but the lawyer *had to*. Unquestionably, the most effective defense for Jean Harris would have been the one known as "extreme emotional disturbance," or EED. Hers is a classic, textbook example of an EED case. It is a defense the jury could have understood. Why was it not used?

The law has always recognized that one who kills in the heat of passion is less culpable than one who kills in cold blood. "Extreme emotional disturbance" is the modern rubric for what used to be called "the heat of passion." Its meaning is strictly legal; it is not a psychiatric term. In the old days, the passion had to be virtually simultaneous with the killing. When New York's penal law was revised in 1967, the definition of EED was modernized in the light of current scientific knowledge. The law now says that jurors "may consider all emotions which in fact influenced . . . conduct, such as, for example, passion, grief, resentment, anger, terror, fright, hatred or excessive excitement or agitation, and these emotions need not necessarily be of sudden or spontaneous occurrence. They may have simmered in the defendant's mind for a long time. . . ." Or, as the Court of Appeals wrote in New York's leading EED case, *People* v. *Pat-*

terson, ". . . it may be that a significant mental trauma has affected a defendant's mind for a substantial period of time, simmering in the *unknowing subconscious,** and then explicitly coming to the fore."

"Jean Harris is *the* person that defense was written for," says Judge Betty D. Friedlander, who, as appellate attorney, represented the defendant in the landmark *Patterson* case.

In the words of New York Supreme Court Justice Peter J. McQuillan, who helped write the revised definition: "EED is there as a vehicle for the jury to express mercy; to say, yes, the defendant is guilty, but in this particular case, we feel that a special understanding is required."

Notwithstanding, the Harris defense decided at the very outset to "go for broke" by denying the jury the option of finding Jean guilty of the lesser EED offense, tying itself to the "tragic accident" defense, and gambling on acquittal. This fateful decision was, in Aurnou's words, "a crapshoot," but he always felt confident of victory.

EED may have been rejected by the Harris lawyers because it implies a homicidal rather than a suicidal state of mind. In truth, Jean's mind was so turmoiled that night as she climbed the spiral staircase with her suicide gun in one hand, flowers in the other, that she was incapable of defining her intent. Jean Harris did not know what was on her mind. Two years later, she still does not know. She will never know, despite her continuing daily and nightly effort to do so. She reflects her ongoing bewilderment when she speaks today of the EED defense as a "cop-out for somebody who doesn't want to plead guilty to murder."

In the spring of 1982, sitting in the prison visiting room, she was discussing the meaning of EED. "I don't think I was ever crazy," she said. Then, suddenly, she threw up her hands, exclaiming, "It was *obvious* I was extremely emotionally disturbed! But I was told that if I were to take that route, I would have to say I murdered Hi. I had a choice of saying I did or did not intend to murder Hi. For me, it was no choice."

A week or two later, Mrs. Harris wrote to her visitor, "What I meant by my comment about being emotionally disturbed is

---

* Italics mine.

simply that you don't get up and walk out of your life if you *aren't* pretty upset by it. Essentially I did commit suicide that night. I just did it the hard way—which seems to be my modus operandi."

The suggestion seems inescapable that Jean was not properly advised, or if advised was incapable of comprehending the legal meaning and significance of the defense of extreme emotional disturbance. Did her lawyers convey to her that EED can be either momentary or long-standing? That it is a seething in the unknown, unconscious part of the mind? That it does not require admission of any mental disease or defect? How would she have responded if her lawyer had put it all in writing for her, and said, "Go study this, and see whether you can accept it. It is *not* an admission of being crazy, and it does *not* mean you would have to say you 'meant to' kill Dr. Tarnower." A lawyer might have asked her three questions: Did you love him? Yes. Did you do it? Yes. Do you remember the fatal shots? No. He might then have told her, "Mrs. Harris, you are the perfect candidate for this defense, and I can prove it in court."

One is left to wonder why competent counsel was seemingly unable fully to apprise this highly intelligent woman of her legal position in all its nuances.

Finally, there is no inconsistency between an EED defense and a "tragic accident" defense. Indeed, one could have caused the other, and Aurnou could have left room to add EED to his "tragic accident" defense at any point during the trial. But he foreclosed his options at the start. He left himself no flexibility. When he opened to the jury with such phrases as "did not intend," and sneered at the prosecutor's suggestion of ". . . another woman! A love triangle—I am not going to waste any time with that . . . ," trained legal ears already could hear the beginnings of a far-off drumroll of doom.

3. *Failure to offer the jury the "mercy" option—first-degree manslaughter.* In the briefest terms, the law divides all homicides into three categories: involuntary manslaughter, voluntary manslaughter, and intentional, cold-blooded murder. *Involuntary manslaughter,* known as manslaughter in the second degree, informally Man II, occurs when a person recklessly, although not intentionally, causes the death of another person.

Voluntary manslaughter, known as manslaughter in the first degree, or Man I, is causing death in the heat of passion, and it may occur in one of two forms: a person is guilty of Man I when, *with intent to cause serious physical injury* to another person, he causes the death of the person; alternatively, a person is guilty of Man I when, *with intent to cause the death* of another person, he causes the death under circumstances that do not constitute murder because he has acted under the influence of extreme emotional disturbance. The fact that the homicide was committed under the influence of extreme emotional disturbance constitutes a *mitigating circumstance* that automatically reduces murder to Man I.

Murder is intent to kill, not in the heat of passion. Unless the victim is a police officer or corrections officer on duty, New York law considers the crime to be murder in the second degree, or Murder II.* There are a number of defenses to Murder II that are known as *affirmative defenses* because the burden of proof shifts from the prosecution to the defense. The one that concerns us here is the one requiring the defendant to prove that he or she was acting "under extreme emotional disturbance for which there was a reasonable explanation or excuse, the reasonableness of which is to be determined from the viewpoint of a person in the defendant's situation, under the circumstances as the defendant believes them to be." If the defendant can prove the foregoing beyond a reasonable doubt, this "constitutes a mitigating circumstance reducing murder to manslaughter in the first degree," and the jury then has an option— the aforementioned "mercy" option—to convict the defendant of the lesser offense.†

The law prescribes maximum and minimum terms of imprisonment for each degree of homicide. Within these terms prescribed by law, the judge exercises his discretion. The minimum term of imprisonment for Murder II is fifteen years-to-life. The minimum for Man I is two to six years. A defendant with a background like Jean Harris's—no criminal record, no danger

---

* The distinction between Murder I and Murder II is useful to those working gradually to reinstate the death penalty in New York State.

† New York Penal Law, section 125.25

to society, maximum social usefulness in the past—could reasonably have expected to receive a minimal sentence.

In the discussion of charges in Judge Leggett's chambers, the prosecutor had said he would be quite satisfied with a Man I verdict based on intent to cause serious physical injury, and he urged the judge to offer the jury this charge. Aurnou objected, saying the evidence could be interpreted as murder or accident, but that there was no evidence whatever of intent to cause serious physical injury, and the judge agreed. Since EED is an affirmative defense, only Aurnou, not Bolen, could have requested a Man I charge based on EED, and Aurnou refused, insisting as he had from the beginning that he wanted to force the jury to make an either/or choice between accident and murder. In his summation, Aurnou had tried to make the point that Jean Harris loved Herman Tarnower so much that she could not possibly have killed him, although poets for centuries have earned their living describing the intertwinings of love and hate. The lawyer had told the jury slowly and emphatically, "Do . . . not . . . compromise. I think you have all understood me from the beginning. . . . I said tragic accident. . . . *Don't compromise!* Search for the truth—we can take it!"

Aurnou had never wavered in his strategy. Back in September he had told a reporter, "At the end of a trial, before the judge charges the jury, it is customary for him to ask the lawyers what the charges should be. Usually it's the defense lawyer who asks to have lesser included offenses charged. In this instance, the DA will ask it, and I will insist that they *not* be. I want to force that jury to choose either murder or acquittal—no compromise."

When the time came, the discussion in chambers went just as Aurnou had said. It was Bolen who asked Leggett to instruct the jury that if they agreed to acquit the defendant of murder, their next option should be to consider a verdict of first-degree manslaughter. Then, if they also acquitted on this charge, he asked that they next be instructed to consider second-degree manslaughter, and after that, criminally negligent homicide. This is the normal, orderly progression of down-charges; in requesting it, the DA was merely sewing things up, protecting his record. It didn't cost him anything. But when Aurnou argued vehemently in favor of omitting the charge of first-degree manslaughter altogether, skipping right over it, Judge Leggett went along with him, agreeing that no evidence had been presented of an attempt to cause serious physical injury which inadvertently resulted in death.

So the choice went to the jury in its most stark form, accident or murder. It went as a gauntlet. They chose murder.

Later Aurnou explained his reasoning. "Like Murder II, Man I is also an 'intent' charge, and I didn't want to give the jury an opportunity to consider intent twice. The last thing you want the jury to dwell on is intent. When you get them past intent—she walks." Another time he said, "Also, I wanted to get her probation. Man I is a mandatory no probation. With Man II, she'd have had a very healthy shot at it." But this jury said later that they never got past consideration of the top charge. They considered it for eight days, and finally, unable to reenact the shooting the way they understood the defense to have described it, they convinced the lone holdout that guilty of murder was the only possible verdict.

After the verdict, Bolen told reporters he would have been happy with a Man I verdict. Other members of the DA's office acknowledged that they would even have considered Man II an acceptable verdict.

Professionals were shocked by the omission of Man I from the down-charges. Supreme Court Justice McQuillan said, "It is so rare *not* to give Man I that I cannot think of a single instance in which it has not been done. I have never heard of its being skipped! That's throwing away a whole lifetime based on technical jazz!"

Many lawyers believe there was a more pragmatic reason why EED was not invoked. George Bolen could scarcely wait to point it out to reporters when he stopped in, flushed with victory, at the impromptu press cocktail party that followed the verdict. The "real reason" Aurnou had insisted on "going for broke," Bolen said, was that he was crapshooting for very high stakes—Jean's $220,000 legacy from Herman Tarnower, and perhaps much more. Unless he could get his client acquitted of intending to murder her lover, the law would prevent her from collecting her inheritance. Furthermore, it would keep her from selling book or movie rights to her ghastly experience, even if she could bring herself to do so. New York's newly passed "Son of Sam" law makes it illegal to profit even indirectly from a murder by selling "rights" to one's criminal misadventures. Such profits rightfully belong to the family of the victim, not to the perpetrator, the new law says. It seems clear that, unless Aurnou got his client past both intent charges, any hope that he might have had of collecting more than his original $25,000 looked slim.

4. Failure to appreciate the impact of the Scarsdale Letter. Legally, the Letter was Jean Harris's property. According to Aurnou, she had the right to dispose of it as she saw fit. But she was never told. Nor was she made aware, except by the promptings of her own instinct, that the Letter could be her undoing. She was told instead that the Letter might become "necessary" to her defense. In retrospect, she thinks the Letter should have been thrown away. "The trouble was, once the Letter was in evidence, Madeira didn't matter anymore. . . ."

But the trouble was much greater. It was that all her advisers, not just Aurnou, misread the Letter and arrived at the fatuous conclusion that the document would show up Tarnower as an utter cad. Letter in hand, the same man who had originally said, "Fellas, you gotta understand my client. She's very much a lady," did the one thing guaranteed to destroy his client's ladylike image: he allowed her to take the stand, which enabled the Letter to be read to the jury. The Letter did not merely destroy the whole premise of a no-jealousy defense; it made Jean seem no lady at all. In fact, the Letter was the work of a lady driven mad by her own demons. Buried resentments pour forth from its pages like the tiny devils with pitchforks that gush from the mouths of victims of demonic possession in medieval paintings.

To have destroyed the Letter early in the game would have been unwise for several reasons: the DA would almost certainly have charged "destruction of evidence"; and some unforeseen development in the course of the trial might have made it necessary to reveal the contents. The Letter thus required a carefully conceived strategy to limit its impact. Regrettably, the lawyers had convinced themselves that the Letter was an asset, not a liability; consequently, no defensive strategy was devised. In retrospect, Dr. Train believes it would have been better to show

the Letter to the jury immediately, as evidence of Jean's internal
chaos and despair, instead of holding it back until it appeared to
be proof of her guilt. He recognized the Letter for what it was:
not proof that Jean was no "lady," but proof that the lady was
psychotic and out of contact with reality. "What that letter
really says," Train explains, "is, 'Please don't call me a liar.
Don't reject me. When you believe Lynne, instead of believing
me, you destroy me. Don't do that.' It is really a plea for *understanding.*"

If the Letter had to go in, Jean would have preferred to have
read it to the jury herself, in order to defuse the prosecution's
exploitation of its contents. She was not allowed to do so.

No one was more shocked by the Letter than Jean's childhood friend, Marge Jacobson. "Little, proper Jeannie! I just
couldn't believe it! I *couldn't,*" she exclaimed.

But Marge, of all people, should have recognized that terrifying voice. For it was the long-suppressed Struvie side of Jean
that finally was heard in those raging pages; all Struvie's fury
and hatred were coming out at last. The part of herself that
Jean had always tried to deny, to muzzle, to keep behind the
iron door, was up on its hind legs now and roaring.

5. *Apparent failure to demand an adequate fee to cover the
work that had to be done.* Law professionals feel that lack of
adequate help for Aurnou was most destructive to Jean Harris's
defense. A lawyer simply cannot handle a case of this nature as
a legal one-man-band. No single individual can take on both the
necessary technical preparation and the daily trial work. One
person cannot keep the citations and codified law in his head at
the same time he is trying the case. If a single lawyer is handling
everything, he cannot also sit back and watch how the trial is
going. He cannot be both actor and audience.

Soon after agreeing to represent Jean Harris for the nominal
fee of $25,000, Aurnou had dissolved his two-year-old law part-
nership, Aurnou, Rubenstein, Morosco and Kelligrew.* It was
a pity; the four-way blend of talents had been about perfect.

---

* Earlier, Aurnou, a Democrat, had been appointed a county judge to fill an
unexpired term. He founded his law firm after failing to be elected when he ran for
the post.

Benjamin Rubenstein is a highly skilled personal injury lawyer; B. Anthony Morosco is technically exceedingly competent and has considerable experience as a former prosecuting attorney. As for John Kelligrew, he is an excellent criminal lawer, experienced and politically well connected. It was Morosco who had doped out the correct federal procedures to follow and the proper U.S. postal forms to fill out, and Kelligrew who had physically retrieved the Scarsdale Letter from the post office, just hours ahead of the DA's men.

By the time his case got to trial, Aurnou was not consulting with any of his ex-partners. His reconstituted legal "team" consisted of Victor Grossman, a bright and personable young lawyer with virtually no criminal experience; Aurnou's faithful and very pregnant secretary, Rose Stern; and four or five other young lawyers and law student volunteers who shuttled in and out on a part-time or unpaid basis. Most professional observers thought that Aurnou made an additional tactical error by not disclosing to his client when he was first retained that the money available was entirely inadequate to cover the expenses necessary for private investigators, expert witnesses, and so on, irrespective of Aurnou's own legal fees.

Although he was working night and day and Saturday and Sunday on the Harris case, Aurnou's abrupt loss of his partners obliged him also to attempt to continue handling his other clients as well. In the long months of preparation and trial, he twice literally collapsed with exhaustion and was ordered to bed by his doctor.

Aurnou put himself into this one-man-band position knowing he could call upon the impressive resources of Jacobson's two-hundred-and-fifty-lawyer firm. And Fried, Frank, Harris, Shriver and Jacobson did provide valuable legal assistance—for example, the twenty-one-page memorandum of law on the admissibility of psychiatric testimony on intent in a noninsanity case. But they were bigtime corporate lawyers with zero experience or savvy in criminal law. As a result, Aurnou's entente with the big firm had a doubly negative impact: he still did not have adequate legal backup, and ultimate control of his own "big case" was in the hands of people who knew less about it than he did. As time passed, the big firm found itself gradually laying out extensive sums for backup legal work during the trial, and later for the very costly preparation of two appeals. Eventually these expenses can be written off, but for the moment, all is being charged to Jean Harris's account. At the end of her first year in prison, she told a visitor she had been advised by William Riegelman that her legal bills then totaled $250,000.

Two thirds of the way through the trial, Aurnou's crippling exhaustion was evident to all. On several occasions he wept openly, both in his office and in the courtroom. The new daily presence of William Riegelman at the defense table made it apparent that the big law firm was reasserting closer control. Between Aurnou's grogginess and Riegelman's unfamiliarity with the details of the case, and with criminal law in general, the defense seems to have missed a critical error during the cross-examination of Jean Harris. Bolen was questioning her closely as to where she had been standing, and which direction she was facing when she first took out the gun. She said she was near the foot of her bed, facing northeast, or slightly toward the bathroom. But she had told MacDonell she was facing southeast, toward the TV set and the glass doors. MacDonell said later, "Her own testimony is inconsistent with what she herself showed me in the room. It is also inaccurate in terms of the physical evidence. Physical evidence does not lie. People under intense cross-examination can get confused." When Jean seemingly misspoke herself, Aurnou failed to call her attention to it, then or later, and get her story straightened out. Bolen, in his summation, pointed out the inconsistency to the jury, and when they attempted to reenact the first shot the way they understood Jean to have described it, they were unable to do so.

6. *Failures in the preparation of the defendant to testify.* Although there is no way for a lawyer to judge whether or not it is wise to put his client on the stand unless, privately, he has been preparing and questioning her all along, it did not happen that way in the Harris case. One Monday, as they were strolling back from the courthouse to Aurnou's office, the lawyer simply said, "Jean, you're going to go on tomorrow."

"I was not looking forward to putting Jean on, believe me. That was a reluctant decision," he told a reporter later. "But look what had happened by then! Roh had said yes, the hand wound *could* have happened in the course of a two-person struggle. But then Leggett wouldn't allow Herb's two-person diagram, which showed *how* it could have happened, into evidence, because Jean had not yet testified.* So now I hadda put Jean on, to say *where* in the room they both were, and how it happened. Only Jean could tell the jury what went on in that bedroom."

But this was not quite accurate. She could tell them everything *but* how the two fatal shots happened to be fired. In these circumstances, the ultimate effect of putting her on the stand was entirely negative.

Like all good trial lawyers, Joel Aurnou has a very quick mind and, to every question, an array of possible answers useful under varying circumstances. The Monday he told Jean she would "go on tomorrow," he added that he had reached his decision over the weekend. Later he said to a reporter, "I wanted to catch Bolen unprepared."

Instead, he caught Jean Harris. Jeptha Schureman, Jean's seasoned divorce lawyer, later wrote, "a criminal defendant who voluntarily takes the stand is at the mercy of the cross-examiner, and is sitting naked before the jury, whose microscope is focussed on little things like nervous mannerisms, argumentativeness, bitchiness, weaseling, imperiousness, personality (alas), and a whole lot of imponderables having nothing to do with credibility. It boils down to whether they like the witness or not."

A judge who followed the case commented later, "Any hope of catching Bolen unprepared reveals Aurnou as no more able to estimate depth of character in the prosecutor than in his client. Bolen started to prepare his cross of Jean from the day he got the case, and was thoroughly prepared for her testimony —witness his skillful buildup to the reading of the Letter."

The eight days Jean Harris occupied the witness box were fatally damaging to her case. Inadequately prepared and re-

---

* The judge had accepted the professor's two other schematic drawings of the trajectory of the bullet that shattered the glass door. One included a figure of Jean Harris, to show her location when she took the gun from her purse. But he excluded the drawing of two figures, Jean and Hi. After Jean's testimony, Aurnou twice reoffered the third diagram, but Leggett continued to refuse to accept it. He was not required to give his reason and he did not.

hearsed, she appeared scornful, spiteful, hypocritical, often foolish, and an unrepentant snob. Her performance was so self-
defeating that afterward many people wondered: had she over-
ruled her lawyers and insisted on taking the stand?

When the question was put to her directly, in prison after the
trial, she replied, "I did not insist. I wanted to testify, because
my middle-class conscience told me that I had to get up there
and tell them the truth. But if they'd all said no, Jean, keep
quiet, I'd have kept quiet until it was all over and then tried to
tell my story in a book."

During portions of her testimony, the jury could not look at
her—always a chilling sign. She herself never looked at the
jurors while she was occupying the witness box, an extraordi-
nary display of insensitivity on her part, and, if her lawyer did
not remonstrate with her, on his. "I assumed you just replied to
the individual who asked you the question," she later confided
to a friend.

Nobody had told her that she was part of a play, and that the
twelve people in the box were the most important audience she
would ever have in her life. "I realize it now. I realize that in a
trial, the end always justifies the means," she said afterward. "I
didn't realize it then."

Nor, says Harris, was she put through any mock cross-examination. Such preparation is so standard an element of criminal
practice that other criminal attorneys say they "cannot believe"
Jean was not prepared. Wrote Schureman: "No courtroom lawyer *ever* lets his clients or his witness testify without first 'horse-
shedding' (an old expression from the days when rural court-
houses had horsesheds next door where lawyers consulted with
their clients), sometimes called sandpapering. We have a dry
run using questions we will ask and the ones we *think* they can
expect from the other side, as a devil's advocate."

Said Herald Price Fahringer, the distinguished appellate specialist who was brought in after the verdict to handle Jean's
appeals, and who later became famous as Claus von Bulow's
lawyer, "If it is true that Jean was not prepared, I am horrified
and shocked."

After Jean was sent to prison, she was requeried on this point
several times. "Well, over the summer before the trial, Jim
Chapman talked to me about it for an hour or two," she once

said defensively. Chapman is an eager young Elmira ex-cop who took police science courses at night and would up as one of Professor MacDonell's corps of volunteer assistants. Bolen had immediately destroyed his usefulness to the defense by forcing the admission under cross-examination that the professor's assistant had never finished high school.*

"Did anybody tell you how to dress?" Jean was also asked. There had been much press criticism of her expensive wardrobe and mink hat.

Lawyer friends had given her some advice over the summer, she said, but when the trial began, "I wore my own clothes. They were my work clothes. They were all I had . . . the same clothes that I wore to teach school."

After the verdict, fashion editors wrote features stories on how Jean's elegant wardrobe had doomed her in front of a working-class jury. One such story quotes Aurnou: "It would be rather presumptive of me to tell Mrs. Harris how to dress." But most defense attorneys routinely go out and buy their clients the "right" clothes, if they do not already own them.

"I don't blame anybody for any of this," Jean Harris says today. "The only thing that bothered me during the trial was not knowing what was going to happen next. I kept saying to Joel, 'I don't know what to expect, Joel. Please tell me what's going to happen now!' But nobody ever did. Joel did tell me a few general things: wait to give my answer until the question was asked, be sure to give Joel time to respond, and answer briefly. And he tried to tell me, in a nice way, not to worry if I cried. I'm sure he meant that crying wouldn't hurt with the jury."

Perhaps Aurnou prepared Jean more than she now recalls. She herself may well have resisted preparation, preferring to stake everything on her ingrained conviction that only telling the absolute truth could set her free. One day she told a prison visitor that she thought the idea of preparing a witness to testify "is like your mother telling you cute little things you did as a child. Finally you think you remember doing them yourself— and I didn't want that to happen."

---

* Chapman had a high-school equivalency diploma, a college degree, and a graduate degree. But Aurnou did not bring these facts out on redirect.

When Aurnou was asked if Jean had perhaps resisted preparation, he said curtly, "In her eight days on the stand, if she had been improperly or not fully prepared, George Bolen could have broken her story."

But it was precisely Bolen's cross-examination that convinced the jury Mrs. Harris was not telling the truth. The defendant's hatred, mistrust, and fear of the prosecutor was consuming; Bolen knew this and turned it to his own advantage, carefully drawing her out, gently provoking, deliberately playing on her unacknowledged jealousy of her rival, knowing just what innocuous-seeming little words would sting and make her lash out. Watching Bolen's cross-examination was a lot like watching a caged animal being poked at with a stick.

7. *Failure promptly to seek access to the scene of the crime.* On December 30, 1981, Jean Harris's bid for a new trial was rejected unanimously by the five justices of the Appellate Division of the State Supreme Court.* Despite the ritual intonation that although Mrs. Harris "did not receive a perfect trial, she received an eminently fair one," the fifty-five-page opinion written by Presiding Justice Milton Mollen criticized the caliber of Mrs. Harris's defense in exceedingly harsh language. Said Fahringer of the bluntness of the judicial attack, "It is most unusual to have this kind of disparagement of counsel in a court opinion. . . ."

In rejecting the various points of the Harris appeal, the judges repeatedly pointed out that it was Aurnou's own actions and inactions, waivers and defaults that had created the very circumstances of which the appeal complained. For example: the appeal claimed that the jurors had improperly attempted to reenact the shooting during their deliberations, thus in effect improperly "manufacturing evidence." But Aurnou, in his summation, had challenged the jurors to do just that. "Try it in the jury room!" The appeal criticized the voluminous pretrial publicity; the judges' brief said that the defense had helped generate the excessive ballyhoo. But the judges reserved their most astringent language to reject the claim that Jean had not received a fair trial because she and her attorneys were denied timely

---

* On November 16, 1982, her second appeal for a new trial was denied.

access to the crime scene, and that in the interval important evidence was lost, such as the blood-stained carpet. In his first appeal, Fahringer wrote, ". . . the carpet would have corroborated Mrs. Harris' testimony concerning where the first shot was fired . . . would have shown he [Tarnower] walked around his bed, into the bathroom where he washed his hands and then returned to the bedroom."* But the police had failed to preserve the carpet after taking their photographs.

The appellate judges pointed out that Aurnou's failure to obtain a court order overruling the defense debarment from the crime scene was "less than prompt," not having been filed until two months after the doctor's death, even though Mrs. Harris "was represented by counsel even before Dr. Tarnower was pronounced dead." In their brief, the judges wrote that Jean Harris was "a victim of her own tardiness."

Such are the euphemisms of bench and bar; when convenient, counsel and client become legally indistinguishable. In fact, during the ten days Mrs. Harris was a patient in United Hospital, she was repeatedly overheard pleading with Aurnou, both in person and on the telephone, "Joel, did you get the court order yet? We've *got to* get into that house!" Although Aurnou continued to reassure his client that he was taking care of the matter, in fact he was taking care of other clients, and even taking a brief vacation, during the sixty days he allowed to elapse before filing the request. "Not only was her request less than prompt; it was actually untimely, and was subject to summary denial," Justice Mollen wrote. Whatever was destroyed, he said, had been made available to the defense for a sufficient length of time, and could have been held longer, had the defense asked for it. "There is no evidence that any representative of the defense ever made a request to the police or to the District Attorney's office to preserve any particular items of evidence." The People's responding brief on this point claims that Aurnou had deliberately failed to make such a request in order to manufacture an issue for the appeal, in the unlikely event that should become necessary.

* * *

* *The People of the State of New York* v. *Jean S. Harris,* Indictment No. 275–80, Appellant's Brief, p. 45.

8. *Failure to resist the malign effects of the media spotlight.*
Close study of the Jean Harris case suggests that the criminal
justice system deals best with the guilty, the artfully criminal;
that defense lawyers should pray to be sent only guilty clients,
the ones they are best trained to handle; and, most frightening,
that the innocent client should pray for utter obscurity. Our
system of justice must be open and public. But to turn the
spotlight of massive modern media attention on any criminal
case, to turn the courtroom into a national arena, is inevitably
to unloose forces unknown to the common law, and unenvi-
sioned by the Founding Fathers. They could not possibly have
anticipated the awesome impact of the mass media. Today's
press and TV not only have the power to transform the old-
fashioned county courthouse into a truly national courthouse,
or national forum, as happened during the congressional Water-
gate hearings. They also have the power to turn an orderly trial
by jury into something like a national bullring.

Much has been written about the public's "right to know,"
and the right of press access to judicial proceedings. Less is
known about the adverse effects of excessive public attention.
Surely daylight is more hospitable to justice than the blackness
of the Star Chamber. But the full attention of the modern media
generates a light much brighter than day, and defendant, accus-
ers, lawyers, judge, and jury—all to a degree are phototropic to
the spotlight's glare. This phenomenon has received insufficient
study as yet by champions of the free press, or by legal scholars.
But most of the latter will agree that, for the criminal defendant, his chances of acquittal are in inverse ratio to the publicity that has been generated.

Joel Aurnou is a man of good heart and strong passions, and
he was deeply affected by his client's plight—too deeply. He lost
the defense attorney's essential objectivity. Losing his emotional
neutrality, letting his big case become too important to him,
impaired his ability to exercise his own best judgment as an
experienced trial attorney. Not only did he convince himself he
could slay the dragon single-handedly. No one was more impressed with Jean Harris as a "lady," to be handled gingerly,
with kid gloves, than was her own lawyer. As a result, says one
former law partner, he failed to administer to her the necessary
"one dozen humility lessons" before trial. With the 20/20 clar-

ity of hindsight, most other trial lawyers say now that when Aurnou's client began to dictate strategy, forbidding him to defend her by attacking Tarnower, for example, he should have walked away. In the words of one colleague, "If a client had said to me, and would not change her mind, 'I am not crazy, and I was not extremely emotionally disturbed that night,' my response would have been, 'Lady, get yourself another lawyer. You have my vow of silence until after the verdict. Then I'm going to say how *I* think the case should have been handled.' "

It is unlikely that a man of Aurnou's intelligence and experience could have been swayed so far off balance were it not for the unaccustomed personal notoriety that suddenly illuminated him the instant he became the lawyer for a tabloid celebrity. Under the relentless attentions of the hundred-odd newsmen and TV people who began besieging his office and swamping his telephones, Aurnou's ego bloomed like a sunflower in August. He took to giving out fulsome interviews on client and strategy as he strutted about his office, the telltale Scarsdale Letter bulging tantalizingly in his breast pocket. He hugely enjoyed his new importance, his words and pictures in the newspapers, his ability to leak tidbits of fact, or fancy, to favored reporters.

Once the trial circus got under way, all defense egos appeared to bloom in riotous profusion. Every afternoon they would march down the hill from the courthouse, Aurnou, Grossman, assistants, and client, collapse into the leather chairs, flip on the local news to check the day's TV coverage, meanwhile rehashing the latest radio and print verbiage. They glowed with a self-generated sense of victory. "They were triumphant about the way Joel was destroying every witness," says a lawyer who saw them almost daily during this period. "Joel's arrogance was infuriating to me. I thought the client's seeming arrogance was something she picked up from him, and that it turned the jury off both of them."

In the courtroom, the effect on Aurnou of the media spotlight's white glare seemed to be to metamorphose a man already known to be gifted in the handling of knotty, abstruse physical evidence into a kind of Walter Mitty of dermatopathology. By the time the exhausted lawyer made his "judgment call" and suddenly rested, his judgment was far from what it used to be.

As media attention to the case increased, a "window-ledge"

mentality became evident among the crowds of spectators who daily lined up at the courthouse in hopes of a glimpse of the defendant and, if lucky, an hour or two in one of the few courtroom seats saved for members of the general public. When a would-be suicide crawls out on a window ledge, and the crowds gather below, when the firetrucks arrive, and the searchlights go on, a voice in the crowd always yells "Jump!" and the chant is taken up by the mob. Something similar happens at witch-burnings, public hangings, autos-da-fé. Something similar happened here. Watching the proceedings, one found it increasingly difficult to convince oneself that the jurors who were marched through these crowds four times daily—every morning, every evening, and in and out for lunch, escorted by deputy sheriffs, to be sure—remained uncontaminated by the circuslike courthouse atmosphere. To attempt to sequester a jury from all this hoopla would have invited difficulties of another nature: jurors tend to become resentful at prolonged total separation from friends, families, sex, drink, and the other comforts of home; and they tend increasingly to identify with the forces of law and order, the sheriffs and marshals who have become their guardians-mentors-jailers, their authority figures.

Jean Harris's remarkable tendency to polarize public opinion already has been noted. In the months before her trial, the gathering public scorn and contempt for this celebrity-defendant became almost palpable. Several old legal hands, experienced in the image-management of unpopular defendants, went to Aurnou to suggest he try to do something to neutralize the overall climate of public hostility to his client before the time came to pick a jury. It might be helpful, they suggested, if Aurnou or Mrs. Harris were to make a public statement to the effect that, since she had no wish to profit from the tragic death of the man she loved, she intended to turn over her $220,000 legacy to a public charity—preferably one in Westchester County.

"That's a very interesting idea," said Joel Aurnou. But Mrs. Harris says he failed to mention it to her.

A ninth defense problem, one that could not entirely be termed a *defense error*, was the notable lack of empathy between defendant and jury, a detachment which seemed to increase as the trial progressed. For whatever reasons, the people in the box never seemed like a jury of her peers, and one was left to wonder uneasily how and whether class, sexual, and racial differences, opacities, and animosities on both sides might affect the outcome. Psyching out the jury is a favorite post-trial pastime. Maybe Aurnou should have taken the ones with blue-green auras, as his psychic had recommended. Herb MacDonell, who has assayed hundreds of juries, says flatly, "Jean Harris was convicted because of class. Nothing including an eyewitness account of the event would have helped with that jury." But the jury did not disbelieve all of Jean's story. They accepted that she had driven to Purchase intending suicide. But they decided that she changed her intent at some time after entering the bedroom—possibly not until she actually had the gun in her hand and her finger on the trigger. Judge Leggett had explained more than once that intent can be formed in a split second.

A prominent Westchester trial lawyer declares: "I have worked in thirty counties, and Westchester juries are the worst. Jean Harris did not have exactly a blue-collar jury, despite what the papers said. Many of these people held supervisory roles. They were more accustomed to giving orders than taking orders. They were persons very much of a law-and-order mentality. They would tend to be against a defendant who came from a moneyed background, *any* defendant."

Each lawyer had twenty challenges, and in the critical matter of jury selection, "Bolen absolutely took the case away from Aurnou. These jurors resented her wealth, or her appearance of wealth. She should have had a more elitist jury. The absence of Jews on the jury was damaging, not just because they're traditionally liberal, but because both the deceased and the entire defense setup was so heavily Semitic. Jews on the jury would not have been offended by this. But some non-Jews may have wanted to punish her for playing the White Goddess to this group. In a case like this one you want, above all, to find people who can relate to an extramarital affair. This generally means a highly intellectual, high income jury, which she certainly didn't have."

When Aurnou was asked how come he had got such a bad jury, he replied, "Eight to four for acquittal on the first ballot is not a terrible jury."

But earlier, appearing on the *Tom Snyder Show*, jury foreman Russell von Glahn had told the audience that their first ballot had been three not guilty, four guilty, and five undecided. Another juror told *The New York Times* that their initial vote had been eight guilty, four for acquittal.

Jean Harris spent her time on the witness stand defending her love instead of her life. The jurors' facial expressions suggested that they found her middle-aged passion sappy and unseemly; a luxury perhaps for the mod rich, but to them a joke. Later, in prison, Jean told a visitor she had once overheard the four alternate jurors literally guffawing at her story while seated backstage in a room adjacent to the judge's chambers.

So yes, Jean did offend her jurors. And yes, at least some of them thought her a snob, and some a joke, and probably they were critical of her way of life in several of its aspects. But they were also extremely conscientious; they listened very hard, and their eight-day debate on the merits of the case constitutes the longest jury deliberation in New York State history. When finally they voted as they did, it must be assumed that their verdict reflected the long accumulation of errors, misapprehensions, and travesties we have here been talking about.

After the case was lost, and Jacobson chose Fahringer to handle the appeal, he kept Aurnou on to assist him, pointing out that only Aurnou knew the details of the case well enough to prepare a speedy appeal. But the decision may have had unfortunate consequences for the defendant in that it precluded arguing on appeal that Jean Harris was deprived of her constitutional right to the effective assistance of counsel. When the Appellate Division opinion upholding Jean Harris's conviction came back stinging in its personal criticism of Joel Aurnou, he was soon quietly dropped.

The law is not perfect, but it is compassionate, and it does have mechanisms to deal with defendants like Jean Harris. But the sum total of defense failures in this case produced a result that made no one entirely happy, not even the judge. (One may exempt the District Attorney's office from this statement on grounds that prosecutors like winning the way sharks like eating; *doing it* is all that counts.) A few months after the verdict, Jean Harris was told that Russell Leggett had said to a friend,

"Mrs. Harris, as I see it, is no threat whatever to the community or to society."

The final travesty in the Harris case would seem to be that the law itself was mocked.

Thus far we have been talking only about the failures of the defense. If the prosecution too committed many errors, it does not matter. They won. But according to A. Bernard Ackerman, M.D., chief defense pathologist and probably the nation's outstanding expert in dermatopathology, a special kind of moral error, deeply offensive to his standards as an academician and as a scientist, was committed by the prosecution. It is Dr. Ackerman's opinion that the People's medical experts, Drs. Roh and Brownstein, misinformed the jury by being too much the DA's advocates, rather than detached scientists. "Is it proper for medical examiners and prosecutors to work together as collaborating colleagues, rather than as independent professionals?" Ackerman asks in a quietly scathing, sixty-page scientific paper prompted by his first courtroom experience as an expert witness.* "Furthermore," says Ackerman, "we physicians submit ourselves to peer-review in every area of medicine except in the courtroom. There a doctor can say anything he likes. The same standards that apply to the pathologist at the autopsy table, behind the microscope, and in the lecture hall of a university medical center should obtain for the pathologist in a courtroom. But did those standards obtain in the trial of Jean Harris?"

Dr. Ackerman's paper points out that Dr. Roh altered his testimony no less than six times. First, over the summer, he changed his opinion about the number of bullets that struck Herman Tarnower from four to three, a change which accommodated the prosecution's new-fledged "defensive wound theory" that one bullet caused two wounds, those in the palm and in the chest. Second, he revised his Autopsy Report in mid-trial to include an "Addendum" that for the first time mentioned three microscopic fragments of palmar tissue. He had not noted these fragments in his original Report, based upon examination

---

* "The Physician as Expert Witness: Is Peer Review Needed?" *American Journal of Dermatopathology,* 1983.

of the same tissue sections from the wound in the chest. This change in the Autopsy Report supported the prosecution's contention that when the defendant fired at the doctor as he was extending his palm in self-defense, the bullet carried palmar tissue into the chest wound.

Furthermore, under direct and cross-examination, Dr. Roh gave a total of four different versions of the kinds of palmar skin the fragments consisted of. Dr. Brownstein, the People's expert dermatopathologist, in court gave an account of the fragments different from that in his own written report about them. Under penetrating cross-examination by Aurnou, Brownstein was compelled to contradict the testimony of Dr. Roh on twenty-three separate issues of medical fact, including the diagnosis of some of the fragments. Brownstein also was forced to admit that, in a note written in his own hand, presumably to the prosecutor, he had proposed that good photographic evidence would "frighten off" still other dermatopathologists from testifying in the case. Since Jean Harris was fully aware of the foregoing, is it any wonder that she was leery of being examined by other expert-witness physicians and psychiatrists hired by the People?

One of several judges who closely followed the trial comments, "A motion could have been made by the defense at the end of all the expert pathology testimony to have it all stricken as prejudicial. One standard for the admissibility of scientific evidence is that its probative value must outweigh its prejudicial effect on the jury. In this case, all those 'could have beens' and 'looks likes' from the People's experts gave the matter undue weight, when the totality of the evidence was that nobody knew for sure what those tiny fragments in the chest wound *were,* only what they *were not.*"

Hidden agendas in this trial were both conscious and unconscious. Surely the conscious ones start with the hopes of the participants to use the media spotlight to further their own ambitions, all splendidly realized. The case earned Aurnou instant national notoriety. After the verdict, and despite it, he was immediately invited to New Orleans to address the annual convention of the American Bar Association. Today his practice flourishes. George Bolen, after receiving lucrative offers from a number of private law firms, accepted a highly remunerative job with a major medical malpractice firm, but a short time later—just a born prosecutor—chucked it to return to his old job. Judge Leggett's new fame made him the Republican party's candidate for the State Supreme Court, and got him the second-highest number of votes in the state. Several jurors sold "the inside story" of their secret deliberations to newspapers and television interview shows. Even the court reporter was hired by NBC and brought to Hollywood as its "consultant" on the network's quickie dramatization of the trial.

Only the psychiatric professionals were left in the shade. Our list of hidden agendas begins with the strange determination to keep them off the stand at all costs. Why?

Aurnou said simply that he had made a "judgment call." Persistent inquiries from others on this point yielded unsatisfactory and inconsistent responses.

Harris to author (March 31, 1981): I was told Halpern's notes said all kinds of indiscreet things which would have looked bad to the jury. Maybe I used some expression like, "Gee, I would have liked to kill Hi for saying that," but I don't remember what I said. After all, I was talking to my psychiatrist.

William Riegelman to author (April 28, 1981): We thought long and hard. We agonized regarding the possibility of psychiatric testimony, and finally, reluctantly, we decided—for a reason which I am unable to disclose to you—that we could not present such testimony.

Marge Jacobson to author (August 19, 1981): Leslie told me it would be an absolute disaster if Abe Halpern got on the stand. His testimony against Jean would be too devastating. . . .

Marge Jacobson to author (August 20, 1981) after double-checking with Leslie Jacobson at author's request: Had they made public the Bloomingdale Report, that would have destroyed Jean's claim of medical privilege, and opened her up to examination by the prosecution's psychiatrists. Furthermore, her comments to her own psy-

chiatrist about Lynne Tryforos, which Halpern indis-
creetly included in his clinical notes, are more savage
than the Scarsdale Letter. They are so damaging to Jean
that we didn't dare let the other side hear them.

John Baer Train, M.D., to author (August 20, 1981): I
have read every page of Dr. Halpern's clinical notes. So
far as I can see, they are routine and utterly harmless.
They certainly contain no statements about Mrs. Harris
wanting to kill or harm Dr. Tarnower or anybody else.

Harris to author (February 18, 1982): Bill Riegelman says
Dr. Halpern's notes are filled with mentions of the book I
was still trying to write, to get the truth out one day, if
my legal difficulties are ever resolved. It was Joel who
first suggested I try to write out what happened, and Dr.
Halpern encouraged me. I used to show him samples
sometimes. Bill says that's what made his notes, and his
testimony, absolutely unusable.

Harris to author (March 3, 1982): Bill Riegelman told me
that Dr. Halpern's behavior in Joel's office—I don't know
what the behavior was—was so bad that they realized
they could just never put him on the stand.

What is going on here? Only after Aurnou had rested did we
begin to hear about the grave dangers contained in Halpern's
notes. The charge is incredible on its face. A very experienced
psychiatrist who expects to testify does not make indiscreet
notes. Train says the notes were harmless. Halpern believes that
the only member of the defense who actually had read his
clinical notes at the time Aurnou rested his case was Bonnie
Steingart, the young Fried, Frank lawyer assisting Riegelman.
She had asked to see them in connection with the confidential
memorandum of law she was preparing on the admissibility of
psychiatric testimony in a non-intent case. Possibly Ms. Steingart alerted her bosses to the news that the notes were replete
with references to a book Jean was working on. Was it to protect this phantom manuscript, which they may never even have
read, from public exposure, or from prosecution hands, that the
master strategists made another "judgment call," deciding to

deep-six Dr. Halpern and his colleagues without recognizing that it might also sink their client?

Another agenda suggests itself. Messrs. Jacobson and Riegelman may not have been eager to encourage a full inquiry into their client's psychological and social past. They might have considered a book potentially as explosive as an EED defense. In an EED defense, everything in Jean Harris's mind—including her extensive knowledge of the private lives of Herman Tarnower's friends and grateful patients—would in theory have been open to discovery. Once cross-examination began, and the fur started to fly, there was no telling what skeletons, or whose, might have come dancing out of the closet. A book could pose similar dangers.

Did Lynne Tryforos have a hidden agenda? If she did, it remains hidden. Mrs. Tryforos was once to have been the prosecution's star witness. Over the summer she complained to friends about Bolen's ceaseless demands on her time for pretrial conferences. The telephone records of her former husband, Nicholas Tryforos, have been removed from phone company files; the Tryforos divorce records are sealed. There is reason to see the hand of the District Attorney in protecting his star witness's past as much as possible from Aurnou's subpoenas. Why did she never appear? Bolen ultimately must have decided that he did not need her, or did not need her enough to expose her to the risk of savage cross-examination. The day the defense rested, Mrs. Tryforos left town for an undisclosed destination; she did not even wait for the verdict.

Why is it that police photographs of Lynne's belongings at the crime scene do not match Jean's detailed recollections? Having minutely compared various sets of police photos taken on different dates, Mrs. Harris has concluded that, two days after the killing, Mrs. Tryforos returned to the roped-off crime scene, reclaimed her personal property, and made the necessary substitutions for the police to find. If this did happen, it would not be unusual.

Did the Van der Vrekens have any hidden agendas? No, they appear to have behaved throughout in the time-honored tradition of loyal servants everywhere.

According to Dr. Halpern, even the dead man had a hidden agenda. "Just as Dr. Tarnower became her symbolic father," says the psychiatrist, "she became his symbolic WASP. Ask yourself: what on earth was Tarnower still doing with Jean Harris? Why did he punish her as he did? I maintain that, through Jean Harris, Tarnower was able to get back at all the WASPs who had excluded him and thwarted him and made him so damned miserable. At one point he did love her; he went wild over her. I'm sure of that. But I'm convinced that the only way one can explain his malignant abuse of Jean, his continuing threats of banishment yet his manifest unwillingness to dump her, is that he kept her because unconsciously he needed continually to revenge himself upon all the WASPs of the world who could not ever quite fully accept this long-nosed Jew."

The hidden agenda of Madeira's Druids has been mentioned. Their policy of silence was not bold but cowardly, not truth but cover-up. In their instinctive reaction to shun publicity, protect themselves, the Druids not only failed to follow Lucy Madeira's quirky motto, they failed to live up to her ideals.

As for that other major constituency in our story, the Century barons and grateful patients, they too drew their wagons in a circle. It was perfectly understandable. Consciously or unconsciously, the natural sympathies of the members of Century, and of the big law firm, would tend to lie more with the victim of the crime than the defendant. They were bound to him not only through friendship and business ties, but by the powerful bonds of class, age, sex, religion, politics, lifestyle, and general outlook and background. There need have been no conscious plan among them to keelhaul Jean Harris. It may be simply that, after Hi died at the hands of an outsider, a stranger, the insiders instinctively drew their wagons into a circle in a purely primitive *shtetl* reaction. In the end, Herman Tarnower was embraced by his club's peerage in the most permanent way possible.

Is it conceivable, then, that the one person in this entire tragedy who had no hidden agenda was Jean Harris, the woman who would not play the grieving widow, would not wear the Peter Pan collars of her childhood, would not "fake it" in any way? The woman who seemed to want absolution, or vindication, more than acquittal? The woman who, to that end, had let everything hang out—her pride, her privacy, her weakness, her shame? Of course not. Jean Harris had admitted everything but one thing, the main thing. She was too much a lady to admit that she was jealous of the office girl. *That* was her hidden agenda. She would rather go to prison for murder than acknowledge it, and she did.

She went there protecting Herman still, silently taking with her the bitter awareness that if it had been any other of Hi's friends who had come to see him that night, distraught, asking only to talk, if the unexpected visitor had been Arthur, or Joe, or John, or Dan, the doctor would not have said, "Shut up!" and closed his eyes and clutched his pillow. He would have sat up, put on the nice robe Jean had given him, and said, "Let's go downstairs and make a pot of tea and talk about it." And quite readily, uncomplainingly, he would have sat up all night with his friend. He very often had. But in the end Jean Harris was not a friend, she was his woman, and the same rules did not apply.

18

The Last Madeira Girl

AFTER THE JUDGE HAD pronounced sentence, the court clerk asked the prisoner's home address. "I don't have any," she replied. "I live in jail, I guess."

Jail is the Bedford Hills Correctional Facility, a ragged agglutination of old red brick and modern prefab spilling down a bare hillside an hour and a half north of New York City. Visiting rules are lenient. Get on a prisoner's approved list and you can see her at any time during visiting hours, daily from nine to three. Any more restrictive arrangement would raise the anxiety level inside these walls to unmanageable proportions. Visitors see only the guardhouse and, across a patch of scaggly grass and steps, the big, stark visiting room furnished with rows of card tables and pink plastic chairs. A wait of ten minutes, and #81G98 comes trotting around the corner wearing a little pair of forest green trousers, spotless white tennis shoes, the hairband. She has transformed the rough muslin prison shirt into an Oxford button-down by resewing the collar and attaching two pearl buttons. Her hair is freshly washed and set, makeup and manicure perfect. She does this every morning when she awakens before daybreak in her six-by-eight-foot cell, which contains a bunk bed, cold-water sink, metal-louvered window with asphalt view, row of pegs for clothes. Prisoners may wear their own footwear, nightwear, underwear, so long as nothing is blue, black, or orange. Those colors are reserved for the guards, of both sexes, who always must be referred to as "correctional officers."

Uniforms are polyester pantsuits, two outfits apiece, one green, the alternate bright yellow, and two muslin shirts. Her other shirt is resewn and embroidered as a cossack-collared overblouse. Its tie-belt is made from the cuffs she cut off when she shortened the trousers. She is almost chic, certainly the best-dressed woman here. Her visitors are made welcome with what she hopes is amusing chitchat about her odd new life: how she requested a "standing appointment" at the prison beauty parlor, and discovered it is stocked only with Afro hair products. How she sent a note of sympathy to a Grosse Pointe women's club that was wondering whether to list her current address in their new directory. *She's* been wondering whether to have her prison number engraved on her new stationery. She burbles on, not complaining ever, trying to make everything into a small entertainment for the visitor. With a small shock you realize *she* is trying to put *you* at ease. Mention the strong fresh paint smell of the visiting room and she automatically apologizes to you on behalf of the State of New York.

It has taken a while to find the right prison job for her. At first she was assigned to menial kitchen and library tasks. When chronic exhaustion overwhelmed her, she was told she could go collapse on her bed. Now that the mood-altering Elavil has had a chance to take hold, she is noticeably steadier. She was next assigned to teach remedial reading, but lacked the patience and stamina. After that, she was made a "grievance counselor" at the "grievance center," which is set up to handle inmate complaints. She had a few small successes untangling bureaucratic red tape, but since every prisoner's chief complaint is harassment by correctional officers, and the "grievance center" is not permitted to handle harassment complaints, she considers the place mostly a sham—a device to drain off prisoner anger—and she began to say as much. The other counselors complained that she was telling aggrieved prisoners the truth, that there is no hope, instead of conning them along as the other counselors did.

At last she has found the right job to absorb her passion; she is deeply involved, and sometimes cries when she talks about it. By the time she finishes describing her work, her listener is apt to be in tears as well. Prisoner #81G98 is a leader among the inmates who help the two volunteer nuns who run the "Parenting Center," and she has become an informed, useful advocate of prisoners' rights. Many new inmates are pregnant. To them the State of New York offers the interesting choice of giving up the infant at birth (in the prison hospital), or keeping it in prison for one year, and then giving it up. Most inmates have several children, often in foster care and often by different fathers, and all this necessitates a great deal of correspondence and negotiation between the women and their various children, foster parents, men, courts, and welfare officials. That she has won sufficient trust and respect from the other prisoners to be permitted to help them handle their personal affairs makes #81G98 very proud.

Prisoner #81G98 is one of 466 inmates, about one third of whom are serving time for killing someone; the others have committed various violent felonies and drug offenses. Their average age is under thirty, but some are toothless crones jailed for trying to augment their Social Security checks by selling a few bags of heroin, and four are sixteen-year-old girls. Most are black or Hispanic; only twenty percent are white. She has never met people like this before. They have never seen anyone like her. She is Bedford's most famous inmate, and much of the others' conversation consists of attempts to define for her the true nature of her new surroundings. "Why don't you go fuck a dead doctor? . . . You don' understand, dis fuckin' place is *jail*. . . . You think it a ol' people's home. . . . Dis no fuckin' Marriott Hotel!"

She has been warned repeatedly to beware, told that she dwells among dangerous criminals, psychopaths, lesbians, sadistic guards, hostile and jealous inmates. But she has never felt afraid. On the contrary, she seems remarkably at ease. She has finally escaped the hounding press. At last she has a room she can go into and close the door and lie down in for as long as she likes whenever she likes. For the first time in her entire life she has no responsibilities, no obligations, no pressures to get things done. She lives once more in a large, closed, homogeneous female community. This one has fewer classes, uglier grounds, but better food, she says. The bread and milk are excellent. Through the visiting-room windows, as from any place in the institution, one can see that all its walls and fences have been newly topped off with silvery coils of aluminum-alloy barbed wire studded with razorblade barbs. A double row of the huge coils encircles the entire institution like a monstrous electrified ruff.

In this community the rules are written down; they just make no sense. When she asked for a prison-issue pantie girdle because she had gained weight from starchy food and lack of exercise, she found herself scheduled for a mandatory gynecological exam. Pantie girdles here are a means to hide pregnancies, not tummies. Useless to point out that she is now fifty-eight years old.

She was inexpressibly thankful when she thought she had found one good friend, Adela Holzer, a Spanish-born businesswoman who was well known in New York as a backer of Broadway shows until she was convicted of grand larceny. Until recently, the two women were each other's best company, eating together in the cafeteria, and after dinner taking a nightly two-mile stroll up and down their corridor.

Though she tries to live inconspicuously, and spends most of her hours alone in her cell reading, writing, and studying prison conditions and the plight of female prisoners across the country, she is still not entirely immune to pressures from the outside. At the request of other prisoners, she helped stage a program aimed at lobbying a prisoners' right-to-work bill through the state legislature. The two-hour presentation, sponsored by the Department of Correctional Services, was opened to legislators and to the press. A reporter who had covered her trial managed to wedge herself into a seat beside her and murmur, "How're you doing in here, Jean?"

"I've a really cozy room . . . and it's blissfully peaceful and quiet," she replied. But her irony was lost on the eager-eared reporter, and a breathless news story immediately flashed around the world that, based on an exclusive prison interview, the writer could report that Jean Harris was very happy in prison. The story made no mention of prisoners' right to work. But it did, finally, produce a letter from a semi-Druid, the wife of a Madeira trustee. "Dear Jean," she wrote, "I'm so glad to read that you're getting on so well and are so happy there."

Despite the oddities and humiliations of her life—inmates pass through sixty locked checkpoints daily and are strip-searched every time they enter and leave the visiting room—Prisoner #81G98 is doing a superb job of making the best of things. She is still trying to teach the others to keep the place clean, and pick up their orange peels. She stands by and observes the hopeless fight to keep them from smuggling drugs and alcohol. People here ferment home brew from raisins pried from cookies.

Near the beginning of her second year behind bars, #81G98 began to write and publish articles in popular magazines calling attention to the severe, unjust, long-range, and hitherto largely neglected problems of the children of female prisoners. She also began work on a deeply affecting book of these children's letters to their inmate mothers, "Dear Mama, Come Home," which she has been collecting and editing in collaboration with another long-term Bedford inmate. Any profits from the book will go to support the activities of the Parenting Center, and of the unique summer day camp for inmates' children, which she has been a leader in setting up behind the barbed-wire walls, and where she is in daily attendance as a teacher and counselor whenever camp is in session. One of her major contributions was to help persuade forty-five families who live in Bedford Village and environs—a very wealthy white community—to take in these ghetto-raised children as temporary overnight boarders when it is time for their mothers to be locked back in their cells each evening.

Except to present herself three times a day for the "count," #81G98 does not have to do much. In the beginning, she constantly read and reread her trial transcripts, tearing apart the testimony of prosecution witnesses point by point. She hand-copied George Bolen's entire summation in multicolored inks and scribbled scornful refutations in the margins. Now she tries not to think about her future. She tries not to think at all. Her only worry is that some aggrieved or crazy person may try to burn out her cell and destroy the precious papers, records, and manuscripts stored under her bed. Her bed is also her desk. After dinner, served at 4:15, inmates are returned to their cell blocks until breakfast. They can exercise and visit in the corridor, or stay in their cells. The steel doors all glide closed at 10:30 P.M. but prisoners can still converse in shouts. Prisoner #81G98 spends most of her time propped up in bed reading and writing. Her backrest is her old mink jacket, the same one she wore driving to Purchase that night, now rolled up and stuffed into a prison pillowcase. Her view is of the sliding metal door and lidless toilet alongside. Even with her door closed and lights out, light from the corridor flows around the door's top and sides, and she never feels entirely entombed.

Her correspondence is voluminous, but phone calls are limited to two five-minute calls per month. She calls her elderly mother back in Cleveland. Mildred Struven is now a bit drifty, and her daughter is not sure she realizes or remembers what has happened, so she never mentions it.

"Where are you calling from, dear? New York! Oh, that's nice." They talk every two weeks.

Sometimes the prisoner thinks her failure to heed her mother's old warning is the real reason she is in this place. She thinks she is being punished for playing Miss Infallible with her lawyers and psychiatrists. It does not occur to her that she *did* listen to them, that she was a good girl right to the end.

"What still makes it easy to be here is that if I get out of here —I don't have a home. I don't know where home is. There isn't any place I'd rather be. There is no place I belong on the outside." So she has ceased to struggle. But there is more than this to her newfound air of resignation. More than the comfort that now, when she feels exhausted, she can just lie down; more to it than the Elavil. The comfort, bleak though it is, seems to be the consequence of having been plunged amid a group of other women whom she may find bizarre, boring, on occasion repulsive, but who nonetheless are innately sympathetic and supportive. They too have killed someone they say they did not intend to kill. They too feel unjustly imprisoned, and are struggling to deal with it. They regard her finally as a sister, and this has generated a profound feeling of acceptance heretofore unavailable.

Which is not to suggest that life at Bedford is easily endured. After a year, the authorities suddenly moved Adela Holzer away, over the pleas of both women, saying that "threats against her life" required she be placed in "protective custody."* In her place they put a woman who sometimes shrieks aloud for three hours describing the various ways she likes to masturbate. Prisoner #81G98 sits with her fingers in her ears, her back against her coat-stuffed pillow, reading. A new favorite author is Viktor Frankl, a writer arrested by the Nazis and kept three years in solitary confinement. One of his sayings is posted above her bed: "What remains is the last of human freedoms, one that cannot be taken from you. It is the ability to choose one's attitude in a given set of circumstances." Another, over the sink, says, "To live is to suffer; to survive is to find meaning in the suffering."

There are no pictures or photographs on her walls. She could not bear to look at them. For the same reason, she spurns a radio or tape deck. Music only makes her remember him, and think what a wonderful dancer he was. So instead she sings to herself, aloud now, mostly the old songs from Rondeau: "Sing, you sinners," "Fish gotta swim . . . ," "We're in the money" in pig-Latin. Sometimes, after the doors are slid shut for the night, the other prisoners sing back. Her neighbors call one another Queen Elizabeth, Eggroll, Thunderthighs, and Blue. She is known matter-of-factly as "The Old Bitch" or "The Mother-Fuckin' Old Bitch." Queen Elizabeth jives at her ceaselessly, but #81G98 doesn't really mind. Queen Elizabeth is bright, and funny, and everybody knows she is "maxing out"—knowingly behaving badly, making it likely that she will have to serve her maximum sentence, because she just doesn't care anymore.

Prisoner #81G98 has tried to help her. Whenever Queen Elizabeth gets out of prison, she sooner or later goes at people with knives, which puts her back in. "Queen Elizabeth, I *know* you can stop doing that. You're a very bright lady."

"Go fuck a dead doctor," Queen Elizabeth says, her standard opening to any conversation.

---

* She was recently released and immediately began peddling a book of prison memoirs, largely based on her "friendship" with Bedford's most famous inmate.

"Queen Elizabeth, you're smart. I'm sure you could stop."

"Yeah, but then I gets to drinkin'. An' when I gets to drinkin', that's when I starts usin' the knives."

But Queen Elizabeth can take care of herself. The prisoner whom #81G98 worries most about is 300-pound Blue. Blue is also "maxing out," and for over a week she has been kept twenty-four hours a day in her six-by-eight-foot cell as punishment for throwing a flatiron at Thunderthighs.

"It ain't *hot!*" Blue said reproachfully as they locked her in. #81G98 fears the huge woman may go crazy confined in the tiny room.

One hot night after everybody has been singing and shouting and jiving and shrieking back and forth for a long time, the corridor falls silent.

Then she hears a big, sorrowing voice. "Queen! . . . Queen!"

"Yeah, Blue. Wha' you wan'?"

"Queen, Ah wrote a song. Wrote it all by mahsef. You wanna hear it?"

"Sure, Blue."

"A prisoner is a person too. A prisoner is a person too. Doo-wacka, doo-wacka, doo-wacka doo."

Postscript

WHEN JEAN HARRIS WAS asked if she had anything to say before the judge passed sentence, she replied, "I want to say that I did not murder Dr. Herman Tarnower, that I loved him very much, and I never wished him ill, and I am innocent as I stand here. For you or for Mr. Bolen [the prosecutor] to arrange my life so that I will be in a cage for the rest of it, and that every time I walk outside I will have iron around my wrists is not justice. It is a travesty of justice." The judge then passed the sentence New York State law required of him. Since Mrs. Harris had been convicted—wrongly, as we shall see—of murder, not manslaughter, she was sent to prison for a minimum term of fifteen-years-to-life, *without possibility of parole by law for fifteen years*. (Italics mine.)

Jean Harris was sentenced March 20, 1981. As I write, five years have passed, and a number of things have happened to render that travesty more grotesque, and to highlight the intractability of the criminal justice system, at least in the special circumstances of the Harris case. Doubtless special circumstances exist in many cases. But the Harris circumstances are ones I have come to know well, and what follows reflects my growing conviction that in this instance, neither truth nor justice nor right nor the people of the state of New York have been well served.

Readers wishing a more complete explanation of what happened to Mrs. Harris at trial will find it in Chapters 16 and 17. This epilogue updates her story and recounts what has happened to her, in and out of courtrooms, since *Very Much a Lady* went to press in December 1982.

Jean Harris is now sixty-three years old. Having served five of her mandatory fifteen years, she has a decade to go. All of this time has been spent in a maximum security women's prison, Bedford Hills Correctional Facility. For nearly three years she lived in a cell block with many other women, each one housed in an "iron cage." For the past two years she has been one of twenty-six "honors prisoners" housed in Fiske House, a separate building.

In the past five years Mrs. Harris has completely recovered from the ten-year amphetamine dependency induced and maintained by Dr. Tarnower. But she has suffered at least two heart attacks. I say "at least" because, after her first serious heart attack, in August 1984, she decided not to report future episodes. It isn't "worth it," she says. She does not so much mind the six mandatory strip searches she must undergo in order to travel back and forth by prison van to the coronary care ward of a nearby hospital. What she cannot stand are the handcuffs, clamped around her wrists and shackled to her waist, which prison regulations also require. They are the iron she spoke of in her speech from the dock. Her hatred of handcuffs is so intense that it took nearly a year before her cardiologist could administer the necessary stress test to determine the correct course of treatment. By the time she got to the hospital, she was too stressed to take the test.

Because of her precarious health, Jean Harris no longer heads the Inmate Liaison Committee, the post to which she was elected by her six hundred sister prisoners to represent them in beefs against the prison administration. "I don't have the strength. I can't run around that much anymore," she says.

"But I still do the dishes in Fiske when it's my turn, and I still wash the stairs."

State corrections officials agree that Mrs. Harris has been a model prisoner, and much more. It almost seems an act of providence that the former boarding school headmistress, and lifetime teacher, should have arrived at this place. In the past five years Jean Harris has made herself an outstanding authority on the special problems faced by children whose mothers are in prison. Hundreds of thousands of such children exist nationwide. No one knows how many there are. Incredibly, no social agency keeps count. What we do know is that, inevitably, many of these children will be among the next generation of prison inmates. Young women entering Bedford today are daughters, and in some cases granddaughters, of onetime inmates. Unless something is done to break the dreadful, destructive, costly cycle of recidivism, the great-granddaughters will be arriving soon. Some women in Bedford are teenagers, and one or two are even older than Jean Harris. But the average age is twenty-eight. Very often the new inmate is pregnant, and the father-to-be is often not her husband, nor the father of her older children. Often she does not know where these children are. They have been placed in foster care, moved about, and—so far as their mothers are concerned—disappeared.

Jean Harris's work is to interfere in the cycle wherever possible, and break it however she can. One way is through education, including sex education. The usual path to Bedford begins with prostitution, at thirteen, leading to drugs, leading to the various felonies that send women to prison. Jean Harris teaches the same basic sex education materials to former prostitutes that she has taught to second-graders all her life. A number of inmates have been convicted of child abuse. Not having received any mothering, they have scant instinct and no knowledge on how to be mothers, only the terrifying biological capability. This spring one twenty-three-year-old prisoner gave birth to her seventh child. The infant is in the prison nursery now, along with twenty-six other infants of inmates.

The nursery is in many ways the heart of Jean Harris's work. The state of New York offers a pregnant prisoner an interesting choice: give the baby up at birth (to a family member if one is available, or to a foster care agency or for adoption) or keep and nurse the infant for one year and then give it up. After all, reasons the state, it is running a prison, not a nursery school. Understandably, many women choose to abandon the newborn at birth; after a year it would be even more painful. Mrs. Harris works very hard to induce these young women to keep their babies with them for the allotted twelve months. This way the infant gets some of the genuine mothering, bonding, and patterning which we have come to understand is vital to future emotional and physical well-being. And the mother gets some opportunity to develop parental feelings; she becomes motivated to seek out her child after her release from prison. Nothing is more important than that first year. When Jean Harris came to Bedford five years ago, the prison nursery had only two babies. Today usually twenty to thirty infants can be found there. Jean Harris considers this her proudest accomplishment.

"What do I do? Let's see. I teach a standard Red Cross course in pregnancy care, and another in care of the newborn. I have a weekly course of teen-teaching: demonstrating good parenting through films, with special emphasis on the education of young mothers." She also takes part in a new, weekly orientation program for new arrivals from the holding pens at Riker's Island, off Manhattan. Sometimes three women arrive, sometimes thirty. They are told how important they are to their children, how important the Parenting Center is to their children, and the importance of good foster care.

"Then, there are constant letters, inquiries from all over the country about what we do here. Many states are interested." Mrs. Harris answers most of the letters. Even letters to Albany often end up on her desk. "I also write lots of thank-you notes. Over a hundred different institutions send Christmas gifts and contributions to the Parenting Center. So there are constant letters, accepting this, thanking somebody for that, maybe asking for something we need.

"Then, inquiries come from all over the country, asking about the Parenting Center, and what we do here. We have the only parenting center in any prison in the United States. And the only nursery. There were a few others, but they've been closing them down." The last, in Florida, was closed in 1981. "You know why? Because they said 'A baby born in prison will

never smile.' Sentimental, mindless rubbish! It's the baby with
no mother, no *mothering,* who will never smile."

Mrs. Harris is talking about the subject she has come to
know and feel most passionately about. Her hands wave, her
eyes flash. "This nation is just beginning to realize something:
Women in prison have *children.* These children have special
needs." Mrs. Harris tries to help find ways to meet those needs
—for mothering, for warmth, play, fun, a sense of belonging.
Her work is not just with the children but with their mothers.
Many mothers who come to Bedford have no idea that their
children need them. That discovery—that they are overwhelm-
ingly important to their own children—gives these young mothers the first sense of self-worth they have ever known.

In the past five years the former boarding school headmistress has made herself "shadow headmistress"—my term—and
guiding spirit of the Parenting Center at Bedford Hills Correctional Facility. Founder and coadministrator of the Center is
the heroic, ebullient Sister Elaine Roulet, who also operates
children's shelters and shelters for battered women throughout
the New York City area, an hour-and-a-half's drive from Bedford Hills. Funds come from Catholic Charities, and individual
and corporate contributions. "I'm just one of a number of inmates who work in here," Jean Harris emphasizes, "though I'm
older than most. Oldest in the Center, by thirty years."

The Parenting Center is a place where inmates' children may
spend the day with their mothers and have lunch in a gaily
decorated playroom filled with children's artwork, books, toys,
and games. It is adjacent to, but very different from the drab
visiting room. A hand-painted rainbow-colored sign loops
across the façade:

JOY IS UNBREAKABLE SO IT IS SAFE
IN THE HANDS OF CHILDREN.

During the school year, buses paid for by Catholic Charities
bring the children from the city on weekends. For three weeks
every summer the Center becomes a kind of indoor day camp,
and the throngs of children spill over into the main visiting
room. When visiting hours end, at 4:00 P.M., buses bring them
to Bedford, Chappaqua, or Mount Kisco, where volunteer families board the children overnight. Over two hundred neighbor-

hood families now participate in the program, most of them recruited by Mrs. Harris and her new friends.

She has made a wall-size decorative quilt for the Center; she has knitted sweaters and caps for all the children. She decorates her room and others' with flowered bedsheets. She has a fine sense of occasion and continually thinks up special surprise presents. Last Christmas she gave her lawyer a three-dimensional knitted American eagle. In addition to working at the Parenting Center, Mrs. Harris has spent time helping care for all the babies in the prison nursery, and assisting in the thirty-bed mental ward. "I bring them games, shampoo, try to find any way to lift their spirits.

"We have six hundred women in here now, and they're talking about adding two hundred more. It'll be a zoo if they do. It's a zoo already. They're talking about dormitories. Dormitories mean *no* privacy. We've got sixty women in dorms now. It takes only one to keep fifty-nine awake all night long. Nice way to warehouse people.

"Mostly what I do in the evenings is read—constantly. I read about schools, education, prisons, anything I can get my hands on. We're just *beginning* to awaken in this country to the many things we're doing wrong. We're just beginning to see the breakup of the black family clearly. The President is wrong about the black family. And soon the same problems they face will be touching all our lives, not just people in the ghetto. It's already happening. The pattern is the same as with drugs: we discovered them when they moved to the suburbs. We're just beginning to see that our concept of how marriage works is wrong. It makes more economic sense *not* to marry, for many black women.

"We've begun to understand that the most important part of a child's life is the first five years. We need more Head Start programs, more nursery schools. Today children go off to begin school already doomed before they get there. Why are there no TV specials on *this?* We still have educators sitting around discussing: Shall we make them take four years of French? Stuff like that has *no bearing on problems.*"

It would be unbearably ironic, a tragedy both for Jean Harris and for the women and children she serves, if her expertise were used as an excuse to keep her behind bars rather than as yet another reason to let her out.

Perhaps this is the place to mention the small amount of good news about Jean Harris. Since going to prison, she has written a book, *Stranger in Two Worlds,* published this month by Macmillan. I have not read her book, save for the first page, which she read to me on the phone from prison the day she wrote it. Its power made me weep. Jean's book manuscript is still undergoing revision and editing. She tells me she has asked her publishers not to show it to me, at least not until it is in its final form. I said that was fine with me—an understatement. I was *thrilled.* "Oh, boy, am I glad not to have to read your book! After all you wouldn't read mine."

Jean had said from the beginning that she did not intend to read *Very Much a Lady,* and maintains she still has not. I believe her. Not only do I know her to be truthful to a fault. She understands that reading what another person might have to say about her and about the man she loved and killed would be needlessly painful.

My reasons for not reading her book are almost equally compelling. I am one of the many people who urged her to write it. I also introduced her to my friend and literary agent, Joy Harris, who in due course became literary agent for Jean Harris. I am also responsible for introducing Jean to my beloved friends and neighbors, Eleanora and Michael Kennedy. Michael is also my lawyer, and his wife is a paralegal. They became interested in the Harris case when Michael Kennedy read *Very Much a Lady* for libel. Eventually, at my urging, under circumstances I shall relate below, Kennedy became Jean Harris's lawyer as well. As I write this chapter, Jean Harris, her publisher, and various advisers are struggling with publishing problems her book may or may not have in relation to New York's "Son of Sam" law, a relatively new statute which requires a criminal who sells book or movie rights to his or her story to turn over the profits to the victim. Whatever the decision, Jean Harris tells me she intends to turn over any earnings to a nonprofit foundation to benefit the children of inmates. I've told her I don't intend to read *Stranger in Two Worlds* until I can buy it in a bookstore.

Before setting down the sorry legal saga of the Harris case, I want to say a few words about the medical testimony, a somewhat less disillusioning tale. On December 30, 1981, in rejecting the original bid of Jean Harris for a new trial, Presiding Justice Milton Mollen of the Appellate Division, Second Department, of the Supreme Court of the State of New York, wrote that although Mrs. Harris "did not receive a perfect trial, she received an eminently fair one."

But three and a half years later, A. Bernard Ackerman, M.D., the widely respected scientist who was an expert medical witness in the case, published a lengthy, most persuasive paper asserting that as far as the crucial medical testimony was concerned, Mrs. Harris had received a singularly *unfair* trial.

Ackerman is professor of dermatology and pathology and director of dermatopathology at New York University School of Medicine. He is an academic; until called by the defense in the Harris case, he had never been asked to serve as an "expert witness" in a court of law. After a meticulous and quietly scathing review of the medical testimony, his paper goes on to discuss several aspects of current American courtroom practice that appear to him to raise substantial questions of medical and legal ethics. "The Physician as Expert Witness: Is Peer Review Needed?" was published in many medical and scientific journals, including *Medical Heritage,* Vol. 1, Number 2, March/April 1985. It has since attracted favorable comment from physicians, medical examiners, and lawyers nationwide. In response to the matters Ackerman raises, resolutions which discipline physicians who give inaccurate, ignorant, or dishonest medical testimony in court are now pending before medical societies in New York and Florida. Other states may be expected to follow.

First, the flawed evidence. Jean Harris's trial was "singularly unfair," Ackerman charges, "because the autopsy findings on Dr. Tarnower were changed in mid-trial." The original autopsy by Drs. Louis Roh, deputy medical examiner, and Gary Paparo, chief medical examiner of Westchester County, and Roh's grand jury testimony, describe four bullet wounds and trace four paths of four bullets entering the body of Herman Tarnower. Nine months later Dr. Roh decided the same wounds were caused by three bullets, not four. "By virtue of that change," says Ackerman, "the evidence now indicated

Jean Harris shot Dr. Tarnower with the *deliberate intention* of killing him."

Harris had never denied shooting Tarnower. "Hurry! Hurry! He's been shot!" she had shouted to the first police officer on the scene.

"Who shot him?"

"I did. Hurry!"

But she also had always said that her intention was suicide, not homicide. When Tarnower struggled to take the gun away from her, he was shot several times. He bled to death in the ambulance before anyone understood the gravity of his wounds.

One month after the start of Harris's trial, the prosecution unexpectedly revised its theory of the crime and suddenly contended, for the first time, that the sleeping doctor, on awakening and seeing Mrs. Harris aiming a gun at him, had held up his hand in a vain attempt to ward off her attack. Thus one bullet had first passed through his hand, front to back, before lodging, fatally, in his chest. Mrs. Harris had always said the first bullet went through Tarnower's hand when he attempted to wrest the gun away as she raised it to her head. The prosecution's new-found "defensive wound" concept was the occasion for defense attorney Joel Aurnou to ask Dr. Ackerman to testify as an expert witness.

In order to prove the new theory, the prosecutor over one weekend in mid-trial had ordered his medical examiner to go back to his preserved blocks of chest tissue and to prepare and stain a new set of slides. To strengthen the new theory, it would be desirable to discover amid the debris of the chest wound some tiny bits of "palmar tissue," i.e., hand skin. The skin of the palm is unique, microscopically different in cellular structure from all other body tissue save for the soles of the feet. Hence such a finding, if provable, would lead a jury to conclude that a single bullet had carried the distinctive palmar tissue through the hand and into the chest. In short, it would show that Herman Tarnower had met his death while attempting to ward off a murderous attack by Jean Harris.

So the medical examiner had returned to his laboratory, had resliced, restained, refocused, and—lo and behold!—three bits of palm skin, or something very like palm skin, or something that *might be* palm skin, but also might be fragments of other cells, or pajama fibers, or plain dirt, was discerned. The actual trial testimony on all this was lengthy, bewildering, and ultimately stupefying as eight physicians, all claiming expertise, debated before a lay jury nuances of cutaneous histology that would have been lost on fourth-year medical students. This portion of the "evidence" in the Harris trial occupied almost nine full days of abstruse medical wrangling—nearly twenty percent of total trial time—and featured much blackboard diagraming and several extended slide shows of human tissue stained purple and green and crimson and magnified to resemble wheat fields and basketballs and doormats.

I sat through every moment of it and found it utterly incomprehensible. Nevertheless, by the time the marathon medical battle was over, a vague but indelible concept of "defensive wound" had been implanted firmly in everybody's mind. When it came time for summation, the defense attorney re-reviewed each one of the bewildering and conflicting cutaneous histology arguments in excruciating detail. The prosecutor shrewdly glossed over them. The judge in charging the jury reviewed the testimony of the eight pathologists once more, emphasizing to the jury that the crucial question before them was the one of intent: Did Mrs. Harris *intend* suicide or homicide? A key to the answer lay somewhere amid the incomprehensible landscapes of pink and purple basketballs and doormats.

In sum, what became crucial physical evidence against Jean Harris was what six out of eight pathologists testified was inconclusive evidence or concocted evidence and what the most qualified of the experts—including Dr. Ackerman—termed "wholly erroneous."

After reviewing these facts, Ackerman addresses wider issues of medico-legal ethics. I here quote from Dr. Ackerman's paper at length, grateful for the opportunity to place the questions he raises before a wider, nonscientific readership. His paper ends with a list of questions, followed by summary comments.

Should the standards for an "expert" in medicine be redefined?

Should physicians be brought to court as advocates for the prosecution or advocates for the defense, or should physicians be placed at the disposal of the Court as advocates of truth?

In the present adversary system of justice, which embroils physicians, should there be a code of ethics that governs the behavior of physicians within that system?

What standards should govern the testimony of forensic and general pathologists in court and should there be penalties for serious violations of those standards?

Is it proper for medical examiners and prosecutors to work together as collaborating colleagues, rather than as independent professionals?

Do fees paid to physicians by defense lawyers or prosecutors tend to compromise the intellectual integrity of physicians?

Can juries of laymen understand evidence in trials in which subtle knowledge of medicine is required?

Should medical students and residents be given formal training in preparation for their possible roles in medical-legal matters?

Should the same standards of peer review that apply in medicine in general be applicable to medical testimony?

Peer review has come to be a means of maintaining high standards in the practice of medicine. . . . The findings from laboratories of clinical pathology are scrutinized by physicians and surgeons who have to manage patients . . . and those findings must at once be judged to be in accord with clinical observations and later with biological course. In short, there is a monitor, a kind of crosscheck, like cross-examination, built into the practice of pathology. . . . Even in the realm of the textbook literature of pathology . . . textual materials . . . are subjected to review before and after publication by able colleagues. Thus, a pathologist's performance is not carried out in an unassailable ivory tower, but before a forum of critical colleagues and the wider community of general and specialized physicians.

A notable exception to ready review of the performance of pathologists and physicians in general occurs in courts of law. Rarely is the actual testimony of a physician in court made known to the community of physicians at large, and even when a physician openly testifies in a case, he may not even look over the transcript of his own testimony, let alone that of other physicians who may also have testified in that case. This special province, the court-room, shelters testifying physicians from corrective peer review that is so critically important to maintaining high standards in pathology and any other discipline of medicine.

Most physicians are fully cognizant of the Hippocratic standards of practice of medicine that obtain equally in a university, a hospital, and a private office. But few physicians, I daresay, are fully aware of the deviation from those standards that all too often occurs in the courtroom.

So much for the medical mess. Now for the legal one. Not being a lawyer myself, I shall have to discuss the various legal maneuverings in English. Members of the bar and others fluent in legalese will.I hope forgive my inability to express myself in their special language. As I have come to see it, after a defendant has had her day in court, and after a jury of her peers has decided which of two contradictory sets of carefully edited and orchestrated "facts" to believe, defense or prosecution, a kind of judicial rigor mortis appears to set in. The legal grounds on which a jury verdict can be overturned are, to this layman, almost unbelievably narrow and circumscribed. It almost seems as if, once the ponderous machinery of the law has at length clanked to a conclusion, no one involved in the tedious process can bear the thought of going through it all again. At any rate, once "justice" has been "done," it is near impossible to get it undone. Almost the only way a defendant such as Mrs. Harris can be granted a new trial is to come up with new evidence, or to claim "ineffective assistance of counsel" in her original trial.

In Jean Harris's case, there seemed to be virtually nothing in the way of new evidence, although routine appeals were filed, and routinely denied, as described in the final paragraph of the Author's Note. As for "ineffective assistance of counsel," this claim was debarred to Jean Harris once it was decided (by others, not by the still-distraught, intermittently suicidal Mrs. Harris) that her trial counsel, Joel Aurnou, should be retained as cocounsel on her appeal, in collaboration with Herald Price Fahringer, a well-known appellate specialist who later became known to a wider public as defense counsel in the first Claus von Bülow trial. Aurnou, that is to say, could scarcely be expected to be coauthor of a brief criticizing his own performance.

The rationale for the Aurnou-Fahringer cocounsel strategy was thrift. It was all explained to Jean Harris in the prison visiting room by the men who devised it, Tarnower's lawyer friends Leslie Jacobson and the late William Riegelman. As partners in Fried, Frank, Harris, Shriver and Jacobson, the giant Wall Street law firm which had helped bring Harris and Aurnou together in the hours following her arrest, Jacobson and Riegelman had exercised ever-closer legal supervision as the four-month trial ground on, and as the immense demands of the case drove Aurnou, working alone, without partners, closer and closer to total collapse. (On two occasions the judge was forced to suspend trial because Aurnou's physician had ordered the exhausted lawyer to bed.) The big law firm had also done a fair amount of legal research, brief-writing and so on which Aurnou alone was unequipped to handle. At least three or four times Aurnou's $25,000 trial fee—in billing time, not dollars—had been "spent" on the defense by Fried, Frank. And the more money Tarnower's old friends "spent," the more control they assumed of strategy and tactics. During the last third of the trial, Riegelman, and sometimes an aide, appeared daily alongside Aurnou at the defense table.

Brief pause for backward glance: Readers will recall that the star-crossed, middle-aged lovers met at a dinner party given by Marge and Leslie Jacobson fourteen years before the stormy night when the distraught boarding school headmistress arrived in her lover's bedroom carrying a bunch of daisies in one hand and a loaded revolver in the other intending suicide but ultimately committing homocide. The purpose of the party was to introduce their distinguished bachelor doctor friend Herman Tarnower to Marge Jacobson's girlhood chum, the smart, pretty, and newly divorced midwestern schoolteacher Jean Struven Harris. The Jacobsons had rejoiced at the sedate romance, which swiftly blossomed into elaborate wedding plans, then withered on the altar steps with Tarnower's abashed decision that at fifty-seven he was too old to become a first-time bridegroom. The romance rebloomed a few months later in somewhat different form when Harris made her fatal but scarcely unusual decision: She loved Herman anyway and any way. And at forty-six she was surely mature enough to conduct her private life without benefit of matrimony. Later, when the doctor took on a second, younger mistress, the Jacobsons were among the many who counseled Jean to walk away. She would not, and perhaps could not. She was not only hooked on Herman, she was unknowingly hooked on Desoxyn, the super-amphetamine that Tarnower ultimately provided her for a decade.

You will also recall that Jacobson's law partner Riegelman, who lived in Westchester just ten minutes from the county police station where Jean Harris was brought after the shooting, was the first attorney to reach Mrs. Harris. When police at the Tarnower home told Mrs. Harris she was under arrest, and advised her to call a lawyer, she phoned the Jacobsons, in New York City, and Jacobson asked Riegelman to take charge until he and his wife could drive up to Westchester. Bill Riegelman was Tarnower's twenty-year buddy at Century Country Club, where the two men occupied adjoining lockers, but he scarcely knew the battered, bruised woman at the police station who now fell sobbing into his arms. Three minutes later a call came in from the hospital: Dr. Tarnower had died. The desk sergeant changed the charge from aggravated assault to murder. Bill Riegelman's wife, Roslyn, a figure in Westchester County Democratic politics, is the person who, in the early morning hours after Mrs. Harris's arrest, first came up with the name of former county judge Joel Aurnou, recently defeated for reelection and now back practicing criminal law.

Aurnou's "go for broke" trial strategy (see below) worked in one sense: after the verdict the defense *was* broke. Mrs. Harris's own meager savings ($25,000) was of course completely gone, and all the money her family and friends had raised was gone too. Since the case was lost, it was now deemed prudent to cut further losses. Aurnou, already thoroughly familiar with the case, would greatly reduce the expense of preparing the appeal. And there—right out the window—went all hope of pleading "ineffective assistance of counsel," though ineffective it had assuredly been.

But no matter that the jury was given wrong facts, or incomplete facts, or incomprehensible facts. No matter that the jury was bamboozled and deceived. No matter that the defendant did not herself know all the facts. No matter that her lawyer didn't either. No matter that he did not fully understand the law, with reference to extreme emotional disturbance, or at least that he misinformed his client as to her legal position.

No matter that the minimum penalty for manslaughter in New York State is two years, whereas the minimum penalty for murder is fifteen years, without possibility of parole. No matter that, notwithstanding the terrible risk, Aurnou was so cocksure of victory that he refused to let the jury consider a compromise verdict of manslaughter. No matter that he knowingly decided to gamble with his client's future, "go for broke," and insist the jurors consider only one charge—murder—and in effect dare them to find his client guilty. As they read the evidence, alas, they could not find her innocent.

No matter that it was Aurnou himself who deliberately withheld from the jury the option to find the defendant guilty of first-degree manslaughter based on "extreme emotional disturbance," or "EED," as it is variously known. No matter that the manslaughter option was denied the jury by Aurnou, in chambers, over the vigorous objection of the prosecutor (who—fearful the jury might well acquit—wanted to be sure the defendant did not get off scot-free). No matter that Aurnou insisted on his client's right to "go for broke" to the dismay and astonishment of the judge, who had structured all his rulings in anticipation of an "extreme emotional disturbance" plea. (The trial record, replete with testimony as to the defendant's long-term emotional distress, her chronic drug dependency, and suicidal despair, is itself proof that an EED plea was anticipated. Otherwise the court would have ruled such testimony remote in time or irrelevant.) No matter that, by opposing a charge of EED, Aurnou denied the jury an opportunity to express a feeling of mercy if they were so inclined. No matter that Jean Harris during her trial was severely drug-addicted, was still taking the powerful amphetamines first prescribed a decade earlier by Tarnower himself, and was probably incapable of cooperating in her own defense. No matter that her psychiatrist had put the Court on notice, by letter, that if the ordeal of his distraught and suicidal patient were permitted to continue, he would not be responsible for her health and safety. No matter that the trial judge, Russell Leggett, now returned to the private practice of law, has recently said several times that he feels Jean Harris is no threat to society, has been punished enough, and no longer belongs in prison. No matter that the day after Leggett first made his statement he received a phone call from Russell von Glahn, foreman of the Harris jury. Von Glahn, a retired school administrator, congratulated the judge for his courage and leadership in speaking out, and said he wanted him to know that most if not all of the other jurors now felt exactly the same way.

It would be hard to disagree with these jurors and, in five years spent traveling cross-country talking about and answering questions about the Harris case, I have yet to find anyone knowledgeable about the facts of the case who does disagree. Now that *Very Much a Lady* has found a paperback publisher, I hope these facts will be taken under consideration by a far wider audience.

A final, personal comment: From the outset, the Harris case was perceived as "a great story." The media went wild. Jean Harris—to add to her suffering—became an instant public figure. "DIET DOC'S AGING MISTRESS," the headlines blared. The criminal trial of a celebrity in 1980s TV America is not always justice. But it is always theater. The proceedings become in fact a kind of daily, true-life soap opera in which *all* participants are apt to become somewhat extremely emotionally disturbed by the outpouring of national attention. I have written about this phenomenon before, in *Anyone's Daughter,* my book on the Patty Hearst case. I am writing about it again in my current work, *Dangerous Games,* a book on the craft of law that focuses on twenty-two defense attorneys and a half-dozen prosecutors and assistants forcibly bound together in the notorious "pizza connection" Mafia drug case. In between, I wrote another book, *Nutcracker,* on a celebrated crime, and that one became a best seller and a TV miniseries.

But the Jean Harris case is different from all the others. Her story alone rises to the level of tragedy, because her character— her mix of unsparing honesty, idealism, integrity, and "ladylike" values—became caught up in forces beyond her control: forces in school, forces in society, and chemical forces unleashed by the "speed" prescribed and supplied to her by Dr. Tarnower. When the media spotlight turns on, everybody goes for broke. The publicity generated by the "DIET DOC" case ultimately led to a "high noon" confrontation between prosecution and defense—and Jean Harris was the one who got shot.

The press coverage was atrocious. *Very Much a Lady* shows readers what the jury never got a chance to see. They saw only the end of the story, the last reel. They didn't see the erosion of a lifetime. Nor did they see it as a love story. Readers of the book did. They understood this as essentially the story of a middle-aged romance, a story of passion, of a woman helplessly in love. People are not fascinated by Harris and Tarnower because the two characters were deviant, but because ordinary people instinctively recognize universal elements. They recognize, too, that the relationship between the lovers, unequal though it became, was by no means all bad.

"But surely she was a terrible masochist, putting up with all that for fourteen years," some people say. I disagree. One must distinguish between sexual and psychic masochism. Every woman in love tolerates pain she would not otherwise tolerate. That is the nature of love. Lovers tolerate the pain—of intimacy —to experience the ecstasy of intimacy, the closeness. Love is making oneself vulnerable, and the psychic "abuse" is the price of that openness.

Is love so different, then, for women than it is for men? I don't know. But I doubt it.

Jean Harris was ready to die for love. She was like Anna Karenina. Poets describe what she felt. Catullus, Sappho, Dorothy Parker, Robert Lowell: "Besides the necessity to stay awake, what is life without the relief of love?" Harris understands the truth of Lowell's line. And she has steered all her life by the wisdom of the great Irish author of "Eileen Aroon." Anon., I think, was his name:

> Youth will in time decay.
> Beauty must fade away.
> Castles are sacked in war,
> Chieftains are scattered far.
> Truth is a fixéd star.
> Eileen Aroon.*

Harris's story proves that the women's movement is off-base when it says, "I am woman. I am strong. I am invincible. I am Jane Fonda. . . ." Women, most women, still need men—need them more, I suspect, than men need women. Despite the ad-

---

* From the poem "Execution" by Robert Lowell, first published *The New York Review of Books,* July 14, 1977. Used by permission of The Estate of Robert Lowell.

vent of "women's lib," many women still suffer in very old-fashioned ways.

As is apparent, Jean Harris and I long ago became friends. Contrary to what one might expect, she is usually the one who cheers me up, sometimes by letter, often by phone (Fiske House residents have the use of a pay phone for collect calls), and always on my occasional trips to see her in prison. She can, on occasion, be salty. Once when she knew I was going to Paris for a vacation, she sent a note urging me to buy us each some black lace underwear, and signed it "Jean Harris, Aging Mistress."

Another time she called up, giggling, "Do you know why the Junior League doesn't endorse group sex?"

"No."

"Too many thank-you notes."

Over the years I have involved myself in efforts to bring wider public attention to Jean Harris's case. The path has taken many unexpected turns. On a return flight from London I was introduced to Utah Senator Orrin Hatch. Impulsively I gave him an advance copy of my book, and at 7:00 A.M. the next morning he was on my phone wanting to help in any way he could.

That Thanksgiving weekend in 1982 Senator Hatch drove to his Senate office, wrote Jean Harris a letter, and had it delivered to my New York home by messenger. The letter said that Hatch, a lawyer, had read her story, and that he believed her although the jury had not. His offer of help began with the firm advice that she seek new, independent counsel. I brought the letter to her in prison. News that a complete stranger believed that she had told the truth made her dissolve into tears. Then she turned the letter over and did something I had been urging for months: She asked a lawyer named Michael Kennedy to please come and see her.

It was more than two years after Jean Harris went to prison when Kennedy agreed to take up her case *pro bono.* He faced a daunting task. Only the discovery of new evidence was now grounds to reopen the case. After a careful reading of the trial transcript Kennedy wrote a brief sailing bravely forth to battle.

His opening salvo states: "Notwithstanding the concurrence of twelve appellate judges of this State that the defendant received an eminently fair trial," the defendant, through counsel, now contends that her trial "is an embarrassment to the criminal justice system of New York," and adds that "a probably incompetent defendant was ineffectively assisted by counsel in a trial that was presided over by a judge who apparently substituted impartiality with indifference to the rights of the accused."

Then began the lengthy, tedious, expensive appeals process: Kennedy first submitted his brief to Westchester County Court Judge Aldo Nastasi. The prosecutor submitted his reply brief. Judge Nastasi denied Harris's motion for a new trial. Kennedy submitted a brief appealing Judge Nastasi's ruling to the judges of the Supreme Court, Appellate Division, in Brooklyn. Four judges were appointed to hear this appeal. Eventually Kennedy received notice that the judges would hear his oral arguments. He was not to speak longer than twenty minutes. The prosecutor would also speak for twenty minutes. Several months later Kennedy learned, first from reporters on the courthouse beat, and later formally from the clerk, that the Harris appeal had been denied. The next step was the Court of Appeals, the highest court in New York State. In November 1985 this appeal was also denied.

All told, two and a half years had ground on before all appeals were written, heard, pondered, denied. The interminable process required tens of thousands of dollars in costs, although Kennedy worked without fee. Jean Harris was destitute. Some but not all of her heavy legal expenses have since been paid for by the Jean Harris Defense Committee, headed by former headmistress and Marine Corps Colonel (retired) Anne Lenox. Board members include Jill Conway, former president of Smith College, the actress Ellen Burstyn, and myself. The Committee accepts contributions, which are tax-deductible to the extent allowed by law, via checks made out to The Bill of Rights Foundation, c/o Anne Lenox, P.O. Box 307, Radnor, PA 19087.

The next step will be an appeal for clemency to New York Governor Mario Cuomo. Clemency is never easy, and 1986—a gubernatorial election year—may be an especially difficult season. Before the end of January 1986 Cuomo had already been savaged by Reagan Republicans for recommending clemency in the case of Gary McGivern, a New York man serving life for murder.

The word *clemency* essentially means "mercy," however, and the Governor is a compassionate man. But there are other difficulties. Normally clemency appeals are not received until a prisoner has served half her minimum sentence. This is not a matter of statute, but of immutable custom. However, in Harris's case, the halftime date will not occur until the end of 1988. Her poor health and the stressful nature of her present existence make it at least questionable that she can live that long.

Every morning Jean Harris passes under the hand-painted rainbow sign which proclaims JOY IS UNBREAKABLE. Not so the human body. If this kindly woman remains in prison, then New York State will be passing the death sentence by default. Jean Harris has spent the last five years teaching others the joys of mothering and childhood and life. She should be allowed to finish out her life in freedom and tranquility.

If I ran the show, I often dream, I would let Jean Harris off now on grounds of what the law calls clemency but what I, not being a lawyer, call Gertrude Stein grounds. "A rose is a rose is a rose," and enough is enough is enough. I am sure the overwhelming majority of her sister prisoners would agree with me. She is their champion, their advocate, their voice. So, too, I am sure, would the majority of other people who have come to know this remarkable, indomitable woman since the steel doors slid closed behind her in March 1981: the professional staff at Bedford Hills, the staff of the Parenting Center, and the thousands of deprived children to whose well-being Mrs. Harris has devoted the past five years of her passionate life.

Those citizens of New York State who have no opinion on Harris one way or the other might be impressed by the argument that to release Jean Harris today would make her prison space available for someone who really is a menace to society, someone whose removal from the community is worth forty thousand taxpayer dollars a year—a poisoner, a child abuser, a loan shark, a dishonest or incompetent doctor; perhaps, dare one say it, an incompetent lawyer.

One day in the visiting room when we were discussing clemency she burst out, impolitic and fatally honest, as always, "I

don't want to *ask* for clemency. I want to *give* clemency for
what they did to me!"

If she is released, I would remind her of that statement. Then
I would do all in my power to make it possible for women
prisoners and their children that this most compassionate and
knowing woman continue to work in their behalf. I can imagine
no greater service, nor servant, to the next generation.

Prison is not redemptive. It is a foolish, bitter, destructive,
debasing, incredibly costly method of human warehousing
which we use because we haven't thought of anything better.
But this is not a lecture on prison reform. I don't have any
answers there. I know of no one who does, with the possible
exception of Jean Harris herself—Harris, the professional educator, topflight headmistress and brilliant woman whom providence five years ago consigned to the Belly of the Beast, to use
Norman Mailer's orchidaceous name for that gray, dead, and
deadly place. Was it divine providence, cruel fate, or a travesty
of justice that sent her there? Call it what you will, something
profound has happened to Jean Harris in these past five years.
At trial she described herself as feeling like a woman in an
empty chair. "I always felt that when I was in Westchester, I
was a woman in a pretty dress and went to a dinner party with
Dr. Tarnower," she told the jury. "And in Washington I was a
woman in a pretty dress and the headmistress. But I wasn't sure
who I was. And it didn't seem to matter . . . I was a person
sitting in an empty chair."

Today the chair is occupied. In it sits a powerful, together,
compassionate woman, sixty-three years old, frail in body, immense in spirit, self-healed—not because of prison but in spite
of it. And yet, in many ways—I am trying now to be as unspar-
ingly honest as Jean Harris herself always is—the self-healing *is*
in part the result of her ordeal, and of the resources she found
in herself to endure it, survive it, master it, and master herself.
Very much a woman, not a "lady," now occupies the once
empty chair. When justice prevails, as I believe it will, her chair
will be outdoors in the sunlight, where it belongs.

Index